Parliament Buildings

Parliament Buildings

The architecture of politics in Europe

Edited by Sophia Psarra, Uta Staiger and
Claudia Sternberg

Guest Editor: Jeremy Melvin

First published in 2023 by
UCL Press
University College London
Gower Street
London WC1E 6BT

Available to download free: www.uclpress.co.uk

A CIP catalogue record for this book is available from The British Library.

ISBN: 978-1-80008-536-7 (Hbk)
ISBN: 978-1-80008-535-0 (Pbk)
ISBN: 978-1-80008-534-3 (PDF)
ISBN: 978-1-80008-537-4 (epub)
DOI: https://doi.org/10.14324/111.9781800085343

*This book is dedicated to our
students and colleagues across UCL.*

Contents

Part II: A contemporary parliament in a historical building

Part III: The material structure of parliaments

Part IV: Political transitions and constructions of legitimacy

Part VIII: Building parliaments for the future
Guest editor: Jeremy Melvin

List of figures

List of tables

List of contributors

Remieg Aerts is Professor of Dutch History at the University of Amsterdam.

Gruia Bădescu is a Research Fellow at the Zukunftskolleg, University of Konstanz.

James Benedict Brown is Associate Professor of Architecture at Umeå University in northern Sweden.

Andrew Borg Wirth is an architect and curator who graduated from the University of Malta and University of the Arts London.

Pol Esteve Castelló is an architect, researcher and teacher affiliated with the Architectural Association and ETH Zurich. They are co-director of GOIG Studio.

Jonathan Chibois is Associate Researcher at the Laboratory of Political Anthropology in Paris, France.

Emma Crewe is Research Professor at SOAS, University of London, and a doctoral supervisor at the University of Hertfordshire's Business School.

Matthew Flinders is Professor of Politics and Founding Director of the Sir Bernard Crick Centre at the University of Sheffield.

Gordana Korolija is Professor of Architecture and Urban Regeneration at the University of Kent.

Naomi Gibson is an architect, Lecturer in Architecture at the University of Greenwich and PhD candidate at the Bartlett School of Architecture UCL.

Sam Griffiths is Associate Professor of Spatial Cultures in the Space Syntax Laboratory at the UCL Bartlett School of Architecture.

Ivan Harbour is an architect and senior partner at RSHP.

Carla Hoetink is Assistant Professor of Political History at Radboud University in the Netherlands.

Tormod Otter Johansen (LLD) is Researcher at the University of Gothenburg Department of Law.

Emilia Kaleva is Assistant Professor in the History and Theory of Architecture Department, UACEG – Sofia.

Amalia Kotsaki is an architect and Professor at the Technical University of Crete (Greece).

Stefani Langehennig is Assistant Professor of the Practice in the Business Information & Analytics Department at the University of Denver's Daniels College of Business.

Gustavo Maldonado Gil is a data scientist and architect at i-DA Design, Data and Analytics.

Alexandra Meakin is Lecturer in British Politics at the University of Leeds.

Jeremy Melvin is Visiting Professor at the Bartlett School of Architecture, UCL.

Paul Monaghan is an architect and Director at Alford Hall Monaghan Morris (AHMM).

Michał Murawski is Associate Professor in Critical Area Studies at UCL's School of Slavonic and East European Studies.

David Nelson is an architect, Senior Executive Partner and Head of Design RCA at Foster and Partners.

Ben Noble is Associate Professor of Russian Politics at UCL.

Philip Norton (Lord Norton of Louth) is Professor of Government at the University of Hull.

Dennis Pohl is Postdoctoral Researcher in Theory of Architecture and Digital Culture at TU Delft.

Alex Prior is Lecturer in Politics with International Relations at London South Bank University and Honorary Research Fellow at the University of East Anglia.

Sophia Psarra is Professor of Architecture and Spatial Design and Director of the Architectural and Urban History and Theory PhD Programme at the Bartlett School of Architecture, UCL.

Kerstin Sailer is Professor in the Sociology of Architecture at the Bartlett School of Architecture, UCL.

Henrik Schoenefeldt is Professor for Sustainability in Architectural Heritage and Director of Graduate Studies at the School of Architecture and Planning, University of Kent.

Julia Schwanholz is a political scientist and senior lecturer at the University of Duisburg-Essen (Germany).

Samuel Singler is Departmental Lecturer in Criminology at the Centre for Criminology, University of Oxford.

Sofia Singler is Junior Research Fellow in Architecture at Homerton College, University of Cambridge.

Uta Staiger is Associate Professor of European Studies and Director of the European Institute at UCL.

Iulia Stătică is Lecturer in Urban Design at the School of Architecture, University of Sheffield.

Claudia Sternberg is Principal Research Fellow and Head of Academic Programmes at the UCL European Institute.

Benedetta Tagliabue is an architect and Principal at Miralles Tagliabue (EMBT)

Mari Takayanagi is a historian of women and parliament in the nineteenth and twentieth centuries, and Senior Archivist at the UK Parliamentary Archives.

Patrick Theiner is Lecturer in Politics and International Relations at the University of Edinburgh.

Harald Trapp is a sociologist, architect, Guest Professor at the University of Innsbruck in Austria and Guest Professor at UACS Skopje in North Macedonia.

Aneta Vasileva is Chief Assistant Professor in the History and Theory of Architecture Department, UACEG – Sofia.

Alexander von Lünen is Senior Lecturer in the History division at the University of Huddersfield.

Ben Worthy is Senior Lecturer in Politics at Birkbeck College, University of London.

Michael Zerafa is an architect and researcher who graduated from the University of Malta.

Acknowledgements

The genesis of this work is in the UCL Grand Challenge of Cultural Understanding, which provided funding for our research project *National Parliament Buildings: The Architecture of Power, Accountability and Democracy in Europe*. We are grateful to them for their support, especially to Siobhan Morris for her continuous encouragement. This project was part of *European Voices*, a special initiative in 2019–20 at UCL intended to showcase UCL's rich work on, and links to, Europe.

The result of this project was two virtual crossdisciplinary conferences combining architecture, the humanities and social sciences, held at the Bartlett School of Architecture in November 2020 and February 2021. We greatly appreciate the contributions of academics and practitioners, beyond those contributing to this volume, who enriched the deliberations at the conferences and subsequent events, providing distinct perspectives on a diverse subject. We are particularly grateful, for their advice, support and chairing roles, to Dr Marc Geddes, Dr Sam Griffiths, Dr Alexandra Meakin, David Mulder van der Vegt (XML), Mariana Pestana, Professor Jane Rendell, Dr David Roberts, Jonas Staal (STUDIO STAAL) and Dr Thanos Zartaloudis, as well as to current and former Deans of the Bartlett School of Architecture, Professor Christoph Lindner and Professor Alan Penn. Professor Emma Crewe and Lord Norton of Louth, both contributors to this book, were also instrumental in advising on research matters related to the subject of the conference.

We are also grateful to the many parliamentarians who gave their time and views on how parliament buildings work for them: Lord Anderson of Ipswich; Lord Best OBE DL; Franziska Brantner, Member of the German Bundestag and Parliamentary State Secretary in the Federal Ministry for Economic Affairs and Climate; Alex Davies-Jones, MP for

Pontypridd; Julian Huppert, former MP for Cambridge; John Lytton, 5th Earl of Lytton; Tulip Siddiq, Labour MP for Hampstead and Kilburn; Lord Smith of Finsbury; and Baroness Smith of Newnham. Special thanks to Dr Graham Riach from Oxford University, who captured these views in two videos, recording our conversations with these parliamentarians.

New parliament buildings are not frequently commissioned. We were fortunate to have contributions from four leading architects who have worked on just such buildings. Guest-edited by Jeremy Melvin, the final section of this volume presents chapters describing architectural designs for two new parliaments resulting from the devolution to Scotland (EMBT) and Wales (RSHP), the refurbishment of the Palace of Westminster (AHMM), and the reconfiguration of the Reichstag building in Berlin (Foster and Partners). We are thankful to Jeremy Melvin and architects Paul Monaghan (AHMM), Benedetta Tagliabue (EMBT), David Nelson (Foster and Partners) and Ivan Harbour (RSHP) for their contributions to the conference in February 2021 and to this book. They shed light on the role architecture plays in how parliaments are conceived, shape political life and communicate with the electorate from the designers' perspective.

Naomi Gibson, Gustavo Maldonado Gil and Avery Anapol provided enormous support in organising the conference and in the final preparations for this volume.

UCL professional services staff from the communications and events teams at the Bartlett School of Architecture, in particular Abi Luter and Ruth Evison, provided logistics support for the two conferences at the height of the COVID-19 pandemic.

Thanks also to Chris Penfold and colleagues at UCL Press for editing and publishing this book, and to our families for their continuous support.

1

Introduction

Parliament buildings and the architecture of politics in Europe

Sophia Psarra, Uta Staiger and Claudia Sternberg

Setting the scene: parliaments between architecture and politics

This book explores European parliament buildings as a nexus of architecture and politics. Situating itself at the intersection of a range of disciplines, and including perspectives from both practice and scholarship, it sets out to examine the relationships between the architectural configurations and the political life of Europe's parliaments. How do parliament buildings and their spaces give form to norms and practices, to behaviours, rituals, identities and imaginaries – and the other way round?

Parliament buildings are instruments and symbols of political life. On one level, parliament buildings enable and carry the imprint of what happens inside them. Parliamentary architecture shapes and reveals how parliamentarians carry out their functions, of representing, deliberating, legislating, authorising expenditure, of making governments and scrutinising the executive (Hague and Harrop 2022). These buildings are where assembly, debate, formal and informal encounters occur, workplaces and much more.

On another level, parliament buildings carry meaning – meaning for those using them and those beholding them, but also meaning beyond the immediate experience of their space and built environment (Goodman 1985). In addition to the meanings associated with lived experience and practice, parliament buildings are symbols (Edelman 1964). They are beacons, signifiers to the country and the outside world as well as to the people filling them with life. They embody how a state and its political elites see themselves, and how they want to be seen (Theiner and Schwanholz in this volume). For example, the storming of the Capitol by Trump

Figure 1.1 Crowd of Donald Trump supporters marching on the US Capitol on 6 January 2021. © TapTheForwardAssist, taken on 6 January 2021. Source: Wikimedia Commons, reproduced on the basis of a CC BY-SA 4.0 licence. Available at: https://commons.wikimedia.org/wiki/File:DC_Capitol_Storming_IMG_7965.jpg (accessed 6 December 2022)

supporters on 6 January 2021 was largely perceived as an attack on the principles and values that the United States of America is founded on.

Parliament buildings play an important role in the legitimation of power. They can, in themselves, develop 'charismatic authority', flowing from architectural features or the display of artwork that heighten the status of the building and the institution itself (Weber 1919 [1970]; Dörner 2000; see Theiner and Schwanholz in this volume). Authority can also be asserted by means of *association* – whether that be with specific architectural styles, languages or forms, or a prominent architect. Architectural references have been used intentionally to link a building, say, with desirable strands of modernity or tradition, with cultural, political or broader historical developments to which a political community aspires, or with a certain collective identity. To be sure, a

Figure 1.2 View east from the Brandenburg Gate towards the Rotes Rathaus, Berlin, under the Nazi regime. © Hans Andres: Berlin. Source: Wikimedia Commons, reproduced on the basis of a CC BY-SA 2.0 licence. Available at: https://commons.wikimedia.org/wiki/File:Berlin_Unter_den_Linden_im_Festschmuck_(49976346608).jpg (accessed 6 December 2022)

building's meaning through association can also work in negative ways, for example when it becomes associated with a reign of terror (Goodman 1985, p. 643).

What is unique about the symbolic significance of parliament buildings is that the legislatures that inhabit them are symbols themselves – symbols of representation. Of course, legislatures represent citizens because they are authorised by them and accountable to them (formalistic representation), or because they somewhat resemble those they represent (descriptive representation), or act in the interest or as an agent of the represented (substantive representation). In addition, legislatures *represent symbolically*, in that they 'stand for' the community they 'make present' in the parliamentary process, due to the meanings they have for those being represented (Pitkin 1967, p. 13). With the advent of photography, the print media, television and, most recently, social media, the radiating power of these buildings has reached ever further. All these developments serve to 'make parliaments present' in the lives of citizens and publics. Parliamentary architecture is a key mediator defining how meanings are constructed and transmitted to people through spaces, forms, images, sounds, narratives, political practices and rituals.

Parliament buildings stand for representative democracy in the 'social imaginaries' by which people picture 'how they fit together with others'. It is these social imaginaries that constitute the 'common understanding that makes possible ... a widely shared sense of legitimacy' (Taylor 2003, p. 23). Parliaments are supporting pillars of the 'necessary political fictions' that make political rule possible (Ezrahi 2012), and specifically the 'foundational fiction' of modern democratic legitimacy, whereby a majority can stand for a whole, and a fictitious 'people' can stand symbolically for society in all its diversity (Rosanvallon 2011, pp. 2–3, 13, 15–72; see Sternberg 2023). In the words of seventeenth-century English philosopher John Locke: "'tis in their *Legislative*, that the Members of a Commonwealth are united, and combined together into a coherent living Body. This *is the soul that gives Form, Life, and Unity*, to the Commonwealth: From hence the several Members have their mutual Influence, Sympathy, and Connexion' (Laslett 1988, p. 407). Parliament buildings are the bodies that contain this soul and prevent 'Dissolution and Death' (Laslett 1988, p. 407). They foster and express collective identity and a sense of unity, and physically embody the body politic (Hobbes, in Tuck 1996; Manow 2010).

More practically speaking, parliament buildings enable and limit the ideologies that orient and inform political practice and policy making (Freeden 1998). They contribute to making how things are done appear 'natural and fixed', as if things could not be otherwise, entrenching relations of domination at the same time as making parliaments, like all institutions, resistant to change (Douglas 1986; Thompson 1990, p. 56; Komarek 2023). And yet, parliament buildings can also inspire people to imagine change. For example, much parliamentary architecture and political reform since the Second World War has aspired to an ideal of open and transparent political decision-making, made tangible in the medium of architectural transparency (Theiner and Schwanholz; Psarra and Maldonado Gil; Zerafa and Borg Wirth in this volume). Of course, architects and architectural theorists have pointed out how transparency can turn into obscurity when glass surfaces act as mirrors (Vidler 1992; Barnstone 2005; Herzog and de Meuron 2016; Theiner and Schwanholz in this volume). A parallel debate in political thought criticises how aspirations to the transparency and openness of decision-making processes tend to gloss over the fact that visibility does not equal accountability or even influence, and definitely not equal access to either (Barnstone 2005; Sternberg 2013, pp. 135–138).

The symbolic significance of parliament buildings, while important and well researched (Edelman 1964; Goodman 1985), is just one of the many functions of parliaments. In this book we acknowledge the significance of symbolic expression, but wish to go beyond the familiar subject of buildings as symbols of power, of memory, of national identity. Our aim is to break ground in investigating how these buildings work as places of political practice and formal and informal encounters, as workplaces; as the places where assembly, debate, back-corridor negotiations, rituals and interpersonal relationships come to life. Understanding the symbolic and the important dimensions of form and space as mutually constitutive, we are interested in how they interrelate, in *how* buildings mean by giving life to practice, rather than merely *what* they mean.

Parliament buildings in Europe

This book focuses exclusively on parliament buildings in Europe. It goes without saying that this is not because other parts of the world do not have fascinating parliament buildings or histories of proto-parliamentary and parliamentary institutions that call for exploration. The book's geographical and historical focus, in addition to corresponding to the editors' areas of research expertise, allows us, however, to delimit the scope of the enquiry, while attending to historical depth both individually and comparatively by exploring transnational features.

Europe's parliament buildings represent an important range of architectural typologies and political histories. Some house one chamber only, others an upper and a lower house; all comprise differing arrangements of associated working spaces. Many European parliaments are situated in repurposed palaces, aristocratic lodgings or monastic sites, which have been adapted from their original use. Others are housed in what were and are prestigious new building projects, with bespoke constructions being built especially for parliaments since the late 1800s (see Gibson et al in this volume). All aspire to a certain grandeur, making use of architectural styles ranging from the neoclassicist (such as the Assemblée Nationale in Paris or the Cortes in Madrid) and neo-Baroque (Berlin's Reichstag or Stockholm's Riksdagshuset) to the neo-Gothic (London's Houses of Parliament or Budapest's Országház) and the (post) modern (Edinburgh's Scottish Parliament or Cardiff's Senedd). They also often sport remarkable features, reflect predominant concerns at the time of building, or raise questions over the symbolic significance of architectural modifications within their national and historical contexts (see, for instance, Tagliabue; Nelson; Harbour in this volume). It is in the context of this European variety and complexity that we set out to explore the intersection of architecture and politics.

But, as we indicated above, parliaments are not only symbols but also *places* of politics, and politics, too, differs across Europe. Members of national parliaments in Europe are voted in by different electoral systems, from plurality and majority to proportional and mixed methods. These return either two large or several smaller parties – and are usually enmeshed in the genesis of distinct political cultures, which are recognisable to politicians and electorate alike. The majoritarian model, which tends to result in a small number of broad parties and single-party governments, is often described as 'exclusive, competitive, and adversarial' (Lijphart 1999, p. 2). It is often called the Westminster model, with the UK Parliament being the prime example. Consensus models, conversely, usually broad multiparty coalitions that share executive power, are characterised by 'inclusiveness, bargaining, and compromise' (Lijphart 1999, p. 2). Most continental European parliaments, for example Belgium, Switzerland – and indeed the European Union

Figure 1.3 A session of the Swiss National Council. © Peter Mosimann, taken 15 June 2005. Source: Wikimedia Commons, free for use without restriction. Available at: https://commons.wikimedia.org/wiki/File:Swiss_National_Council_Session.jpg (accessed 6 December 2022)

Figure 1.4 A European Union ceremony in the Strasbourg semicircle. © the European Parliament, taken on 22 November 2022. Source: Wikimedia Commons, reproduced on the basis of a CC BY-SA 2.0 licence. Available at: https://commons .wikimedia.org/wiki/File:The_European_Parliament_at_70-_%E2%80%9CThe _voice_of_citizens_and_democratic_values%E2%80%9D.jpg (accessed 6 December 2022)

itself – illustrate this model. Considering the fraught political history of Europe, not least since the inception of parliamentary politics in the early 1800s, these 'patterns of democracy' (Lijphart 1999) provide us with a rich pool of sources and cases to examine political culture as it relates to parliamentary architecture.

At the same time, in a complementary way, the focus on Europe allows us to explore the main typologies of plenary designs that form the interior heart of parliament buildings – oblong halls with opposing grandstands (see Melvin in this volume), the now dominant semicircle (including variations such as the horseshoe and the circle, see for example Theiner and Schwanholz; Psarra and Maldonado Gil; Sailer in this volume), and the classroom model (Gibson et al; Murawski and Noble in this volume). This range of plenary designs allows us to illustrate ongoing discussions – outlined below – over the extent to which parliamentary architectures may shape, or may be shaped by, the patterns of democracy and political practice. Their additional architectural ramifications, often overlooked, are here also of political significance – the size of the plenary hall, the distribution of seats, the positions members speak from, the orchestration of sightlines, and the procedures that regulate debate or voting (Psarra and Maldonado Gil; Gibson et al in this volume). These features come in addition to parliaments' organisation of complementary spaces for work, formal and informal meetings, and the space allotted to public access (Crewe 2015, 2021; Norton 2019; Norton, Chibois, Takayanagi in this volume).

European parliaments as we know them today emerged out of classical, medieval and early modern traditions of gathering, deliberation and interest representation with kings and local rulers. These proto-parliamentary institutions, in the form of general assemblies of citizens, estates, provinces or counties, are noteworthy not least as they display a considerable continuity of rhetoric and ritual with the parliaments emerging after the early 1800s (Feuchter and Helmrath 2013). The British Parliament, which in its earliest forms dates to the thirteenth century, formally began to share power in government in 1689, and has been housed in a palace at Westminster for over 900 years, is a particularly significant example in this context (see Melvin in this volume). But the watershed moment for the increasing prominence of parliaments in the governance of European states – the *parliamentarisation* of politics – remains the late eighteenth and early nineteenth centuries. The American and French Revolutions promulgate a notion, which may have become naturalised since but is not therefore any less groundbreaking: the concept of the people as a body politic with an authority to rival the king's (Manow 2010). The ideal of parliament consequently metamorphosed from a tightly circumscribed aristocratic representation into one that stood for (most of) the population. And 'parliamentary buildings may be the best illustration of the spread of [this] ideal of parliament' (Aerts and van den Berg 2019, p. 7).

We should take note, however, that parliament buildings and parliamentary processes are not marked by unswerving similarity and continuity across Europe. Indeed, parliaments *qua* institutions of popular representation are intimately related to particular national histories, political cultures and societal self-images (Goodsell 1988; Vale 2008; Gibson et al in this volume). In his 1867 *The English Constitution*, Walter Bagehot famously claimed that parliamentary government was a matter of 'national characteristics' (Bagehot 1867 [1963], p. 239) – and therefore not suited, really, for anyone but the English. Certainly not the French, whose disorderly proceedings in the Assemblée compared rather unfavourably with the sober exchange of arguments in Westminster, 'the model and envy of nations', as the *Illustrated London News* had it in 1852 (te Velde 2019, p. 27). Parliamentary buildings in Europe may thus not only consolidate their standing as legal and constitutional institutions but reflect idiosyncratic and diverse political cultures – which also change over time.

Yet, as some have argued, European parliaments and their buildings did not grow in isolation; they are an 'outcome of an ongoing process of interchange, borrowing, reproduction and adaptation' (Aerts and van den Berg 2019, p. 6). Well before our modern globalised world, European elites acquainted themselves with other nations' parliamentary buildings and practices, witnessed and discussed them, and notably adapted them for their own contexts. As historians have noted, Jeremy Bentham for example, advised Count Mirabeau on the longstanding but impenetrable rules of Westminster. In the heydays of parliamentary prestige, French and British aristocrats paid mutual visits to each other's parliaments to hear well-known orators speak. The Dutch parliament building first emulated the French assembly, then the British-style bicameral system, showing the importance of both models and their adaptability in different contexts (te Velde 2019, pp. 28–29). Today this conceptual and practical transnationalism is well established, with a British architect reworking the German, and a Catalan architect designing the Scottish Parliament (see Nelson and Tagliabue in this volume). As David Nelson explains, German officials visited the Commons chamber at the Palace of Westminster for the remodelling of the Reichstag by the British architectural firm Foster and Partners (see Nelson in this volume).

Further to these shared histories of adaptation and exchange, European parliaments also share a history of crises. These are linked to unfulfilled expectations of the electorate, increasing scepticism, and challenges to legitimacy – from the late nineteenth century to the interwar years, the desolation of the Second World War, the economic crises in the 1970s, and seemingly recurringly in the past two decades. Indeed, parliaments have often been the sites of protest and challenge – not just over policy differences, but the nature of the institution itself. Think, for example, of the suffragettes' 1910 march to the UK Houses of Parliament to request the vote for women. Think also of the attempted *coup d'état* in the Spanish Cortes in 1981, or, indeed, of UKIP MEPs' 2019 anti-EU protests in the Strasbourg semicircle. But even without overt protests, parliamentarians are increasingly aware of public demands for access, inclusivity and transparency. These demands, as well as modern exigencies of efficiency, have influenced new practical and symbolic solutions for the buildings, as a look at Germany's state parliaments

Figure 1.5 Section of a working women's picket: a suffrage procession. Photograph taken 17 February 1917, caption 'Wage-Earners Marching to the White House Gates' from *The Suffragist*, 5(61) (24 March 1917) via the Library of Congress. Source: Wikimedia Commons, reproduced on the basis of Public Domain. Available at: https://commons .wikimedia.org/wiki/File:Section_of_Working_Women%27s_Picket_160016v.jpg (accessed 6 December 2022)

Figure 1.6 Scene around the National Assembly of Bangladesh in Dhaka. © Micah Parker, 19 May 2005. Source: Wikimedia Commons, reproduced on the basis of a CC BY-SA 2.0 licence. Available at: https://commons .wikimedia.org/wiki/File:National_Assembly_of_Bangladesh,_Dhaka _(26).jpg (accessed 6 December 2022)

(Theiner and Schwanholz), the Swedish Riksdag (Johansen) or the European Parliament (Esteve Castelló and Pohl) in this volume testifies.

In addition, European parliaments have developed explicit links over and above their national space. There is the legacy of colonialism and empire, with nations emerging from colonial rule facing the question whether or to what extent to adopt the political systems, constitutional models and parliamentary buildings originally imposed or represented by the colonising states (Goodsell 1988; Kumarasingham 2013). There are also cooperative networks, most significantly in our context the Inter-Parliamentary Union, created in 1889 as a forum for multilateral parliamentary cooperation, and at first a 'European peace movement, aiming at international arbitration' (te Velde 2019, p. 35). It is also worth recalling that in recent decades, in the wake of the European integration process, the role of national parliaments has been transformed. Today, the parliaments of EU member states cooperate to an extent with the European Parliament, with many arguing, however, that national parliaments need to be further empowered – or reclaim competences – so as to strengthen democratic legitimacy in and of the EU (Kröger and Bellamy 2016). The European Parliament itself, seen as both a symbol of and a possible solution to Europe's 'democratic deficit', acutely reflects the demands of an institution that seeks to entrench its transnational, responsive and transparent credentials (Sternberg forthcoming). This also includes the structures and adaptation of its building – visually, spatially and communicatively (Sailer; Esteve Castelló and Pohl in this volume).

This book is thus not a cohesive history nor a comprehensive catalogue of European parliament buildings. It is, however, the first bespoke volume that explores the wide range of parliament buildings in Europe from a cross-disciplinary perspective. In turns national and regional, comparative and transnational, thematically and diachronically focused, the volume offers an eclectic deep dive into the complex nexus of architecture and politics in Europe.

Introducing literature on parliament buildings and the architecture of parliaments

Studies on parliaments and parliament buildings diverge into different subjects, engaging a range of audiences and paradigms of knowledge. This is not surprising as parliaments are embodiments and expressions of many things, 'an idea, a process, a place, a building, a time and a symbol' (Crewe 2021, p. 7).

> You can't study parliament without a sense of architecture to fathom the building; geography to consider how people navigate space and place; history to see what unfolds over time including movements in power, relationships or values; linguistics for perusing speechifying and written texts; legal studies if tracking law-making; psychology to uncover the pressures people face and how they respond to them and so on (Crewe 2021, p. 14).

In this book we discuss what scholars in architecture, the humanities and social sciences, as well as architectural practitioners who have designed parliament buildings in the last three decades, have said about parliaments, and open up questions for further research. If one looks at parliaments and their history, at where politicians, officials and staff sit, what rituals they perform and how they go about their daily routines, much is revealed about a nation (Crewe 2021). Our starting point is that architectural scholars can expand their engagement with parliaments and institutional buildings by seeing their discipline through a range of other perspectives. Equally, scholars in disciplines engaging parliamentary studies can enrich their approaches by seeing architecture as a political force in its own right (Bell and Zacka 2020).

Architecture, politics and power

Although parliaments are by definition sites of politics, ritual and rules, they are not the only institutions that exercise power, express collective values and channel political behaviour. Since Plato, who in *The Laws* discussed how the geographical location and features of his proposed city of Magnesia affect the ease or difficulty of creating a virtuous city (Schofield and Griffith 2016), architects, political theorists and artists have studied and imagined physical layouts, from early classical examples (the Greek agora, the Roman forum) to phalansteries, utopian communities and visionary designs. Space and politics have also been explored as theoretical subjects in a range of disciplines and epistemological perspectives (Foucault 1977; Adorno 1979; Habermas 1989; Soja 1989; Latour 1991; Lefebvre 1991; Latour and Yaneva 2017).

And yet, no other thinker has more systematically reflected on the relationship between space and power than Michel Foucault. Defining power as a 'co-ordinated cluster of relations' (Gordon 1980, p. 198) that operates both from above and below, Foucault (1977) considered Jeremy Bentham's *Panopticon* prison as a model for the disciplinary apparatus of society founded on practices of hierarchical observation. He explained that placing categories of people and objects in separate locations, and using surveillance as a tool for ordering, monitoring and ranking them, defined the foundational principles of many institutional building types, from schools to museums and libraries and from hospitals to mental asylums and prisons. Foucault's main interest was the abstract principles defining a 'technology of power' (Gordon 1980, p. 148), rather than the link between the physical configuration of buildings and sociopolitical life:

> [A] whole history remains to be written of spaces – which would at the same time be a history of powers (both these terms in the plural) – from the great strategies of geopolitics to the little tactics of the habitat, institutional architecture from the classroom to the design of hospitals, passing via economic and political installations (Foucault in Gordon 1980, p. 149).

Writing the history of spaces and powers is the task architectural theorist Thomas Markus undertook in *Buildings and Power* (1993). The institutional buildings in which we now work and live express the battles fought over class, division of labour, and some of the fiercest ideological battles of the early nineteenth century. Markus considers buildings as classifying devices, organising asymmetries of power as well as tensions between control and freedom: 'The places of political assembly, lawmaking, or the administration of justice – council chambers, parliamentary assemblies and lawcourts – share some features with teaching spaces.' However, the resemblance is superficial as what is 'produced in these spaces is not knowledge, but legal and political structures' (Markus 1993, p. 229).

Markus's work is an advance on Foucault, identifying a diversity of institutional building types and studying their history and spatial morphology. However, parliament buildings – a typology that also emerged in the age of reason and the nineteenth century – remain outside his purview in *Buildings and Power*.

In *Architecture, Power and National Identity* (2008), architectural and urban theorist Lawrence Vale takes a close look at national parliament buildings and the districts that surround them.[1] Discussing the complex meanings of these environments, Vale explains that the physical designs of architects are equal in importance to the political designs of government officials and the meanings these hold for the people. Grand symbolic buildings need to be understood not only in terms of their architectural history and precedents, but also in terms of the political and cultural contexts that helped bring them into being. Drawing from Nelson Goodman's four ways by which buildings mean (1985), Vale mainly focuses on the history and representational function of capital cities and capitols rather than their political culture and inner life.

In *Framing Places* (1999), architectural theorist Kim Dovey argues that built forms of architecture frame life, mediating, constructing and reproducing power relations of class, gender, race, culture and age. His account of the Australian parliament building in Canberra, designed by the Italian-American architect Romaldo Giurgola, draws a distinction between the spatial programme developed by government officials and the architects' work.[2] Spatial relations in the building, such as four separate entrances for four different classes of people whose paths rarely cross, the distance from the access corridor for ministers' offices coupled with a back entry/exit, were the work of bureaucrats and demonstrate a shift of power from the parliament to the executive. Dovey explains that the architect's influence in the design was mainly through forms

Figure 1.7 The parliament houses of Canberra, the new house in the foreground, looking towards the old house in the background. © Dietmar Rabich, 20 October 2019. 'Canberra (AU), Parliament House and Old Parliament House – 2019 – 1767'. Source: Wikimedia Commons, reproduced on the basis of a CC BY-SA 4.0 licence. Available at: https://commons.wikimedia.org/wiki/File:Canberra_(AU), _Parliament_House_and_Old_Parliament_House_--_2019_--_1767.jpg (accessed 6 December 2022)

of representation and composition. Locating the Parliament House on Capital Hill, Giurgola resisted the impulse for an imposing building:

> Instead the building excavates several storeys off the natural landscape which it then reconstructs artificially. This tactic enables a very large building to blend into the landscape and one enters the parliament as if into the land it stands for—Parliament House as a hill rather than on the hill. Citizens could initially walk on top to produce a potent legitimating image, although that access is now sadly denied (Dovey 2018).

Dovey's and Markus's emphasis on spatial relations is influenced by Bill Hillier and Julienne Hanson's approach, known as space syntax (1984).

Architectural theorists Hillier and Hanson and their colleagues at UCL (Penn et al 1999) have studied spatial systems, uncovering deep social structures in buildings and urban settlements. These are translated into networks and analysed by measuring the number of spaces one needs to traverse from every room to every other space, capturing similarities and differences in a wide range of layouts that architectural and sociological discourse would find difficult to categorise, lacking a nonverbal language of spatial configuration. In *The Social Logic of Space* (1984), Hillier and Hanson explain that buildings interface 'inhabitants' who have control over the building with 'visitors' who may enter a building regularly but have no control over it. Traditionally, inhabitants occupy rooms that are located 'deeply' in a layout, for example in houses, religious buildings and theatres – what Hillier and Hanson call 'elementary buildings'. The relation of power to depth tends to be reversed in hospitals, asylums, prisons and schools, locating visitors in the deepest spaces and placing them under surveillance, as in Foucault's disciplinary institutions. Parliament buildings would naturally fall into the first category, positioning visitors into easily accessible areas, and politicians and staff into deeper locations in the building.

Markus, Dovey, and Hillier and Hanson extend Foucault's theory of disciplinary power into the specific characteristics through which spaces internalise sociopolitical relationships.[3] Their approach expands the study of institutional settings into the practices of power and control beyond the expression of historical narratives, identity or political legitimacy. The aim is not to supersede symbolism, but to open up research in architecture as an autonomous field – resulting from the simultaneous presence of relations rather than extraneous associations – and explain similarities and variations in the physical design of institutions. If indeed every parliament were an individual expression of a nation's distinct historical and national narratives, one would expect to find in the collected examples of parliaments considerable variety in building forms in the same period as well as over several generations. Yet clearly it is possible to discern distinct physical similarities, despite historical and political differences, ruptures or transformations, and beyond territorial and temporal states.

This is one of the key findings in *Parliament*, a study of the assembly halls of 193 United Nations member states by XML architects, exploring typology of shape, seating arrangement and political system. As the authors explain, regardless of political regimes, ranging from authoritarian to democratic, and major differences between countries, cultures and traditions, a limited number of typologies, already mentioned above, emerges for the shape of this hall: the opposite benches derived from

Figure 1.8 The parliament buildings in Astana, Kazakhstan. © msykos, 12 June 2008. Source: Wikimedia Commons, reproduced on the basis of a CC BY-SA 2.0 licence. Available at: https://commons.wikimedia.org /wiki/File:Kazakh_Parliament_Astana.jpg (accessed 6 December 2022)

the medieval hall, the neoclassical semicircle of the nineteenth-century nation-states, the horseshoe that is a hybrid of the previous two, the rare typology of the circle and the authoritarian typology of the classroom. For the authors, these typologies survive as visions of the past, posing the question of what role architecture can play beyond ornamental or symbolic representations of national values in rethinking and shaping politics.

Even a superficial look at the comprehensive catalogue of assembly halls by XML reveals historical and political exports to Europe (Cyprus, Malta), Australia and America where chambers were shaped by opposite-facing benches. Similarly, former socialist states of central and eastern Europe, such as Estonia, Bulgaria and North Macedonia, use the classroom layout despite their transition to multiparty democracy (see Gibson et al in this volume). Further, reappropriating historical buildings for contemporary use as in Foster and Partners' design of the Reichstag building in Berlin, opens up contestations about the relationship between old regimes and newly forged political narratives (see Nelson; Bădescu and Stătică; Kaleva and Vasileva in this volume). These phenomena show a loose relationship between architectural form and political system. They also confirm the persistence of forms over time as opposed to changing value systems, socioeconomic and political realities.

Yet, even if similar architectural forms have been used by different political cultures, these forms are clothed in particular materials and styles, and display the stamp of architects' idiom. Taking the UK Houses of Parliament for example, the debate over architectural styles – classical or Gothic – in the nineteenth century shaped the reconstruction of the building after the fire in 1834. Charles Barry, who won the Westminster competition for the reconstruction, used a classical plan but clothed the building in Gothic appearance and details, skilfully produced by Augustus W.N. Pugin, 'the most fertile and passionate of the Gothicists' (Bradley and Pevsner 2003, p. 215). As David Anderson (Lord Anderson of Ipswich) explained in an interview about the architecture of the Houses of Parliament:

> The building conveys an early Victorian pastiche of a democracy which … was wished to trace back to the Middle Ages. So in a sense the decoration is highly political in terms of the message that it seeks to convey, just as in parts of the world law courts look like Roman temples, because someone wished to convey the impression that there was an unbroken line of Jurisprudence going back to Justinian. So the House of Lords, to lesser extent the House of Commons, is constructed as a medieval environment to demonstrate the unbroken strength of our institutions for hundreds of years[4] (Psarra and Riach 2020).

If, traditionally, parliament buildings expressed symbolic messages about the nation-state, its history and its practices of democracy, a question that arises is whether in the face of global transformations, architecture has lost its resonance, 'as the nation state is in decline and the global neoliberal consensus holds sway' (Dovey 2018). Not quite so, as Deborah Barnstone (2005) suggests, arguing that the relationship of architectural form and political expression takes new dimensions in contemporary contexts, as in parliament buildings produced in the second half of the twentieth century in Germany, through the use of transparent materials.

The Reichstag building in Berlin is one of the examples studied by architectural scholar Thomas Markus and linguist Deborah Cameron in their book *The Words Between the Spaces* (2002), in which they examine how various types of discourse, such as treatises and manifestos, texts intended for teaching, guidance and regulation, design briefs and guides, inscriptions and labels, texts in media and the press, Acts of Parliament and legal documents of various sorts affect the production and use of the built environment. Another example the authors explore is the Scottish

Parliament in Edinburgh designed by Enric Miralles and Benedetta Tagliabue (see Tagliabue in this volume). They explain that like many symbolic structures, parliaments are characterised by a clash of discourses of power. In the case of the competition brief for the Scottish Parliament, the political/ideological discourse on *democracy*, *transparency*, *openness* and *accessibility* of the parliament stood in stark contrast to 'an hierarchical and static idea of power as something exercised by the state *over* the people' (Markus and Cameron 2002, p. 76), who must be strictly monitored and controlled. Markus and Cameron bring to the fore a key factor in the study of institutions, that is, language, what texts say, how they say it, and what are the explicit and implicit consequences for gender, race and class relations. One should extend the study of texts to written texts, spoken discourse and image affecting relations of power, perceptions and shared experiences of people (Griffiths and von Lünen in this volume).

Political practices and architectural space

The work of Vale, Barnstone, and Markus and Cameron is useful both for venturing into the architectural expression of political regimes – a widely researched subject – and textual influences, and for providing a counterargument to any claim about architectural autonomy in the study of parliaments and institutional buildings. A primary lesson from the architectural theorists reviewed here is that these settings mean different things to architects, the institutions that inhabit them and the public, calling for contributions by other disciplines and modes of inquiry. The scholarship that is most relevant to this book from knowledge fields outside architecture outlines the importance of the relationship between spatial organisation and sociopolitical practices in the construction of political culture (Goodsell 1988; Puwar 2004; Parkinson 2009; Malley 2012a, 2012b; Norton 2019; Geddes 2020).

In 'The Architecture of Parliaments', political scientist Charles Goodsell sees architecture as a subject of interest to political scientists, since parliament buildings and the rooms inside them 'are in themselves artefacts of political culture, the shared norms of governance and underlying patterns of political behaviour' (Goodsell 1988, p. 287). He explains that parliament buildings make three contributions to political culture: they perpetuate the past over long periods of time (preservation), they manifest the present (articulation), and they condition the future (formation). In terms of preservation, parliament buildings express narratives of historical continuity, national integration, newly created national orders, foundational acts, and the values of stability, dignity and legitimacy. Articulation is a form of nonverbal language, communicating ideas that otherwise would be difficult to reveal. For example, the two houses in bicameral systems are usually expressed as being equal by some manifestation of architectural equality. Formation refers to how the 'physical dimensions of chambers and the spatial relationships between houses and the parliament, versus the executive' can affect thoughts, actions and behaviour (Goodsell 1988, p. 287). Stretching from the symbolic operation of these institutions to behavioural norms, Goodsell's analysis defines the physical configuration of parliament buildings neither as backdrop nor as a system of signs, but as constitutive of political life in its own right.

Asking why particular forms such as the opposite benches and the modern semicircular seating plan came to prevail in particular countries, political economist Philip Manow takes a different position to Goodsell's approach to these plans as expressing political culture. Manow reaches to the premodern origins of our political institutions to argue that the semicircular plan was neither an import from classical antiquity, nor a form of legitimation of modern left-right semantics. Further, it does not express consensual politics or fragmentation into different parties. Rather, as previously mentioned, it offers a pictorial imagery that legitimates a system of rule that dissolved with the French Revolution, the *body politic*, conveying 'an ideology of political unity derived from corporeal analogies in evidence from the Middle Ages until late Absolutism' (Manow 2010, p. 37). The point after the French Revolution, Manow explains, was 'to develop new symbols of national unity, once the king's body could no longer serve as a symbol of political rulership and will formation' (Manow 2010, p. 39).

Whereas Manow focuses on assembly chambers as ideological spaces and imaginaries, anthropologist Emma Crewe studies parliaments through an ethnography, stressing the importance of 'the stable and the unstable, the continuities and the dynamism, the patterns at different times, places and scales' (Crewe 2021, p. 9; see also Crewe 2015). She regards parliaments as microcosms of society because in them are representatives of all people (nearly) in a nation (see above on Pitkin's 'descriptive representation', 1967). Crewe explores parliaments as the workplace of politicians where political culture is made through the everyday interactions of people. By studying the relationship between parliaments and political culture as processes rather than as products, Crewe brings together ideology, space, time and sociopolitical practices, offering an inquiry into rituals, diaries and appointments observable in offices, streets and parliamentary buildings.

A number of other scholars in political science, anthropology, sociology of the built environment and architecture point to the importance of place, design and architecture in parliaments (Flinders et al 2018; Crewe and Sarra 2019), the significant functioning of the corridors and social spaces of the Palace of Westminster as settings for informal encounters (Bold 2019; Geddes 2020) and the consequences of the use of informal spaces for gatherings of members (Norton 2019).

Drawing from ethnographic research and his own experience of sitting in the UK House of Lords, Philip Norton (Lord Norton of Louth) explains that the use of space to meet informally in tea rooms, dining rooms and lobbies is very important in understanding the processes of institutionalisation, socialisation, information exchange, lobbying, mobilising political support and the exercise of influence (Norton 2019; see also Norton in this volume). Norton explains that informal discourse and behaviour is 'power behind the scenes' and by its nature difficult to observe, justifying the absence of scholarly research in this area.

Drawing from social anthropology and their personal experience of working *with* people, Crewe and Norton show that 'the inter-subjective cultures of parliaments accommodate multiple social entanglements without which democracy would die' (Crewe 2021, p. 29). A crucial point in these entanglements is the expansion of interactions to virtual space for formal and informal discourse between members. Understanding the impact of digital communications in legislatures is crucial, particularly during the COVID pandemic, when parliaments around the world shifted to a hybrid format, with physical participation of a limited number of members and virtual input by the majority of elected representatives.

Key themes, contributions and overview of the volume

Two key observations emerge from this brief review of existing works on parliament buildings and political culture. On one hand, research focusing specifically on the architecture of parliaments often concerns the shape of plenary halls (XML 2016), historical analysis of built (Bradley and Pevsner 2003) and unbuilt designs (Sharr and Thornton 2013) and the emblematic expression of power, political ideology and national identity (Barnstone 2005; Vale 2008). With the exception of XML, for the most part architectural scholarship is focused on a few cases of parliament buildings rather than a wider spectrum. More importantly, these contributions have little to say about parliament buildings as dynamic institutions facilitating spatial and political practices.

On the other hand, significant works in political theory, the social sciences and the humanities focus on political discourse, culture, ritual, social relations in parliaments and metaphoric expressions of the body politic (Manow 2010). A particularly studied example here is the UK House of Commons and House of Lords (Crewe 2005, 2015, 2021; Norton 2019). However, with a few exceptions, studies engaging the role of architecture and space in these knowledge fields are lacking. A relevant book dedicated to the intersection of architecture and political theory is by Duncan Bell and Bernardo Zacka (2020). This, however, does not examine parliaments, but rather politics and architecture in general, addressing abstract notions of spatiality in political processes.

By contrast, it is the key contention of this book that the spatial layouts of legislatures are intricately enmeshed with political cultures. Parliament buildings are best approached using a multidisciplinary understanding of legislatures, cultures of political assembly, forms of interaction and perceptions both nationally and across Europe. As such, the book brings together scholars from architecture, history, art history, history of political thought, sociology, behavioural psychology, anthropology and political science to explore and compare parliament buildings in depth. These are complemented with contributions from practitioners and architects, who have led and are leading on some of the most iconic parliamentary design and renovation projects – including the Scottish Parliament, the Welsh Senedd, the German Reichstag and the UK House of Commons (see Part VIII of this volume, guest edited by Jeremy Melvin).

Considering the concrete specificity of architecture as a semi-autonomous field (Hays 1998) and the larger historical, social and political context of parliament buildings, the book offers theoretical and methodological innovation, analysing parliamentary spaces through architectural history, political theory, interviews, participant observation, spatial analysis, text analysis and design-led exploration.

The book does not intend to be comprehensive or favour one particular type of discourse over others. The chapters it presents begin from the premise that architecture might not determine political culture and political life, but it conditions our thoughts, actions and discourses in these environments. Our aim is to demonstrate the intersecting trajectories of the disciplines represented when it comes to the study of parliaments in particular, and in a more general sense of the built environment. In so doing, we build on but go beyond existing literature, charting connections between parliamentary space, political life, history, culture and identity in legislatures in Europe, extending our knowledge of how parliaments work, exposing the breadth of political activity both inside the buildings and the context they are situated in, and exploring alternative visions for parliamentary space, political behaviour, participation and public engagement.

This diverse engagement with parliament buildings and the architecture of politics centres around several lines of inquiry that serve to structure the book into nine different parts.

Part I Rhythms of space and time

Part I presents a group of chapters that look at parliaments through the lens of social ethnography, focusing on formal and informal practices, gatherings and the flow of people inside parliament. The chapters in this section consider questions such as: what kind of work do members of parliament do (Crewe)? How do they meet and work in parliament buildings (Norton)? How do politicians, staff and the public use parliamentary spaces, both collectively and individually, and why does this matter (Chibois)? What types of epistemologies and knowledge are critical in achieving in-depth understanding of people, bodies, interactions, language, routines and rituals? What kinds of sociotechnical practices and traditions was parliament engaged with in managing its spaces, the diversity of participants, politicians, lobbyists, clerks, campaigners, staff and visitors (Schoenefeldt)? In this part, a political practitioner, two anthropologists and an architect look at how parliaments inhabit the entire space devoted to them with emphasis on informal communications (Norton), route structures for different social groups (Chibois), rhythms of space and time (Crewe) and sociotechnical networks of engagement of users with the functioning of the building (Schoenefeldt).

Part II A contemporary parliament in a historical building

The Palace of Westminster, home to the UK Houses of Parliament, is possibly the most iconic of parliamentary buildings in Europe. In this section, entirely dedicated to Westminster, three political scientists, an urban historian, a parliamentary historian and archivist, and a scholar in the digital humanities approach the building(s) to explore how they 'speak' to multiple users and groups – politicians, officials, citizens – and how these in turn invest the Palace with meaning and agency. Looking outwards, how can a centuries-old institution in a relatively modern, if historicised building, represent itself to and engage with the contemporary public?

What is its *corporate identity*, what does it stand for (Prior)? In the case of refurbishment and renovation, are there opportunities to break the link between history and the architectural form of the institution; how can we use an *architectural imagination* to reveal the hidden politics of architectural design, and consequently, envision it otherwise (Flinders)? Turning inward, how has the Palace shaped the behaviour and emotional response of some of its key constituents, the elected members and the officials working therein – and how, consequently, has this attachment shaped policy decisions about the building's own future (Meakin)? Indeed, in the grand narratives of the UK Parliament's history, what kinds of politically engaged groups were de facto rendered invisible in the building; how did they both form part of and increasingly challenge the institutional culture of parliament (Takayanagi)? And what can literary fiction, particularly if written by one of the nineteenth century's most prominent prime ministers, Benjamin Disraeli, tell us about the intersection between parliament *qua* building and parliament *qua* institution, between the political and the fictional discourses of *Young England* (Griffiths and von Lünen)?

Part III The material structure of parliaments

Political scientists and political theorists typically approach parliament and assembly buildings or courthouses in essence as containers for action and discourse. Architects and architectural scholars, on the other hand, are primarily preoccupied either with the physical configuration of these buildings, matters of architectural heritage, or some abstract notions of spatiality in social and political processes. Part III explores the relationship between parliamentary architecture and material structures, on one hand, and the life and culture of politics, on the other. How does the spatial organisation of parliament buildings shape political practices, rituals and traditions and become shaped by them? Is there a difference between expressing political culture and actively shaping this culture (Psarra and Maldonado Gil)? How is political culture constituted by space and architectural parameters? How is it expressed through the spatial form of the buildings and their appearance (Theiner and Schwanholz)? Presenting chapters by two political scientists, two architectural scholars and two historians, this part addresses these questions by looking at the UK Parliament and the German Bundestag in the Reichstag building (Psarra and Maldonado Gil), and the material culture of 16 new political institutions in Germany since the Second World War (Theiner and

Schwanholz). The final chapter (Aerts and Hoetink) reviews the work of European and American historians analysing parliament buildings in various countries, with a focus on how they contributed to our understanding of the nexus between politics and the spaces within which it is mediated.

Part IV Political transitions and constructions of legitimacy

This part examines political transitions, and what happens when a political system changes radically but the architectural forms housing its institutions persist, or when architectural forms are modified to signal supposed political change or democratic aspirations. In doing so, it challenges the notion of a deterministic relationship between society and space. Straddling eastern and southern Europe, from Bucharest to La Valletta and from Moscow to Sofia, the chapters in Part IV explore variations of three questions: how authoritarian regimes shape their parliaments; how these spaces are reshaped during transitional periods and by aspirations to democracy; and how protest and civic engagement challenge architectures that supposedly express the power of the people. Can architectures of power be associated with both authoritarian and democratic regimes (Bădescu and Stătică; Vasileva and Kaleva)? What kinds of politics, aesthetics and morphology are behind decisions to renovate parliaments and their spaces? What is the role of canonical architectural typologies in the redesign of parliamentary settings (Murawski and Noble)? And how, finally, do contemporary designs and imageries of democracy give agency to the public (Borg Wirth and Zerafa)? The part brings together an anthropologist of architecture and cities, a political scientist, a social scientist of architecture and three architects and architectural scholars.

Part V Mediated parliament and digital interactions

Television entered plenary chambers in parliaments in the second half of the twentieth century. Broadcasting parliamentary interactions widely to their nations gave parliaments new means of increasing public interest, and allowed politicians to appeal to voters in their constituencies. Since the turn of the twenty-first century, social media and digital platforms provide yet more possibilities for visibility, scrutiny and surveillance. Diverse publics outside institutional spaces can engage with political affairs in a more multifaceted and direct manner. Such a bridging of physical and mediated spaces does not come without its attending risks, however, as it can give rise to new inequities and interfere with democratic deliberation. In this part, architects and political scientists examine the role of TV and digital media in the context of the UK Parliament (Worthy and Langehennig; Brown) and the European Parliament (Esteve Castelló and Pohl). How do broadcasts, news and media platforms heighten and hide aspects of the Palace of Westminster – how is parliament *mediated* – and what can we learn from the point of view, quite literally, of its liminal, adjacent broadcasting spaces (Brown)? Has the arrival of new technologies, purportedly serving to allow citizens a closer look into and engagement with parliamentary affairs, brought about a new *monitory* democracy – and what might this mean in terms of surveillance, misrepresentation and intrusion (Worthy and Langehennig)? How can large institutions such as parliaments – not least the European Parliament – develop their own media approaches and adapt their spaces to foster remote, distributed and active forms of democratic engagement; and how do they fall short (Esteve Castelló and Pohl)? Across these chapters, Part V seeks to cautiously weigh up the benefits of digital communication technologies, opening up parliamentary space and its potential pitfalls, as our parliaments continue to adapt their physical and their digital spaces.

Part VI The spatial production of assemblies

If the history of European nations has been diverse in its rhythms of power and decline, the European nation-states do share important forms, experiences, discourses and interactions that give them some coherence. One site where such coherence may be demonstrated is in the parliament buildings of European states (Gibson et al) and the European Parliament (Sailer). The rise of modern democracies in Europe found expression in the staged unity of the parliamentary seating plan, that the chambers themselves have partly helped to shape (Manow 2010). This staged unity has its origins in the open-air circles of the Teutonic 'Thing' as well as in the *ecclesiasterion* and the *comitium* of the Greeks and the Romans (Trapp). It is also routed into the origins of the parliamentary debate as a philosophical category in the Enlightenment (Korolija). However, if similar typologies and forms were used for a variety of political systems (XML 2016), the forms alone are not sufficient registers for differences in power dynamics. A closer look at parliamentary chambers reveals rich variety depending on where the legislature, the executive and the chair sit; the customs around seating arrangements for MPs and MEPs; the rituals and rules of plenary proceedings. This session by four architects discusses the history and spatial construction of assemblies and politics, in the context of the EU plenary chamber (Sailer) and the 28 parliament buildings in the EU, the UK included (Gibson et al), with special emphasis on seating arrangements (Sailer; Gibson et al), ideology (Korolija), the evolutionary history of assemblies and representational structures (Trapp).

Part VII Sovereignty, scale and languages of representation

Marked differences between cultural and political boundaries often result in disputes concerning autonomy and self-determination. Architecture, the spatial and visual form of parliament buildings, their rituals and symbolism, can thus become caught in contentious debates. Likewise, constitutional change can result in gaps opening up between the new constitutional order and engrained parliamentary ritual or form. This part explores negotiations of parliamentary architecture, form and symbolism in a variety of contexts: the political tensions between nation-states and indigenous peoples, which may have no tradition of large-scale immovable structures (Singler and Singler); constructions of national identity of newly established states, semi-autonomous tributary states and suzerain states (Kotsaki); or the adaptation of parliamentary ceremony, ritual and symbolism to shifts in constitutional order (Johansen). What architectural forms and trajectories capture the emergence of modern nation-states (Kotsaki)? What visual languages, material cultures and architectural forms might capture the imaginaries of indigenous peoples and their struggles for political representation (Singler and Singler)? How do contemporary parliaments adapt their forms and ritual symbolically to represent the historical innovation and reinvention of state, nation and democracy (Johansen)? In Part VII, two architecture scholars and two legal scholars explore these questions in the context of the cultural-administrative centre of Sajos, which houses the Sámi Parliament of Finland (Singler and Singler); the seven parliamentary buildings situated in today's Greek territory (Kotsaki); as well as the ceremonial practices of the Swedish Riksdag (Johansen).

Part VIII Building parliaments for the future

In a speech to the House of Commons in October 1943, Winston Churchill connected the process of government and the architectural character of the spaces in which it takes place. The war was still raging when he gave that speech, with the famous phrase 'we shape our buildings and afterwards they shape us', which is probably his best-known comment on architecture. In this part, guest editor Jeremy Melvin discusses the long evolution of the House of Commons, both as a building and as an institution, in the light of that quote (Melvin). He argues that several centuries of the Commons shaping the building are followed by another few centuries of the building shaping how the Commons (and indeed, how the British Parliament) works. Based on this introduction, Melvin offers a context for the following chapters presenting designs of contemporary parliament buildings in the UK and Germany. This context concerns the critical dialogue between political evolution and political rupture or a new beginning, creating the need either for an entirely new parliament building, such as the Scottish Parliament designed by Miralles Tagliabue EMBT (Tagliabue) and the Welsh Senedd by RSHP (Harbour), a remodelled building such as the German Reichstag by Foster and Partners (Nelson), or a temporary accommodation such as the project by AHMM Architects for a temporary UK Commons chamber (Monaghan).

Outlook

We hope that this book might guide the design of future parliament buildings, providing a lasting resource and inspiration not only for academics, but also designers and political practitioners regarding how to improve the physical dimensions of politics for greater transparency and legitimacy in parliaments. At this particular moment in time, a number of restoration projects of parliaments are under way, including in the UK, Austria and Canada, while the Cypriot parliament is awaiting its resettlement into its permanent building from temporary spatial arrangements. All these projects require systematic knowledge of how to adapt a historic fabric to contemporary political challenges, or an established political system to a new building. Equally important is the need to understand how potential transformations from devolved parliaments to national parliaments (Scotland), or tensions between sovereign state, indigenous or stateless people (such as the Sámi) put pressure on the spatial structure and architectural language of expression of parliament buildings. Finally, as political changes affect confidence in the shared values and constitutional orders of many nations (including Brexit Britain), it is imperative that we explore how parliaments can stay relevant, meaningful and accessible to the citizens whom they serve. In the hope that this book will be useful as a work of reference for scholars and practitioners alike, we are providing a focused, comparative and multidisciplinary study of parliament buildings across Europe and across history.

Notes

1 From early designed capitals in North America and Europe to Chandigarh, Brasília and four postcolonial capitol complexes (Papua New Guinea, Sri Lanka, Kuwait and Bangladesh).

2 Dovey reinforces Foucault's idea that power is not something held by agents, but a system of micropractices of everyday life that produces a disciplined subject. Dovey, K. (2018).

3 These relationships concern opposite forces, such as the preservation of hierarchical differences, professional statuses and norms of behaviour on the one hand, and the need to interface different social categories, construct solidarities and forms of surveillance on the other.

4 A series of filmed interviews were conducted with members of the House of Lords and the House of Commons in the UK Houses of Parliament, discussing the building in terms of how it is perceived by parliamentarians, the impact of the coronavirus pandemic in parliamentary proceedings, its symbolic and expressive function and its future in light of the Restoration and Renewal Programme. The interviews took place from July to October 2020. They were subsequently edited and presented in two short films directed by Graham Riach and produced by Sophia Psarra and the UCL European Institute (available from: https://www.parliamentbuildings.org.uk/video/inside-parliament-the -architecture-of-democracy).

References

Adorno. T. (1979) 'Functionalism Today' [translation by J.O. Newman and J. Smith], *Oppositions*, 17, pp. 31–41.

Aerts, R. and van den Berg, J.Th.J. (2019) 'The Ideal of Parliament in Europe Since 1800: Introduction', in R. Aerts, C. van Baalen, H. te Velde, M. van der Steen and M.-L. Recker (eds) *The Ideal of Parliament Since 1800*, Palgrave Studies in Political History, Cham: Palgrave Macmillan/Springer Nature Switzerland, pp. 1–22.

Bagehot, W. (1867 [1963]) *The English Constitution*, Ithaca: Cornell University Press.

Barnstone, D.A. (2005) *The Transparent State: Architecture and Politics in Postwar Germany*, Abingdon and New York: Routledge.

Bell, D. and Zacka, B. (eds) (2020) *Political Theory and Architecture*, London and New York: Bloomsbury.

Bold, J. (2019) 'Familiar Ordinary Things: The Corridor in English Architecture', *Transactions of the Ancient Monuments Society*, 63, pp. 41–78.

Bradley, S. and Pevsner, N. (2003) *London 6: Westminster*, New Haven and London: Yale University Press.

Crewe, E. (2005) *Lords of Parliament: Manners, Rituals and Politics*, Manchester: Manchester University Press.

Crewe, E. (2015) *The House of Commons: An Anthropology of MPs at Work*, London and New York: Bloomsbury.

Crewe, E. (2021) *The Anthropology of Parliaments: Entanglements in Democratic Politics*, Abingdon and New York: Routledge.

Crewe, E. and Sarra, N. (2019) 'Chairing UK Select Committees: Walking Between Friends and Foes', *Parliamentary Affairs*, 72(4), pp. 841–859. DOI: 10.1093/pa/gsz036.

Dörner, A. (2000) 'Der Bundestag im Reichstag. Zur Inszenierung einer politischen Institution in der, "Berliner Republik"', *Zeitschrift für Parlamentsfragen*, 31(2), pp. 237–246.

Douglas, M. (1986) *How Institutions Think*, Syracuse: Syracuse University Press.

Dovey, K. (1999) *Framing Places: Mediating Power in Built Form*, Abingdon and New York: Routledge.

Dovey, K. (2018) 'Architecture and Power: How to Fix Australia's Parliament House'. Available from: https://www.themandarin.com.au/92899-architecture-and-power-how-to-fix-aus tralias-parliament-house (accessed 9 February 2023).

Edelman, M. (1964) *The Symbolic Uses of Politics*, Urbana: University of Illinois Press.

Ezrahi, Y. (2012) *Imagined Democracies: Necessary Political Fictions*, Cambridge: Cambridge University Press.

Feuchter, J. and Helmrath, J. (eds) (2013) *Parlamentarische Kulturen vom Mittelal ter bis in die Moderne. Reden – Räume – Bilder*, Beiträge zur Geschichte des Parlamentarismus und der politischen Parteien, 164. Düsseldorf: Droste.

Flinders, M., Cotter, L.-M., Kelso, A. and Meakin, A. (2018) 'The Politics of Parliamentary Restoration and Renewal: Decisions, Discretion, Democracy', *Parliamentary Affairs*, 71(1), pp. 144–168. DOI: 10.1093/pa/gsx012.

Foucault, M. (1977) *Discipline and Punish: The Birth of the Prison* [translation by A. Sheridan], London: Allen Lane.

Freeden, M. (1998) *Ideologies and Political Theory: A Conceptual Approach*, Oxford: Oxford University Press.

Geddes, M. (2020) *Dramas at Westminster: Select Committees and the Quest for Accountability*, Manchester: Manchester University Press.

Goodman, N. (1985) 'How Buildings Mean', *Critical Inquiry*, 11(4), pp. 642–653. Available from: https://www.jstor.org/stable/1343421.

Goodsell, C. (1988) 'The Architecture of Parliaments: Legislative Houses and Political Culture', *British Journal of Political Science*, 18(3), pp. 287–302. DOI: 10.1017/S0007123400005135.

Gordon, C. (ed.) (1980) *Power Knowledge: Selected Interviews and Other Writings 1972–1977 by Michel Foucault*, New York: Pantheon Books.

Habermas, J. (1989) *The Structural Transformation of the Public Sphere: An Inquiry into a Category of Bourgeois Society*, Cambridge, MA: MIT Press.

Hague, M. and Harrop, M. (2022) *Comparative Government and Politics: An Introduction* (12th ed.), London: Bloomsbury Academic.

Hays, M.K. (1998) *Architectural Theory since 1968*, New York and Cambridge, MA: Columbia University in the City of New York and MIT Press.

Herzog, J. and de Meuron, P. (2016) *Treacherous Transparencies*, New York: Actar Publishers.

Hillier, B. and Hanson, J. (1984) *The Social Logic of Space*, Cambridge: Cambridge University Press.

Komarek, J. (ed.) (2023) *European Constitutional Imaginaries: Between Ideology and Utopia*, Oxford: Oxford University Press.

Kröger, S. and Bellamy, R. (eds) (2016) *National Parliaments and the Politicization of European Integration, Comparative European Politics* (Special issue), 14(2).

Kumarasingham, H. (2013) *A Political Legacy of the British Empire: Power and the Parliamentary System in Post-Colonial India and Sri Lanka*, London: I.B. Tauris.

Laslett, P. (ed.) (1988) *Locke: Two Treatises of Government, Student Edition*, Cambridge Texts in the History of Political Thought, Cambridge: Cambridge University Press.

Latour, B. (1991) *We Have Never Been Modern*, Cambridge, MA: Harvard University Press.

Latour, B. and Yaneva, A. (2008) 'Give Me a Gun and I Will Make Buildings Move: An ANT's View of Architecture', *Ardeth*, 1. Available from: http://journals.openedition.org/ardeth/991 (accessed 28 July 2023).

Lefebvre, H. (1991) *The Production of Space* [translation by D. Nicholson-Smith], Oxford: Blackwell.

Lijphart, A. (1999) *Patterns of Democracy: Government Forms and Performance in Thirty-Six Countries*, London: Yale University Press.

Malley, R. (2012a) *The Institutionalisation of Gendered Norms and the Substantive Representation of Women in Westminster and the Scottish Parliament*. PhD thesis. University of Bristol. Available at: https://research-information.bristol.ac.uk/en/theses/the-institutionalisation -of-gendered-norms-and-the-substantive-representation-of-women-in-westminster-and -the-scottish-parliament(afc27afb-884e-4c97-8416-f5126d81cb61).html (accessed 19 October 2019).

Malley, R. (2012b) 'Feeling at Home: Inclusion at Westminster and the Scottish Parliament', *The Political Quarterly*, (83)4, pp. 714–717.

Manow, P. (2010) *In the King's Shadow: The Political Anatomy of Democratic Representation* [translation by P. Camiller], Cambridge: Polity Press.

Markus, T. (1993) *Buildings and Power: Freedom and Control in the Origins of Modern Building Types*, London and New York: Routledge.

Markus, T.A. and Cameron, D. (2002) *The Words Between the Spaces: Buildings and Language*, London and New York: Routledge.

Norton, P. (2019) 'Power Behind the Scenes: The Importance of Informal Space in Legislatures', *Parliamentary Affairs*, 72(2), pp. 245–266. DOI: 10.1093/pa/gsy018.

Parkinson, J. (2009) 'Holistic Democracy and Physical Public Space', in M. Kinwell and P. Turmel (eds) *Rites of Way: The Politics and Poetics of Public Space*, Ontario: Wilfrid Laurier University Press, pp. 71–84.

Penn, A., Desyllas, J. and Vaughan, L. (1999) 'The Space of Innovation: Interaction and Communication in the Work Environment', *Environment and Planning B*, 26(2), pp. 193–218. DOI: 10.1068/b4225.

Pitkin, H.F. (1967) *The Concept of Representation*, Berkeley: University of California.

Psarra, S. and Riach, G. (2020) 'Inside Parliament: The Architecture of Democracy', film created in collaboration with the UCL European Institute. Available from: https://www.parliamentbuildings.org.uk/video/inside-parliament-the-architecture-of-democracy/ (accessed 1 March 2022).

Puwar, N. (2004) *Space Invaders: Race, Gender and Bodies Out of Place*, Berg: Oxford.

Rosanvallon, P. (2011) *Democratic Legitimacy: Impartiality, Reflexivity, Proximity*, Princeton: Princeton University Press.

Schofield, M. and Griffith, T. (eds) (2016) *Plato: Laws*, Cambridge Texts in the History of Political Thought, Cambridge: Cambridge University Press.

Schwanholz, J. and Theiner, P. (2020) *Die Politische Architektur Deutscher Parlamente, Von Häusern, Schlössern und Palästen*, Wiesbaden: Springer Verlag.

Sharr, A. and Thornton, S. (2013) *Demolishing Whitehall: Leslie Martin, Harold Wilson and the Architecture of White Heat*, Farnham: Ashgate.

Soja, E.W. (1989) *Postmodern Geographies: The Reassertion of Space in Critical Social Theory*, London: Verso.

Sternberg, C. (2013) *The Struggle for EU Legitimacy: Public Contestation, 1950s–2005*, Basingstoke: Palgrave Macmillan.

Sternberg, C. (2023) 'Ideologies and Imaginaries of Legitimacy from the 1950s to Today: Trajectories of EU-Official Discourses against Rosanvallon's Democratic Legitimacy', in J. Komarek (ed.) *European Constitutional Imaginaries: Between Ideology and Utopia*, Oxford: Oxford University Press, pp. 92–117.

Taylor, C. (2003) *Modern Social Imaginaries*, Durham, NC: Duke University Press.

te Velde, H. (2019) 'Between National Character and an International Model: Parliaments in the Nineteenth Century', in R. Aerts, C. van Baalen, H. te Velde, M. van der Steen and M.-L. Recker (eds) *The Ideal of Parliament Since 1800*, Palgrave Studies in Political History, Cham: Palgrave Macmillan/Springer Nature Switzerland, pp. 25–40.

Thompson, J.B. (1990) *Ideology and Modern Culture: Critical Social Theory in the Era of Mass Communication*, Stanford: Stanford University Press.

Tuck, R. (ed.) (1996) *Hobbes: Leviathan*, Cambridge Texts in the History of Political Thought, Cambridge: Cambridge University Press.

Vale, L.J. (2008) *Architecture, Power and National Identity*, London and New York: Routledge.

Vidler, A. (1992) *The Architectural Uncanny: Essays in the Modern Unhomely*, Cambridge, MA: MIT Press.

Weber, M. (1919 [1970]) 'Politics as a Vocation', in H.H. Gerth and C.W. Mills (eds) *From Max Weber: Essays in Sociology*, London: Routledge, pp. 77–128.

XML (2016) *Parliament*, Amsterdam: XML.

Part I
Rhythms of time and space

2
Making use of space
The unseen impact of mixing informally
Philip Norton

Introduction

Legislatures matter because they are law-effecting institutions. Studies of their roles and members' behaviour focus primarily on the publicly observable and the formal – the deliberations in the chamber and committee rooms. Citizens in many nations are able now to watch proceedings of their legislature on television or the internet. What they see usually are members engaged in public debate or questioning witnesses in a committee room. The cameras rarely follow members away from the formal arena. This chapter examines the underexplored behaviour of members of parliament in the less formal settings of the legislature and how that behaviour matters for the work and output of the institution.

Creating space

Space in legislatures is not distributed randomly. The design of parliamentary buildings and allocation of space within them is ultimately a political decision. When the chamber of the British House of Commons was destroyed by enemy bombing in May 1941, the decision to build a new chamber in the same form as the old one was justified by the prime minister, Winston Churchill, on the basis of his perception of the nature of parliamentary politics in the United Kingdom (Cocks 1977). The use of space within the chamber is characterised by what Anthony King identified as the opposition mode of executive-legislative relations (King 1976). Two principal parties face one another in an adversarial relationship. The aim, as King noted, is not accommodation, but domination. The design of the chamber reflects and reinforces that relationship, one side sat facing its

Figure 2.1 Portcullis House Interior Cafe. © Colin, 'Portcullis House Interior Cafe', 19 September 2015. Edited for publication. Source: Wikimedia Commons, reproduced on the basis of CC BY-SA 2.0 licence. Available at: https://commons.wikimedia.org /wiki/File:Portcullis_House_Interior_Cafe_2015-09-19_(27694442083).jpg (accessed 29 November 2022)

opponent party. The rules governing the conduct of the house are largely predicated on the existence of a government and a formal opposition. The concept of an official opposition is a notable feature of parliaments that have followed Westminster in adopting a distinctive executive-centred, adversarial parliamentary system (Kaiser 2009), the parties competing to win the argument rather than achieve consensus (Norton 2022). This sets it apart from the other legislatures covered in this volume.

Political decisions determine the sheer size of a parliament building and how space is allocated within it. Structures and processes are then agreed for the institution to operate. They help shape the use of space. That usage takes two forms, one essentially observable and measurable. The other is largely unseen and unmeasurable. The former is much studied in the political science literature. The latter is largely ignored – and will be the focus of this chapter.

Configuration of space in legislatures matters not only for the transaction of formal business, but also for the extent to which it enables members to mix informally with one another, free from formal constraints and direction by party leaders.

Studies of the use of space in legislatures tend to focus on dedicated space for formal gatherings – the chamber and committee rooms – where proceedings are rule-based, observable and recorded. Such space may also be used for private meetings (as, for example, of parliamentary parties), but these are also normally scheduled, subject to rules and often with a record kept (see Norton 1994, 2013). What is less studied is what is essentially unseen behaviour: members gathering informally in the dining and tea rooms, corridors, lobbies and lounges. Here other modes of relationship identified by King – notably the intraparty and non-party modes – come more to the fore. Such informal contact is not rule-based, formally observable or measurable. It can, however, have significant consequences.

The form and use of informal space

Space for members of either house of the UK Parliament to meet informally with one another takes different forms, has changed over time, and differs between the two houses. Although both houses sat primarily in the Palace of Westminster from 1548 onwards, they did not always meet there. The Parliament of 1625, for example, met at Oxford, the Commons sitting on the ground floor of the new Divinity School and the Lords on the top floor. Lecture halls were used as committee rooms, with colleges and other spaces for members to meet one another. A gallery was designated as a conference space.

When the new Palace of Westminster was built following the great fire of 1834, space was included for members to meet informally. Over time, the space has grown as the parliamentary estate has expanded. This has been especially the case in the twenty-first century with the addition of Portcullis House, discussed below. Opportunities for members of both houses to mix informally have also expanded as a result not only of the development of Portcullis House, but also changes in rules governing the use of space exclusive to members.

The timing of the building of the new Palace of Westminster, and the architect who designed it, were fortuitous in terms of creating space for members to meet informally. The new building was designed when gentlemen's clubs had become fashionable in London. The architect, Charles Barry, had designed one of them (the Travellers Club), and he created discrete facilities, away from public areas, for the use of members:

> The most important of these new facilities for Members and Peers lay on the principal floor, with libraries and refreshment rooms on the river-side of the new building, located away from the street and the public entrance through Westminster Hall, and adjacent to the Chambers, the heart of Parliamentary life (Church 2000, p. 164).

Members were able to relax and mix informally in the Commons in the bars, dining rooms, smoking room, and tea room, as well as in the library and spacious corridors, and on the terrace. The absence of offices for members encouraged such mixing.

The capacity to mix informally was thus created as part of the design of the new Parliament and the members were culturally attuned to mixing in such space. The demands made of them in terms of business were not great – it was only towards the end of the century that public business dominated in place of private legislation – and many were not assiduous attenders, but the opportunity to meet with one another in a relaxed environment was a feature of the institution.

In the late twentieth century, there were substantial changes in the use of space as more rooms were taken over to provide offices for members, not least through converting what previously was accommodation within the Palace for officers of either house, and through the acquisition of adjoining property, such as the Norman Shaw buildings, formerly housing Scotland Yard. Previously, members had a locker in which to keep their papers or if they were lucky, had a desk in a shared room (facilitating informal contact with others in the room); otherwise, it was a case of using the shared space: 'It was bewildering, in those days you didn't have a desk, you just did your work in the corridors until they allocated you something, or you squatted on someone's desk' (Ann Widdecombe, quoted in Peplow and Pivatto 2020, p. 87). With the acquisition of more space, a growing number of MPs had their own rooms. The process of ensuring each MP had an individual office was completed in the twenty-first century with the opening in 2001 of a new parliamentary building,

Portcullis House, next to the Palace of Westminster and linked to it by a tunnel. This provided office space for more than 200 members.

The creation of more offices encouraged MPs, and their staff, to spend time in what a former government chief whip described as their 'rabbit hutches' (former chief whip to author), reducing the opportunities for informal interaction with other members. This was exacerbated by email replacing paper mail as the principal mode of contacting MPs. MPs no longer congregated in the Members' Lobby, by the chamber, to collect messages left in their trays and to chat to fellow members. They now spent time in their offices dealing with electronic communications, including 'dear colleague' emails from other members.

Interaction between MPs was also affected by the location of Portcullis House and the design of its ground floor atrium. The building occupies a key geopolitical space within the parliamentary estate. It sits at the intersection of other parliamentary buildings – occupants of those buildings have to pass through Portcullis House to get to the Palace of Westminster – and the atrium provides substantial space for members to meet informally, not necessarily with one another, but rather with visiting guests, members of the House of Lords, and journalists. As one MP noted, lobby journalists based in Parliament 'are often scattered among the tables awaiting a passer-by to have a good old gossip with' (Phillips 2021, p. 62). The atrium is served by a restaurant, cafe and coffee shop, drawing members and staff throughout the day. It is normally crowded and becomes full of MPs whenever a division is called as they rush from their offices upstairs or in the adjoining buildings. They often engage in animated conversation as they troop to the Palace.

The facilities for members of the second chamber to mix informally are not as substantial, at least in terms of physical space, as in the House of Commons. There are dining rooms and bars, but not the equivalent of the tea room and smoking room. However, there is a cultural difference that encourages informal contact between members of different parties not experienced in the Commons. MPs tend to dine, and mix in the tea room, on a party basis. As former prime minister Harold Wilson told one new Conservative MP, 'we have segregation here' (Teddy Taylor, quoted in Peplow and Pivatto 2020, p. 89). Peers, in contrast, adopt the long table principle – if dining alone, they join whoever is already at the peers' long table in whichever dining room they use. This ensures informal interaction between members and on a crossparty basis.

Members of each house also have the opportunity to mix informally with members of the other on a more extensive basis than before as a consequence of a rule change enabling members of one house to use some of the dining and drinking facilities of the other, previously restricted to members only of that house. Peers who are ex-MPs already had dining rights in the Commons, but now there is greater fluidity in the use of facilities. This change followed a change in sitting hours of the House of Commons, with earlier sittings meaning MPs did not need to remain on the premises in the evening to the extent they did when a 10.00 p.m. vote was expected. The need for dining outlets to maintain custom appears to have prompted more competition to attract customers beyond the members of the house.

The key points are thus that there is space within the Westminster parliamentary estate for parliamentarians to meet informally with one another and that the configuration of that space has changed over time. The extent and nature of this space is particular to the Westminster Parliament, but the use to which it is put is not.

Consequences

The existence and use of informal space can contribute to the institution-alisation of a legislature. It facilitates members staying in the parliament building and enables them to feel part of the process. The more extensive the space available in different forms (lounges, dining rooms, tea rooms, reading rooms), and the greater its use, the more established members become in operating within the institution. The existence and use of dedicated informal space contribute to the complexity and the autonomy of the institution, both features of institutionalisation (Polsby 1968; Patterson 1995). Members develop patterns of behaviour over time (see Crewe in this volume). The facility and use of social space serve to hold members' emotional attachment: 'The place has such a phenomenal hold on the MPs', as one of their number wrote, 'institutionalised doesn't come close to describing it' (Phillips 2021, p. 71).

The use of space to mix informally also has significant consequences for members. An analysis of the UK Parliament has identified four: socialisation, information exchange, lobbying and raising political support (Norton 2019).

The use of such space serves to facilitate *socialisation* – getting to know the norms of behaviour as well as fellow members. Members may get to know the norms from publications, induction meetings and observation. Bill Rodgers recorded that in his first two-and-a-half years in Parliament – he was elected in a by-election in 1962 – he made only ten speeches. 'I felt no compelling need to speak more often when getting to know my colleagues in the lobbies, corridors, bar and tea rooms and absorbing the atmosphere of the place seemed the more important part of learning' (Rodgers 2000, p. 74). Observation may be complemented by more active engagement, seeking out other members to draw on their knowledge and advice on how to conduct themselves and how to make the most of their membership of the institution. This may occur through arranging a meeting or more spontaneously when wishing to take part in proceedings and not being sure of what to do, asking a nearby member for guidance. Even if not sought, guidance may be offered. One senior MP, Edward du Cann, often took it upon himself to explain procedures and behaviour to newly elected members, noting, 'I wish the same service had been available to me when I was a new boy in the House' (du Cann 1995, p. 219).

The existence and use of informal space can be significant for female members, especially in parliamentary systems with male-orientated adversarial politics to the fore in formal space, especially the chamber. The use of formal space may be off-putting, not least given the numerical dominance of male MPs in most legislatures. Having space where members can meet one another in a less adversarial manner may help female members feel more integrated into the institution. This may be enhanced where such space is exclusive to female members. In each house of the UK Parliament, women members have their own room (Ridge 2017; Honeyball 2015; Knight 1995). Such space may help draw into the institution those women who, as Sarah Childs put it, do not want 'to act like men' (Childs 2004, p. 10; see also Norton 2019).

The use of space to mix informally also facilitates *information exchange*, members sharing their views as well as information gleaned from other sources. Some of the contact can be the result of proactively seeking views and information and in other cases may be more passive, listening to what members are saying. As one MP who sat in the house from 1918 to 1929 recalled, 'The central social magnet in my day was the Smoke-room where … Members who might have been assailing one another most bitterly in the Chamber were wont to meet and discuss the affairs of the world in genial accord' (Brittain 1949, p. 169). It can also range from information on high policy to more personal comment and gossip (see Mitchell 1982); indeed, one MP, Arthur Griffith-Boscawen, first returned at the end of the nineteenth century, described the smoking room as 'a hotbed of gossip' (Griffith-Boscawen 1925, p. 42). Such comments possibly mask the value of the informal exchanges as a form of political intelligence. Members get to know what fellow members are thinking. It also offers opportunities for party whips and leaders to get an idea of attitudes among party members, attitudes that may not be expressed publicly. As one MP recorded, 'whips equipped with bionic hearing are known to loiter' (George 2002, p. 63). Such political intelligence can be useful to ensure backbench disquiet is addressed before it ever becomes public.

Informal space, thirdly, is used for *lobbying*, members with a particular cause seeing other members to press their argument. As Griffith-Boscawen also recorded of the smoking room, 'a good deal of political wirepulling goes on in there' (Griffith-Boscawen 1925, p. 42). Members may lobby fellow backbenchers or use the space to press ministers on a particular policy. It is not unknown for ministers to use the space to lobby backbenchers to support their case or even to persuade them to be critical of policies they do not actually support. It is also useful for candid discussions among party members. As Labour MP Jess Phillips observed:

> There is a lot of plotting that goes on in politics, lots of quiet little meetings without notetakers. This is usually where party politicking goes on and trying to find allegiances with others to make demands – sometimes of the government, but, let's face it, a lot of this is to find a way to pressure your own party to do what you want. Every single faction of politics does this plotting (Phillips 2021, pp. 62–3).

In the UK House of Commons, voting in division lobbies ensures ministers (including the prime minister) are physically present to vote and, once in the voting lobbies, can be approached by other members to argue their causes. This is one of the principal reasons that parliamentarians make the case for retaining voting physically rather than electronically. When in the division lobby, there is no escape for ministers. They can be and are approached by other members.

Using informal space for lobbying is long established. A valuable case study, drawn from the interwar years, demonstrates how a member can achieve a reputation for deploying such space effectively. Eleanor Rathbone was a female MP in a very male house and an independent MP in a party-dominated house, but she was an exemplar of how to deploy both formal and informal space to achieve her goals. She is largely credited with, among other things, achieving the introduction of family allowances, but she lobbied on a range of issues. She would stalk the corridors of the Palace of Westminster waiting to waylay ministers. As Harold Nicolson recorded:

> Benign and yet menacing, she would stalk through the lobby, one arm weighed with the heavy satchel which contained the papers on

family allowances, another arm dragging an even heavier satchel in which were stored the more recent papers about refugees and displaced persons; recalcitrant Ministers would quail before the fire of her magnificent eyes (Nicolson 1946, quoted in Norton 2016, p. 7).

She proved remarkably effective, but in an institution where such behaviour is common, with members waiting in the tea room or corridors to approach fellow members to press them to support a particular cause. Some may do it on a sporadic basis; others, like Rathbone, may always have one or more causes on the go.

Ministers and those wishing to be ministers may also utilise informal space to *mobilise political support* for their own career progression. Being seen and listening to other members helps establish one's credentials as a potential candidate for promotion or, if already in office, keeping supporters in place. Among prime ministers, James Callaghan was particularly adept at spending time in the Palace of Westminster and being seen by backbenchers (Norton 2020a). Neglect of informal space – failing to be seen and to mix with fellow members – can harm or even destroy a political career. Neglecting to use informal space to build support when their leadership was under challenge was viewed as contributing to the loss of the UK Conservative party leadership by both Edward Heath in 1975 and Margaret Thatcher in 1990 (Norton 2019). More recently, Theresa May's failure as prime minister to mix regularly with her backbenchers – she was noted for her lack of 'clubbability' (Prince 2017, p. 334) – left her vulnerable when her leadership came under pressure.

These consequences are thus substantial. It is impossible to appreciate fully the life of the Westminster Parliament, and some political outcomes, without understanding how parliamentarians utilise the opportunities afforded by the space within the parliamentary estate to mix informally with one another.

The pandemic challenge

The importance of informal space is highlighted when it ceases to be available or is constricted or modified. The coronavirus crisis of 2020–21 forced legislators to decant, wholly or in large measure, the legislature and to operate as discrete entities away from the building (Study of Parliament Group 2021). Although it became possible to transact formal business by virtual or hybrid (part virtual, part physical) means, and with committees operating online, it proved less feasible to replicate the space for members to mix informally. Although members may use social media, creating WhatsApp groups and texting one another, there is not the same capacity to meet someone unexpectedly and strike up a conversation. What may be termed the serendipity of informal contact is lost. That is especially the case with contact between members of the two houses. Members are more likely to maintain contact informally with members of their own house and to meet members of the other in the course of moving around the parliamentary estate. Yet it is this contact between members of the two houses that can be crucial in affecting outcomes, often constituting a key form of political intelligence.

The constricted or non-existent ability for members to mix informally has significant political consequences. Constricted opportunities for socialisation may leave new members especially feeling isolated. MPs newly elected in the December 2019 general election had little time to acclimatise to the norms and procedures of Westminster before the pandemic forced them to leave Parliament and operate remotely. Once they were able to return to Westminster, they were unsure of how to proceed and utilise the opportunities available to them, indeed were uncertain in some cases as to what those opportunities were. Some sought out other members for guidance and advice. At least one turned to this writer, as a specialist on Parliament, for tutoring on how to be effective in utilising space within the Commons.

Limiting informal contact between members, and hence the exchange of information, strengthens the executive (Norton 2020b). Sharing information among members via social media may prevent the executive being a monopoly supplier of information, but the process of sharing takes time and is likely to be reactive. For the executive, limited opportunities for members to meet informally are beneficial in that they reduce the likelihood of spontaneous plotting and rebellions.

Restoration and renewal

By the early twenty-first century, the Palace of Westminster was showing its age, its infrastructure in a parlous state and with a danger of some basic services suffering a catastrophic failure. Firewatchers were employed on a 24-hour basis. There was asbestos in over 1,000 locations and instances of falling masonry. There was recognition by government and the parliamentary authorities that constant repairs were inadequate and that a programme of restoration and renewal, entailing a full or partial decant by both chambers, was required. How to proceed proved controversial and challenging (see Flinders in this volume). In 2018, both houses voted for a full decant. It was expected that the programme would take five to ten years, as opposed to 30 or more that may be required in the event of a partial decant. The Parliamentary Buildings (Restoration and Renewal) Act 2019 created both a sponsor body and a delivery authority to deliver the programme. The House of Commons was scheduled to move to a purpose-built replica chamber in Richmond House on the northern part of the parliamentary estate and the House of Lords to a nearby conference centre.

There were twentieth-century precedents for members of both houses having to move out of the chambers. After the destruction of the Commons' chamber by enemy bombing in 1941, both houses met briefly in Church House, Westminster, before the Commons returned to sit in the chamber of the House of Lords and the Lords sat in the Robing Room. Meeting principally in the Palace meant that opportunities for informal gatherings remained. What limitations there were on such gatherings were affected more by the absence of many members on active service than by the physical constraints (Norton 1998). Given that the parties were united in the chamber in the prosecution of the war, space away from the chamber was used both for the parliamentary parties to retain their identity and continue meeting (Norton 2013) and for members who may have doubts about the conduct of government to formulate and share their views; some 'ginger groups' of members came into being (Norton 1998), that is, unofficial groups to keep ministers on their toes or to promote a particular issue. In the 1980s, the House of Lords also moved out of the chamber briefly, meeting in the Royal Gallery, following a partial ceiling collapse, but the use of space for informal contact was not greatly affected.

The Restoration and Renewal (R&R) Programme poses two distinctive challenges in creating space for members to meet informally and indeed for members of one house to mix with members of the other. The first covers the period in which both houses leave the Palace of Westminster. During this period, the two houses will not be on the same estate. They will face the challenge of being separated by buildings and roads. The different configuration of space for informal gatherings will take time for members to adapt to and will be especially problematic in facilitating informal contact between members of the two houses. For MPs, Portcullis House will still be in operation and accessible on the same estate as the new chamber. For peers, getting over to Portcullis House will entail a walk of several hundred yards and crossing two busy roads. Building an underground tunnel would be expensive and the cost may render it politically difficult to sustain. The problem is one recognised by the team responsible for the programme: 'There has been some early work undertaken by officials of both Houses to consider how the implications of the Houses operating on different sites should be addressed; this will obviously need to be addressed in more detail' (Restoration and Renewal 2020, p. 32). This has included talking to peers about how much time they spend at events or meetings with MPs. However, by late 2021 no concrete proposals had emerged.

The second challenge is that of the extent to which the space for informal contact will be maintained and indeed enhanced in the restored Palace of Westminster. There is no evidence that the space will be reduced, but equally there is no explicit statement in the *Vision and Strategic Themes* for the programme of a desire to protect and enhance it. There is an emphasis on accessibility and inclusion in terms of the outward face of Parliament, to enhance public engagement to provide space for members of both houses 'to meet constituents, the public and the media', but no mention of members meeting one another. In terms of functionality and design, there is the aim of creating 'a flexible, effective and enjoyable working environment in the Palace', but no acknowledgement of the importance, indeed centrality to the work of Parliament, of enabling members to meet informally. There is a danger of the emphasis on the public face of the institution obscuring the need for members to be able to meet informally and privately. The R&R programme offers an unrivalled opportunity to think creatively about the form and nature of space available to members and how to enhance that which presently exists. There is the danger of the opportunity being lost.

Conclusion

What this chapter has sought to demonstrate is that, without understanding and factoring in the impact of the use of informal space, it is not possible to understand fully the behaviour and impact of members of parliaments. There is more to a parliament than what happens formally in the chamber and committee rooms. How space is allocated matters, not only for enabling each house to meet formally and publicly, and for members of each to meet members of the public as well as be seen by and interact with the media, but also for members to meet with one another informally. Mixing informally has consequences, both for the institution and for members. Those consequences impact on the political life of the nation. Enhancing space to meet informally enhances parliament in its relationship to the executive. Constraining members in meeting with one another other than in formal space removes a potential constraint on the executive.

The use of space for members to mix informally, being by its nature away from the public gaze and, insofar as it may be seen (through anthropological study or casual observation, for example by journalists in shared space), difficult to measure, has been relatively neglected in the study of legislatures (Norton 2019). The neglect results in a skewed picture of parliamentary life, obscuring activity that has significant political consequences. The focus of this chapter has been the UK Parliament. Space for members to mix informally is configured in a particular way in the Palace of Westminster – and now the wider parliamentary estate – but the existence of space for members to mix informally with one another is not peculiar to Westminster. There is a need to take the study global.

References

Brittain, H. (1949) *Happy Pilgrimage*, London: Hutchinson.

Childs, S. (2004) 'A Feminised Style of Politics? Women MPs in the House of Commons', *British Journal of Politics and International Relations*, 6(1), pp. 3–19.

Church, D. (2000) '"New Furniture of a Suitable and Proper Character": The Working Interiors 1849–60', in C. Riding and J. Riding (eds) *The Houses of Parliament: History, Art, Architecture*, London: Merrell, pp. 163–77.

Cocks, B. (1977) *Mid-Victorian Masterpiece*, London: Hutchinson.

du Cann, E. (1995) *Two Lives*, Upton upon Severn: Images Publishing (Malvern).

George, A. (2002) *A View from the Bottom Left-Hand Corner*, Penzance: Patten Press.

Griffith-Boscawen, A. (1925) *Memoirs*, London: John Murray.

Honeyball, M. (2015) *Parliamentary Pioneers: Labour Women MPs 1918–1945*, Chatham: Urbane Publications.

Kaiser, A. (2009) 'Parliamentary Opposition in Westminster Democracies: Britain, Canada, Australia and New Zealand', in L. Helms (ed.) *Parliamentary Opposition in Old and New Democracies*, Abingdon: Routledge, pp. 1–26.

King, A. (1976) 'Modes of Executive-Legislative Relations: Great Britain, France and West Germany', *Legislative Studies Quarterly*, 1(1), pp. 11–34.

Knight, J. (1995) *About the House*, London: Churchill Press.

Mitchell, A. (1982) *Westminster Man*, London: Thames Methuen.

Nicolson, H. (1946) 'Eleanor Rathbone', *The Spectator*, 11 January.

Norton, P. (1994) 'The Parliamentary Party and Party Committees', in A. Seldon and S. Ball (eds) *Conservative Century*, Oxford: Oxford University Press, pp. 97–144.

Norton, P. (1998) 'Winning the War, But Losing the Peace: The British House of Commons During the Second World War', *The Journal of Legislative Studies*, 4(3), pp. 33–51.

Norton, P. (2013) *The Voice of the Backbenchers. The 1922 Committee: the first 90 years, 1923–2013*, London: Conservative History Group.

Norton, P. (2016) *Eleanor Rathbone: An Independent Force of Nature*, Hull: University of Hull.

Norton, P. (2019) 'Power behind the Scenes: The Importance of Informal Space in Legislatures', *Parliamentary Affairs*, 72(2), pp. 245–66.

Norton, P. (2020a) 'Staying in the Saddle: James Callaghan and Parliament', in K. Hickson and J. Miles (eds) *James Callaghan: An Underrated Prime Minister?* London: Biteback, pp. 55–70.

Norton, P. (2020b) 'Written Evidence, Constitution Committee, House of Lords', *The Constitutional Implications of COVID-19*. Available at: https://committees.parliament.uk/writtenevidence/8704/pdf/.

Norton, P. (2022) 'Is the Westminster System of Government Alive and Well?' *Journal of International and Comparative Law*, 9(1), pp. 1–24.

Patterson, S.C. (1995) 'Legislative Institutions and Institutionalisation in the United States', *The Journal of Legislative Studies*, 1(4), pp. 10–29.

Peplow, E. and Pivatto, P. (2020) *The Political Lives of Postwar British MPs*, London: Bloomsbury Academic.

Phillips, J. (2021) *Everything You Really Need to Know About Politics. My Life as an MP*, London: Gallery Books UK.

Polsby, N. (1968) 'The Institutionalisation of the US House of Representatives', *American Political Science Review*, 62(1), pp. 144–68.

Prince, R. (2017) *Theresa May*, London: Biteback Publishing.

Restoration and Renewal, Houses of Parliament (2020) *Restoration and Renewal Members' FAQs*, London: Restoration and Renewal Programme.

Ridge, S. (2017) *The Women Who Shaped Politics*, London: Coronet.

Rodgers, B. (2000) *Fourth Among Equals*, London: Politico's.

Study of Parliament Group (2021) *Parliaments and the Pandemic*, London: Study of Parliament Group. Available at: https://studyofparliamentgroup.org/wp-content/uploads/2021/01/Parliaments-and-the-Pandemic.pdf.

3

Rhythms of navigating time and space in the UK House of Commons

Emma Crewe

Introduction[1]

Parliamentary scholars tend to classify the work of Members of Parliament (MPs) into roles and measure their activities, votes and outputs. They thereby miss the contradictory, performative and ambivalent processes in politics. Influenced by Goffman's (1959) theatrical analogy in *The Presentation of Self in Everyday Life*, I have tried to shift attention towards everyday processes by writing about performance and relationships in MPs' political work. However, critical of my own former bias towards mind, knowledge and temporal perspectives, in my recent book *An Anthropology of Parliaments* (2021) and in this chapter, I bring bodies and space more directly into the centre of my analysis. Building on ethnographic studies of space in parliaments (Abélès 2000; Floret 2010; Puwar 2014; Rai 2014; Norton 2019), and following Lefebvre's rhythmanalysis (2013), I will propose a systematic way to research the diversity of MPs' work by looking at the *rhythms of performance* through time and space, using examples from my own ethnographic research into the House of Commons (2015).

According to Lefebvre (2013), rhythms can be sequential – where people follow each other; harmonious – where people perform in concert; cyclical with a beginning, a peak and a decline; or out of sync, multiple or problematic (Lefebvre 2013, p. 25). Whether in public or private space, rhythmed patterns reveal who is meeting whom, how often and for how long, and although finding out about the significance of meetings needs further investigation, rhythms can be a generative starting point. An inquiry into the rhythms – the patterns created by where people go, with whom and to do what, but also how those patterns change – reveals much about how politicians accomplish their political work: what they prioritise,

Figure 3.1 Lifting the lid. © Edward J.T. Walker

who they include and exclude in their encounters and how they respond
to changing circumstances. Both similarities and differences between
politicians are revealed, as are the seasonal shifts in political work,
influenced by whether or not Parliament is sitting, parties are holding
conferences, elections are being held. An abrupt change to rhythms,
such as a special sitting in the event of war, tells an observer when
Parliament is facing a critical event. So, tracing the rhythms is a method

and theory for achieving multidisciplinarity – a way of systematically studying the sociology, history and geography of politics with a sense of proportion.

Shapeshifting into and across parliamentary sociopolitical spaces

Political work is in part about navigating space. MPs get into Parliament by joining a political party and being (or at least seen as being) 'local' to a constituency. According to research by Campbell and Cowley (2014), the identity marker that most strongly influences constituents to vote for candidates is their belonging to their area: they have to be 'local', that is, to belong to the space in order to represent it. Getting inducted as an MP means in part learning to move around rooms, corridors, bars and speaking chambers, the routes to travel between and within them, and where and when they are expected to congregate, sit, stand, speak or walk. Groups of MPs share rhythms in common – mostly planned in the UK (such as attending a select committee), and others spontaneous (like sitting regularly with your allies in a particular bar), while many rhythms are idiosyncratic (visiting particular businesses in their constituency annually). You need to learn that the Commons tea room is a good private spot for gossiping with MPs from your own party; the Sports and Social bar is more popular with staff than politicians; Portcullis House atrium is where journalists lurk, so the most exposed place for a private meeting in Westminster; the division lobby, where you are expected to vote, is a good opportunity for lobbying your own frontbenchers, and so on. When you look also at how MPs create aggregated patterns, then you begin to get a fuller picture, as these rhythms of movement reveal not only individual experience but the shared social processes for various groups. Take voting as described by the lobby journalist Marie Le Conte, as an example:

> When MPs are required to go and vote on a bill or an amendment, the division bell will start ringing across the estate (and in nearby pubs and buildings), meaning that MPs have exactly eight minutes to get into the voting lobbies if they want to be counted. What this means in practice is that on days of important votes, parts of the Palace suddenly get invaded by parliamentarians sharply walking together and having seemingly come out of nowhere, flooding corridors like a stampede of buffaloes finally reaching a body of water. As it is usually not known precisely when votes will happen,

the dreaded bell gives Westminster life a peculiar rhythm, where meetings and drinks can be abandoned at a moment's notice, and idle chats in corners of the building are interrupted by a cabinet minister sprinting past (Le Conte 2019, pp. 6–7).

As MPs learn the ropes and develop their political strategies, rhythms provide continuity in social relations, which makes it possible for MPs to navigate their changeable social world and shapeshift between private, public and hybrid audiences. It allows them to develop and maintain key

Figure 3.2   Shapeshifting. © Edward J.T. Walker

social relationships and have some continuous sense of self in relation to the world around them. The different spaces hold associations and, over time, memories that create emotional resonance. This perhaps partly explains why MPs are extremely reluctant to move out of the Palace of Westminster so it can be restored, despite the huge costs and inconvenience of doing the work with politicians still using the building (for more on restoration of the Palace, see Meakin in this volume).

While the space of the Commons is travelled around like a frenetic city, with many outbuildings and a high turnover of politicians at each election, the House of Lords is more like a less mobile gilded village. Peers' membership is for life and they occupy a far more restricted space; their far more confined use of space both creates but also reveals a completely different culture and politics from that of the Commons. In the UK the key embodied spaces – the Palace of Westminster, committee rooms, TV studios, constituency and others – once signposted politicians' most important sites and relationships in their political work. Now they have to show up in digital space as well: Facebook, Twitter, TikTok and so on, meaning that increasingly MPs appear in not just two but multiple spaces at the same time. To understand these embodied and virtual rhythms you need to study the differential impact of space on different actors and audiences.

Figure 3.3   MPs responding to different audiences. © Edward J.T. Walker

Hierarchical space in the Palace of Westminster

One of the world's most famous buildings, the Palace of Westminster is revered in some people's imagination as a symbol of Britain's glorious past:

> The past is everywhere: soaring arches, the luxuriance of sculpted dead kings sprouting from mouldings, painted historical tableaux on the walls, marble statues of deceased parliamentarians. ... For its devotees, the House is a shrine to this beloved, majestic, patriotic saga, conjuring endless genial associations, while still being thoroughly alive in the present (Crewe 2005, p. 9).

For others it is a reminder of Britain's historical colonising vandalism and class privilege. The public school appearance is as alienating for some as it is resonant for others. Nirmal Puwar portrays the Palace of Westminster as a space designed for specific sorts of masculinities; women and racialised MPs are bodies out of place – even 'space invaders' – while the default idea of an MP is assumed to be male and white (Puwar 2014, p. 234). This has been occasionally disrupted, most notably by the suffragettes when they padlocked themselves to the grille of the Commons ladies' gallery, handcuffed themselves to statues in St Stephen's Hall and hid in a cupboard on census night. These invasions into a masculine space underline how the exclusion of women was the norm (Puwar 2014, pp. 237–239).

Gender is not the only hierarchy. In both houses, spaces and rhythms are gendered, racialised and aged but also infused with class. Minority MPs tend to create more frantic rhythms as they grapple with the additional work of dealing with a mixture of prejudice, backlash and supporting others facing marginalisation. In the main debating chamber of Parliament, it is the seating that educates participants and observers about the political hierarchies, alliances and divisions where these informal inequalities are reinforced by the dominance of privileged white men in the formal hierarchies. The government is always on the right of the Commons or Lords speaker, the opposition on the left and those with frontbench (ministerial or shadow) positions are on the lowest benches nearest to the table. Political parties sit in blocks and allies tend to often sit together. The speaker (and deputies) preside on a raised chair, facilitating good debate and refereeing on the procedural rules, while clerks sit at a table just in front of the speaker's chair ready to give advice. Civil servants are kept at a distance but on the floor of the House, symbolically depicting that the government is both inside Parliament, but should not interfere in the democratic scrutiny of the executive. In the building more broadly, the positioning of your office often betrays your relative status – the nearer you are to the chamber, the more powerful you are. Some of those who have lost power are rewarded with a large office and, even better, a good view of the River Thames. So, parliaments can be a 'kind of spatial projection of the political field' (Bourdieu 1991, p. 186); the inequalities of society show up in the organisation of which bodies occupy which spaces.

When you look at how people, objects and documents travel you discover how political process works. Tracing how bodies (politicians, officials), objects (the mace, the speaker's chair) and documents (the standing orders, draft bills) are placed, position themselves and travel around the Palace tells you what kind of work is going on. It is not just people who have rhythms. Documents too travel around in predictable ways as part of the process of being transformed from one thing (draft, bill) to another (final version, Act). When I researched the making of law, one of the critical processes of any legislature, I followed a 250-word clause for two years as it made its way through both Houses of Parliament. If you only study the texts alone, you will fail to discern the full picture because the impression given is that only politicians influenced the revision of a bill. However, by watching where thousands of people met to discuss this particular clause – in consultations online, select committee rooms, in the debating chambers, in charities' offices – I gathered an historical picture of how it was a network of people gathering in shared spaces that brought about Parliament's approval to critical amendments (Crewe 2015, chapter 6).

To understand whipping within political parties too, you have to look at space. Whips are the politicians within a political party who are responsible for finding out what their members are likely to support and, once the party line is fixed, coaxing their membership to support it. They do this via digital means but also by sitting both in the chamber and just outside it in both houses with sufficient proximity to when MPs or peers vote in order to persuade them to go into the right division lobby. To be effective, whips need to renew how they circulate around both physical spaces, but also digital media, to keep up with the changes caused by technology development and shifts in MPs' habits. During COVID restrictions, the House of Commons introduced electronic voting, but they tellingly restored embodied voting once the pandemic reduced in intensity – in recognition of the importance of face-to-face contact for encouraging party loyalty. As the sense of belonging to party weakens, and frustration with party leaders heightens (Crewe 2021, pp. 48–49), the significance of face-to-face interaction for intensifying social bonds within parties becomes more and more significant each year.

Knowledge of constituency as place

When an aspiring politician stands as a candidate to represent a constituency in the UK Parliament, then they need to know, symbolise and embody a place. Canvassing to gain the support of voters increasingly depends on digital media – especially since the pandemic has constrained face-to-face interaction – but usually winning a seat in an election also means walking the streets and knocking on doors. This pacing of the streets together when campaigning creates a heightened sense of belonging to one party – or *communitas* as the anthropologist Victor Turner (1974) put it – helping MPs forget the factions and divisions that beset parties in normal times. When getting coverage in the media, the TV and political parties make use of space in specific ways to create a sense of drama. The cameras get as close as possible to the small group of party workers huddled around the candidate to create the impression of a large and ebullient crowd in a way that you can only see if you are an embodied observer.

Once in, MPs' knowledge of the issues and people within their constituency is needed partly for reelection. One MP told me he has canvassed every Saturday for as long as he has sat in the House of Commons, getting around the whole constituency between elections and putting a letter of introduction through the letterbox of all new residents who move in. Knowledge is also needed to respond to constituents' problems. MPs and their staff undertake the equivalent of an ethnography of their constituency – getting to know the public services, the charities, the areas that need attention and the people who can solve problems. After visits to nine constituencies, and discussing constituency work with over 65 MPs, I discerned that women MPs seemed to be more at ease with highly emotional 'surgery' meetings than men MPs. Far more caseworkers (that is MPs' staff dealing with problems rather than policy issues) were female, while researchers tended to be male.

Whether for policy or case work, the politician needs to convey a sense of belonging to the space so that constituents feel represented, constantly talking about landmarks and ongoing projects, famous characters or new restaurants opening (pre-COVID). The growing importance of the constituency in UK politics is evidenced by the frequency of visits by MPs, usually weekly or at least fortnightly for non-London politicians.

If we discovered more about what spaces they are travelling to in their constituency, and who they meet when they get there, we might enhance the accountability of politicians considerably.

A Friday in the life of an MP in her constituency

This government MP's Scottish constituency is four hours' travel from Westminster. Her constituency is a mix of rural and urban. She stays there from Thursday afternoon until Monday morning, returning to London to attend Parliament from Monday afternoon until Thursday morning.

9.00–10.00	Meeting in a local hospital to discuss possible closure of one department
10.00–12.00	Surgery in MP's office: six meetings with individual constituents facing severe and multiple problems and challenges when accessing local services; one meeting with a group of environmental campaigners; one meeting with a group of parents complaining about a local school
12.00–12.30	Meeting with MP's staff to make decisions about follow-up on individual constituents' cases and phone calls to council for the most urgent case
12.30–13.45	Walk to meet local party officials to review tactics for campaigning for local elections and eat a sandwich along the way
13.45–15.30	Canvass for local government elections (also reconnecting with constituents by knocking on doors), meeting up with neighbouring MPs from the same party, and giving a speech to party workers
15.30–16.30	Interview with local journalist about the possible hospital closure
16.30–17.00	Meeting with staff in MP's office to discuss latest developments in a campaign to raise funds for a local charity
17.00–18.30	Walk to and then visit a housing association to discuss complaints received from tenants
18.30–19.30	Open a new social enterprise, creating jobs for adults with learning difficulties; give speech and meet those involved

| 19.30–20.45 | Back to office to go through emails, postbag and Twitter and respond to requests from constituents, journalists, other MPs and party workers |
| 21.00 | Home to catch up with family who live in the constituency |

Extract from a series of imagined days in the life of MPs (Crewe 2021, p. 114)

A Tuesday in the life of a backbencher MP in Westminster

His constituency is in the north of England, too far from London to visit during the week.

9.30–10.00	Spoke in a debate in Westminster Hall about 'Children Missing from Care Homes'
10.00–10.30	Interviewed by a journalist about why children go missing from care homes
10.30–11.00	Discussing various urgent constituency issues on the phone with staff in his constituency office
11.00–12.00	Spoke at a meeting of the All-Party Parliamentary Group on Children about children accessing social care services
12.00–13.00	Met with other backbench MPs to discuss abuse on social media
13.00–13.15	Grabbed a sandwich
13.15–14.15	Met with a group of representatives from children's charities to discuss improving the educational prospects of children in care and strategies for responding to upcoming legislation
14.30–15.30	Attended, as a member of the International Development select committee, an oral evidence session on sexual abuse and exploitation in the aid sector
15.40–16.30	Participated in the urgent debate: Learning Disabilities Mortality Review in the main chamber

	of the House of Commons, asking the minister a question
16.30–17.00	Met with his whip to explain why he plans to vote against the party in an important vote next week
17.00–17.15	Went to his office in Portcullis House and discussed commitments for the week with his Westminster office staff
17.30–18.30	Opened a charity function in one of the House of Commons function rooms for raising funds for a children's charity with a brief speech about their work
18.30–19.30	Went to the House of Commons to collect some research findings the library researchers had compiled for him and wrote his speech for an important debate the next day
19.30–21.00	Dinner with colleagues in the party; discussion of campaigning tactics for the local elections in their region (and how the leadership is doing)
After dinner	Caught up with emails
1.00 am	Home to his rented flat

Extract from a series of imagined days in the life of MPs (Crewe 2021, p. 115)

Nomadic symbolism of select committees

My shift towards researching political work took a new turn when working with Nicholas Sarra, a psychotherapist and group analyst from Exeter University. We wrote an article on the basis of a collaborative mini ethnography about how committee work is embodied. We concluded that: 'Committee chairs, members and staff are constrained by the architecture, rules and rituals in their bid to achieve plausibility, but at the same time find the room to express individuality in the ways that they manage emotions and communicate with others through words, silence, bodily movements, or facial expressions' (Crewe and Sarra 2019, p. 841).

Departmental select committees in the House of Commons are confined by specific spaces (Crewe and Sarra 2019, p. 845) but also how they are configured. When committees meet their room is set up in a rigid way – usually with the members' chairs arranged around a horseshoe-shaped table, the witness table forming a line to close the horseshoe and (a few) chairs for the public behind the witnesses. Politicians sitting on select committees are constrained by hierarchies, limits to power, rules and routines, but also, and simultaneously, find ways to create room for manoeuvre or, to put it another way, breaks in the rhythm. Such breaks can provoke acts of disciplining. Committee members, and especially the chair, often watch the clerk to see whether their faces are expressing disapproval. The select committee in action constitutes 'an embodied affectual display of impression management in which the poker face, the smirk, the "look", the frown, the appearance of engagement or disengagement, all play their part' in managing the emergent situation (Crewe and Sarra 2019, p. 14).

Literal and symbolic space can interweave. The committee chair presides over the meetings by sitting in the middle of the table with the clerk to their left. The chair represents the committee to the outside world – including the visitors sitting beyond witnesses as well as those watching via television or online – and embodies it as well; one MP chair even said to us, 'I am the committee'. This embodiment is clearest when the chair operates in spaces away from committee meetings on their own (giving an interview to a journalist or sitting on the committee of committee chairs – the Liaison Committee) and represents the whole committee. At other times, the embodiment has to be relinquished. The clerk manages the plans and staff of the committee so their relationship with the chair is the cornerstone of the operation of a committee. The rhythm of authority – who is in charge of the committee at any one moment – is revealed by what happens between these two key characters and the paperwork they produce. During the formal 'sittings' of the committee, the chair is the authority, but in between meetings the clerk symbolically holds the committee in a parliamentary outbuilding in Tothill Street, about 10 minutes' walk away from the Palace of Westminster (Crewe and Sarra 2019, p. 847). Before and after a meeting, the chair and the clerk confer as the committee is symbolically handed over from one to the other. When the clerk then carries the paperwork of the committee to or from the office in which staff look after it between meetings, and especially (pre-COVID) the physical copy of their 'reports', then the committee has a nomadic quality as it moves around the parliamentary estate and even, very occasionally, on outreach trips to other parts of the UK and even overseas.

Conclusion: an embodied theory of parliaments

The rhythms of parliamentary life require an inquiry into seasons, diaries and appointments observable in offices, streets and parliamentary buildings. Such an inquiry into rhythms can only be achieved if you track what happens through time and across space in everyday embodied interaction both literally and symbolically. This theoretical and methodological approach illuminates three neglected areas in the study of parliaments: first, a better understanding of diversity and relationships. We can systematically study the similarities, differences and relationships between MPs, seeing how rhythms vary between political parties, women versus men, on the basis of class and so on, but also between countries. Second, the rhythms in the performance of politics are deeply affected by how public versus private the space is to which groups, because reputation for politicians is such a precious commodity. They are continually worrying about the optics so the more public the space, and the larger the audience, the more they will be vigilant about the appearance of expertise and success. And finally, considering how minds and bodies are entangled in time and space allows us to compare politicians with different social groups. We all engage in politics – at work and play – so we all need rhythms to navigate our entangled social and political worlds. But politicians do politics with the dial turned up because they walk with even more friends and foes, and engage in more bitter power struggles, than the rest of us. The dial indicates intensity – of emotion, pleasure, pain, cultural significance, political impact – meaning that what politicians do as they navigate space tends to be a magnified version of the politics engaged in by ordinary people. In summary, studying the rhythms of political work can be a powerful research strategy for seeing what makes politicians both ordinary and extraordinary.

Note

1 This chapter is part of a project that has received funding from the European Research Council (ERC) under the European Union's Horizon 2020 research and innovation programme (Grant agreement No. 834986).

References

Abélès, M. (2000) *Un ethnologue à l'Assembleé*, Paris: Odile Jacob.
Bourdieu, P. (1991) *Language and Symbolic Power*, Cambridge: Polity.
Campbell, R. and Cowley, P. (2014) 'What Voters Want: Reactions to Candidate Characteristics in a Survey Experiment', *Political Studies*, 62(4), pp. 745–765.

Crewe, E. (2005) *Lords of Parliament: Manners, Rituals and Power*, Manchester: Manchester University Press.

Crewe, E. (2015) *House of Commons: An Anthropology of the Work of MPs*, London: Bloomsbury.

Crewe, E. (2021) *An Anthropology of Parliaments: Entanglements of Democratic Politics*, London: Routledge.

Crewe, E. and Sarra, N. (2019) 'Chairing UK Select Committees: Walking Between Friends and Foes', *Parliamentary Affairs*, 72(4), pp. 841–859.

Floret, F. (2010) 'European Political Rituals: A Challenging Tradition in the Making', *International Political Anthropology*, 3(1), pp. 55–77.

Goffman, E. (1959) *The Presentation of Self in Everyday Life*, New York: Anchor Books.

Le Conte, M. (2019) *Haven't You Heard? Gossip, Politics and Power*, London: 353 Books.

Lefebvre, H. (2013) *Rhythmanalysis: Space, Time and Everyday Life*, London: Bloomsbury.

Norton, P. (2019) 'Power Behind the Scenes: The Importance of Informal Space in Legislatures', *Parliamentary Affairs*, 72(2), pp. 245–266.

Puwar, N. (2014) 'The Archi-Texture of Parliament at Westminster', in S. Rai and R. Johnson (eds), *Democracy in Practice: Ceremony and Practice in Parliament*, Basingstoke: Palgrave Macmillan, pp. 234–250.

Rai, S. (2014) 'Political Aesthetics of the Political Nation', *Interventions: International Journal of Postcolonial Studies*, 16(6), pp. 898–915.

Turner, V. (1974) *Dramas, Fields, and Metaphors: Symbolic Action in Human Society*, Ithaca, NY: Cornell University Press.

4

The ephemeral architecture of socioenvironmental practices in the UK Houses of Parliament, 1836–1966

Henrik Schoenefeldt

Introduction: hidden networks of convention and routine

This volume is concerned with the study of parliament buildings, seeking to shift the focus from the study of their monumental expression towards the spatial construction of political practices and traditions. This objective, however, raises the important question of what we consider eligible for inclusion under the terms of political practices and traditions. The Palace of Westminster, which was built after a large fire in 1834 had destroyed an earlier, largely medieval, complex of buildings, was designed to incorporate spaces required to support inherited and newly invented political practices. Among the newly invented traditions was the ceremonial approach for state opening and a voting system involving the use of two division lobbies. Its design was also shaped by more technical requirements, of which the provision of adequate ventilation and indoor climates was the most prominent. The Palace of Westminster was equipped with complex systems for ventilation, and the debating chamber provided with an early form of air conditioning. Meeting these environmental requirements, however, was not solely a matter of technology, but also relied on complex social processes.

These processes had the characteristics of what the historian Eric Hobsbawm describes as 'networks of convention and routine'. Hobsbawm uses this phrase to describe traditions that have evolved in response to practical needs, which, in contrast to many political traditions, do not have 'significant ritual or symbolic functions' (Hobsbawm 2012, p. 3). In Westminster these involved managing the interaction between human and technological functions in the task of providing environmental control. As such, they could be considered a historic example of sociotechnical design. Sociotechnical design is concerned with the study of 'technology and its associated work structure', and although it is a modern concept that was unknown in the nineteenth century (Mumford 2006, pp. 317–42), it offers a lens through which to view the social processes underpinning the operation of historic technologies.

These sociotechnical practices were first introduced and trialled inside the temporary Houses of Parliament, which had been erected after the fire as preliminary facilities for Parliament. They were designed by the architect Robert Smirke (1780–1867), but they also incorporated experimental systems for ventilation and climatic control that had been developed by the physician David Boswell Reid (1805–63). The trials, which lasted from 1837 to 1852 in the House of Commons and from 1839 until 1847 in the House of Lords, enabled Reid to test and refine technical arrangements but also to collaborate with the institution in the development and implementation of sociotechnical practices that underpinned their day-to-day operation (Schoenefeldt 2014, pp. 175–215). These were subsequently applied within the Palace of Westminster, first in the House of Lords, which opened in 1847, and subsequently in the House of Commons, which was occupied in 1852. These sociotechnical practices might at first appear insignificant and marginal to the political business. However, archival research has shown that MPs, Lords and senior officials were directly involved in the day-to-day operation of the systems of ventilation and climate control, functioning as human actors within the sociotechnical network of convention and routine.

Focusing on the period from 1852 until 1966, this chapter examines the ephemeral architecture of these social practices, and how they were integrated into the technological operations. Instead of providing a study of historic technologies it will focus on the social processes underpinning their operation. Through site investigations and archival research, using historic records held by the estate archives, Historic England, National Archives and Parliamentary Archives, it retraces the evolution of these practices and elucidates their role in enabling MPs and Lords to participate in the day-to-day management, assessment and improvement of their working environment. The first section examines the institutional organisation of the network and their physical facilities, such as the network of hidden spaces and circulation routes. The second section examines the impact of the first technological changes introduced in 1854.

The institutional organisation of sociotechnical practices

The design of sociotechnical practices was shaped by technology as well as institutional structures. To fully understand the nature of these practices, it is critical to distinguish between two sets of human functions in the operation of the nineteenth-century technologies. The first set was comprised of technical operations, which, aside from the operation of machinery (such as humidification, heating and cooling equipment or the boilers and engines of the steam-powered fans), also involved the delivery of control and monitoring procedures. In contrast to the automated controls of modern systems, these functions were performed entirely manually. As a direct result, environmental control was a question of human organisation and its success relied on the tight coordination of manually performed technological procedures. The second set of human functions was the engagement of MPs, Lords and officials in the day-to-day operations.

Before discussing these functions in detail, it is important to examine the organisation of the operational staff. The management of the environmental systems across the Palace of Westminster was undertaken by the Department of Ventilation, Warming and Lighting,[1] under the direction of a superintending engineer (House of Commons 1865). For the first seven years, this role was held by Alfred Meeson, a civil engineer of Charles Barry's office. For the first five years he oversaw the operation of the Lords chamber, but in November 1852 his responsibility was extended to the House of Commons (Schoenefeldt 2018a). His department was responsible for the whole Palace of Westminster, but complex systems of climate control with facilities for cooling, heating, humidification and air purification were only provided inside the two debating chambers.

The operations were largely invisible to parliamentarians as most of the staff operated inside a network of hidden spaces and circulation routes. This included the large air chambers below and above the two houses (Figure 4.1), boiler and engine rooms inside the basement (Figure 4.2, ix and x) as well as a back-of-house office (Office of Works 1852). The historic records show that the main offices, which the ventilation department used for the central administration of the technical operations performed throughout the Palace of Westminster, were located on the ground floor, north of the Members' Lobby (vii) (Reid 1847, 1851a). By 1852 the department had also established several subsidiary offices within the public areas on the principal floor, which provided them with an interface with users, including MPs, Lords, officials and other staff. One of these offices, which was referred to as 'warming and ventilating office'

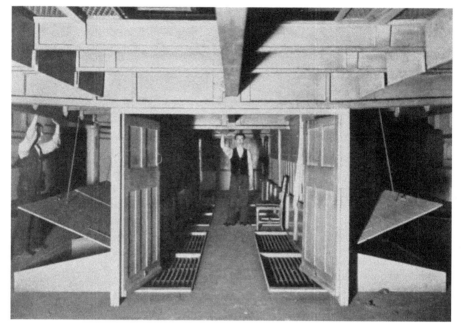

Figure 4.1 Photograph showing attendants and valves in the interior of the air chamber below the House of Commons (Wright and Smith 1901, p. 272). © British Library

in a historic drawing, was located in the south-west corner of the central lobby (Barry 1852; see Figure 4.2, i). The operational staff in charge of the House of Commons had a small subsidiary office (ii) inside the Members' Lobby, which was immediately adjacent to the staircase leading to the main office below. The subsidiary office for the Lords (iii) was located in the south-west corner of the Peers' Lobby (Office of Works 1914), next to the entrance of the debating chamber. It was also close to a hidden door and staircase inside the east division lobby (iv) which gave direct access to the air chambers on the ground floor. And another staircase (v), situated on the west side of the lobby, connected to the air chambers above the ceiling.

Although many of the technical operations were invisible, their management relied on close collaborations with senior officials within the two houses, who, although they did not have technical backgrounds, were important actors within the system. During sittings, the system in the House of Commons was under the supervision of the office of the serjeant at arms, a senior official responsible for order and security in the chamber. Among his staff were messengers, and a 'chief attendant on

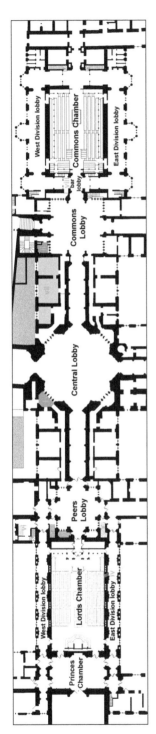

Figure 4.2 Floor plan of principal floor showing the debating chambers, lobbies and the offices of the operational staff. © Henrik Schoenefeldt

ventilation', who, during sittings, coordinated the operations undertaken by technical staff (House of Commons 1852a, p. 6; House of Commons 1873, p. 23). The messengers, who were authorised to enter the chamber and surrounding lobbies during sittings, supported the operations by collecting personal feedback from MPs and taking hourly readings from ten thermometers within the chamber, which were recorded in paper registers. One historic book of registers, covering the years 1853 and 1854, shows that the interior was equipped with 19 thermometers. Two thermometers were located within the galleries inside the debating chamber, and eight on the principal floor, while two were located in the division lobbies and inside the Members' Lobby.

The serjeant at arms acted as a mediator between MPs and the technical staff. Lord Charles Russell, who held the post of serjeant at arms between 1848 and 1875, reported that he was the 'medium of communication, as respects the ventilation' (House of Commons 1852b, Q255–56). The serjeant reviewed feedback received from individual MPs and, if necessary, sent requests to the attendant for ad hoc adjustments to the temperature or ventilation. The historic logbooks contain records of requests and feedback received from the serjeant. On 22 April 1853, for instance, the attendants had noted a '[g]ood many complaints of draughts' from the serjeant and on 7 April 1854 they wrote that 'Lord John Russel wished the House a little Cooler' (Ventilation Department 1854). As such the serjeant and his staff were an important channel for the communication of quantitative and qualitative feedback on the interior condition. A hidden door and ladder (Figure 4.2, viii), located in the north-west side of the bar lobby, enabled them to directly communicate with the staff inside the air chamber below (Reid 1851b).

A similar approach was adopted in the House of Lords. The indoor climate was continually monitored using an array of conventional thermometers. Some of these are shown in historic photographs of the interior (Wright and Smith 1901, p. 244). John Percy, who acted as superintendent from 1862 until 1889, reported that thermometers were read every 30 minutes in six to seven locations and recorded in registers (House of Lords 1869, Q100–05; House of Lords 1883, Q344). Staff were instructed to regulate the climate and ventilation based on measurements and attendance levels, but also to undertake ad hoc adjustment based on feedback and requests sent by senior officers (House of Commons 1852b, Q255–56; House of Lords 1854, Q75). As in the Commons, the senior officers were charged with the responsibilities for the collection, review and communication of feedback from peers. The officials had dedicated seats inside the house, enabling them to directly interact with the peers about issues of thermal comfort or air quality. The lord high chancellor, who was the presiding officer, sat on the Woolsack in the centre and the Usher of the Black Rod occupied a box at the opposite end. During sittings, the Black Rod and his deputy, the yeoman usher, acted as intermediaries between the Lords and the technical staff (House of Commons 1852b, Q544–46). In 1852 Sir Augustus Clifford, who served as Black Rod from 1832 until 1877, reported that they reviewed any critical feedback received from peers and, if necessary, sent orders to the superintendent for ad hoc adjustments to the temperature or ventilation (House of Commons, 1852b, Q544–46).

These procedures facilitated socially sustained feedback loops, which were important as they allowed environmental control procedures to be informed by user experience alongside measurements. Through these feedback loops, staff acquired detailed knowledge of the environmental conditions – and how these affected Lords, MPs and other users. The feedback offered insights into the full range of thermal stimuli that were affecting users but were not routinely measured. This included the cooling sensations produced by currents entering through the perforated floors.

The historic records show that thermal comfort and ventilation were of sufficiently serious concern to MPs and Lords. In the House of Commons, the performance of Reid's system, which was only operational for two years, was the subject of multiple debates and two inquiries, led by select committees in 1852 and 1854 (Schoenefeldt 2021, pp. 201–16). The system in the House of Lords was also subject of a critical appraisal, which was conducted by another select committee in 1854 (Schoenefeldt 2022). These inquiries resulted in substantial modifications to the systems of both houses. They also required the sociotechnical practices to be adapted. These modifications were based on a scheme by the English physician Goldsworthy Gurney (1793–1875), who from 1854 to 1862 also acted as the superintendent.

First alterations with sociotechnical implications, 1854

These changes included the remodelling of the ventilation and the introduction of the new facilities for cooling, heating, humidification and air purification. It also involved the introduction of a supplementary system of natural ventilation, using openable windows. The latter was a small, yet significant intervention, as the original houses had been designed to be permanently sealed spaces with fixed glazing inside the windows, and ventilation was provided through apertures within the floors and ceilings. In the House of Commons, 12 openable windows were introduced within the clerestory windows above the gallery (Office of Works 1902), while the large Gothic windows in the House of Lords were altered to accommodate 24 openable sections (Figure 4.3) (Office of Works 1854; Barry 1854). These were side-hung and operated from the outside with the aid of ropes (Office of Works 1943) which in 1945, when the windows underwent repairs due to war damage, were replaced with a more sophisticated system of windings gears (Ministry of Works 1943). Both systems were operated from the roofs above the division lobby, which staff could access through the two staircases at the east (Figure 4.2, no. v) and west (vi) sides of the Peers' Lobby.

As a direct result of these changes, the role of officials was extended, providing them with the responsibility for monitoring and supervising the operation of the windows and external sun blinds. In the House of Commons, this responsibility was held by the speaker and the chairman of ways and means, who acted as the speaker's deputy (House of Commons 1854, Q213–15). Figure 4.4 shows the extended network and actors of the feedback system in the House of Commons, which remained largely

Figure 4.3 Interior of House of Commons chamber, 1869, showing open windows inside clerestory (Harrington 1869, plate IX). © British Library

unchanged until 1941. The historic logbooks from the 1920s provide a detailed record of any ad hoc adjustments made to the windows. On 10 July 1924 one entry said: '4 windows opened on east side of House, 2.55 pm, by order of Mr Speaker' and on 6 June 1928: '4 windows opened on east side of House, 5.15 pm, by order of chairman'. On 30 July 1925 the attendants wrote: '1.40 pm 1 window closed, east side, Sergeant-at-Arms order with consent of Mr Speaker' (Ventilation Department 1928).

In the House of Lords these responsibilities were held by the lord chancellor. Hugh Cairns, who had served as lord chancellor from 1874 until 1880, reported that he routinely instructed windows to be opened at 5.00 pm during the summer, but also that he gave orders for the ad hoc adjustments, based on his experience or in response to feedback from peers. During a debate on 18 July 1878, for instance, he instructed five windows to be opened at 5.00 pm, and to be increased to 11 windows at 6.30 pm. Through this role the lord chancellor also acquired close insights into the impact of the use of natural ventilation and shades on the internal environment. Cairns, for instance, observed that heat from the sunlight could become a problem in summer. During the day, he noted, it was necessary to deploy blinds in order to 'prevent the House, as far as possible, from being heated through the windows' (HL Deb 22 July 1878). During daylight hours, windows were ordered to be opened only on the shaded side, while the windows on the opposite were closed and protected with solar blinds.

These arrangements are significant, as they gave individual peers and MPs agency within the control of the indoor environment. As the primary users, they had the ability to influence the way the windows were operated during sittings. Similar to the control of temperatures, the opening and closing of windows was the subject of disagreements between individual peers and MPs. Cairns and Percy reported difficulties with managing conflicting requests. In the summer of 1869, Percy described a case where he had multiple responses within a single evening. At 7.00 pm, he noted, Cairns had formally instructed him to open the windows, but one hour later Lord Talbot, who spoke to him directly, asked for them to be closed again. At 11.00 pm he received yet another request, this time from Lord Salisbury, who wished the windows to be reopened (House of Lords 1869, Q97). Cairns gave a similar account in 1883. He reported that the atmosphere could feel 'insufferably close' if the chamber was crowded, and that one individual would make an appeal 'to open the windows, and on the windows being opened, there is a counter appeal made by somebody else who feels the draught very much, to have the windows shut' (House of Lords 1883, Q327).

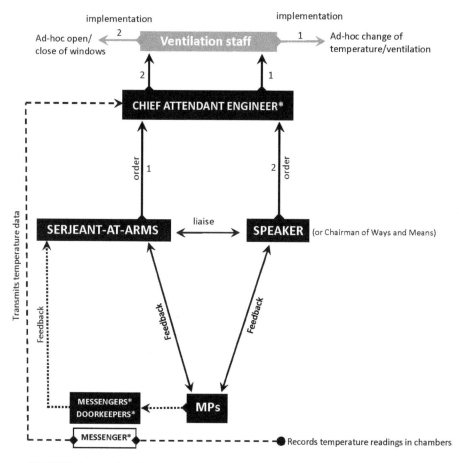

Figure 4.4 Sociotechnical network, House of Commons, 1854–1941. © Henrik Schoenefeldt

Evidence of such disagreements can also be found in transcript of parliamentary debates. In 1869, for instance, as the Marquess of Salisbury voiced. He believed that 'the more we discourage these artificial systems of ventilation … and resort to the natural remedy of opening the windows, the better it will be for our general comfort'. Similarly, criticism was expressed by the Earl of Camperdown during a debate held on 2 March 1886. He said that ventilation 'would be all that could be desired if they would open the windows and dispense with the elaborate system they had introduced' (HL Deb 2 March 1886). In contrast, Lord Granville noted in 1878 that the chamber is 'most oppressive during hot weather' and attributes it to the fact that the lord chancellor permitted windows to be opened on request from some peers (HL Deb 22 July 1878).

This practice, however, did not only lead to tensions between peers. It also resulted in operational responsibilities being shared between two parties that held a different view on how the climate ought to be managed. It needs to be stressed that the technical staff did not have direct control over the windows or shades. Their control was governed by instructions issued by the lord chancellor, drawing either on his own observations or feedback received from peers. Their instructions did not always adhere to the control regimes advocated by the engineers, but instead reflected the subjective views of members.

Percy, who was the superintendent from 1862 until 1889, was highly critical of this practice. In his view, the influence of peers in the operation of windows was impediment to realising an effective cooling strategy, arguing that the interior could be kept cooler if it remained sealed and supplied with cooled air through the floor. In hot weather, he believed, open windows would cause internal temperatures to rise, and cool or windy conditions could produce 'downdraughts of air on the heads of Peers' (House of Lords 1869, Q97).

Technological disruption of historic sociotechnical practices, 1950–66

After the changes of 1854, the sociotechnical procedures remained largely unchanged until the twentieth century. In the House of Commons these practices were followed until the destruction of the chamber in 1941 (Schoenefeldt 2018b). The chamber was completely rebuilt between 1944 and 1950 with modern air conditioning, resulting in many of the historic operational practices becoming redundant. These were replaced by semi-automated control and monitoring systems, utilising electromechanical technology. These systems comprised an extensive network of electric sensors, connected to controls, electromechanical indicators screens and strip chart recorders. Although these enabled the routine control operations to be partly automated, new social practices were adopted for qualitative monitoring and user engagement.

Activities and attendance within the chamber were monitored with the aid of a microphone and periscope, while MPs were instructed to call the resident engineer about any issues with the climate. Like his nineteenth-century predecessors, the resident engineer kept a diary of reports from MPs and liaised with the control engineers about adjustments. Some of the feedback, however, was still mediated by the minister of work and parliamentary secretary, who engaged with MPs through personal conversations and written correspondence (Schoenefeldt 2020). The system of openable windows was briefly reexamined by a select committee in 1944, but was not reinstated. Oscar Faber, the engineer of the new system, advocated a permanently sealed environment to protect the interior from external pollution, and to prevent the opening of windows from interfering with the air conditioning system. The idea had been initially opposed by MPs on the committee, who wished the historic practices to be reintroduced. In a report, dated 25 October 1944, the committee wrote that members were 'at first not in favour of the permanently closed windows the engineers has prescribed for the chamber, and preferred to feel that they could, if required, to be flung open to admit fresh air in fine weather' (House of Commons 1945, p. 6).

In the House of Lords, which survived the war largely unscathed, the nineteenth-century system was not decommissioned and replaced with mechanical air conditioning until 1966. Over this period, measures taken to displace human labour through technology did not go beyond the installation of thermostats for the automation of heating controls (1960) and a small electromechanical monitoring system (1950) which, equipped with an indicator screen and a network of seven electric sensors (Ministry of Works 1951; Cunliffe 1960), enabled staff to take temperature readings remotely from a central control panel.[2] The historic approach to user engagement, involving the Black Rod and lord chancellor as mediator, were reinstated in 1951 and continued for another 20 years after the war (Denbon 1956; Lord Chamberlain 1963). The utilisation of openable windows was only discontinued after the introduction of air conditioning, when the space became a permanently controlled environment. The technological changes of 1966 also resulted in most of the technical operations becoming automated. However, the user engagement remained a prominent feature of its operational design. According to reports of the Ministry of Works from November 1963, the system incorporated an automated control and monitoring system, involving a network of electric sensors. It was also provided with facilities that allowed the climate to be manually adjusted 'according to desires of the occupants' (Knight 1963) and to accommodate 'individual response to comfort' (Chief Mechanical Engineer 1963).

Conclusion: the persistence of the social

The operational history of the Houses of Parliament has yielded insights into the ephemeral architecture of sociotechnical practices in the context of environmental control. This was characterised as a participatory approach, in which operational staff, MPs, Lords and officials were important actors within a wider sociotechnical network of environmental control. It has shown how technology had affected both the design and function of social networks. While the operation of the original nineteenth-century system had relied entirely on socially sustained feedback mechanisms, after the war sociotechnical aspects were revisited in the light of new technologies. Although some of the original nineteenth-century sociotechnical practices were lost due to automation, the operation of the new systems, completed in 1950 and 1966, respectively, were still dependent on socially sustained feedback mechanisms. These changes resulted in the emergence of two types of feedback loops, one of which was sustained technologically, utilising quantitative data, one socially, which focused on qualitative evaluations. The latter, which relied on direct participation of users alongside technological and non-technical staff, suggests that the social processes persisted, but were refocused.

This research has focused on elucidating a more ordinary, domestic aspect of the history of parliamentary architecture. Similar to other practical matters, such as building repairs or cleaning, it belongs to the sphere of facilities management. The engagement of historical research with such practical matters, however, is important as it offers insights into the social history of environmental design in architecture.

This social history is significant because it illuminates the character of nineteenth-century environmental technologies and the specific challenges of their application within a large and complex institutional building. The research has shown that the delivery of a process of user participation was underpinned by institutional structures. As a direct result of this participatory approach, however, the practical questions of how to provide ventilation or thermal comfort became part of what could be interpreted as the politics of environmental control. These politics manifested themselves in the tensions between opposing positions between users and technologists as well as in the disagreements between individual peers or MPs. The study of the history of these tensions shows that it was not the view of technical specialists or the authority of their scientific data, but the views of the most vocal users that became the ultimate measure of building performance. This was due to the fact that the primary occupants of the chambers were not ordinary users, but holders of political power. It was a relationship of servant and served, and this manifested itself not only spatially, but also in the institutional structures within which interactions between 'users' and 'operators' of the building were performed.

Notes

1 The staff of the Department of Ventilation was employed by the Commissioners of Woods and Forests, and after 1854 became HM Office of Works (1854–1940).
2 The original indicator and switch were located in the dimmer room and have survived to this day. It has a rotary switch to select individual sensors in seven positions. These were labelled 1. 'throne east', 2. 'throne west', 3. 'princes chamber', 4. 'division lobby east', 5. 'division lobby west', 6. 'table', 7. 'bar'.

References

Barry, C. (1852) Palace of Westminster, Plan of the principal floor. The National Archives. Catalogue reference: WORK 29/5028.

Barry, C. (1854) Letter to Thornbarrow, 11 December. The National Archives. Catalogue reference: WORK 11/7/7/10.

Chief Mechanical Engineer (1963) Letter to K. Newis, 10 December. The National Archives. Catalogue reference: WORK 11/588/62.

Cunliffe, W. (1960) Letter to Captain Mackintosh, 10 August. The National Archives. Catalogue reference: WORK 11/588/27–28.

Denbon, H. (1956) Memorandum, 13 January. The National Archives. Catalogue reference: WORK 11/588/3.

Harrington, J. (1869) *The Abbey and Palace of Westminster*, London: S. Low, Son, & Marston.

HL Deb (2 March 1886) vol. 302, col. 1664.

HL Deb (22 July 1878) vol. 241, cols. 2018–21.

Hobsbawm, E. (2012) *The Invention of Traditions*, Cambridge: Cambridge University Press.

Knight, J.C. (1963) House of Lords feasibility study on air-conditioning, 29 November. The National Archives. Catalogue reference: WORK 11/588/59.

Lord Chamberlain (1963) Letter to G. Rippon, 24 July. The National Archives. Catalogue reference: WORK 11/588/45.

Ministry of Works (1943) Drawing, 'Proposed gear operating side hung casement', 17 October. The National Archives. Catalogue reference: WORK 11/443.

Ministry of Works (1951) Press notice, 'The House of Lords chamber', 23 May. The National Archives. Catalogue reference: WORK 11/525.

Mumford, E. (2006) 'The story of socio-technical design: reflections on its successes, failures and potential', *Information Systems Journal*, 16(4), pp. 317–42. DOI: /10.1111/j.1365-2575.2006.00221.x.

Office of Works (1852) Drawing, 'Palace of Westminster, plan of ground floor'. Historic England Archive: Work 29/5027.

Office of Works (1854) Letter to Huxley, 2 October. The National Archives. Catalogue reference: WORK 11/7/7/8.

Office of Works (1902) Drawing, 'Plan of the first floor'. Strategic Estates Archive: Office of Works drawing 1010693.

Office of Works (1914) Drawing, 'Plan of the principal floor'. Strategic Estates Archive: Office of Works Drawing 176/3/2A.

Office of Works (1943) Report, 'Proposed re-installment of original Peers chamber windows', 4 November. The National Archives. Catalogue reference: WORK 11/443.

Parliament. House of Commons (1852a) *Estimates for Civil Services* (HC 1851–1852 211) HMSO.

Parliament. House of Commons (1852b) *Second Report from the Select Committee on Ventilation and Lighting of the House* (HC 1852 402) HMSO.

Parliament. House of Commons (1854) *Ventilation of the House of Commons – the Second Report* (HC 270 1854) HMSO.

Parliament. House of Commons (1865) *Estimates for Civil Services* (HC 1864–1865 I.-VII 21) HMSO.

Parliament. House of Commons (1873) *Estimates for Civil Services* (HC 1872–1873 112) HMSO.

Parliament. House of Commons (1945) Select Committee on House of Commons (rebuilding) (HC 1944-1945 109-1) HMSO.

Parliament. House of Lords (1854) Select Committee Appointed to Inquire into the Possibility of Improving the Ventilation and Lighting of the House, 'First report' (HL 1854 (384)) HMSO.

Parliament. House of Lords (1869) Office of the Clerk of the Parliaments and Office of the Gentleman Usher of the Black Rod, 'Report' (HL 1869 (278)) HMSO.

Parliament. House of Lords (1883) Construction and Accommodation, 'Report' (HL 1883 (147)) HMSO.

Reid, D.B. (1847) Plans and sections of offices for ventilation, 19 August. The National Archives. Catalogue reference: WORK 29/3104.

Reid, D.B. (1851a) Drawing, 'Plans and sections of office for ventilation', 6 November. The National Archives. Catalogue reference: WORK 29/3106.

Reid, D.B. (1851b) Drawing, 'Plan of south-west corner of House', 6 November. The National Archives. Catalogue reference: WORK 29/3109.

Schoenefeldt, H. (2014) 'The Temporary Houses of Parliament and David Boswell Reid's architecture of experimentation', *Architectural History*, 57, pp. 175–215. DOI: 10.1017/S0066622X00001416.

Schoenefeldt, H. (2018a) 'The historic ventilation system of the House of Commons, 1840–52: revisiting David Boswell Reid's environmental legacy', *Antiquaries Journal*, 98, pp. 245–95. DOI: 10.1017/S0003581518000549.

Schoenefeldt, H. (2018b) 'The House of Commons: a precedent for post-occupancy evaluation', *Building Research and Information*, 6, pp. 635–65. DOI: 10.1080/09613218.2019.1547547.

Schoenefeldt, H. (2020) 'Delivery of occupant satisfaction in the House of Commons, 1950–2019', *Buildings and Cities*, 1(1), pp. 141–63. DOI: 10.5334/bc.57.

Schoenefeldt, H. (2021) *Rebuilding the Houses of Parliament – David Boswell Reid and Disruptive Environmentalism*, Abingdon: Routledge.

Schoenefeldt, H. (2022) 'Technological transitions in climate control: lessons from the House of Lords', *Buildings and Cities*, 3(1), pp. 68–92. DOI: 10.5334/bc.161.

Ventilation Department (1854) 'Registers of temperature control and ventilation for the House of Commons, 1853–54', London: Parliamentary Archives. Catalogue number: OOW 5/1.

Ventilation Department (1928) 'Register of temperature control and ventilation for the House of Commons, February 1923–December 1928', London: Parliamentary Archives. Catalogue number: OOW 5/3.

Wright, A. and Smith, P. (1901) *Parliament Past and Present*, London: Hutchinson.

5

Inhabiting the Palais Bourbon together

Sharing, allocating and regulating parliamentary space among its multiple users at the French National Assembly

Jonathan Chibois

Introduction

For more than two centuries, the lower house of the bicameral French parliament – the National Assembly – has been housed in the Palais Bourbon in central Paris, which was a princely residence before the French Revolution. This place has gradually been configured to meet its needs, and even expanded in the 1970s by adding on other buildings in the neighbourhood. Despite these efforts, the Palais Bourbon remains a place where space is limited while the historical character of the site prohibits making the significant changes necessary to make it truly functional for modern legislative work. The idea of building a new, fully equipped and serviced building has often been suggested (Gardey 2015, pp. 78–86), but has never been fulfilled. Indeed, not only would the cost of such a project be monumental, but the idea of abandoning this symbolic place is also controversial. The Assembly has little choice but to make do with it.

When, in the early 2000s, the Assembly authorities[1] decided to open the doors of the Palais Bourbon to citizens in the name of openness and democratic transparency, these issues took on a new dimension. How do we make room for a crowd of people in a place that is already too small for legislative activities and is compelled to be converted? Yet the Assembly's spatial organisation also raises questions that go beyond mere material and logistical aspects. As we shall see in this chapter, the architectural constraints inherited from the past can contribute to shaping the political life of a nation by ensuring the survival of certain parliamentary practices or by forcing the authorities of the institution to make compromises when new democratic expectations emerge (Goodsell 1988).

In order to meet the challenge of opening the Palais Bourbon to the public, a systematic control of access to the different buildings of the Assembly was introduced in 2002 (Chibois 2019, pp. 83–86). Since then, any non-elected person walking through the corridors of the Palais must wear an individual badge indicating the category of user to which they belong. Officially presented as a response to a security threat, I will show here that, more particularly, this new procedure offers a means for the parliamentary administration to plan and distribute the various spaces of the Palais among its many users. Moreover, it allows the interactions between deputies and users of the Palais to be guided and controlled, favouring some users and banning others. I will thus argue that this policy of opening up the Assembly and that of closing access to its buildings are inseparable, as paradoxical as that may seem. They both carry the same hopes of modernisation and the same conservative rigidities.

For the anthropologist, studying this policy of movement is a rich opportunity to question the implicit hierarchy of values on which the parliamentary order is based and, therefore, to reflect on 'how parliament thinks' (Douglas 1986). My approach here is an anthropology of parliaments (Crewe 2021), although my focus is not on the symbolism and the rituals at the centres of power (Abélès 1997; Rai and Johnson 2014). Rather, I am interested in the sociotechnical materiality of institutional life, its architecture as well as its everyday objects and working tools. I argue that this approach provides insider access to the structures of social relations and collective activities that anthropology is interested in. In doing so, I take advantage of the large percentage of human interactions that is instrumentalised by sociotechnical devices, by which they are facilitated as well as made invisible, institutionalised or framed (Winner 1980; Warnier 2009; Lemonnier 2012).

I will begin by briefly outlining the historical problems of access and circulation in the Palais Bourbon to explain how the architectural problem emerged at the French National Assembly in the 1980s and 1990s. I will then detail the solutions that the parliamentary administration devised to address the new challenges it faced alongside the practical and political consequences of these solutions. Finally, I will discuss the paradoxical effects of the policies of managing the circulation of individuals, pointing out the singular dynamics of transformation that are particular to parliaments.

A two-century closure process

The history of the French National Assembly is closely linked to the spatial movement of people within the institution. Revolutionary times gave rise to numerous artistic representations showing the people of Paris cheering the debates of the self-proclaimed Assembly (see Figure 5.1), which helped to create the myth of the public as onlookers who were passionate about the verbal jousting of their elected representatives. What these paintings do not show is that the presence of the crowd was soon considered invasive because it was deemed noisy, fickle and impatient. From the very first months of the National Assembly's existence, this led to attempts at regulating public access. Because of several riots and popular revolts, protecting the Assembly's deliberations against the crowds became an essential requirement when it chose to move to the Palais Bourbon in 1798 (Chibois 2019, pp. 74–76).

Throughout the nineteenth century, several events added further pressure on the Assembly to isolate itself, two of which were decisive. First, the coup d'état of 1852, where the army's intrusion into the Palais was literally experienced as 'rape' (Gardey 2015, p. 106), made the Assembly durably suspicious of the executive's abuses. Second, two attacks at the end of the nineteenth century made it clear that it was not only the crowds, but also such isolated acts, that should be feared. As a result, the institution started developing its own defences in order to make the area an autonomous zone.

Beginning in the 1880s, with the formalisation of the parliamentary administration into a modern bureaucracy and the arrival of the golden age of French parliamentarism (under the Third Republic), a complementary dynamic emerged as a result of the need to make the Palais Bourbon the 'home of deputies' (members of parliament). To this end, it was felt necessary to erase the intrusive activities within the Palais walls, such as wandering journalists, citizens waiting to be received by their deputies, or mail carriers coming and going, as much as possible in order to bring peace of mind. Here, the installation of the telephone at this time was an important instrument for the quietening of the parliamentary space (Chibois 2017), allowing for remote discussions with deputies or the parliamentary administration.

After this two-century policy of closure, the use of the parliamentary space has been shaken up by three major changes within the institution. First, in the late 1970s, the Assembly's authorities decided to buy and construct additional buildings to provide personal offices for deputies. Second, the status of 'deputies' staff' (*assistant parlementaire*) was created in the 1980s to support the work of deputies and groups. Third,

Figure 5.1 Helman I.-S., Duclos, A.-J. and Monnet, C., *Serment du Jeu de Paume à Versailles le 19 juin 1789*, 1792. Engraving, 27.5 × 43.5 cm. Public domain. It shows the Tennis Court Oath ('Serment du Jeu de Paume' in French) that the representatives of the French population took on 19 June 1789, a pivotal event in the Revolution. The presence of the crowd is depicted in the background, in front of the windows on the left and in the passageway on the right. Source gallica.bnf.fr / © Bibliothèque nationale de France

with anti-parliamentary discourse rising from the 1990s onwards, the institution increased the number of initiatives to make the Palais more of a 'people's house' (Abélès 2001). These initiatives include the creation of a parliamentary TV channel, a children's parliament and, above all, the development of guided tours of the Palais.

Unlike the UK House of Commons or the German Reichstag (see Psarra and Maldonado Gil in this volume), no one can attend the guided tours of the Palais without being invited by a deputy. The only exceptions to this rule are special events such as the European Heritage Days, when the Assembly turns the opening of its doors into a celebration. The deputies can choose to carry out the visits themselves or, as is most often the case, to entrust the task to the parliamentary administration, which has some 50 staff specially trained for this purpose. These guided tours are partly an opportunity to discover the symbolic places of legislative activity, but above all for the institution to share its architectural and artistic heritage with the public. This initiative was a great success. In

2015, the communications service told me that it managed to achieve the high rate of 1,000 visitors per day, or between 150,000 and 170,000 people per year.

A policy of 'separation of movement'

Thus, within two decades, the Palais, which was a small space reserved for a limited number of regulars, saw its surface area suddenly fragmented with the multiplication of buildings outside the historical walls of the Palais, and its level of attendance explode with the multiplication of new users. The right of movement, as it had been implemented and patiently built since the Assembly was installed in the Palais, was suddenly faced with a paradox. It was necessary to make the Palais both the 'house of the deputies' as well as the 'people's house'. In other words, the Palais needed to become a private as well as a public place while clearly emphasising its symbolic and heritage dimensions.

To take up this challenge, the parliamentary administration has set up a policy known as the 'separation of movement' (*séparation des flux*) (Assemblée nationale n.d.). It consists, on the one hand, of assigning dedicated entrances to the various categories of users of the Palais, and, on the other hand, assigning them authorised areas in which they can move (see Figure 5.2). But movement jams appear, especially in central areas such as the 'sacred perimeter' (*périmètre sacré*), which is the most significant one in terms of the Palais' political and architectural heritage. This is the reason why individual patterns of movement could vary dynamically, depending on the hours of the day, the days of the week and the weeks of the year.

For instance, on days when the Assembly is not in session, there is no activity around the semicircle, so the sacred perimeter is entirely devoted to guided tours, and some rooms can accommodate public lectures. On days when the Assembly is in session, this sacred perimeter is reserved exclusively for deputies, with some places adjacent to the meeting places for deputies and journalists. On these days, guided tours take a different route so that they can only visit the semicircle from the public galleries.

This separation of movement is backed up by an elaborate system of access badges, which not only allows security officers to visually check that no one oversteps their rights of movement, but also to take advantage of the automation provided by digital access control technologies. In most functional areas, far from the view of visitors and television cameras, movement controls are carried out automatically by detecting the type of badge that each individual bears. In the most mediatised or sensitive places, the parliamentary officers carry out the sorting and control by their discreet presence which, in addition to the flexibility offered by human

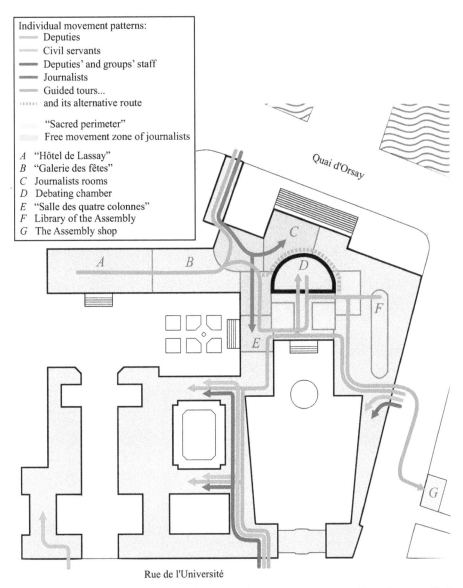

Individual movement patterns:
— Deputies
— Civil servants
— Deputies' and groups' staff
— Journalists
— Guided tours...
⋯⋯ and its alternative route

"Sacred perimeter"
Free movement zone of journalists

A "Hôtel de Lassay"
B "Galerie des fêtes"
C Journalists rooms
D Debating chamber
E "Salle des quatre colonnes"
F Library of the Assembly
G The Assembly shop

Quai d'Orsay

Rue de l'Université

Figure 5.2 Simplified diagram of the circulation patterns regarding the so-called 'separation of movement' of the users of the Palais Bourbon as recreated by the ethnographer during his fieldwork. © Jonathan Chibois

judgement, has the great advantage of making access limits invisible, thus suggesting to the uninformed eye that the place is opened to the greatest number of people.

It should be noted that, since the early 2000s, all staff and visitors have been required to wear their badge visibly in all circumstances in order to make identification and verification possible. However, there are two notable exceptions to this general rule: (1) deputies, whose faces staff must have memorised and (2) citizens taking part in guided tours, whose presence is supervised by a guide. From the point of view of these two categories of users, nothing seems to hinder traffic in the Palais Bourbon, making it truly appear as a place welcoming to all. We are therefore dealing with a symbolic expression of openness, where the presence of the public 'is part of the show' (Bennett 1988). Visitors come to see the heritage of the Assembly building as they are walking across the Palais, which aims to portray the opening of the institution to the public.

Controlling interactions between users

For those who are neither deputies nor visitors, the parliamentary space is, on the contrary, a very fragmented space, both geographically and socially. For them, the badge does not symbolise the privilege of access to the focal point of the Republic, but rather a constraint that limits their freedom to move and therefore their freedom to interact with deputies and other categories of users. Indeed, it is important to understand that in managing movement, the control of interactions is what is fundamentally at stake. The two-century-old policy of keeping spectators away from the periphery of the building and dedicating the heart of the Palais to the deputies alone has been transformed into a policy aimed at controlling who interacts with whom in the Palais and, above all, who interacts with the deputies.

As an ethnographer, I had to deal with this reality personally during my research (Chibois 2019). While carrying out fieldwork, which lasted almost 10 years, I held several positions – mainly as staff member, journalist and private citizen – which forced me to juggle with different badges (see Figure 5.3) and rights of movement necessary in order to conduct my study. I had the opportunity to experience the Palais differently and understand that parliamentary life is broadly dependent on the category of users to which one is assigned. The policy of separating movement in the Palais is so effective that it is as if it contains several parallel social worlds, each with its own rules, logic and uses.

For example, by virtue of their badges, the deputies' staff are only authorised to circulate in corridors where the deputies' offices are and where their political group is located. This circulation rule regulates them to a strict role of 'invisible' workers (Star and Strauss 1999), where they are recognised by the institution as only having the right to assist the deputies – but never to stand in for or collaborate with them (Beauvallet

Figure 5.3 Examples of various badges worn by the ethnographer during his research at the French National Assembly. © Jonathan Chibois

and Michon 2018). Having been a staff member myself allowed me to understand an important issue: the institution's desire to reduce as much as possible the capacity for political action by those who work in the Palais without possessing the legitimacy granted by being elected, as if there were a risk that they might interfere with the political game by being 'matter out of place' (Douglas 1984, p. 36).

Furthermore, journalists' badges give them access to specific places only. These are the press rooms to which they are assigned, the galleries of the semicircle, and the Four Columns Hall (*Salle des quatre colonnes*). The last one is the only place where they are allowed to interview deputies after the sittings. This space is unique in that it is always guarded by an official whose job is to ensure that journalists speak to deputies according to an established code of conduct and, above all, they do not cross the red ribbon separating them. These rules show that journalists hold the roles of super-spectators: privileged observers who are offered opportunities to report on debates and ask questions, but are kept out of certain types of action in the Palais at the same time.

Finally, civil servants' badges give them access only to those areas of the Palais that are necessary for their tasks. This category of users is the most complex, not only because of the many sub-categories it contains, but also because of their role in organising the separation of user flows. Although civil servants have a fully recognised place in the Palais – because they have been selected by the Republic through a competitive examination – they are not elected by the public. This intermediary position does not require their presence to be totally invisible, like deputies' staff members, but discreet, similar to the presence of domestic staff in nineteenth-century bourgeois houses (Gardey 2015, pp. 163–65).

A conservative conception of democracy

It is important to understand that this policy of separation of movement by different kinds of users currently produces two structural effects. On the one hand, it tends to make the presence of non-elected users in the French National Assembly imperceptible. This reveals an elitist conception of democracy by the institution, where the presence of some individuals in the Palais Bourbon is necessary but not fully recognised as legitimate according to the national democratic ideology, so their agency is limited. The administration of the Palais therefore keeps certain activities on the periphery where possible, limiting their interaction with deputies and other users. On the other hand, the presence of citizens and deputies, for whom the Palais is supposedly their 'home', is not only highly noticeable, but is also promoted through institutional communication. The latter two categories of users are not on an equal footing, however, since the initiative for guided tours is a privilege reserved for deputies alone. When they are at the Palais, citizens must therefore be considered guests of their representatives.

This policy regarding users' access and movement appears to be conservative (Urbinati 2006). It serves the myth of national sovereignty, developed at the end of the eighteenth century during the Revolution, on two levels. First, by concealing the presence of deputies' staff and journalists, restricting the movement of civil servants and staging the presence of private citizens, the republican liturgy aims to showcase the deputies above all. Within French democratic ideology, the principle of election is not only a pragmatic way of appointing political representatives. It is also a process by which individuals temporarily and symbolically emerge from their condition as ordinary citizens (Manin 2010), and are put on a pedestal within the institutions of the Republic.

Second, this spatial organisation helps to give concrete expression to a strict opposition between the status of *spectators* and *protagonists* in debates (Heurtin 1994). The French democratic ideology does not tolerate any intermediate position, with the sole exception of civil servants who work for the parliamentary administration. Indeed, the hierarchy of circulation patterns goes hand in hand with an implicit symbolic hierarchy that organises the users of the Palais according to their degree of involvement with legislative work. From a spatial point of view, this hierarchy means that the more individuals are protagonists in legislative work, the closer they are allowed to get to the heart of the parliamentary space that is the semicircle. The more they are in the official position of spectators, the more they are kept on the periphery of the building. From a relational point of view, the more individuals are protagonists, the more their interactions with elected officials tend to be face-to-face; the more they are observers, the more their interactions with elected officials are mediated by communication tools such as video broadcasting, telephone, text messages or email.

Consequently, we can see that this policy of the 'separation of movement' does not call into question the complete opposition between the figures of the deputy and the public – between the protagonist and the observer – but rather reinforces it. Opening up the parliamentary space in the French National Assembly does not mean making the public protagonists, nor does it mean getting them to work with deputies. On the contrary, it means erecting virtual glass walls around the deputies so that the public can get as close as possible to the deliberations and become a kind of super-onlooker. This is an approach similar to the one taken in the German parliament where the public has an elevated view into the plenary chamber under a transparent dome (Waylen 2014; Psarra and Maldonado Gil in this volume). The Assembly's response to the recent rise of anti-parliamentary discourses, and more generally to the demand for greater accountability in democracy, does not aim at altering the communication between the deputies and public (in the direction of a more participatory democracy) but at consolidating republican elitism and the elite status of elected representatives.

Conclusion

In conclusion, apart from allowing a large number of individuals to move inside the Palais Bourbon while also maintaining its security, the main interest of this policy of 'separation of movement' is to ensure that different categories of users remain invisible to each other. This policy allows the institution to demonstrate that the Palais is both the 'house of the deputies' and the 'people's house', simultaneously making clear that the latter are the former's guests.

In the process, these institutional practices shape a contradictory image of the Assembly. On the one hand, it is the emblematic place where deputies and people meet. That is, it is the place where deputies are meant to protect citizens' interests in the face of the threats – according to Claude Bartolone, the Assembly's president between 2012 and 2017 – of the growing power of Europe, of the state's decentralisation process in France, of financial capitalism and more broadly of the globalised world (Bartolone and Winock 2015). On the other hand, they make the Assembly function as the custodian of a representative democracy whereby political work remains the exclusive prerogative of deputies. Here is a stance against citizens' demands for greater recognition of their rights to participate in the conduct of the nation's business – for instance, through an extended right of petition or a citizens' right to amend a bill – or to evaluate the deputies' actions – for instance, through statistics of their attendance and activities.

Note

1 For the sake of simplicity, I use the term 'the Assembly's authorities' to refer to the combination of the three bodies – the presidency, the Bureau and the Conference of Presidents – which have many members in common.

References

Abélès, M. (1997) 'Political Anthropology: New challenges, new aims', *International Social Science Journal*, 49(153), pp. 319–32.

Abélès, M. (2001) *Un ethnologue à l'Assemblée*, Paris: Odile Jacob.

Assemblée nationale (no date) 'La sécurité à l'Assemblée nationale', Assemblée nationale. Available from: https://www2.assemblee-nationale.fr/decouvrir-l-assemblee/role-et-pouvoirs-de-l-assemblee-nationale/l-administration-de-l-assemblee-nationale/la-securite-a-l-assemblee-nationale (accessed 14 January 2021).

Bartolone, C. and Winock, M. (2015) *Refaire la démocratie. Rapport du groupe de travail sur l'avenir des institutions*, Assemblée nationale. Available from: http://www2.assemblee-nationale.fr/14/commissions-permanentes/avenir-des-institutions.

Beauvallet, W. and Michon, S. (eds) (2018) *Dans l'ombre des élus: Une sociologie des collaborateurs politiques*, Villeneuve d'Ascq: Presses Universitaires du Septentrion.

Bennett, T. (1988) 'The Exhibitionary Complex', *New Formations*, 1(4), pp. 73–102.

Chibois, J. (2017) 'The Chamber's Telephonists: Communication infrastructure and division of labor at the Palais Bourbon under the Third Republic', *Revue française de science politique (English Edition)*, 67(4), pp. I–XX.

Chibois, J. (2019) *'L'Assemblée du 21e siècle'. Anthropologie et histoire des infrastructures de communication d'une institution politique d'État*, PhD thesis, EHESS.

Crewe, E. (2021) *The Anthropology of Parliaments: Entanglements in democratic politics*, London: Routledge.

Douglas, M. (1984) *Purity and Danger: An analysis of the concepts of pollution and taboo*, London: Routledge.

Douglas, M. (1986) *How Institutions Think*, Syracuse: Syracuse University Press.

Gardey, D. (2015) *Le linge du Palais-Bourbon: corps, matérialité et genre du politique à l'ère démocratique*, Bordeaux: Le Bord de l'Eau.

Goodsell, C. T. (1988) 'The Architecture of Parliaments: Legislative houses and political culture', *British Journal of Political Science*, 18(3), pp. 287–302. DOI: 10.1017/S0007123400005135.

Heurtin, J.-P. (1994) 'Architectures morales de l'Assemblée nationale', *Politix*, 7(26), pp. 109–40.

Lemonnier, P. (2012) *Mundane Objects: Materiality and non-verbal communication*, Walnut Creek: Left Coast Press.

Manin, B. (2010) *The Principles of Representative Government*, Cambridge: Cambridge University Press.

Rai, S. and Johnson, R. (2014) *Democracy in Practice: Ceremony and ritual in parliament*, London: Palgrave Macmillan.

Star, S. L. and Strauss, A. (1999) 'Layers of Silence, Arenas of Voice: The ecology of visible and invisible work', *Computer Supported Cooperative Work (CSCW)*, 8, pp. 9–30. DOI: 10.1023/A:1008651105359.

Urbinati, N. (2006) *Representative Democracy: Principles and genealogy*, Chicago: University of Chicago Press.

Warnier, J.-P. (2009) 'Technology as Efficacious Action on Objects ... And Subjects', *Journal of Material Culture*, 14(4), pp. 459–70. DOI: 10.1177/1359183509345944.

Waylen, G. (2014) 'Space and Symbols: Transforming parliamentary buildings in South Africa and Germany', in S. Rai and R. Johnson (eds) *Democracy in Practice: Ceremony and ritual in parliament*, London: Palgrave Macmillan, pp. 211–33. DOI: 10.1057/9781137361912_10.

Winner, L. (1980) 'Do Artifacts Have Politics?' *Daedalus*, 109(1), pp. 121–36.

Part II

A contemporary parliament in a historical building

6

Trapping the architectural imagination

Restoration, renewal and denial at Westminster

Matthew Flinders

Introduction

A great body of writing and research has in recent years voiced significant concerns about the health of democracy. This is reflected in narratives of death and decline, crisis and complacency, which all tend to suggest that a gap – as characterised in Peter Mair's (2013) notion of 'ruling the void' – has emerged between the governors and the governed. Globally this is captured in concerns regarding democratic 'deconsolidation', 'backsliding' and the rise of 'pitchfork politics' (Alizada et al. 2021). In the UK, the Hansard Society's 2019 *Audit of Political Engagement* provided a stark insight into the extent of democratic disaffections. Seventy-two per cent of those surveyed suggested that the system of governing in the UK needs 'quite a lot' or a 'great deal' of improvement, and 75 per cent thought the main parties were so divided they cannot serve the best interests of the country. More worryingly, these feelings of disengagement appear to have created an appetite for *il*liberal political shifts, with 54 per cent saying Britain needs 'a strong leader who is willing to break the rules' and 42 per cent thinking that the country's challenges could be dealt with more effectively 'if the government didn't have to worry so much about votes in Parliament' (Hansard Society 2019, p. 5).

In this context, this chapter explores power, architecture and democracy through a focus on what is termed *the architectural imagination*. The intellectual heritage of this term is to be found in the work of C. Wright Mills and one of the main aims of this chapter is to illustrate the value of his arguments concerning 'the promise' and 'the trap' for the fields of architecture and design. My baseline position that architectural (re)design is an instrument of political power is particularly important in relation to parliaments and legislatures – due to their functional and symbolic position at the apex of democratic systems. Charles Goodsell argued over three decades ago that 'the physical architecture of parliaments is – or should be – of interest to political scientists, not just architects or architectural historians' (Goodsell 1988, p. 287). However, research and writing at the intersection of political science, architecture and design remains, with just a few notable exceptions (see, for example, Vale 1992; Parkinson 2012; Bell 2020), a largely barren intellectual terrain. Instead, I want to suggest, with Harold Lasswell, that 'the literature of politics, law, and government has given rather casual attention to the topic [the political and symbolic significance of architecture and design]. Treatises, textbooks and monographs reflect the traditional disregard of these relationships. Scattered here and there, nevertheless, are suggestive propositions' (2016 [1979], p. ix). The aim of this chapter is to develop the conceptual tools available to those who seek a more detailed and nuanced understanding of the relationship between political power, on the one hand, and architectural design, on the other.

The chapter is divided into three sections. The first focuses on Mills' *The Sociological Imagination* (2000 [1959]) to briefly explore its core arguments and broader significance. The second section develops this focus by taking Mills' insights, for the first time, into the realm of architecture and design. Also drawing upon the work of Pierre Bourdieu, Peter Hall, Noam Chomsky, Kim Dovey, Carl DiSalvo and others, I seek to flesh out the intellectual scaffolding originally provided by Mills to develop a politicised 'architectural imagination'. The third section seeks to demonstrate the empirical relevance of the architecture imagination through a brief review of the evolution of the Restoration and Renewal Programme (R&R) in the UK Houses of Parliament. Trapping the architectural imagination within a dominant elite vision of what democracy '*is*' and how it should '*be*', I argue, is increasingly at odds with the view of large sections of the public that British democracy is failing.

The sociological imagination

The notion of the sociological imagination developed by Mills provides a lens that: (i) focuses attention on the role of structures in shaping individual lives and (ii) raises questions about the role of academics in exposing and politicising these relationships. As a sociologist, Mills did not study architecture and design. However, he was concerned with social change and why an increasing proportion of the public appeared to be feeling trapped within a social structure they no longer understood.

Nowadays people often feel that their private lives are a series of traps. They sense that within their everyday worlds, they cannot overcome their troubles, and in this feeling, they are often quite correct. What ordinary people are directly aware of and what they try to do are bounded by the private orbits in which they live. Their visions and their powers are limited to the close-up scenes of job, family, neighbourhood and other milieu, they move vicariously and remain spectators. And the more aware they become, however vaguely, of ambitions and of threats which transcend their immediate locales, the more trapped they seem to feel (Mills 2000 [1959], p. 3).

For Mills, the role of the social scientist was to help those people who felt trapped to understand the nature of social change and, through that, to help people generate a sense of belonging and control. This was 'the promise' that inspired all of Mills' work and writing. The 'sociological imagination' was – through this lens – the ability to forge and make clear the connections between broad social structures and everyday life. The aim of this was to make what were often viewed as personal troubles into public issues by exposing how the roots were structural and beyond the control of any one person: 'That is its task and its promise … from the most impersonal and remote transformations to the most intimate features of the human self' (Mills 2000 [1959], p. 6).

Mills, therefore, focused attention on the role of academics in society. Three quick points serve to underline the contemporary relevance of his work. First, a vast literature on the 'left behind', the 'peripheral' and 'strangers in their own land' (see, respectively, Wuthnow 2018; Guilluy 2015; Hochschild 2018) – not to mention the burgeoning body of work on 'disaffected democrats' – suggests that the themes of social anomie, frustration and anger have grown in significance over the last 50 years. The second issue revolves around the debate within academe about 'the tyranny of impact' (Flinders 2013) and the degree to which scholarship should demonstrate more non-academic relevance and value. Mills' work was critical about the evolution and professionalisation of academe, particularly the social sciences. What he referred to as 'grand theory', 'abstracted empiricism' and 'the bureaucratic ethos' had failed to nurture the 'quality of mind' that allowed scholarship to help the public regain a sense of connection with a world in flux. In the context of contemporary debates concerning research and relevance in the academia (see Eisfeld and Flinders 2021), Mills' work is hugely relevant.

Third, the insights of the sociological imagination are applicable beyond the discipline, Mills held.

> I hope my colleagues will accept the term 'sociological imagination'. ... Political scientists who have read my manuscript suggest 'the political imagination'; anthropologists, 'the anthropological imagination' – and so on. The term matters less than the idea. ... Nevertheless, I use 'sociological imagination' because: (1) every cobbler thinks leather is the only thing and, for better or worse, I am a sociologist; (2) I do believe that historically the quality of mind has been more frequently and vividly displayed by classic sociologists than by other social scientists; (3) since I am going to examine critically a number of curious sociological schools, I need a counter term on which to stand.
>
> (Mills 2000 [1959], p. 19)

In the 60 years since its publication, different scholars have developed Mills' 'idea' within the parameters of their own discipline to forge new insights (see, for example, Young 2011; Willis 2000), but architectural scholarship has, so far, remained beyond this process despite the fact that the notions of 'the promise' and 'the trap' offer significant theoretical and empirical potential. The 'promise' relates to the ability of architecture and design specialists to understand and expose the role that buildings, and the public spaces they exist within, have in terms of encouraging power hoarding or power sharing forms of behaviour. The notion of the 'trap' relates to a situation in which the role of these same factors in 'locking-in' a specific model of politics, and certain forms of political inequality, were either denied or overlooked. The public is, in essence, trapped within a dominant institutional configuration made real in the form of buildings and courtyards, layout and levels – yet unable to grasp the symbolic and practical ways in which those structures actively shaped politics and democracy.

Mills' sociological imagination is thus, above all, a sensitising concept – 'the term matters less than the idea' (Mills 2000 [1959], p. 19). And 'the idea' can be summarised as consisting of two core elements. The first one is the intersection between personal biography, on the one hand, and social structures and institutional frameworks, on the other. Mills wanted the existence of socially embedded structural inequalities to be recognised so that individuals would not be blamed for issues that were, in reality, beyond their control, and for politicians to be held responsible for resolving those issues through social and political reform (Dowding 2020). The second element is the commitment to non-academic engagement – scholars should not just study but also take the results of their study into society more broadly. This places a professional responsibility on the shoulders of professors of architecture or design to engage with the public – working with multiple groups in a variety of ways – to nurture an understanding of how and why the (re)form of parliaments and other public buildings matters. Taken together these two elements, as Mills' appendix 'On Intellectual Craftsmanship' demonstrates, provide a flexible framework for one key question: how can we conceptualise 'the architectural imagination'? This forms the focus of the next section.

The architectural imagination

I suggest that the architectural imagination allows us to interpret architectural debates about parliaments and public buildings as *political* issues with democratic consequences. This is the promise of the architectural imagination. But how might we realise this promise in terms of an analytical toolkit? To ask this question is not to suggest that the fields of architecture and design lack imaginative zeal or energy. Even the most cursory glance at the literature suggests a clear imaginative emphasis, such as Brook Muller's *Ecology and the Architectural Imagination* (2014), Martin Bressani's *Architecture and the Historical Imagination* (2014), Angeliki Sioloi and Yoonchun Jung's *Reading Architecture: Literary Imagination and Architectural Experience* (2018) and Dean Hawkes' *The Environmental Imagination* (2019). Other works focus on 'tracing the architectural imagination' in specific urban environments – such as Sophia Psarra's *The Venice Variations: Tracing the Architectural Imagination* (2018), Robert Govers' *Imaginative Communities: Admired Cities, Regions and Countries* (2018) and Paul Dobraszczyk's *Future Cities: Architecture and the Imagination* (2019). These works tend to use the notion of 'imagination', however, without an explicit focus on the intersection between a *politics of architecture* and an *architecture of politics*.

By contrast, by highlighting the relevance of Mills' sociological imagination, I want to look more explicitly at how architecture and design, closely intertwined with notions of imagination, creativity and aesthetic significance, shape political behaviour and public attitudes. Indeed, if the essence of Mills' approach is a focus on the ability to move up and down the ladder of abstraction from the macro to the micro, then it is possible to suggest that the existing architecture and design literature offers more of a dichotomy than a blend.

What I mean by this is that it is possible to identify two pools of scholarship. The first tends toward a high-level analysis of the historic and symbolic significance of architecture with a clear political texture and tone. The second offers highly detailed institutional analyses of specific buildings or design phases. Examples of the former macro-level seam of scholarship might include Harold Lasswell's *The Signature of Power* (2016 [1979]), Jules Lubbock's *The Tyranny of Taste* (1995), the collected essays of Bernard Tschumi in *Architecture and Disjunction* (1997), Juhani Pallasmaa's *The Thinking Hand* (2009) and *The Eyes of the Skin* (2012), Philip Manow's *In the Shadow of the King* (2010) through to Carl DiSalvo's *Adversarial Design* (2012). They offer a high – or what Mills might have called 'grand' – level of theorising that rarely reaches down to the specific case study, let alone to everyday lived experience. This body of work offers significant value in terms of understanding the link between architecture and the notion of 'the trap' (that is, the symbolic complexity of physical structures and therefore the existence of powerful path dependencies), but generally less about 'the promise' (that is, the emancipatory potential of architecture or design).

The macro-level studies thus remain somewhat aloof from the day-to-day machinations and messiness of political life; they focus on bold themes and big ideas rather than the practical minutiae of everyday politics. The second (micro-level) seam, by contrast, offers a mirror image, with detailed scholarly accounts of architectural history and institutional design, rarely accompanied by any developed awareness of social structure or political dynamics. With a shared focus in the Palace of Westminster, examples could include the work of Chris Miele (1998) on 'the battle for Westminster Hall', Edward Gillin's (2018) analysis of architectural science and Henrik Schoenefeldt's (2014) work on the design of heating and ventilation systems (see Schoenefeldt in this volume). Although rich in descriptive historical and technical detail, these studies can lack an explicit thematisation of what Mills termed 'the big picture' – such as the growing sense of unease surrounding the relationship between the public and the architecture of politics. This brings us back to a focus on Charles Goodsell's argument that a focus on physical architecture should be of great interest to political science due to the manner in which buildings and spaces preserved cultural values, articulated political attitudes and contributed to the formation of a broader political culture (Goodsell 1988). Goodsell was promoting exactly the mid-range position that is largely absent from the contemporary research base.

Mills' arguments and insights, too, operate at a fairly high level of abstraction. To operationalise them for the disciplines of architecture and design, where they have not so far appeared in an explicit manner, I now want to focus on three mid-range or 'connective' concepts that, when taken together, might provide the basis of an 'architectural imagination' approach.

Thinking within and beyond

An analysis that possessed the architectural imagination would demonstrate a rare connective capacity to shift the focus of analysis from the micro to the macro (and vice versa). The focus would be society's interaction with a building or group of buildings that shared a specific design heritage or spatial position, and the building(s) interpreted as a 'signature of power' – to paraphrase Lasswell (2016 [1979]) – that both structured and symbolised specific relationships. The great value of the architectural imagination, therefore, would be its ability to range from a discussion about very specific issues (for example, visitor facilities, constituency offices, digital systems, educational materials, works of art, public space, seating layouts, rituals, language and petition processes) to far broader debates concerning social structures, historical trends and technological change. The architectural design of public buildings in general, and parliaments in particular, therefore becomes a core component of the social structure and is, in this way, ultimately

Figure 6.1 *The Palace of Westminster from the River after the Fire of 1834.*
Anon. circa 1934, Painting. Oil on Canvas. © Museum of London Collection

politicised. This is a key point. The architectural imagination goes beyond the notion of the public as mere spectators of a built environment or passive users of public buildings and is instead attuned to the role and power of 'sensory democracy' (Flinders and Ryan 2017).

As such, the architectural imagination brings the political centre stage in a way that challenges, or at the very least questions, dominant 'self-evident truths' about 'insiders' and 'outsiders' (Ostrom 2000). By revealing the structural manifestation or 'hidden politics' of architectural design, the architectural imagination exposes layers of architectural sedimentation and accretion. Indeed, if architecture reflects, materialises and eternalises images of an idealised polity, then the architectural imagination challenges that view. Instead, it highlights what might be termed the pathologies of everyday architecture. It also highlights the 'potentiality of consciousness', a term taken from Merleau-Ponty's *The Visible and the Invisible* (1969), in terms of how awareness and understanding can rekindle a sense of self, being, energy, agency and even anger.

This turns Mills' emphasis on multi-levelled positionality and relationships back within the analytical approach in order to expose the existence of what might be termed *imaginative architectural gradations*. This draws upon public policy theory, particularly Peter Hall's (1993) analysis of policy change. As Table 6.1 illustrates, Hall identifies three levels – first, second and third order – which are nested. (First order) adjustment options exist in relation to specific policies (second order) which, in turn, are defined by a dominant (third-order) paradigm. The great value of this three-level framework is that it highlights the notion (or trap) of 'thinking within', by which I mean the restriction of policy debates and therefore policy choices *within* an established dominant paradigm. It is only by challenging what appear to be settled assumptions or self-evident truths that new options and opportunities can be identified. The additional benefit of Hall's framework is that it aids understanding in relation to historical institutionalism and path dependencies. Historical institutionalism simply highlights the ways in which decisions taken in the past structure options for the future. The layout of roads, design of keyboards and investment in buildings, for example, all frame the costs and benefits associated with potential changes or reforms in the future (they create logical policy pathways that can be resistant to change). This explains the notion of institutional 'stickiness', which is highly relevant in relation to parliamentary buildings because once embedded and built, the institutional architecture flowing out of a dominant ideational paradigm

Table 6.1 Adversarial design as a third-order focus

Level	Focus	Parliamentary architecture example	Scope	Link to DiSalvo's thesis
Third order	Dominant ideational paradigm	Majoritarian (power-hoarding) representative democracy	Macro-political or 'mega-constitutional'	'adversarial design' / 'political design'
Second order	Technique, policy or design choice	Imposing and inaccessible building supporting agonistic oppositional design.	Meso-level or mid-range	'Design for politics' / 'Designing for democracy'
First Order	Adjustments or tinkering	Public galleries, social space, visitor centres, digital engagement, etc.	Micro-political or 'everyday'	'Design for politics' / 'Designing for democracy'

can be resistant to change. This, in turn, explains why the literature on radical policy change emphasises the role of crises in disrupting the status quo, thereby opening 'windows of opportunity' through which third-order changes may be implemented.

The notion of 'thinking within' seeks to raise awareness of dominant ideational and structurally embedded paradigms and how they might trap the capacity of individuals or organisations to (re)imagine a completely different way of living. The architectural imagination promotes thinking *beyond* rather than *within*. This notion of thinking beyond rather than just within complements a second mid-level focus on adversarial design.

Adversarial design

In seeking to develop the notion of 'thinking within', Carl DiSalvo's *Adversarial Design* (2012) provides a valuable intellectual reference point for at least three reasons. First, as a style of scholarship it is committed to ranging across disciplinary boundaries and promoting public conversations. At root, DiSalvo seeks to politicise the realm of design and 'look beyond'. Second, DiSalvo offers a key distinction between 'design for politics' or 'designing for democracy', on the one hand, and 'adversarial design' or 'political design', on the other, which resonates with Peter Hall's work on policy paradigms I discussed above (see final column of Table 6.1).

Put simply, 'design for politics' or 'designing for democracy' relates – in DiSalvo's analysis – to 'improving the mechanisms of governance and increasing participation in processes of governance' (2012, p. 3) *within* already existing structures. This might include improving access to petitions, balloting, voting, or promoting citizenship education. In other words, it refers to projects that apply design thinking to politics in order to support an established way of governing. It is focused on first- and second-order issues but does not challenge the dominant third-order paradigm. Third, and consequently, DiSalvo foregrounds the importance of 'adversarial design' – and with it, a theory of agonism.

The theory of agonistic pluralism is essentially a commitment to cultivating constructive conflict and challenge instead of accepting the existence of any settled consensus. Theories of agonism emphasise the affective aspects of political relations and accept that disagreement and confrontation are forever ongoing. This is what Chantal Mouffe (2000) labels 'the paradox of democracy'. Consequently, agonism supports non-antagonistic forms of confrontation and critical political spaces to question rather than accommodate a hegemonic rationality or mode of governing. 'For democracy to flourish, spaces of confrontation must exist, and contestation must occur', DiSalvo writes (2012, p. 5), 'perhaps the most basic purpose of adversarial design is to make these spaces of confrontation and provide opportunities for others to participate in contestation.' The core argument about agonism is pertinent to the analysis of public buildings, parliaments and legislatures due to the way in which it seeks to expose the political values and assumptions embedded within the glass, concrete, wood or tiles. In essence, DiSalvo promotes 'thinking beyond' what currently exists and towards what 'might be': it is intolerant towards silent complicity. This approach – when combined with Hall's emphasis on levels of reform – allows us to identify a number of (imaginative) architectural gradations. Or, to put the same point slightly differently, what DiSalvo's adversarial emphasis pushes architectural analysts towards is a deeper focus on uncovering and challenging the dominant third-order paradigms that are themselves embedded in the design and form of buildings (see Table 6.1).

Silent complicity

DiSalvo's work on adversarial design seeks to explicitly politicise the role of designers: he almost ascribes to them a set of professional responsibilities to the public and to supporting democracy. In doing so, his work chimes with Mills' admittedly more robust views about the responsibilities of academics to realise 'the promise' of the social sciences and help the public escape a multitude of 'traps'. It also brings us to a focus on professional complicity and a consideration of Kim Dovey's work on the notion of 'silent complicity' (2002, 2010). The starting point for Dovey is Pierre Bourdieu's argument that, 'architectonic spaces whose silent dictates are directly addressed to the body are undoubtedly among the most important components of the symbolism of power, precisely because of their invisibility' (in Prigge 2008, p. 46). Following on from this, Dovey suggests that 'we live in the world first and look at it second' (Dovey 2002, p. 31). Individuals, groups and communities tend to exist within a spatial world that they have 'already silently imbibed and embodied' (Dovey 2002, p. 33).

Dovey's 'silent complicity' describes the link between architecture and social order, and the former's role in shaping the latter in ways that are rarely articulated. 'There is no zone of neutrality in which to practice and a primary imperative is to strip the design professions of the illusion of autonomy. Design is the practice of "framing" the habitat of everyday life, both literally and discursively' (Dovey 2002, p. 38). The intersection between individual biography and historical sweep is connected beautifully in Dovey's observation that the events of everyday life 'take place' within the clusters of rooms, buildings, streets and cities we inhabit. To which I would add: through the architecture of politics and the politics of architecture.

Echoing Mills' notion of entrapment, Dovey seeks to reveal the hidden politics of place and physical structure by politicising what is too often defined as neutral or apolitical. Following on from this, the opposite of 'silent complicity' might be defined in terms of 'critical noise' in the sense of challenging and confronting established modes of being or acting within specific public spaces. Andrew Filmer (2013) provides a wonderful example of 'disrupting the silent complicity of parliamentary architecture' through his study of an impromptu choral performance in the foyer of Australia's new Parliament House. And yet it is possible to push the notion of silent complicity even further and to develop what might be termed a 'double-dimension' that focuses on both exposing the structural influence of architecture – Filmer's (2013, p. 275) emphasis on being 'noisy' – and DiSalvo's emphasis on 'adversarial design'. In short, the suggestion is that if those with the capacity to articulate a little imaginative capacity and make a little noise in society fail to do so, then they are also engaged in a form of professional 'silent complicity'.

Restoring, renewing, not (re)imagining

The final section of this – primarily conceptual – chapter seeks to illustrate the practical, intellectual and professional value of the theoretical approach outlined in the previous sections through a brief discussion of a globally significant case study – the planned R&R of the Palace of Westminster. This is a 'mid-Victorian masterpiece' – to paraphrase the title of Cocks' (1977) book on the history of the building – that arose after the fire of October 1834 under the supervision of Charles Barry and Augustus Pugin. As several detailed technical reports have underlined in recent years, the building is in a state of advanced structural decay with the likelihood of a catastrophic incident increasing as the structure collapses. Common day-to-day challenges for those working at Westminster include falling masonry, leaking roofs, sewage leaks, rodent infestations, inadequate lighting, limited facilities, electrical failures, asbestos risks, fires and inadequate heating. The jumble of pipes, wires, ducts and conduits in the basement floor that runs the length of the building has been described by a former clerk of the House of Commons as 'a cathedral of horrors' (Thurso 2015).

The current patch-and-mend approach adds £150 million a year to general running costs. But restoring and renewing a Grade I listed building and world heritage site is also costly – and complex. Existing analyses suggest that the most low-risk and efficient way of undertaking the required works would involve a full decant of Parliament for a period of around a decade and at a cost of £4 billion. Staying in the building by working through different zones of the building would be far more costly and inefficient (possibly up to 40 years and over £10 billion). But the fundamental refurbishment of the building must happen. This, in turn, creates a window of opportunity within which to consider (i) how the architecture and design of the Palace of Westminster was intended to embed and perpetuate a certain form of politics (elite, male-dominated, remote, aggressive, adversarial), and (ii) whether an appetite exists to create a building that is more suited to the principles and values of the twenty-first century (inclusive, participatory, transparent, conciliatory).

Decline and disaster, therefore, provide opportunities to break from the past. The fire that destroyed the South African Parliament at the beginning of 2022 sparked exactly this debate. The building's neoclassical columns and Cape Dutch additions served as a physical and symbolic reminder of the country's colonial past; numerous commentators thus suggested that the need for a complete rebuild provides an opportunity to create something that better reflects South Africa's culture, history and diversity. 'Architecture tells stories', the leading South African architect Mphethi Morojele argued in February 2022, 'and those [colonial] buildings didn't really tell our story' (Filhani 2022). Morojele was essentially calling for a reimagining of the link between architecture, politics and power. Yet when it comes to the R&R of the Palace of Westminster, a combination of political forces has conspired to close down any public debate about whether the story the building tells is still suitable, or what designing for a different type of democracy might look like. More specifically, the current architectural design serves to accommodate, reflect and possibly even to lock in a two-party system. Therefore, the leaders of the two main political parties have little incentive in opening up debates about issues that might ultimately affect their position and power.

This is not new. In the wake of the fire of 1834 and the bombing of the Palace in May 1941, suggestions were made by a small number of backbenchers and peers that different options should at least be discussed (new locations, different chamber layouts, new facilities). On both occasions, the government of the day very quickly decided that rebuilding should occur on a 'like-for-like' basis (Flinders, McCarthy Cotter and Meakin 2019; Flinders and Cotter 2019). The fact that government controls the framing of any reform agenda, and can – in all but the most extreme of circumstances – effectively veto any measures that threaten its position, might therefore be seen as a form of 'trap' which prevents the potential 'promise' of redesign from being realised. To speak in terms of 'the trap' and 'the promise' reintroduces the framing of C. Wright Mills and encourages us to utilise the three strands discussed above.

Indeed, in many ways the whole discussion and decision-making process surrounding R&R has been dominated by 'thinking within'. Rebuilding what exists already is the dominant default assumption, with any minor reform ideas focusing on adjustments and tinkering (Table 6.1). In this sense, and as I have explored elsewhere in detail (see Flinders, Meakin and Anderson 2019), the R&R programme risks perpetuating a historical cycle whereby the link between architecture and politics is almost denied. Indeed, what is interesting about the R&R programme is that, from its inception, it has been framed by politicians and policymakers as little more than a technocratic exercise in project management and building maintenance that has absolutely nothing to do with politics or architecture at all. And yet the design and architecture

Figure 6.2 Speculating a pop-up parliament. 2020. © James Cook jamescook artwork.com

of the building, as Shirin Rai (2014) and Sarah Childs (2016) have illustrated, serve to impose certain values and put beyond contestation the everyday workings of the institution. In an argument that resonates with the architect Morojele, Nirmal Puwar (2010, p. 298) argues that the Palace of Westminster serves as 'a memorial to a particularly selected and crafted history of politics and the nation'. Nevertheless, although the Public Accounts Committee argued in its March 2017 report on R&R that the building 'belongs to the people and the nation and [is] a symbol of our democracy' (House of Commons 2017, p. 9), the democratic potential of what is in reality a vast 'mega-project' has largely remained hidden (for a discussion see Bercow 2018).

This flows into our second focus on adversarial design. Despite a sociopolitical context that is rich in anti-establishment fervour, the R&R programme has been the focus of almost no radical thinking, provocation or contestation from the professional architecture and design communities. This might reflect a simple acknowledgement and pragmatic understanding of the political situation. As a result, the reform proposals surrounding the project have generally been within DiSalvo's notion of 'designing for democracy' within existing frameworks, rather than embracing an 'adversarial design' that would have explicitly sought to politicise and challenge the framing currently surrounding R&R. This is not to suggest that the professional community is not aware of such issues. In March 2015, for example, the Design Commission published *Designing Democracy: How Designers Are Changing Democratic Spaces and Processes* with a great deal of this book reflecting on the relevance of parliamentary buildings. William Baker and Nick Hurley pick up themes that have already been emphasised in this chapter with their observation that 'for eight centuries our democracy was just as much about excluding people as it was about participation' (2015, p. 10); and in light of this, Kate Jones from the Design Council asks:

> With such changes to the nature of democracy here in the UK, how can design update and support the spaces and systems in which British democracy takes place? Arguably, one of the biggest opportunities is the restoration and renewal of one of the world's most iconic homes of democracy, the Palace of Westminster (2015, p. 20).

To what degree have the architecture and design communities sought to take a public stance, offering adversarial design options? The architectural competitions that led to the building of the Scottish Parliament in Edinburgh and the National Assembly of Wales in Cardiff had been explicit in their recognition of how 'we shape our buildings, and then they shape subsequent behaviour and culture'. There was a clear desire for buildings that physically reflected an inclusive, open and democratic approach to 'doing' politics.

This brings us to a final focus on our third strand and to the notion of 'silent complicity'. In structural terms, the Palace of Westminster is a building that has reached crisis point. Doing nothing is not an option, and crises create opportunities. 'During decant when colleagues will necessarily operate in a temporary, alternative Chamber, different ways of doing politics might usefully be trialled', the speaker of the House of Commons suggested in 2016, adding that 'the only limitations on us are those which we allow to constrain our ambitions and our imagination' (Bercow 2018). In 2019 the director of the Institute for Government, Bronwen Maddox, re-emphasised the rare constitutional opportunity awarded by a decant and warned Parliament and the government not to 'squander the opportunity that the upheaval represents – to reimagine in more radical terms how the eight acres on the banks of the Thames might be used' (Maddox 2019). But these calls remain rare and go unheard – there has been no national conversation. This is the silent complicity that arguably needs to be made 'noisy' (qua Dovey 2002); or, to recast the same point, those with knowledge of how the architectural imagination is being trapped or denied have themselves some professional and public responsibility to break the silence.

Conclusion

This chapter has focused attention on the structuration of politics through architecture and design. Through a focus on C. Wright Mills' work, I have discussed how what we might term 'the architectural imagination' can make clear what might otherwise remain hidden in everyday life. It has led us to assess how the architecture and design of the Palace of Westminster affects and influences everyday political life. Moreover, Mills' focus on 'the trap' and 'the promise' encouraged academics and experts (architects and designers in our case) to reflect upon the democratic implications of their knowledge and to take that into society. If the architectural imagination exposes why structure and form matter, then it also highlights how crises bring opportunities for change. Thinking *beyond* (rather than *within*) by grasping the value of adversarial design provides a way not only of demonstrating one's architectural imagination but also of avoiding accusations of co-option, control and silent complicity.

References

Alizada, N., Cole, R., Gastaldi, L., Grahn, S., Hellmeier, S., Kolvani, P., Lachapelle, J., Lührmann, A., Maerz, S. F. and Pillai, S. (2021) *Autocratization Turns Viral. Democracy Report 2021*, University of Gothenburg: V-Dem Institute. Available from: https://www.v-dem.net/static /website/files/dr/dr_2021.pdf.

Baker, W. and Hurley, N. (2015) 'Designing Direct Democracy', in Design Commission (ed.) *Designing Democracy: How Designers Are Changing Democratic Spaces and Processes*, London: Design Commission, pp. 10–13. Available from: https://www.policyconnect.org.uk/research /designing-democracy-essay-collection

Bell, D. ed. (2020) *Political Theory and Architecture*, London: Bloomsbury.

Bercow, J. (2018) 'Designing for Democracy: The 2016 Crick Lecture', *Parliamentary Affairs*, 71(4), pp. 845–852. DOI: 10.1093/pa/gsw037.

Bressani, M. (2014) *Architecture and the Historical Imagination*, London: Routledge.

Childs, S. (2016) *The Good Parliament*, Bristol: Bristol University Press.

Cocks, B. (1977) *A Mid-Victorian Masterpiece*, London: Hutchinson.

DiSalvo, C. (2012) *Adversarial Design*, London: MIT Press.

Dobraszczyk, P. (2019) *Future Cities: Architecture and the Imagination*, London: Reaktion Books.

Dovey, K. (2002) 'The Silent Complicity of Architecture', in J. Hillier and E. Rooksby (eds) *Habitus: A Sense of Place*, Aldershot: Ashgate, pp. 267–280.

Dovey, K. (2010) *Becoming Places*, London: Routledge.

Dowding, K. (2020) *It's the Government, Stupid*, Bristol: Policy Press.

Eisfeld, R. and Flinders, M. (eds) (2021) *Political Science in the Shadow of the State*, London: Palgrave.

Filhani, P. (2022) 'South Africa's parliament fire: How it offers a break from the past', *BBC News*, 2 February. Available from: https://www.bbc.co.uk/news/world-africa-60215615.

Filmer, A. (2013) 'Disrupting the "Silent Complicity" of Parliamentary Architecture', *Performance Research*, 18(3), pp. 19–26. DOI: 10.1080/13528165.2013.818309.

Flinders, M. (2013) 'The Tyranny of Relevance and the Art of Translation', *Political Studies Review*, 11(2), pp. 149–167.

Flinders, M. and Cotter, L. (2019) 'The Place of Westminster: Another Window of Opportunity', *Parliamentary History*, 38(1), pp. 149–165. DOI: 10.1111/1750-0206.12418.

Flinders, M. and Ryan, H. (2017) 'From Senseless to Sensory Democracy', *Politics*, 38(2), pp. 133–147. DOI: 10.1177/0263395717700155.

Flinders, M., McCarthy Cotter, L. and Meakin, A. (2019) 'The Double-Design Dilemma', *Journal of Legislative Studies*, 25(2), pp. 250–277. DOI: 10.1080/13572334.2019.1603224.

Flinders, M., Meakin, A. and Anderson (2019) 'The Restoration and Renewal of the Palace of Westminster: Avoiding the Trap and Realising the Promise', *Political Quarterly*, 90(3), pp. 488–495. DOI: 10.1111/1467-923X.12730.

Gillin, E. (2018) 'The Parliament that Science Built: Credibility, Architecture, and Britain's Palace of Westminster', *Endeavour*, 42(4), pp. 189–195. DOI: 10.1016/j.endeavour.2018.07.005.

Goodsell, C. (1988) 'The Architecture of Parliaments: Legislative Houses and Political Culture', *British Journal of Political Science*, 18(3), pp. 287–302. DOI: 10.1017/S0007123400005135.

Govers, R. (2018) *Imaginative Communities: Admired Cities, Regions and Countries*, London: Reputo.

Guilluy, C. (2015) *La France périphérique*, Paris: Flammarion.

Hall, P. (1993) 'Policy Paradigms, Social Learning, and the State', *Comparative Politics*, 25(3), pp. 275–296. DOI: 10.2307/422246.

Hansard Society (2019) *Audit of Political Engagement 16*, London: Hansard Society.

Hawkes, D. (2019) *The Environmental Imagination*, London: Routledge.

Hochschild, A. (2018) *Strangers in Their Own Land*, New York: New Press.

House of Commons (2017) *Delivering Restoration and Renewal, 45th Report of the PAC* (HC 2016–2017 1005). London: House of Commons.

Jones, K. (2015) 'The Future of the Palace of Westminster', in Design Commission (ed.) *Designing Democracy: How Designers Are Changing Democratic Spaces and Processes*, London: Design Commission, pp. 20–22. Available from: https://www.policyconnect.org.uk/research /designing-democracy-essay-collection.

Lasswell, H. (2016 [1979]) *The Signature of Power*, Somerset: Taylor and Francis.

Lubbock, J. (1995) *The Tyranny of Taste*, Cambridge: Cambridge University Press.

Maddox, B. (2019) 'Parliamentary reform can come from Parliament's renovation', The Constitution Unit Blog, 21 May. Available from: https://www.instituteforgovernment.org.uk /blog/parliamentary-reform-can-come-parliaments-renovation.

Mair, P. (2013) *Ruling the Void*, London: Verso.

Manow, P. (2010) *In the Shadow of the King*, Cambridge: Polity.

Merleau-Ponty, M. (1969) *The Visible and the Invisible*, Evanston, IL: Northwestern University Press.

Miele, C. (1998) 'The Battle for Westminster Hall', *Architectural History*, 41, pp. 220–244.

Mills, C. W. (2000 [1959]) *The Sociological Imagination*, Oxford: Oxford University Press.

Mouffe, C. (2000) *The Democratic Paradox*, London: Verso.

Muller, B. (2014) *Ecology and the Architectural Imagination*, London: Routledge.

Ostrom, E. (2000) 'The Danger of Self-Evident Truths', *PS: Political Science and Politics*, 33(1), pp. 33–46. DOI: 10.2307/420774.

Pallasmaa, J. (2009) *The Thinking Hand*, London: Wiley.

Pallasmaa, J. (2012) *The Eyes of the Skin*, London: Wiley.

Parkinson, J. (2012) *Democracy and Public Space*, Oxford: Oxford University Press.

Prigge, W. (2008) 'Reading the Urban Revolution', in K. Goonewardena, S. Kipfer, R. Milgrom and C. Schmid (eds) *Space, Difference and Everyday Life*, London: Routledge, pp. 46–62.

Psarra, S. (2018) *The Venice Variations: Tracing the Architectural Imagination*, London: UCL Press.

Puwar, N. (2010) 'The Archi-texture of Parliament', *Journal of Legislative Studies*, 16(3), pp. 298–312. DOI: 10.1080/13572334.2010.498099.

Rai, S. (2014) *Democracy in Practice: Ceremony and Ritual in Parliament*, London: Palgrave.

Schoenefeldt, H. (2014) 'The Temporary Houses of Parliament and David Boswell Reid's Architecture of Experimentation', *Architectural History*, 57, pp. 175–215. DOI: 10.1017/ S0066622X00001416.

Sioloi, A. and Jung, Y. (2018) *Reading Architecture: Literary Imagination and Architectural Experience*, London: Routledge.

Thurso, J. (2015) 'The Cathedral of Horrors', BBC2 broadcast on 3 March 2015. Available from: https://www.bbc.co.uk/programmes/p02l6cbw.

Tschumi, B. (1997) *Architecture and Disjunction*, Cambridge: MIT Press.

Vale, L. (1992) *Architecture, Power and National Identity*, London: Wiley.

Willis, P. (2000) *The Ethnographic Imagination*, Cambridge: Polity.

Wuthnow, R. (2018) *The Left Behind*, Princeton, NJ: Princeton University Press.

Young, J. (2011) *The Criminological Imagination*, London: Polity.

7

'It was as though a spell has been cast on them'

The relationship between the Palace of Westminster and the UK Parliament

Alexandra Meakin

Introduction

Legislative buildings are not simply collections of bricks and mortar but can shape the behaviour of the people within. One particular legislative building: the home of the UK Parliament – the Palace of Westminster – is said to have such power over those who work within the building that it has been argued, by a parliamentarian, that 'it was as though a spell has been cast' on his colleagues (Blunkett 2017). This chapter considers the nature and impact of this 'spell' by analysing the emotional attachment felt by parliamentarians and officials to the Palace of Westminster. It draws on 35 semi-structured elite interviews with members of parliament (MPs), members of the House of Lords (peers) and parliamentary officials to consider attitudes towards the building, and complements the interview data with extensive textual analysis and archival research. It thus sheds light on how at key points in the history of the building – most notably, the 1834 fire and the bomb damage caused in the Second World War – the emotional attachment felt by parliamentarians shaped the policy decisions taken for the future of the Palace. This chapter then develops this analysis by considering the impact of this emotional attachment on the current Restoration and Renewal Programme of the Palace of Westminster.

Understanding legislative buildings

It is recognised that legislative buildings act as symbols both of national identity and of the institution they house (Sawyer 2003). This chapter focuses not on the power of legislative buildings over the population in general, however, but the way the buildings shape the behaviour of actors – primarily elected members but also non-elected officials – working within. This occurs, Goodsell argued, in three ways: legislative buildings 'perpetuate the past, they manifest the present and they condition the future' (1988, p. 288). On the latter point, Goodsell stressed that the effect of legislative buildings was not to 'deterministically control the attitudes and behaviour of people' but to 'condition their thoughts and actions in preliminary, subtle and interactive ways' (1988, p. 288). It is not, therefore, a simple causal relationship between building and behaviour. For example, while the layout of the House of Commons chamber is closely associated with the majoritarian two-party politics of the UK, as Peschel (1961) has noted, the two-party system has also flourished in the US despite a very different chamber layout. Rather, the effect of the building on its inhabitants has been to foster an emotional attachment, which has, in turn, shaped policy decisions about the building's future.

The 'spell'

When construction of the Palace of Westminster began in 1042, the building was intended to be a royal residence, not a parliamentary building (Joint Committee on the Palace of Westminster 2016). Over the course of centuries the building evolved, becoming one of the meeting places used by the Commons in 1258 and then, in 1547, the permanent home of the House of Commons and Lords, with separate chambers within the same building (Given-Wilson 2009; Bryant 2014). After fire destroyed much of the old Palace in 1834, Charles Barry and Augustus Welby Pugin created a 'New Palace at Westminster', constructed in a neo-Gothic style, decorated with gilded wallpaper and encaustic tiles, filled with paintings and sculptures celebrating great statesmen and military victories (Port 1976). The building process was lengthy and complex: the House of Lords chamber was completed in 1847, the Commons chamber in 1850. But the overall Palace was still being built and altered into the 1860s (Shenton 2016).

The overall effect of the building is powerful: David Judge (1989, p. 400) has described how the 'architectural splendour' of the Palace has 'enchanted' people. Aileen Walker, then director of public engagement in the House of Commons, noted in 2012 that 'visiting Parliament makes a strong impact … the buildings can be intimidating in their splendour' (Walker 2012, p. 274). The effect is no less for those working within the building. Lord Naseby, who has spent 48 years as a parliamentarian, described the building as 'magical' (Naseby 2018). Multiple MPs and peers interviewed for this research used the word 'love' unprompted, to describe their feelings towards the Palace.

For some MPs, the 'spell' of the building is in the feeling of a physical connection to their predecessors, transmitted through the Palace – and its location – itself. This was present prior to the fire. John Wilson Croker MP 'opposed further consideration' of any changes to the Commons chamber in 1831, arguing that they were 'quite needless' (HC Deb 11 Oct 1831, c560). Instead, he explained his commitment to the existing chamber in St Stephen's Chapel:

> He could not forget that it was the place in which the Cecils and the Bacons, the Wentworths and Hampdens, the Somers's and the St. Johns, the Walpoles and the Pulteneys, the Pitts, the Foxes, the Murrays, and the Burkes, had 'lived, and breathed, and had their being' … as long as the human mind was susceptible of local associations, he could not disregard the beneficial effect that might be felt from their continuing to assemble on the scene where so many illustrious actors had performed such splendid parts. If patriotism could grow warmer on the plain of Marathon, and piety amid the ruins of Iona, the zeal and talents of British senators might also be exalted by the religious and legislative sanctity with which time and circumstances had invested the ancient chapel of St. Stephen (HC Deb 11 Oct 1831, c558–559).

This speech took place during a debate over the future of the old Palace, following calls for a new Commons chamber. Over a century later, when decisions were again to be made about the future of the Commons, after the new Palace was damaged by Luftwaffe bombs during the Second World War, the same predecessors were again invoked, demonstrating how the emotional attachment had transferred to Barry and Pugin's building on the same site. Dr Russell Thomas MP argued for Parliament to stay within the same building where 'Burke, Sheridan, Charles James Fox, Pitt and others there laid down the foundations' of parliamentary democracy (HC Deb 28 Oct 1943, c452). Another 75 years later, another MP, Ian Paisley, would also look back to the building's past:

> I try to have that sense of place, that understanding, that sense of history, I mean every time I walk through St Stephen's Hall I try to think of the words of William Wilberforce echoing for *28 years* trying to change slavery, you know, all of those things just are in this building and in this fabric (Paisley 2018).

Paisley also drew on more recent – and personal – history to explain his connection to the building through his predecessors: 'When I got elected it felt like coming home. You know, my Dad [Ian Paisley Sr, MP for North Antrim, 1970–2010] brought me here when I was a wee boy' (Paisley 2018).

For other parliamentarians, the spell of the building is in its symbolic value. Sir Edward Leigh MP described it as the 'iconic picture of the nation' (Leigh 2018). Lord Birt praised the Victorian parliamentarians for 'investing in the future' and creating 'for ever a symbol understood the world over of all that is best in this cradle of democracy' (HL Deb 16 Nov 2021, c69GC). The debates over rebuilding the Commons chamber in the Second World War demonstrated how the very design of Barry and Pugin's chamber was seen as symbolic of a golden age of parliamentary democracy (HL Deb 14 May 1941, c171). Nearly 80 years later, Sir John Redwood MP would make a similar claim:

> I agree with those who think there is something very special about this place and something important about it for our democracy. This is the mother of Parliaments and this building does have great resonance around the world, being associated with the long history of freedom, and the development of the power of voice and vote for all adults in our country (HC Deb 31 Jan 2018, c918).

The symbolic value of a building may reflect the intentions of an architect or decision maker (Jones 2011) or be unintentional as a result of their own biases or assumption, but further, it may also, as Edelman (1995, p. 84) argues, 'diverge radically from whatever the architect intended', affecting how occupants, as well as the country at large, view the building. Indeed, Laura Pidcock, then a Labour MP, argued that the symbolism of the Palace is negative rather than positive: 'The Palace of Westminster is a beautiful, historic building. We have to recognise, however, that for many in this country it is also a symbol of corruption, power, dominance, greed and suffering' (Pidcock 2017).

Symbolic value is thus subjective, making it even more critical to understand the role it plays in policymaking for legislative buildings.

Shaping policy decisions – the past

The long history of the Palace of Westminster as the home of the UK Parliament has meant there have been multiple times when the future of the building has been considered, due to the need for expansion or repairs or due to changes to the institution itself. At each of these points, the emotional attachment of the building's inhabitants to the Palace has shaped the decision taken. Three years after John Wilson Croker's arguments against a new Commons chamber, noted above, the building was destroyed by fire. Any suggestion that Parliament should leave Westminster, even temporarily, was rejected by the prime minister, Lord Melbourne, who warned the king that such a move risked changing the 'character' of the Commons (Melbourne 1889, p. 214). Instead, Parliament decided to rebuild the Palace and even stayed on site during the building works. While Barry and Pugin's new Palace was, in theory, built as a legislature, the commitment to the old Palace and the politics of the time meant that, as David Cannadine (2000, p. 15) described, it remained 'more a royal residence than a democratic legislature', focusing on the monarch and the Lords, with the Commons in a secondary role. Edward Gillin has argued that 'as far as architecture goes, the Palace is the ultimate symbol of political power. Though to look at the Houses of Parliament building is not to see a bastion of democracy, but a fantastic shrine to the medieval powers of monarchy, church, and aristocracy' (Gillin 2017, p. 1x).

When the new Palace was damaged during the Second World War, the prime minister, Winston Churchill, invoked his own personal attachment to the old Commons as a reason to rebuild as before:

> We shape our buildings and afterwards our buildings shape us. Having dwelt and served for more than 40 years in the late Chamber, and having derived fiery great pleasure and advantage therefrom, I, naturally, would like to see it restored in all essentials to its old form, convenience and dignity (HC Deb 28 Oct 1943, c403).

This view was shared by his colleagues: only three MPs voted against the decision to preserve the essential features of the old Commons chamber in the rebuilding process (HC Deb 28 Oct 1943, c473). The personal relationship members had with the physical building was clear: Arthur Greenford, acting as leader of the opposition, invoked this relationship when explaining why he agreed with the prime minister:

> This is not a party question. It is a question that affects all of us. I remember that Sunday morning. I was the first member of the Government to see the blazing Chamber. I found it very difficult to express my feelings at that time. I felt a sense of personal loss, which I knew would be shared by all Members of the House, and, I am

bound to say, an intensified sense of bitterness against the author of the damage (HC Deb 28 Oct 1943, c409).

Shaping policy decisions – the future

At the present time, parliamentarians are once again considering the future of the building in which they work. These discussions have not been prompted by fire or war damage, but are seeking instead to preempt a catastrophe of similar status. Decades of neglect since the rebuilt Commons chamber opened in 1950 (and, with regards to the infrastructure serving the building as a whole, since Barry and Pugin's Palace was constructed a century earlier) led a joint select committee to conclude in 2016 that: 'The Palace of Westminster, a masterpiece of Victorian and medieval architecture and engineering, faces an impending crisis which we cannot responsibly ignore' (Joint Committee on the Palace of Westminster 2016, p. 5).

One potential solution to the impending crisis – moving to a purpose-built building, rather than a royal palace – was not considered by the joint committee. The idea had been ruled out at an early stage of the decision-making process by the internal governance bodies of the Commons and Lords. There was almost no appetite among parliamentarians for moving to a new building. The idea was not seen as a serious prospect or even desirable, demonstrating the strength of the attachment to the Palace (interviews with MPs, peers and officials 2018).

Instead, the joint committee endorsed the adoption of a major refurbishment – known as the Restoration and Renewal of the Palace of Westminster – including a 'full decant' during which the Commons and Lords would leave the Palace entirely, returning some five to seven (or more) years later. As in 1834, the prospect of parliamentarians moving out, even temporarily, has been controversial. Sir Edward Leigh MP, while accepting that the building did require repairs, argued that such a decant 'would be tearing the heart out of politics' (Leigh 2018). Neil Gray, then an MP for the Scottish National Party, referred to the impact of this emotional attachment on the decant discussions among MPs: 'I think there was just a romance around remaining in the Palace of Westminster forever more, and that you know British democracy had to stay within the Palace of Westminster in order to stay legitimate, which I disagree with' (Gray 2018).

While affection for the Palace was given as a reason not to leave the building, it was also mobilised as a reason to support decant. The then speaker of the House of Commons, John Bercow, explained how his position changed between 2012, when he was 'very sceptical' about a major programme of works, and 2015, when he described himself as 'slightly influenced by one or two other people you know, in the House, among members, you know, who I know love the place just as much as I do, and who sort of said to me "you know, well, I don't think there's much alternative"' (Bercow 2018).

Sir David Natzler, the then clerk of the House (the most senior official in the Commons), said that the argument he used with decant-sceptic MPs was: 'Because you love the building you have to save it' (Natzler 2018). He was successful: in January 2018 the House of Commons voted to approve the Restoration and Renewal Programme with a full decant of Parliament, a decision endorsed the following week by the House of Lords. It marked a significant policy change in the institution of the UK Parliament.

The passage of the Restoration and Renewal Programme since its approval in 2018 has not been without obstacles – the potential cost of the project remains an issue of significant concern for parliamentarians, particularly in light of the economic damage caused by the pandemic. Indeed, the full decant may not survive such concerns, with the governing bodies of the Commons and Lords recommending 'an incremental approach to the work' (House of Commons Commission 2022). But on all sides of the debate, the connection to the physical building of the Palace remains clear. Labour Peer Baroness Andrews described the central place of the Palace in the UK's national identity:

> This place—and it is a place, not just a building—has been at the heart of our religious and political life for a millennium. In the past two centuries, it has spoken aloud the biography of this nation—and it still contains its original function, when so few historic buildings do. That makes it extremely important (HL Deb 8 Jul 2019, c1639).

The then leader of the Commons Jacob Rees-Mogg echoed the symbolic importance of the building, citing 'Westminster's long history as the centre of our national life, of our island story' when calling on MPs to save the Palace, adding a reference to the religious history of the Palace and neighbouring Westminster Abbey: 'So when, eventually, St Peter returns with his heavenly choir, he will look from his abbey across to a building that he will be able to report back to a carpenter's son is one that he can be proud of' (HC Deb 20 May 2021, c910).

Conclusion

This chapter has shown how UK parliamentarians report an emotional attachment to the Palace of Westminster through their 'love' for its architecture and beauty, a feeling of walking in the footsteps of

Figure 7.1 The Elizabeth Tower, undergoing vital restoration work in 2018. ©
Alexandra Meakin

illustrious predecessors or a commitment to its symbolic value. In turn, this attachment has helped to shape policy decisions around the Palace and ensured that it will remain the permanent home of the legislature. In this way, the evidence supports Goodsell's claim that parliamentary buildings 'perpetuate the past, they manifest the present and they condition the future', at least in relation to their own futures (Goodsell 1988, p. 288). This chapter has also shown, however, that while the emotional attachment to the building has acted as a deterrent to changing the building, it was harnessed in 2018 to persuade parliamentarians to back a major refurbishment, the Restoration and Renewal Programme, which aims to create a building that 'accommodate[s] the needs of a 21st Century Parliament' (Deloitte 2014), potentially opening the opportunity for significant change to the Palace.

The approval of the Restoration and Renewal Programme demonstrates how emotional attachment to a building does not need to prevent evolution. Lord Blunkett, who had compared the Palace to an old church, described how he both appreciated the history of the Palace and supported changes to modernise and repair it:

> I like old churches, I like their smell, their aura, I like the history that you can feel exuding from the walls, which you particularly can feel in the big Westminster Hall which is really the old part that's been saved from the Second World War bombing. And that's very nice and I occasionally myself like to stand there for five minutes, and then move out and go back into the real world. And so, understanding and differentiating between enjoying heritage, but not living in it, is quite important (Blunkett 2018).

As the Restoration and Renewal Programme proceeds, parliamentarians will have to grapple with finding the balance referred to by Lord Blunkett, ensuring there will be further evolution in the relationship between the institution and the Palace it calls home.

References

Bercow, J. (2018) Interviewed by Alexandra Meakin, September 2018, London.
Blunkett, D. (2017) 'The Allure of the Palace of Westminster is More Than Even a Radical Spirit Can Take', *The Crick Centre*, 9 October. Available from: http://www.crickcentre.org/blog/blunkett-palace-of-westminster/ (no longer available).
Blunkett, D. (2018) Interviewed by Alexandra Meakin, 6 July 2018, Sheffield.
Bryant, C. (2014) *Parliament: The biography, Volume 1, Ancestral voices*, London: Black Swan.
Cannadine, D. (2000) *The Houses of Parliament: History, art, architecture*, London: Merrell.
Deloitte (2014) *Palace of Westminster Restoration and Renewal Programme, Independent Options Appraisal, Final Report, vol. 1*, London: Deloitte. Available from: https://www.parliament

.uk/globalassets/documents/lords-information-office/2015/Independent-Options
-Appraisal-final-report-A4.pdf. Accessed 7 May 2017.

Edelman, M. (1995) *From Art to Politics: How artistic creations shape political conceptions*, Chicago:
University of Chicago Press.

Gillin, E. J. (2017) *The Victorian Palace of Science*, Cambridge: Cambridge University Press.

Given-Wilson, C. (2009) 'The House of Lords 1307–1529', in C. Jones (ed.) *A Short History of
Parliament*, Woodbridge: The Boydell Press, pp. 16–28.

Goodsell, C. T. (1988) 'The Architecture of Parliaments: Legislative houses and political culture',
British Journal of Political Science, 18(3) pp. 287–302. DOI: 10.1017/S0007123400005135.

Gray, N. (2018) Interviewed by Alexandra Meakin, 27 June 2018, London.

HC Deb (11 October 1831), vol. 8, col. 560. Available from: https://hansard.parliament.uk
/commons/1831-10-11/debates/5606cc53-0ae9-4e51-8317-c42b2d2efac5/Accommodatio
nsInTheHouseOfCommons. Accessed 2 February 2023.

HC Deb (11 October 1831), vol. 8, col. 558–559. Available from: https://hansard.parliament
.uk/commons/1831-10-11/debates/5606cc53-0ae9-4e51-8317-c42b2d2efac5/Accommod
ationsInTheHouseOfCommons. Accessed 2 February 2023.

HC Deb (28 October 1943), vol. 393, col. 452. Available from: https://hansard.parliament.uk
/commons/1943-10-28/debates/4388c736-7e25-4a7e-92d8-eccb751c4f56/HouseOfCom
monsRebuilding. Accessed 2 February 2023.

HC Deb (28 October 1943), vol. 393, col. 403. Available from: https://hansard.parliament.uk
/commons/1943-10-28/debates/4388c736-7e25-4a7e-92d8-eccb751c4f56/HouseOfCom
monsRebuilding. Accessed 2 February 2023.

HC Deb (28 October 1943), vol. 393, col. 473. Available from: https://hansard.parliament.uk
/commons/1943-10-28/debates/4388c736-7e25-4a7e-92d8-eccb751c4f56/HouseOfCom
monsRebuilding. Accessed 2 February 2023.

HC Deb (28 October 1943), vol. 393, col. 409. Available from: https://hansard.parliament.uk
/commons/1943-10-28/debates/4388c736-7e25-4a7e-92d8-eccb751c4f56/HouseOfCom
monsRebuilding. Accessed 2 February 2023.

HC Deb (31 January 2018), vol. 635, col. 918. Available from: https://hansard.parliament.uk
/commons/2018-01-31/debates/12231195-A66F-4D6B-A901-340BD27BD5F4/Restoratio
nAndRenewal(ReportOfTheJointCommittee). Accessed 2 February 2023.

HC Deb (20 May 2021), vol. 695, col. 910. Available from: https://hansard.parliament.uk
/commons/2021-05-20/debates/B5FC8D4C-FD99-447B-B27D-287747FCB845/Restorati
onAndRenewalOfThePalaceOfWestminster. Accessed 2 February 2023.

HL Deb (14 May 1941), vol. 119, col. 171. Available from: https://hansard.parliament.uk/lords
/1941-05-14/debates/a5e23dee-79a3-476c-89c0-aefe7d028dab/SympathyWithTheCom
mons. Accessed 18 May 2023.

HL Deb (8 July 2019), vol. 798, col. 1639. Available from: https://hansard.parliament.uk/Lords
/2019-07-08/debates/DEEFBAB8-AD5A-424A-8FEF-686CF54886F6/ParliamentaryBuild
ings(RestorationAndRenewal)Bill. Accessed 18 May 2023.

HL Deb (16 November 2021), vol. 816, col. 69GC. Available from: https://hansard.parliament.uk
/lords/2021-11-16/debates/CA0DFF10-B7F9-46CA-94DC-32987C09F585/Parliamentary
WorksSponsorBodyAnnualReport. Accessed 18 May 2023.

House of Commons Commission (2022) *Joint statement from the House of Commons and House of
Lords Commissions 18 March 2022*. Available from: https://committees.parliament.uk
/committee/348/house-of-commons-commission/news/164938/joint-statement-from
-the-house-of-commons-and-house-of-lords-commissions/. Accessed 14 June 2022.

Joint Committee on the Palace of Westminster (2016) *Restoration and Renewal of the Palace of
Westminster*, HL 41, HC 659. London: House of Commons.

Jones, P. (2011) *The Sociology of Architecture: Constructing identities*, Liverpool: Liverpool
University Press.

Judge, D. (1989) 'Parliament in the 1980s', *Political Quarterly*, 60(4) pp. 400–412. DOI:
10.1111/j.1467-923X.1989.tb00783.x.

Leigh, E. (2018) Interviewed by Alexandra Meakin, 16 May 2018, London.

Melbourne, W. L. (1889) *Lord Melbourne's Papers*, London: Longmans, Green, and Co.

Naseby, L. (2018) Interviewed by Alexandra Meakin, 8 May 2018, London.

Natzler, D. (2018) Interviewed by Alexandra Meakin, 12 July 2018, London.

Paisley, I. (2018) Interviewed by Alexandra Meakin, 27 June 2018, London.

Peschel, K. (1961) 'Council Chambers of the Great Parliaments', *Parliamentary Affairs*, 14 pp. 518–533. DOI: 10.1093/oxfordjournals.pa.a053628.

Pidcock, L. (2017) 'It's 2017 – So Why Does Parliament Still Feel Like a Gentlemen's Club?' *CLASS*, 9 August. Available from: http://classonline.org.uk/blog/item/its-2017-so-why-does-parliament-still-feel-like-a-gentlemans-club. Accessed 14 June 2022.

Port, M. H. (1976) *The Houses of Parliament*, New Haven: Yale University Press.

Sawyer, S. (2003) 'Delusions of National Grandeur: Reflections on the intersection of architecture and history at the Palace of Westminster, 1789–1834', *Transactions of the Royal Historical Society*, 13, pp. 237–250, Cambridge: Cambridge University Press. DOI: 10.1017/S0080440103000136.

Shenton, C. (2016) *Mr Barry's War*, Oxford: Oxford University Press.

Walker, A. (2012) 'A People's Parliament?' *Parliamentary Affairs*, 65(1) pp. 270–280. DOI: 10.1093/pa/gsr054.

8

Symbolic representation in public space, and the UK Parliament's corporate identities

Alex Prior

Introduction

The UK Parliament is an ancient institution, symbolised by (and partially housed in) the Palace of Westminster, a comparatively modern building that nevertheless invokes antiquity. Both characteristics are a hindrance to establishing a corporate identity, that is to say, to managing public experiences and perceptions of Parliament. As a term, corporate identity is typically discussed vis-à-vis Parliament only in terms of its absence, and how it may be achieved. This chapter examines the reasons for, and significance of, this supposed absence. It does so by utilising a conceptual framework based on symbolic representation. It focuses on the physicality of Parliament – specifically, the building(s) symbolising and housing it. Through this examination, we can identify existing obstacles to the way the UK Parliament presents itself to the public, and discern realistic prospects for addressing them. This is particularly significant in the context of plans for the Restoration and Renewal of the Palace of Westminster, which have galvanised discussions of the Palace (and Parliament) as both space and place (see Flinders, and Meakin in this volume).

Engagement and identity

The importance of corporate (or any other) identity is premised upon the significance of public engagement, that is to say, the involvement of publics in decision making.[1] The UK Parliament's (self-identified) responsibility to engage publics is a comparatively recent phenomenon.

Figure 8.1 *Houses of Parliament* [unfinished] [oil on canvas]. © Ellen Spafford 2016. Reproduced with permission of the artist

It was only in 2004 that the Select Committee on Modernisation of the House of Commons observed that:

> The legitimacy of the House of Commons, as the principal representative body in British democracy, rests upon the support and engagement of the electorate. The decline in political participation and engagement in recent years, as well as in levels of trust in politicians, political parties and the institutions of State should be of concern to every citizen. But it should be of particular concern to the House of Commons (Select Committee on Modernisation of the House of Commons 2004, p. 9).

MPs, by contrast, have a longstanding history of engaging publics – typically, their own constituencies, given the importance of strong local connections to gaining a seat in Parliament. They continue to play a key role in 'humanis[ing] governance, representing it to people, and people to it, in humane and accessible terms' (Coleman 2005, p. 12). Nevertheless, individual members vary considerably in the degree to which this form of interaction is valued (or, indeed, sought), especially in situations that do not relate directly back to political (electoral) utility. It is therefore important to acknowledge recent institutional efforts to promote public engagement, which are not (entirely) reliant on the individual energies of members. These efforts pull away from an image of Parliament as beholden to temporal (and often unpopular) forces: individual policies, politicians and administrations. Cristina Leston-Bandeira acknowledges the importance of this development, identifying:

> A clear effort in public engagement to encourage attachments that rely on more symbolic ideas such as democracy and the country's historical heritage, hence a strong focus on educational and cultural public engagement activities. These events potentially enable the development of different intersubjective interpretations according to each participant's context, stimulating different types of connections between the public and the institution of parliament (Leston-Bandeira 2016, p. 513).

Fostering these interpretations and connections is one means of addressing a longstanding dilemma of public engagement, one that is particularly (though not exclusively) relevant to Parliament. This dilemma concerns the lack of a single, coherent institutional identity, or perhaps more accurately, the existence of a plurality of institutional identities. This phenomenon is partially attributable to bicameral roles, as demonstrated in Alexandra Kelso's discussion of media strategies: '[t]he two separate Houses of Parliament have traditionally conducted media relations in their own different ways, which in itself crystallises the problems associated with talking about a "parliamentary" strategy towards anything' (Kelso 2007, p. 368). However, the identity under discussion is not merely bicameral but disaggregated. As Kelso observes, 'Parliament does not function as a "unified" institution, and largely lacks any kind of corporate identity, and therefore also lacks the means to approach political disengagement in a holistic fashion' (Kelso 2007, pp. 365–366).

Thus far we can establish two key contextual points, first of which is a concerted institutional effort to foster more symbolic (and intersubjective) connections with publics. The second is a lack of corporate identity, which the aforementioned institutional effort stands, at least potentially, to address. In order to discuss the prospects for the former in addressing the latter, we must first establish an understanding of corporate identity and symbolic representation.

What (and where) is corporate identity?

Corporate identity is a difficult term to define, even within its own relevant literature. T.C. Melewar and Elizabeth Jenkins attribute this difficulty to the status of the term as a construct – acknowledged to be largely conceptual and subjective (2002). They do, however, cite Wally Olins' definition of corporate identity: 'the explicit management of all the ways in which the organisation presents itself through experiences and perceptions to all its audiences' (1995, cited in Melewar and Jenkins 2002, p. 77). This presupposes – or at the very least requires – a strong central strategy and/ or identity. This is a particular – even definitive – challenge for parliaments, which are aggregations of different identities and intentions (Shepsle 1992). They must manage numerous conflicting, and even contradictory, responsibilities, such as balancing representative functions with security concerns:

> Where once assembly buildings were open and accessible to citizens, most are now protected by heavy security both internally and externally. Certain kinds of purposive citizen – those who have active, democratic purposes in coming to the building – are set apart in the galleries unable to interact, sometimes even held behind thick layers of bullet-proof glass. The kinds of visitors who are welcomed at many assemblies are tourists and school children, and are taught about democratic citizenship in a building that strictly curtails their ability to express that citizenship (Parkinson 2013, p. 448).

The understanding of corporate identity as 'explicit management' of experiences and perceptions (insofar as they *can* be managed) applies itself to many different departments and services, inside and outside of a parliament. In this sense, a successful approach relies upon a holistic cross-institutional strategy, transcending individual (or even collective) members, whose efforts nonetheless shape public experiences and perceptions.

Nevertheless, a lack of corporate identity is not *intrinsic* to a parliament. The Scottish Parliament, for example, possesses corporate identity guidelines that, despite referring specifically to formatting details, indicate broader representative principles: that '[e]veryone should have the same opportunity to engage', and for corporate identity 'to reflect the values of the Scottish Parliament in the balance between authority and openness' (The Scottish Parliament 2017, pp. 5–6). The Welsh Parliament also exemplifies a link between corporate identity and the legislature's responsibility to engage, in this context, to 'deliver advertising, publicity, campaigns or other engagement methods that target the public bilingually' (National Assembly for Wales Assembly Commission 2013, p. 18).

In the case of the Scottish and Welsh parliaments – both comparatively young institutions – there is an evident understanding and appreciation of the value of corporate identity to accessibility and engagement, as well as the way in which this corporate identity constitutes a form of 'representative claim-making' (with a significant emphasis on unity and accessibility), a term we will discuss in the following section. Considering the relative youth of these legislatures it is possible that this distinction is attributable to a comparative absence of (or perhaps freedom from) heritage and tradition, concepts that are continually recreated and entrenched within Westminster. Barry Winetrobe, in a rare scholarly case of discussing parliaments in explicitly 'marketing' terms, observes that one of 'the defining characteristics of an effective Parliament [is] an underlying vision and purpose' (Winetrobe 2003, p. 1). Winetrobe relates this to concepts of marketing and corporate identity in order to emphasise the importance of thinking not only of functions, but identity and 'customers'. Identity matters, not only for parliaments but for their publics. The myriad perspectives and interpretations of these publics can be better understood through the lens of symbolic representation.

Parliament(s) through a symbolic lens

The theoretical framework for symbolic representation was provided by Hanna Pitkin's *Concept of Representation* (1967). Pitkin's theoretical groundwork (on representation in general) has been subject to extensive critique by academics such as Michael Saward (2010), who stress a more performative and dynamic element to representation. This performativity is encapsulated by the theory of a 'representative claim' and the necessity of an audience to validate it. From the 'claim-making' viewpoint, representation is a performative construct rather than a universal truth. This represents a substantial departure from Pitkin's original conceptualisation: a 'three-dimensional structure in the middle of a dark enclosure' which we may only glimpse through 'flash-bulb photographs' (Pitkin 1967, p. 10).

Nevertheless, Pitkin's discussion of *symbolic representation* – as representation ('speaking for') on the basis of inference and suggestion rather than resemblance (1967, pp. 92–111) – remains highly influential in emphasising the role of symbolism, ritual and ceremony within political practice and institutions (Parkinson 2009; Waylen 2010; Rai 2010, 2015; Leston-Bandeira 2016). Gerhard Loewenberg points out that symbolic representation is distinctly (and continually) significant in terms of the inferences made by institutions: 'Although it would appear to be the most abstract aspect of representation, symbolic representation finds a specific application in the contribution that legislatures make to nation building, to giving a set of separate communities the sense that they belong together as a nation' (Loewenberg 2011, pp. 33–34). The 'meaning' of Parliament thereby exists in its meaning to publics (or to its members) and as such is not 'set' or self-explanatory. Saward, in emphasising this point, critiques the traditional notion that 'political makers of representations tend to foreclose or fix the meanings of themselves and their actions' (2006, pp. 303–304).

If what Parliament represents is subjective (and often nebulous), we must also acknowledge that Parliament itself – as a physical entity – can be just as difficult to define. Though Parliament is in some sense a physical institution, it would be reductive to conceptualise it in the same manner as other symbolic objects – the US flag, for example, which corresponds with information (50 stars corresponding with 50 states) and 'symbolizes (suggests, evokes, arouses feelings appropriate to) the honor and majesty of the United States' (Pitkin 1967, p. 98). The reason is that while we might all define a flag (especially one specific flag) in similar ways, definitions of 'Parliament' (or *a* parliament) are myriad, with little or nothing in common. In this case it is useful to refer back to Saward's theory of the representative claim, in which '[a] maker of representations (M) puts forward a subject (S) which stands for an object (O) which is related to a referent (R) and is offered to an audience (A)' (Saward 2006, p. 302). Leston-Bandeira provides a useful example in applying this framework to the Arts in Parliament programme, coinciding with the 2012 Olympics in London: 'One representative claim may be the Houses of Parliament (M) utilising its own space to share contemporary art (S) as evocative of perceptions of democracy (O), to the public (A)' (Leston-Bandeira 2016, p. 512).

It is also possible, however, to conceptualise Parliament as the *subject*, rather than the *maker*, of the representative claim. For example, let us draw on a statement made in early January 2018 by former Labour MP Stephen Pound in the context of Restoration and Renewal:

This building is not just a matter of stone, porphyry, marble and stained glass. It is not just a structure; it is a home, a statement and a place of democracy. It stands for something in this nation and beyond, far more than mere bricks and mortar. This is the place where democracy lives. It is so easy to say that we could move elsewhere and that it would still be a Parliament, but it would not be the Palace of Westminster. It would not be the building that has survived fire and bombing – it has survived the most horrendous impacts and we have somehow come through – and it is crucial that that footprint be retained and we maintain our presence in this building (HC Deb 31 January 2018).

Here we observe a politician (M) describing the Palace or, specifically, its structure and location (S) as definitively central to the UK Parliament (O) and its associations of democracy and nationhood (R) to the Commons chamber (A). Thus the 'specific application in the contribution that legislatures make to nation building' (Loewenberg 2011, pp. 33–34) is

Figure 8.2 *Westminster Hall* [oil on canvas]. © Ellen Spafford, 2016. Reproduced with permission of the artist

reinforced. This also validates the especial consideration we must give to symbolic representation when discussing corporate identity (or lack thereof) in the UK Parliament.

The importance of corporate (non)identity

Conceptualisations of corporate identity and symbolic representation are highly complementary. Both are fundamentally based upon (re)-presentation through experience and perception. In combining both of these theoretical approaches, we can better understand not only the significance of an 'absent' corporate identity, but also the nature of the absence itself. The theme of an absent identity is often raised in relation to the physicality of Parliament. For example, David Beetham cites a conversation with former Labour MP Tony Wright in which Parliament was described as 'simply a building, in which a multitude of activities is carried on, but without any corporate identity' (2011, p. 125). There is a causal connection to be made here, namely that a lack of corporate identity could in this case be *because of* the building(s). As Melewar and Jenkins attest, architecture and location are key components within the construct of corporate identity, albeit components that are overlooked by much of the relevant literature (2002, p. 82).

In terms of both architecture and location (among many other factors), the UK Parliament's heritage problematises a coherent corporate identity. This is especially apparent when comparing it with nearby legislatures. The Scottish Parliament, for example,

> was intended to be very different, and the articulation of that difference by the Scottish Constitutional Convention and the Consultative Steering Group can be summed up in the well-known CSG principles – *sharing the power, accountability, access and participation and equal opportunities.* This 'CSG vision' provides an underpinning mission statement for the Parliament, and certainly contributed to the successful creation of a brand in the last four years, as well as to a palpable sense of purpose in its members and staff ... the Scottish Parliament has several advantages, not least that sense of purpose which the 'CSG vision' provides ... and the obvious modernity of some of its procedures and practices compared with Westminster (Winetrobe 2003, pp. 6–7).

This 'obvious modernity' contrasts sharply with Westminster's obvious, or in some cases invoked, antiquity. Norton points out that 'Westminster Hall aside, the Palace of Westminster is a relatively new building', featuring a 'mock-Gothic façade [which] is suggestive of Parliament's long history' (Norton 2013, pp. 215–216). Another study notes that parliamentary renovations successively ask: 'Which heritage should it follow and which boundaries should it produce anew'? (Puwar 2010, pp. 298–299). That is to say, this particular building *suggests* a history that it does not *span*. The Scottish Parliament, in contrast with Westminster, 'has no historical baggage, and, up till now, it has not operated in such historic or famous locations as to deflect from the image of a modern institution' (Winetrobe 2003, p. 7).

This 'deflection' from modernity reflects two key points. First, the issue is not, as Kelso describes it, a lack of corporate identity (2007, pp. 365–366). Rather, Parliament is replete with identities, just as it is replete with symbolism. The issue here concerns what Parliament symbolises, and the identities it is seen to encapsulate. Second, the issue is also not as Labour MP Tony Wright (as quoted by Beetham) describes it: Parliament being 'simply a building' (2011, p. 125).[2] Speaking objectively, the UK Parliament is not *a* building but several buildings, with Wright's observation showing how 'Parliament is still seen solely in terms of the Palace of Westminster' (Norton 2013, p. 216). The very fact that Wright (among others) associates Parliament *with* one building shows us *that Parliament is not simply a building*. If Parliament were indeed just a building – or even just a few buildings – the problems of an absent corporate identity would be less pervasive (perhaps even nonexistent). Parliament's buildings – and its location – both stand for something. Precisely what Parliament (and its physicality) stands for – in terms of both positive and negative associations and connections – is an essential consideration as part of the Restoration and Renewal project, within which these questions of corporate identity and symbolic representation have never been so important (nor so possible) to address.

Conclusion

This chapter has focused on the significance of the institution of Parliament – that is, a physical and discursive construct – to what goes on inside its constituent buildings. This reflects the focus of this volume, but it also reflects the paramount importance of buildings to political behaviour. As this chapter has illustrated, buildings themselves are sites of political and democratic engagement. They also present a physical and conceptual nexus between publics and governance. Discussing 'corporate identity' with respect to the UK Parliament remains a nebulous process.

Greater academic attention should be afforded to the buildings and the behaviour of those who inhabit and visit them (and of course, those who do neither). Through this process, we can gain a better understanding of corporate identity, symbolic representation and Parliament itself, with constant reference to the publics through whom this institution is defined and forever (re)constructed.

Notes

1 This involvement ranges from informing and educating publics (before and/or after the relevant decisions have been made) to working collaboratively with publics. This is reflected in several nuanced definitions of public engagement. See: Arnstein 1969; Walker et al. 2019.
2 Incidentally, Wright's observation is not even shared among Labour MPs. Consider, for example, MP Stephen Pound's aforementioned description of Parliament transcending 'bricks and mortar'.

References

Arnstein, S. (1969) 'A ladder of citizen participation', *Journal of the American Institute of Planners*, 35(4), pp. 216–224. DOI: 10.1080/01944366908977225.

Beetham, D. (2011) 'Do parliaments have a future?' in S. Alonso, J. Keane and W. Merkel (eds) *The Future of Representative Democracy*, Cambridge: Cambridge University Press, pp. 124–143.

Coleman, S. (2005) Direct representation: towards a conversational democracy. London: IPPR Exchange.

HC Deb (31 January 2018) Vol. 635, Col. 913. Available from: https://hansard.parliament.uk/Commons/2018-01-31/debates/12231195-A66F-4D6B-A901-340BD27BD5F4/RestoratioNAndRenewal(ReportOfTheJointCommittee)#contribution-24691707-845F-4ADB-B79F-43B3FFB9E6F6 (accessed 1 October 2018).

Kelso, A. (2007) 'Parliament and political disengagement: neither waving nor drowning', *The Political Quarterly*, 78(3), pp. 364–373. DOI: 10.1111/j.1467-923X.2007.00865.x.

Leston-Bandeira, C. (2016) 'Why symbolic representation frames parliamentary public engagement', *The British Journal of Politics and International Relations*, 18(2), pp. 498–516. DOI: 10.1177/1369148115615029.

Loewenberg, G. (2011) *On Legislatures*, Boulder: Paradigm Publishers.

Melewar, T.C. and Jenkins, E. (2002) 'Defining the corporate identity construct', *Corporate Reputation Review*, 5, pp. 76–90. DOI: 10.1057/palgrave.crr.1540166.

National Assembly for Wales Assembly Commission (2013) Official Languages Scheme. Cardiff. Available from: https://senedd.wales/Laid%20Documents/GEN-LD9401%20-%20Assembly%20Commission%20Official%20Languages%20Scheme%20-10072013-248001/gen-ld9401-e-English.pdf.

Norton, P. (2013) *Parliament in British Politics*, New York: Palgrave Macmillan.

Parkinson, J. (2009) 'Symbolic representation in public space: capital cities, presence and memory', *Representation*, 45(1), pp. 1–14. DOI: 10.1080/00344890802709781.

Parkinson, J. (2013) 'How legislatures work – and should work – as public space', *Democratization*, 20(3), pp. 438–455. DOI: 10.1080/13510347.2013.786544.

Pitkin, H.F. (1967) *The Concept of Representation*, Berkeley: University of California Press.

Puwar, N. (2010) 'The archi-texture of Parliament: flaneur as method in Westminster', *The Journal of Legislative Studies*, 16(3), pp. 298–312. DOI: 10.1080/13572334.2010.498099.

Rai, S.M. (2010) 'Analysing ceremony and ritual in Parliament', *The Journal of Legislative Studies*, 16(3), pp. 284–297. DOI: 10.1080/13572334.2010.498098.

Rai, S.M. (2015) 'Political performance: a framework for analysing democratic politics', *Political Studies*, 63(5), pp. 1179–1197. DOI: 10.1111/1467-9248.12154.

Saward, M. (2006) 'The representative claim', *Contemporary Political Theory,* 5, pp. 297–318. DOI: 10.1057/palgrave.cpt.9300234.

Saward, M. (2010) *The Representative Claim,* Oxford: Oxford University Press.

Select Committee on Modernisation of the House of Commons (2004) *Connecting Parliament with the public* (Cmnd HC 368, 2003–04). London: The Stationery Office. Available from: https://publications.parliament.uk/pa/cm200304/cmselect/cmmodern/368/368.pdf.

Shepsle, K. (1992) 'Congress is a "They," not an "It": legislative intent as oxymoron', *International Review of Law and Economics,* 12(2), pp. 239–256. DOI: 10.1016/0144-8188(92)90043-Q.

The Scottish Parliament (2017) *Scottish Parliament Brand Guidelines* [online]. Available from: https://archive2021.parliament.scot/PublicInformationdocuments/BrandGuidelines_Jan 2020.pdf (accessed 2 August 2023).

Walker, A., Jurczak, N., Bochel, C. and Leston-Bandeira, C. (2019) 'How public engagement became a core part of the House of Commons select committees', *Parliamentary Affairs,* 72(4), pp. 965–986. DOI: 10.1093/pa/gsz031.

Waylen, G. (2010) 'Researching ritual and the symbolic in parliaments: an institutionalist perspective', *The Journal of Legislative Studies,* 16(3), pp. 352–365. DOI: 10.1080/13572334.2010.498103.

Winetrobe, B. (2003) 'Political but not partisan: marketing parliaments and their members', *The Journal of Legislative Studies,* 9(1), pp. 1–13. DOI: 10.1080/13523270300660001.

9
The UK Parliament as a historical space for women
Mari Takayanagi

Introduction

On census night in 1911, suffragette Emily Wilding Davison hid overnight in a broom cupboard in the Palace of Westminster. This was so she could claim to be resident in the Parliament building on the census form and stake a claim to the same political rights as men. And yet, an examination of the census records shows that as well as Davison, there were 67 women resident in Parliament that night (Takayanagi and Hallam Smith 2023). These were housekeeping and kitchen staff in the House of Lords and House of Commons, as well as wives, daughters and servants living in official residences such as Speaker's House.

As this demonstrates, women have always been present in the UK Parliament – living there, working there, watching debates, giving evidence to committees, lobbying and campaigning. However, this is largely invisible in the building, amid the much more prominent visual grand narratives of monarchs and male politicians through political history (Unwin 2018). The visitor tour route through the Palace of Westminster today begins with Arthurian legends portrayed in the Robing Room, and works its way via Tudors and Stuarts in Princes Chamber, through the English Civil War and Glorious Revolution. Virtually all women pictured are queens, present only by virtue of their birth and office. It is sometimes assumed that there were no women in the House of Commons until Nancy Astor arrived as the first woman MP to take her seat in 1919, and no women in the House of Lords until the first four women life peers arrived in 1958. Only relatively recently has it been realised that there is a much longer women's history in the building, which can help shed light on the political culture and practices within (Takayanagi, Unwin and Seaward 2018).

This chapter will consider the Palace of Westminster as a space for women from a historical perspective, c. 1818–1960. First, it will examine women as politically engaged visitors, using first a 'ventilator' and later a 'cage' to watch debates in the House of Commons. Second, it will analyse the physical activities of women lobbyists and campaigners in parliamentary spaces in the period before the First World War. Third, it will consider the experiences of the early women MPs in the House of Commons and the 'tomb', the nickname for their restricted office space, as well as the arrival of the first women peers in 1958. Finally, it will rediscover the women staff who lived and worked in the building, without whom Parliament could not have operated.

The ventilator and the cage: women as politically engaged observers

The UK House of Commons and House of Lords have sat at the Palace of Westminster since medieval times. In the old building, which was destroyed by fire in 1834, the House of Commons banned women from its public galleries following an incident in 1778. After this, although women continued to attend as observers in the Lords, there was no official provision for women wanting to watch proceedings in the Commons until the current building was built after 1834. Instead, women found their way up to an attic space high above the Commons chamber, known as the 'ventilator' (see Figure 9.1), from which they could see and hear proceedings (Gleadle 2009; Richardson 2013). This room was created following ventilation improvement work in the early nineteenth century (Hallam Smith 2019). The first woman known to have used the ventilator was the prison reformer Elizabeth Fry, to watch a Commons debate in February 1818. As described by Frances, Lady Shelley, on a visit in April 1818:

> On my arrival I was conducted by Mr Bellamy through a number of winding passages, up and down stairs, and over the roof of St Stephen's Chapel. On reaching a dark niche in the wall Mr Bellamy warned me to preserve absolute silence, and opened a small door. I found myself in a room about eight feet square, resembling the cabin of a ship. There was a window to admit air, two chairs, a table, and a thing like a chimney in the centre (Shelley 1913, pp. 7–8).

Many women visitors, including Fry, Shelley, novelist Maria Edgeworth and Emma Wedgewood (later Darwin), were actively interested in political events and issues such as slavery, sati (the practice of widows

Figure 9.1 Sketch of a ventilator in Ladies' Gallery Attic in St Stephens, 1834. Pencil drawing by Frances Rickman. © Parliamentary Art Collection, WOA 26

being burned on their dead husband's funeral pyre in India) and the plight of the poor. Their correspondence and diaries show active commentary and knowledge of participants and subjects. Women were also occasionally able to watch debates from the ventilator when the public and reporters' galleries were ordered to be cleared. Although most women in the ventilator were clearly of a high social elite, there was also a working-class presence – their servants, and house staff who worked and lived in the nearby attic space. Amy Galvin has considered the ventilator using the discipline of feminist geography, and argues that through this shared political experience, women created a lived political identity that was distinctly female, with its own constructed space, viewpoint and understanding (Galvin 2020). It was, however, not created as a viewing gallery but as an attempt to improve ventilation in the Commons chamber. The acoustics were surprisingly good, but it was an uncomfortable space, with smoke and heat rising up into spectators' faces (Hallam Smith 2019).

The ventilator was destroyed, along with almost all the medieval Palace, in a great fire in October 1834, after which the current Victorian building was built by Charles Barry, assisted by Augustus Pugin. Barry made provision for women to watch proceedings in the House from a Ladies' Gallery positioned high above the speaker's chair. This gallery had a heavy metal grille covering its windows to prevent the male MPs being able to see women watching them – it was thought this would be a distraction for the men. The grille made the space hot, stuffy and smelly, and difficult to see or hear, and gave it the nickname of the 'cage' (Figure 9.2). As described by Millicent Fawcett, suffrage campaigner and also the wife of a blind MP:

> One great discomfort of the grille was that the interstices of the heavy brass work were not large enough to allow the victims who sat behind it to focus, so that both eyes looked through the same hole. It was like using a gigantic pair of spectacles which did not fit and made the Ladies' gallery a grand place for getting headaches (Fawcett 1920, p. 166).

As with the ventilator, the cage was used by women who were politically engaged to view debates. Galvin has traced changes in women's behaviours over time as they engaged with the gallery space and adopted new attitudes and responses to the debates in the House of Commons (Galvin 2020). As time went on, the gallery space increasingly became used by women actively lobbying and campaigning for political and social change.

Women as lobbyists and campaigners

For centuries before the vote was won, women influenced Parliament through lobbying, including by signing and presenting petitions. They might ask for relief in personal matters, to bring political change, or both. Women occasionally petitioned in person from the bar of the house, such as Ann Fitzharris, who asked for relief following the execution of her husband in 1681 (Wright and Smith 1905). However, even though the women were not usually physically present, the process brought their voices indirectly into the business of both houses. The petitions were sent in writing or sometimes brought in person to the building by petitioners, and then formally laid before the House of Commons or House of Lords by an MP or peer. They were noted either in the Journal, the official record of proceedings in both houses, or in the House of Commons Select

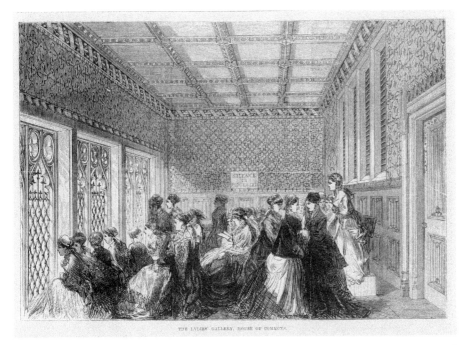

Figure 9.2   The Ladies' Gallery, *Illustrated London News*, 1870. Photomechanical print by Unknown and *Illustrated London News*. © Parliamentary Art Collection, WOA 3938

Committee on Public Petitions reports. For example, Mary Prince, born enslaved in Bermuda and now living in London, petitioned the House of Commons on 19 June 1829 for her freedom, the first woman of colour known to have petitioned Parliament, and the words of her petition are reproduced in the House of Commons Journal. Sometimes petitions led to mentions in parliamentary debates by the MPs who laid them. The long campaign for women's suffrage began with petitions. The first received from an individual, a Mary Smith from Stanmore in Yorkshire, was the subject of a speech by Henry Hunt MP in the House of Commons on 3 August 1834. The first mass organised petition for votes for women was brought to Parliament by Elizabeth Garrett and Emily Davies on 7 June 1866, and John Stuart Mill MP spoke on it in the Commons a few weeks later, on 17 July.

Another parliamentary platform for women's political agency was select committees. Women gave evidence in person in Parliament as experts, for example educational expert Mary Carpenter to a Select Committee on Criminal and Destitute Juveniles in 1852, and social reformer

Isabella Tod to a Select Committee on Married Women's Property in 1868 (Takayanagi 2012). Nor were all such women from the upper and middle classes. Recent research by Galvin has shown that reformers Elizabeth Fry and Josephine Butler both brought working-class women, some accused and even convicted of crimes, into parliamentary committee rooms to give personal testimony (Galvin 2020). In the pre-1834 Palace navigated by Fry, committee rooms were disorganised and inadequate, and it was noted in 1825 that it had become a habit to use 'the long gallery, where Members were customarily sworn in, the smoking room, the Members' waiting room and the chamber itself for committee purposes' (Fisher 2009). The presence of women may, therefore, have been clear well beyond the committee room itself. In the post-1834 Palace, women would have walked through the grand surroundings of St Stephen's Hall, Central Lobby and the Lower Waiting Hall on their way to committee corridor on the first floor – the rooms themselves being similarly grandly decorated with large paintings and wood-panelled walls. Butler referred to the committee space as a 'lion's den' and her experience as akin to taking an exam (Galvin 2020).

In the early twentieth century, women came to use increasingly direct action in the long campaign for the vote. Some women embarked on militant action such as chaining themselves to statues, jumping on chairs, and attempting to 'rush' the building (Puwar 2004). Up in the Ladies' Gallery, the grille became both a physical and metaphorical symbol of women's exclusion from parliamentary politics. As such, it was targeted by suffragettes in a famous protest by the Women's Freedom League in 1908, when two women chained themselves to the grille while a third lowered a banner into the chamber (Eustance 1997). The grille had to be removed so the women could be cut off, breaching the spatial barrier between men and women. The gallery remained closed for some time before the grille was reinstated. The grille was finally removed permanently in August 1917 and can today be seen screening the internal windows of Central Lobby.

The tomb: early women MPs and peers

The Representation of the People Act 1918 gave the parliamentary vote to women over the age of 30 who met the property qualification for the local government franchise. This meant occupying either a dwelling-house of any value, or land or premises of a yearly value of not less than £5. These provisos excluded approximately one third of the adult female population. Women finally got the vote on the same terms as men ten years later, by the Equal Franchise Act 1928. Also in 1918, the Parliament (Qualification of Women) Act enabled women to become MPs. The first elected was Constance Markievicz, elected in December 1918, who as a Sinn Fein MP never took her seat at Westminster, instead sitting in the first Dáil Éireann in Dublin. The first woman to take her seat at Westminster was Nancy Astor, elected in 1919. Other women followed but only in very small numbers. This did not change substantially until 1997. Astor and the other early women faced a huge amount of hostility in the overwhelmingly male environment of the House of Commons (Brookes 1967; Harrison 1986; Thane 2020).

Away from the chamber, the women MPs often found themselves either formally or informally excluded from spaces such as dining rooms and smoking rooms, and confined to the Lady Members' Room which was shared by women of all parties and nicknamed the 'tomb' thanks to its uninviting atmosphere. The first Lady Members' Room was on the ground floor next to the river front, and later moved further down corridor. As described by Ellen Wilkinson in 1932:

> When I got into Parliament seven years ago, there were four of us to share the room that had been set apart for Lady Astor's own use when she was the only woman there. Then came eight women, then ten, but still only that same little cubby-hole with one tiny glass pane for ventilation and NO MIRROR! To reach the toilet-room provided for us meant a walk of nearly a quarter of a mile along three long corridors and up two flights of stairs (Wilkinson 1932).

Meanwhile, Viscountess Rhondda, a hereditary peer in her own right, fought an unsuccessful battle to take her seat in the Lords in the 1920s. A feminist, former suffragette and businesswoman, she brought her case to the House of Lords Committee for Privileges where she was defeated by the Lord Chancellor, Lord Birkenhead (John 2013). Many peers opposed the physical presence of women in their comfortable, all-male club, exemplified in this speech by the Earl of Glasgow in 1958:

> Many of us do not want women in this House. We do not want to sit beside them on these Benches, nor do we want to meet them in the Library. This is a House of men, a House of Lords. We do not wish it to become a House of Lords and Ladies (HL Deb 31 October 1957).

Despite such attitudes, women were finally able to sit in the Lords as life peers after the Life Peerages Act 1958, and as hereditary peers from the

Peerage Act 1963 (Sutherland 2000). The early women peers met with more overt courtesy than the women MPs had, but fought similar battles over facilities (Takayanagi 2008).

Necessary women: staff in Parliament

The final part of the picture of Parliament as a historical space for women is that of parliamentary staff. Women lived and worked in the building over many centuries, in households of men such as the speaker, or employed by the Commons or Lords, or as contractors and entrepreneurs. They worked as housekeepers, maids, cleaners, cooks and firelighters, sold oranges in the members' lobby, and ran stalls in Westminster Hall (Takayanagi, Unwin and Seaward 2018; Takayanagi and Hallam Smith 2023). When Elizabeth Garrett and Emily Davies arrived with the first mass women's suffrage petition in 1866, they had to wait for John Stuart Mill in Westminster Hall. Feeling conspicuous, they hid the large, rolled petition underneath the cart of an old woman selling apples. As well as being necessary for parliamentary operations, their presence could affect the nature of the building. Sarah Smith, Commons housekeeper in the 1720s, for instance, refused to light fires in advance of the chamber sitting because they made her own rooms too hot, leading to further work on ventilation in the House of Commons (Hallam Smith 2019).

From the late nineteenth century, women arrived in secretarial roles, both working for Parliament and for individual MPs. Wartime then accelerated change. The First World War saw the temporary employment of four girl porters in the House of Commons, replacing male porters on war service; while in the Lords, May Court rose to become the first woman accountant, running an all-female department for many years and retiring with an OBE in 1944. In the Second World War, the Commons employed Kay Midwinter as its first woman clerk in 1940 and Jean Winder, the first woman Hansard reporter, in 1944. Both Midwinter and Winder experienced discrimination and were paid less than men doing the same job – Winder fought a long and ultimately successful battle for equal pay (Takayanagi 2016; Takayanagi and Hallam Smith 2023). Midwinter reflected later on how her physical presence as a woman in the chamber caused controversy:

> During the war I was standing behind the Speaker's Chair about 5 or 6 yards from Churchill while he made all his famous war speeches. He used to glare at me as much to say, 'What's this woman doing?' but he never challenged me. I was expecting to be ordered to be

removed from the Chamber, but it was great fun and then when it came to laying the Report on the table of the house—you know, my male colleagues said 'Oh you'd better not do that, you know, it has never been done by a woman before!' So I said 'Well, for that reason I'm going to do it!' So there we are. But really one was up against male prejudice throughout (Midwinter 1990).

Midwinter left the Commons for a job at the Foreign Office in 1943. The next woman clerk was not appointed until 1969. Jean Winder worked in Hansard to her retirement in 1960. The next woman Hansard reporter was also not appointed until 1969.

Conclusion

Today, as recorded in the most recent analyses from the House of Commons and House of Lords libraries, there are 225 women members of Parliament, approximately 35 per cent of the total, and 231 women members of the House of Lords, approximately 28 per cent (Taylor 2021; Kelly 2022). These are significant numbers, although a long way off a 50:50 Parliament. Women make up 46 per cent of staff in the Commons and 54 per cent of staff in the Lords, although they are under-represented at higher grades (House of Commons 2022; House of Lords 2022). Despite the presence of so many women, to walk through the Palace of Westminster today is still to see an overwhelmingly masculine space, dominated by a Victorian historical narrative decorated with scenes from which women are almost entirely absent except as queens (Unwin 2018). This contributes to women MPs today still feeling unwelcome and unrepresented, as identified in Sarah Childs' report *The Good Parliament* (Childs 2016).

Yet as this historical overview of women has demonstrated, women have always been present in the physical spaces of the UK Parliament – working as staff, petitioning, lobbying, influencing and demonstrating. The Works of Art committees in both houses have begun to take steps to increase the representation of women in their collections, for example commissioning *New Dawn* by Mary Branson (Figure 9.3). This permanent, large-scale contemporary light sculpture celebrates the women's suffrage movement in Westminster Hall, the oldest part of Parliament. *New Dawn* is a magnificent achievement, but should be a starting point and not an end point for shedding light on the history of women in the UK Parliament.

Figure 9.3 *New Dawn*, sculpture by Mary Branson. © Mary Branson, Parliamentary Art Collection, WOA S753

References

Brookes, P. (1967) *Women at Westminster: An Account of Women in the British Parliament, 1918–1966,* London: Peter Davies.

Childs, S. (2016) *The Good Parliament,* Bristol: University of Bristol. Available from: https://www.parliament.uk/globalassets/documents/commons-committees/reference-group-representation-inclusion/good-parliament-report-july-2016.pdf.

Eustance, C. (1997) 'Protests from Behind the Grille: Gender and the Transformation of Parliament, 1867–1918', *Parliamentary History,* 16(1), pp. 107–126. DOI: 10.1111/j.1750-0206.1997.tb00576.x.

Fawcett, M.G. (1920) *The Women's Victory – and After,* London: Sidgwick and Jackson.

Fisher, D.R. (ed.) (2009) 'VII. The Procedure and Business of the House', in *The History of Parliament: The House of Commons 1820–1832.* Available from: https://www.historyofparliamentonline.org/volume/1820-1832/survey/vii-procedure-and-business-house.

Galvin, A. (2020) *From Suffragette to Citizen: female experience of parliamentary spaces in long-nineteenth century Britain,* PhD thesis, University of Warwick. Available from: http://wrap.warwick.ac.uk/153040/.

Gleadle, K. (2009) *Borderline Citizens: Women, Gender and Political Culture in Britain, 1815–1867,* Oxford: Oxford University Press.

Hallam Smith, E. (2019) 'Ventilating the Commons, heating the Lords, 1701–1834', *Parliamentary History,* 38(1), pp. 74–102. DOI: 10.1111/1750-0206.12414.

Harrison, B. (1986) 'Women in a men's house: the women MPs, 1919–1945', *Historical Journal,* 29(3), pp. 623–654. Available from: https://www.jstor.org/stable/2639051.

HL Deb (31 October 1957) ccv, col. 690. Available from: https://api.parliament.uk/historic-hansard/lords/1957/oct/31/constitution-of-the-house-of-lords#column_690.

John, A.V. (2013) *Turning the Tide: The Life of Lady Rhondda,* Cardiff: Parthian.

Kelly, R. (2022) *Female Members of Parliament,* research briefing, House of Commons Library. Available from: https://commonslibrary.parliament.uk/research-briefings/sn06652/.

Midwinter, K. (1990) Recording and transcript of oral history, *MS Eng. c. 4718, 4733.* United Nations Career Records Project, Bodleian Library, University of Oxford.

Parliament. House of Commons (2022) *House of Commons Pay Gap Report 2021.* Available from: https://www.parliament.uk/business/news/2022/february-2022/house-of-commons-and-parliamentary-digital-service-publish-2021-pay-gap-data/.

Parliament. House of Lords (2022) *Gender and Ethnicity Pay Gap Report 2021.* Available from: https://www.parliament.uk/globalassets/hl-gender-and-ethnicity-pay-gap-report-2021.pdf.

Puwar, N. (2004) *Space Invaders: Race, Gender and Bodies Out of Place,* Oxford: Berg.

Richardson, S. (2013) *The Political Worlds of Women: Gender and Politics in Nineteenth Century Britain,* London: Routledge.

Shelley, F. (1913) *Diary of Frances Lady Shelley 1817–1875, vol. ii,* R. Edgcumbe (ed.), London: John Murray.

Sutherland, D. (2000) 'Peeresses, Parliament and prejudice: the admission of women to the House of Lords, 1918–1963', *Parliaments, Estates and Representation,* 20(1), pp. 215–231. DOI: 10.1080/02606755.2000.9522108.

Takayanagi, M. (2008) 'A changing house: the Life Peerages Act 1958', *Parliamentary History,* 27(3), pp. 380–392. DOI: http://dx.doi.org/10.1111/j.1750-0206.2008.00045.x.

Takayanagi, M. (2012) *Parliament and Women c1900–1945.* PhD thesis, King's College London. Available from: https://kclpure.kcl.ac.uk/portal/en/theses/parliament-and-women-c19001945%2834708cef-2efd-4389-9382-5e847fd50189%29.html.

Takayanagi, M. (2016) 'The Home Front in the "Westminster Village": women staff in Parliament during the Second World War', *Women's History Review,* 26(4), pp. 608–620. DOI: 10.1080/09612025.2016.1148509.

Takayanagi, M. and Hallam Smith, E. (2023) *Necessary Women: The Untold Story of Parliament's Working Women,* Cheltenham: The History Press.

Takayanagi, M., Unwin, M. and Seaward, P. (eds) (2018) *Voice and Vote: Celebrating 100 Years of Votes for Women,* London: History of Parliament Trust/St James' House.

Taylor, R. (2021) *Lords Membership: How Many Women Have Sat in the Lords?,* research briefing, House of Lords Library. Available from: https://lordslibrary.parliament.uk/research-briefings/lln-2018-0014/.

Thane, P. (2020) 'Nancy Astor, women and politics, 1919–1945', *Open Library of Humanities*, 6(2), p. 1. DOI: 10.16995/olh.542.

Unwin, M. (2018) 'New Dawn: Celebrating feminist collective action in the landscape of the heroic male parliamentarian', *Feminism in Museums,* vol. 2, pp. 106–137.

Wilkinson, E. (1932) 'Woman-to-woman close-ups', article, 30 Jan. Parliamentary Archives, RUN/1.

Wright, A. and Smith, P. (1905) *Parliament Past and Present,* London: Hutchinson and Co.

10

Parliament and the language of political agency in Disraeli's 'Young England' trilogy

A corpus linguistic approach

Sam Griffiths and Alexander von Lünen

Introduction

Benjamin Disraeli (1804–1881) was a towering figure of nineteenth-century British politics, of the Conservative party and of conservative thought. His two periods as prime minister (1868 and 1874–1880) were characterised by pioneering reformist legislation on the domestic front, including the Public Health Act (1875), and abroad by the advancement of Britain's imperial interests, most notably the purchase of the Suez Canal (1875). Disraeli was also a prolific writer, author of 16 completed novels, as well as plays, poetry and nonfiction works of biography and political thought. Although not generally considered as a major literary figure, his novels were widely read and have attracted limited but serious critical attention since their publication (Blake 1966).

The dual trajectories of Disraeli's remarkable career inevitably raise the question of the relationship between his political life and literary corpus (Weeks 1989; O'Kell 2013). A key pivot of this relationship is 'Young England', the adopted name of a small parliamentary grouping of Conservative MPs in the 1840s (c.1842–1847) of which Disraeli was a member. Disraeli embraced Young England not only as a political identity but also as a literary motif that distinguishes the trilogy of novels comprising *Coningsby, or The New Generation* (1844), *Sybil, or The Two Nations* (1845) and *Tancred, or The New Crusade* (1847) that he wrote at this time (Blake 1966, pp. 190–194).

The novels of Disraeli's Young England period offer his biographers a valuable literary key to the development of his political views. The trilogy was written after his election to Parliament as a backbencher in 1837 and completed well before the onset of his ministerial career in the 1850s. Conversely, Disraeli's parliamentary career provides useful critical context for exploring the political themes of the Young England novels. In this essay we triangulate these disciplinary approaches by focusing on the Westminster Parliament as a site-specific *topos* at the intersection of the political and fictional discourses of Disraeli's Young England, where the language of parliamentary representation and the literary representation of Parliament were in flux.

Disraeli's early parliamentary career coincided with a period of acute industrial distress and widespread political agitation in England in the 1840s. This was associated with the rise of the working-class Chartist movement that campaigned for sweeping democratic reforms of the constitution. Although a party-political Conservative, Disraeli was deeply concerned with the popular legitimacy of constitutional government. As an ambitious young MP he recognised that the changing socioeconomic conditions of urbanising, industrial England demanded a political vision that could articulate and respond to new social realities, while also mobilising support within and without Parliament (Faber 1987).

Widespread debate over the value of Parliament is pressing once again in our own time with long-held assumptions about the relationship between government and governed being renegotiated in an age of digitally enabled communication. Here we focus on how discourse can help us to disentangle the metonymic relationship between 'parliament' the building and 'Parliament' the institution, noting how its architectural form is used to signify the system of government it embodies. We pursue this through a mixed method approach, combining *close readings* of Disraeli's Young England novels with *distant reading* exercises from quantitative text analyses, or corpus linguistics.

Young England as a political identity

Disraeli's membership of the intimate Young England group enabled him to forge a political reputation soon after his election to Parliament. Young England were in opposition to Robert Peel's Conservative-led administration (1841–1847). They objected to what they saw as the connivance of Peel's Conservative party in the degradation of English political life by its adoption of a utilitarian, materialist political philosophy and indulgence in narrow-minded factionalism that undermined the constitutional pillars of monarchy, aristocracy and the Church. This betrayal was symbolised for Disraeli in Peel's acceptance of the political settlement following the 1832 Parliamentary Reform Act that extended the franchise to the urban middle classes, and his subsequent decision to repeal the Corn Laws 1846, a move that lowered food prices by opening up the agricultural economy of landed estates to foreign competition. For a short period in the mid-to-late 1840s the political opposition to Peel orchestrated by Disraeli helped establish Young England as a distinctive voice in the Conservative party and in Parliament before the group eventually dissolved in the later part of the decade.

Young England held that widespread social division in the country reflected not only a lack of moral principles but also a lack of political imagination among the governing class, posing the question of whether Parliament as an institution was capable of representing nineteenth-century England as a national community. Its members advocated national renewal on a heroic model of aristocratic government, legitimised by its paternalistic and religious duty to ameliorate the conditions of the working classes and defend the interests of labour against those of commerce. Young England was not a title deliberately chosen by the parliamentary group themselves (it was bestowed in satirical vein by a critic who accused them of romanticising 'old England') but it served to express their desire for a new political vision of national life (Faber 1987, p. 46). *Coningsby*'s subtitle *The New Generation* alludes to the political ideals of the Young England group. The frontispiece from the 1904 edition (Figure 10.1) is indicative of how Coningsby (for whose character Disraeli drew on the Young England member of Parliament George Smythe) embodied a kind of romantic call to arms, here represented as a paragon of medieval chivalry.

The novels of the Young England trilogy address the three estates of pre-industrial England: the aristocracy (*Coningsby*), the people (*Sybil*) and the Church (*Tancred*), respectively (Maurois 1931, p. vi). The trilogy is widely understood to be Disraeli's response to what Thomas Carlyle (1795–1881) had termed the 'condition of England' question. Disraeli himself intended the three novels as a trilogy exploring the political, social and religious themes of his day (Watson 1954, p. 6). For the critic Raymond Williams (1961, pp. 108–110), *Sybil* is one of the 'industrial novels' that documented the social changes of the nineteenth century. He places it alongside novels such as Elizabeth Gaskell's *Mary Barton* (1848) and Charles Dickens' *Hard Times* (1854) as an example of nineteenth-century social realism. Yet only *Sybil* among the Young England novels takes the reader into industrial areas, and it is the strain of romantically

Figure 10.1 Frontispiece of 1904 Brimly and Johnson edition of *Coningsby* – illustration by Byam Shaw. © Griffiths and von Lünen

inspired medieval revivalism, for example with regard to his description of alms-giving ceremonies, that arguably leaves the more characteristic impression. *Coningsby*, by contrast, is set in the aristocratic world of town houses and rural estates, and much of *Tancred* in the Middle East. Rather than social documentary then, Disraeli's Young England offers an alternative political reality in which social division of the industrial age would be overcome by a kind of benevolent feudalism. O'Kell (2013) characterises Disraeli's career as a 'romance of politics'; the Young England novels credibly justify the label of 'political romances'.

Representing Parliament and the people in the Young England novels

Each of the three Young England novels tells the story of a leading male aristocratic protagonist: Harry Coningsby, Charles Egremont and Tancred Montacute, in their search for the social, political and religious identities appropriate to the rapidly changing world in which they find themselves. It is revealing of Disraeli's literary strategy that Coningsby, Egremont and Montacute initially reject the parliamentary life that is their birthright – thereby directing the narratives of the novels elsewhere. Disraeli would rather concentrate on the personal epiphanies of his protagonists that made a political, morally serious life an imperative.

The historically minded reader turning to Disraeli's Young England novels for documentary accounts of parliamentary life is likely to be disappointed, as would be the architectural historian looking for descriptions of the parliamentary interior. While it is less surprising that Parliament does not feature largely in Disraeli's ten or so 'silver fork' high society romances, written before he entered Parliament, its relative absence from the avowedly political Young England novels is more noteworthy. The Victorian equivalent of what contemporary political commentators call the 'Westminster bubble' extended the political life of Parliament to the clubs, town houses and country seats of the governing elite – settings that recur in Disraeli's novels. Yet while the gossip generated by parliamentary intrigue is the currency of the social circles in which the aristocratic protagonists of Disraeli's trilogy all move, the choreography of party-political events at the Palace of Westminster themselves is consistently at a remove from the principal narratives. Disraeli only ever shows the reader Parliament from the outside. For someone so completely immersed in the political life of the House of Commons and ambitious to succeed there, one is entitled to ask why the political agency of Parliament is so repressed in the Young England novels. It appears that Parliament itself did not interest Disraeli on an imaginative level.

It is indicative of Disraeli's imaginative distance from Parliament that no mention is made throughout the Young England trilogy of the fire of October 1834 that consumed most of the medieval Tudor Palace of Westminster. This despite the fact that the novels are set in the period from the late 1830s to mid-1840s. The formative years of Disraeli's parliamentary life were, therefore, spent in the House of Commons' makeshift accommodation in the Lesser Hall of the Palace of Westminster that had survived the blaze intact, moving to its new premises (and current home) in Barry and Pugin's neo-Gothic masterpiece only in 1852. By the time Disraeli was writing *Coningsby* (published in 1844) the process of rebuilding Parliament had been under way for almost a decade. All the Young England novels were published before it was completed. Given this upheaval in parliamentary routines, it seems surprising that Disraeli assigns no explicit narrative or metaphorical significance to the fire.

Interestingly, several publishers clearly think that Disraeli's *Coningsby* is (or should be) about what goes on *inside* Parliament. They use pictures of the pre-1834 or post-1852 House of Commons for the novel's cover to make their point.[1] Inevitably, the reading of Disraeli's Young England novels in more recent times is informed by the author's reputation as a former prime minister, a point we shall return to in the final section (Blake 1966, p. 191). Disraeli himself, though, was more concerned with the symbolism of other kinds of institutional architecture in his novels, rather than parliament buildings.

Some of the most evocative architectural descriptions in Young England are reserved for the ruins of religious buildings. In his account of the fictional Marney Abbey in *Sybil*, Disraeli reveals a romantically inspired sensibility towards the sacred landscape of pre-Reformation, pre-industrial England that he shared with many of his generation, including Pugin (Hill 2007; Moore 2016). Egremont, we are told, was 'almost born amid [the] ruins' of Marney Abbey (in a spiritual sense). It was the place where he first encountered Sybil, the pre-Raphaelite image of ancient English virtue who first awakened in him a sense of the oppression of ordinary people. Subsequently 'never without emotion could he behold these unrivalled remains' (*Sybil*, p. 65). For Egremont, Marney Abbey represents a kind of prelapsarian ideal of 'merrie England', a more benign world where the rich took care of the poor.

While aspects of the historic English landscape might be romanticised, Disraeli's Young England novels also seek to engage 'old England' with contemporary contexts of social change. Sybil herself remarks that the new railway has brought benefits in making Marney Abbey more accessible (*Sybil*, p. 88). In *Coningsby*, Disraeli has the well-travelled Jewish financier Sidonia declare the 'Age of Ruins is past' (*Coningsby*, p. 101). The context is Coningsby's statement of his wish to visit Athens, but the 'Age of Ruins' equally serves Disraeli as a broader metaphor for the decrepitude of the English governing class when faced with the vitality of human life to be found in Manchester (*Coningsby*, pp. 135–137). If Disraeli can imagine Parliament the institution as a metaphorical ruin, however, he appears reluctant to represent parliamentary buildings as ruins even in a literal sense.

In *Sybil*, Disraeli describes the Palace of Westminster that captures his heroine's gaze as 'those proud and passionate halls' (*Sybil*, p. 281). In reality, all Sybil could have seen in the late 1830s and early 1840s when the novel is set was a gutted ruin encased in scaffolding (Figure 10.2). Rather than explicitly evoke the metaphorical potential of the fire in the novel, however, Disraeli prefers to present Sybil with the historical Palace of Westminster apparently intact. This exposes a tension in the metonymic relationship of Parliament the building(s) and Parliament the institution. If Disraeli's own view of the historic Parliament buildings is inflected by the romantic sensibility of the early nineteenth century, it clearly does not extend to the institution of Parliament itself, 'that rapacious, violent, and haughty body' as he calls it (*Sybil*, p. 281).

Disraeli's description of a 'Christian church and a Mohometan mosque' on Mount Sinai in *Tancred* offers an additional insight into why he may have chosen *not* to represent the Parliament buildings in ruinous state. Setting the scene for Montacute's imminent vision of the divine presence, Disraeli asks rhetorically of the two sacred buildings 'Why are they in ruins? Is it that human structures are not to be endured amid the awful temples of nature and revelation' (*Tancred*, p. 288). It becomes apparent that for Disraeli the ruin of religious buildings testifies to how

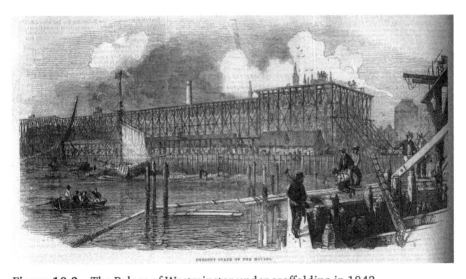

Figure 10.2   The Palace of Westminster under scaffolding in 1842.

Source: Wikimedia Commons, reproduced on the basis of Public Domain. Available at: https://commons.wikimedia.org/wiki/File:Palace_of_Westminster_1842.jpg (accessed 10 July 2023)

the utilitarian human world has lost sight of its divinity. But the material ruination of these buildings in *Sybil* and *Tancred* is redeemed by their transcendent significance as the sites of Egremont's and Tancred's awakening to the spiritual poverty of the modern age.

The same could not be said of the burnt out House of Commons, whose physical degradation did nothing to change (in Disraeli's eyes) its malign institutional status as an instrument of social and moral desolation. To represent the Palace of Westminster as a ruin in the romantic idiom, therefore, would be to risk bestowing on it a sanctity that would be problematic for Disraeli in symbolic and didactic terms. The manipulated image of the parliamentary buildings as unruined in *Sybil*, then, serves as the necessary metaphorical correlate of his polemical critique of the institution itself. Even to represent the buildings in their scaffolding would be metaphorically complicated from this perspective because Disraeli is not concerned with documentary realism of reconstruction, but with the possibility of constructing alternative political realities. In a reversal of the romantic trope, the Palace of Westminster's apparently timeless intactness admits the possibility of Parliament's institutional redemption in the imaginary of Young England, not in the transcendent sense of a source of eternal virtue but rather as a contingent, worldly site of political action.

Disraeli concludes *Sybil*'s brief meditation on the Palace of Westminster with his own rhetorical question: 'Could', he wonders, 'the voice of solace sound from such a quarter?' (*Sybil*, p. 281). This speaks directly to Disraeli's and Young England's political agenda. The question of whether Parliament can ultimately serve as an agent of social reconciliation in nineteenth-century England is left open, but in *Sybil* Disraeli represents the buildings and institution alike as weighed down by the burden of their long histories. The buildings appear to endure as a husk while the institution of parliamentary government retreats into increasing irrelevance behind their ancient walls.

In *Coningsby*, 'solace' arises from the marriage of the aristocratic Coningsby to Edith Millbank, the sister of his friend and daughter of a wealthy manufacturer, who represents the 'new money' of industrial England. In *Sybil*, it emerges from the mutual understanding and love affair of the aristocratic Egremont with Sybil herself, daughter of Chartist leader Walter Gerard. In *Tancred*, Montacute's reverence for Eva, the beautiful 'Jewess' of Bethany he meets on pilgrimage to Jerusalem, hints at Jewish-Christian reconciliation as the precondition of England's spiritual renewal, a fantasy in which, as a Christianised Jew, Disraeli was himself personally implicated. Eventually, Coningsby and Egremont *do* become members of Parliament (Montacute's destiny is left open) in fulfilment of their personal vocations to the betterment of national life rather than to service the interests of their aristocratic families. Even so, the reader is never invited to follow them into the House of Commons.

It is not hard to see why this is, since at the point at which they become politicians, they must become constrained by parliamentary codes and conventions, no matter how lofty the ideals they wish to pursue. Yet social exclusivity was not Young England's target: it was the failure of the ruling classes to rise to the moral and imaginative challenge of urban-industrial England to which they objected. Developing a political idiom capable of articulating this challenge was the project of the Young England group who relied on literary productions rather than political speeches from the backbenches to disseminate their ideas (Faber 1987, p. 48). Disraeli was already an established novelist when he entered Parliament, but it was his association with the Young Englanders that stimulated him to compose his political romances while his status as a politician identifies 'Young England' as both a fictional and a politically situated discourse.

Languages of political agency in Disraeli's Young England

This section presents the initial results of exploratory corpus analysis combining Disraeli's parliamentary speeches and literary works.[2] The analysis offers clues to how far the relationship between the political and literary languages of Disraeli's Young England were defined by the institutional and material boundaries of Parliament, and how far these boundaries were porous in terms of the discourses deployed. The first part presents a thematic, textual analysis of the Young England novels (YEN) in comparison with the corpus of all Disraeli's novels (DN) minus YEN,[3] to get a sense of the extent to which words associated with the representation of Parliament (as an x) and parliamentary representation (as a y) distinguish between YEN and DN. The thematic analysis provides a qualitative dimension because the selection of search terms reflects the authors' own critical priorities for the purposes of this essay. In this it offers a useful framing for the quantitative methods of corpus analysis, which uses computational methods to identify keywords without any preselection (Mahlberg 2010, p. 292). A reference corpus of a sample of 20 nineteenth-century British novels was also created (C19N) in order to assess whether Disraeli's style was different from that of his contemporaries.[4]

Techniques from corpus linguistics to analyse novels have been used extensively by scholars (Fischer-Starcke 2010; Mahlberg 2010). In these types of analyses it is usually a good point of departure to look at a list of 'raw' frequencies and find possible candidates of words for further analysis.[5] Naturally, many words will be common terms encountered in any kind of novel, but a frequency list might already give a good initial idea of the specifics of Disraeli's linguistic style. The word 'parliament', for example, is found 149 times in the YEN; at the same time, it is also found 148 times in the DN corpus (only 40 times if the autobiographical *Endymion* published in 1880 is excluded).[6] In the nineteenth-century novels that were compiled as reference corpus, 'parliament' appears a mere 76 times. Already, this indicates that this word played a relatively bigger role in Disraeli's thought. The normalised frequencies of 'parliament' amplify this; it is 128.09 for the DN (40.7 with *Endymion* excluded), 308.65 for the YEN, but only 27.03 for the C19N. This preliminary analysis shows how 'parliament' features disproportionately in YEN when compared to the other novels by Disraeli, let alone contemporary British novels. Above average references to the 'House of Commons' and 'House of Lords' can also be found in Disraeli's novels.

Figure 10.3 represents the occurrences of 'parliament' in DN and YEN that can be read left to right in chronological order. It shows how infrequently 'parliament' appears in the pre-YEN phase of Disraeli's novels and how rarely afterwards, other than in *Endymion*. This analysis clearly indicates how Disraeli's imaginative distance from Parliament is not achieved by its absence from the YEN lexicon. It suggests that Disraeli chose to represent Young England as a particular vantage point on the parliamentary *topos* rather than ignoring it altogether. The recurrence of the term 'government' – even higher when excluding *Endymion* – as well as 'conservative' lends support to the critical characterisation of YEN as Disraeli's political novels.

In this context, the significance of the high prevalence of 'the people' bigrams (two consecutive words) in YEN becomes clearer. While there is a lesser but still pronounced presence of the 'aristocracy', the 'middle class' or 'middle classes' are relatively marginalised. In general, Disraeli uses a more extensive vocabulary of class to describe 'the people' (working, labouring, humbler, degraded) and 'the aristocracy' (privileged, prosperous, superior) in YEN. The middle classes barely feature other than as 'influential'. The analysis suggests that Disraeli's imaginative distance from Parliament in YEN is paralleled by a lack of interest in the commercial middle classes. The increased influence of this demographic characterised the post-Reform Peelite Parliament of which Young England so disapproved. It is not that Disraeli disliked commerce or industry as such, but he wanted to see it firmly tethered to the romantic paternalism of the feudal nobility.

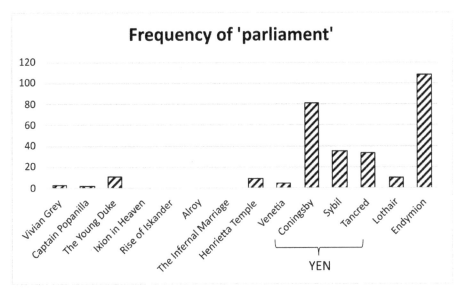

Figure 10.3 Plot showing incidence of 'parliament' in all Disraeli's completed novels excluding *Contarini Fleming* (1832). © Griffiths and von Lünen

Other descriptions of the built environment feature disproportionately in YEN. Most notable are 'castle'[s] (n = 203 – a larger number than for 'parliament' in absolute terms), including those belonging to the families of Coningsby, Egremont and Tancred, and 'cottage' (n=61), especially the home of Sybil and Walter Gerrard in *Sybil*. As key sites where the narratives unfold, these buildings reflect Disraeli's advocacy of the traditional rural society of England. Yet the relatively high incidences of 'town', 'street' and 'club' also indicate how these narratives involve character movement between the urban and rural worlds of the landed rich and the poor. The below average occurrence of 'park', in the sense of the walkable gardens belonging to a landed estate, is consistent with the fact that YEN are not primarily 'country-house' novels. Religious buildings such as Abbey (n=63 – all in *Sybil*) feature strongly in absolute but less prominently in relative terms. The term 'church' (n = 196) is referred to in an institutional or theological sense more often than in reference to a specific building, but either way appears only to have been a little more characteristic of YEN than DN overall. The thematic analysis reveals Young England as a world view that sought to decentre the *topos* of the Westminster Parliament as a site of political agency and rework the historical built environment of 'old England' into a political imaginary of contemporary English nationhood in which a range of characteristic building types are prominent. The high incidence of the toponym 'Jerusalem' (n = 118, all but two in *Tancred*) suggests how for Disraeli this world view extended beyond 'old England' to embrace the cosmopolitan Judeo-Christian civilisation from which he drew inspiration.

One may speculate how the relative absence of 'horse' in YEN compared to DN may be indicative of a preference for description and dialogue over movement. More revealingly the seemingly generic noun 'room' has a relatively low incidence in YEN. For Disraeli, rooms are usually 'drawing', 'dressing', 'dining', 'ball-', 'muniment' and 'smoking'. Taken with the strikingly below average occurrences of the female pronoun 'she' in YEN, one can legitimately associate the prioritisation of the architecture of the feudal aristocracy, public buildings and exterior spaces over domestic interiors and gardens in YEN with the dominance of male protagonists. By contrast, the sites which are most exclusively associated with key female characters, including the upper-middle-class house of Edith Millbank (*Coningsby*) and the walled garden of Eva (*Tancred*), are relatively localised within the narratives.

The exception is Sybil who, as the heroine, if not strictly speaking the protagonist, of the novel that takes her name, is key to Disraeli's purpose of animating his vision of Young England from cottage (the people), to castle (the aristocracy) and Church (Christianity) alike. The status of the parliamentary *topos* in this context is ambiguous. Sybil herself finds London alienating, though it is when she is in London, gazing disconsolately at the 'proud and passionate halls' of the Palace of Westminster, that she decides to read a periodical account of a debate in the House of Commons in which she discovers Egremont's advocacy of social justice for working people. Sybil reflects on how 'one voice that had sounded in that proud Parliament … free from the slang of faction, had dared to express immortal truths' (*Sybil*, p. 281).

No doubt Egremont's 'voice of solace' was how Disraeli dared to envisage his own orchestration of Parliament's moral redemption. The novelist could report on a fictional speech that would have been neither procedurally straightforward nor, one can assume, professionally expedient for the politician to introduce in the House of Commons. Disraeli himself noted in the preface to the fifth edition of *Coningsby* (written in 1849) that while it had not been his original intention to use fiction as an 'instrument to scatter his suggestions', he had come to see it as 'a method which, in the temper of the times, offered the best chance of influencing opinion' (Disraeli 1849). This prompts the hypothesis that YEN offered Disraeli an opportunity to escape the institutional constraints of parliamentary discourse by empowering him to make speeches in fictional spaces, deploying a different lexicon to do so. In this respect, it is the high proportion of 'speechmaking' in the form of character dialogue that is significant.

This thematic textual analysis provides a qualitative framework for the corpus analysis. This compares Disraeli's language in YEN and DN with his political speeches during the 1840s, approximately the Young England period (YPS), to explore whether YEN and YPS have distinctive linguistic markers when compared with the novels (DN) and speeches (DS) of his career as a whole. The corpus analysis indicates how Disraeli used extra-parliamentary discourse – represented by the amount of dialogue content between the characters in his novels – to make the speeches he could not make in Parliament. It reveals the textual strategy he deployed in his novels to create the extra-parliamentary platform he needed to advance Young England's political agenda. It suggests how Disraeli conceptualised Parliament as an institutionalised space where such an agenda could not be routinely articulated, a feeling expressed by Sybil's uneasiness as she gazed upon the Palace of Westminster.

The first analysis of dialogue ratios was prompted by the fact that 'said' appears as the most frequently used word in YEN when prepositions and articles are excluded. The top ten bigrams are in the form 'said x' when x is the title or name of a person, suggesting the novels are heavy in character dialogue. The amount of character dialogue in DN and YEN was then measured using the count of words between inverted commas (see Mahlberg et al. 2019) and compared with the extent of Disraeli's speechmaking in Parliament (DS and YPS, measured as the number of spoken words recorded in Hansard). The mean average quantity of character dialogue in all of Disraeli's novels is 6.38 per cent (standard deviation: 2.8). *Coningsby* is below this average (5.25 per cent) while *Sybil* is above (7.37 per cent) and *Tancred* about even (6.43 per cent). Interestingly, all YEN feature considerably more dialogue than the corpus of the 20 representative English novels of the nineteenth century, which have a mean average of 4.35 per cent dialogue content (standard deviation: 1.81).

In contrast, Disraeli's speeches accounted for 2.5 per cent of all recorded words in Parliament throughout his career as MP, while in the 1840s it was just 1.4 per cent. Given the political themes of YEN, the analysis supports the hypothesis that, in certain respects, character dialogue in these novels substituted for parliamentary speeches for Disraeli during the 1840s. The extensive use of character dialogue in YEN indicates how the form of fiction provided Disraeli with the space he needed to present political arguments that his junior position and the lexical conventions of parliamentary speechmaking made it difficult for him to articulate in the debating chamber.

It follows from this that Disraeli's language in YEN and of YPS might be expected to deploy distinctive lexicons rather than share the linguistic markers of Young England. Indeed, this appears to have been the case. A corpus analysis of keywords in YPS (target corpus) compared with YEN (reference corpus) showed that there were 898 words that appeared in the speeches but not in the novels, with only 34 words attaining a relevant keyness score.[7] The three most distinctive keywords in YPS were 'majesty', 'measure' and 'commercial' – fairly conventional words in the context of parliamentary speeches – although 'government' appearing in the YEN represents an overlap to a limited extent. When the comparison is reversed (YEN as target corpus and YPS as reference corpus), the discrepancy is even starker, with over ten thousand distinct words appearing in the novels but not in the parliamentary speeches.[8] Overall, the analysis shows that Disraeli's word choices in YEN and YPS are not strongly reflected in one another. We conclude that Disraeli's choice of parliamentary and literary language during his Young England period mirrored his fictional intention of representing the world within and without the parliamentary *topos* as separate spheres.

A keyword analysis of YEN (target corpus) and DN (reference corpus) suggests that Disraeli's choice of words does not differ markedly across all novels other than in the use of proper nouns. This finding qualifies the preliminary analysis from above that used terms selected on the basis of their thematic importance to the narrative. In the corpus linguistic analysis which takes into account *all* words used in a text, the difference in word choice as measured by the keyness value alone is not sufficient, of itself, to distinguish the YEN from the DN lexicon (especially with *Endymion* in the corpus). Interestingly though, a comparison of YEN (target corpus) with the corpus of nineteenth-century novels (reference corpus) identifies 'political', 'government', 'conservatism' and 'parliament' among others as significant enough keywords of YEN, again justifying their classification as political novels.

While YEN does not appear to be strongly differentiated from DN as a corpus in terms of word choice, YEN and YPS *are* clearly distinctive. The particular qualities of the Young England novels as political romances fulfilled a distinctive role for Disraeli as a backbencher in the 1840s by allowing him to represent Parliament from the outsider standpoint of the imagined nation he wanted Young England to bring into being. As a Conservative member of Parliament, the Young England novels enabled Disraeli to articulate his political identity in a manner that would have been difficult through the conventional and stylised medium of political debates alone.

Contemporary resonances of a crisis of parliamentary legitimacy

There is some irony in the fact that Disraeli's Young England novels, which consistently put Parliament at distance, have been frequently invoked in parliamentary debates themselves – mainly in the House of Commons but also in the Lords. Yet in many respects, this is consistent with their author's ambition to reimagine the meaning and possibilities of parliamentary representation for the nineteenth century. The Hansard at Huddersfield database records how the first mention of *Coningsby* in the House of Commons was as early as its year of publication in 1844 and the most recent 2019, for *Sybil* 1860 and 2019 and for *Tancred* (by far the least popular) 1921 and 2014 (Figure 10.4). Overall, there have been 115 speeches naming the Young England novels in this time, with *Sybil* featuring the highest number (85) followed by *Coningsby* (26) and *Tancred* (4).

It is interesting to note that the phrase 'Young England' itself appeared in just 12 parliamentary speeches during Disraeli's political career. No fewer than ten of these were in 1844, one of which was Disraeli's (Hansard 1844). Since 1880 it has featured 11 more times in debates in the House of Commons and the House of Lords, only four of which make explicit reference to the Young England grouping or to Disraeli's novels – the most recent of these in 1986. 'Young England' appears even less frequently in the texts of YEN, just twice as a reference to a parliamentary-political allegiance, both in *Tancred*. For all its historical poignancy, Young England has little continuing rhetorical impact beyond the national and international contexts of the 1830s and 1840s, when it might have drawn parallels with the populist Young Italy and Young Germany movements.

Disraeli's characterisation of England as two nations, 'the Rich and the Poor', in *Sybil* has proved a more recurrent motif than Young England (*Sybil*, p. 73). It has been widely invoked in multiple political debates by MPs of different political parties. It has also led to the labelling of a particular kind of consensus-politics Conservative as a 'one-nation' Tory – an increasingly contested political identity referred to in speeches no fewer than 85 times since 1996 (17 times in 2019, 26 times in 2020). It is indicative of how Young England's romantic idea of Parliament as a site of solace has become normative in political discourse while its realisation seems no closer.

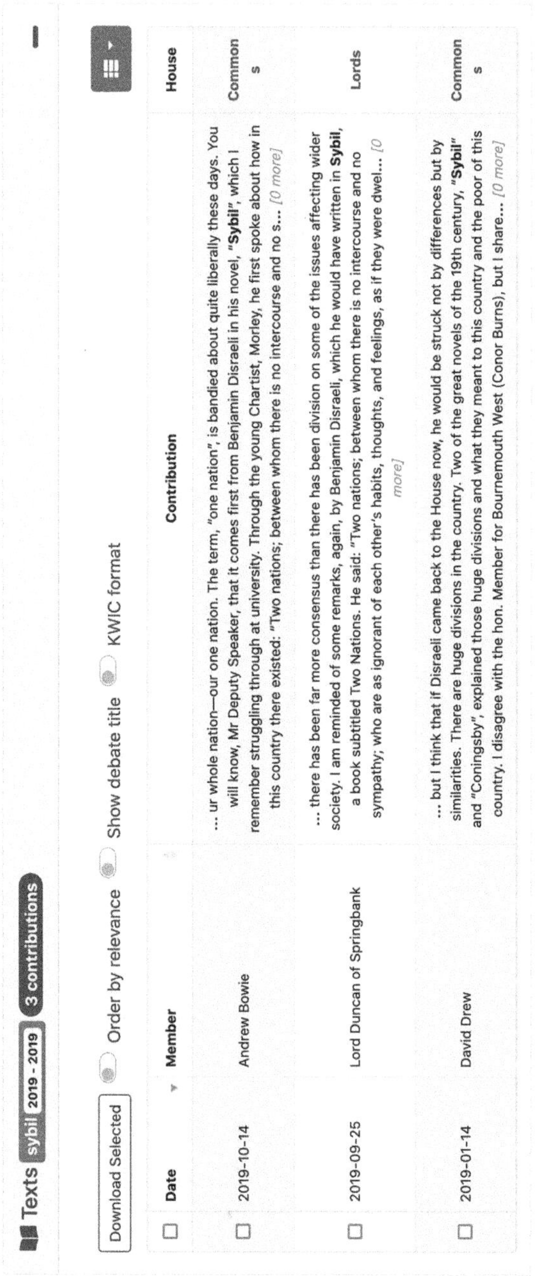

Texts sybil 2019 - 2019 | 3 contributions

Download Selected · Order by relevance · Show debate title · KWIC format

	Date	Member	Contribution	House
☐	2019-10-14	Andrew Bowie	… ur whole nation—our one nation. The term, "one nation", is bandied about quite liberally these days. You will know, Mr Deputy Speaker, that it comes first from Benjamin Disraeli in his novel, **"Sybil"**, which I remember struggling through at university. Through the young Chartist, Morley, he first spoke about how in this country there existed: "Two nations; between whom there is no intercourse and no s… *[0 more]*	Commons
☐	2019-09-25	Lord Duncan of Springbank	… there has been far more consensus than there has been division on some of the issues affecting wider society. I am reminded of some remarks, again, by Benjamin Disraeli, which he would have written in **Sybil**, a book subtitled Two Nations. He said: "Two nations; between whom there is no intercourse and no sympathy; who are as ignorant of each other's habits, thoughts, and feelings, as if they were dwel… *[0 more]*	Lords
☐	2019-01-14	David Drew	… but I think that if Disraeli came back to the House now, he would be struck not by differences but by similarities. There are huge divisions in the country. Two of the great novels of the 19th century, **"Sybil"** and "Coningsby", explained those huge divisions and what they meant to this country and the poor of this country. I disagree with the hon. Member for Bournemouth West (Conor Burns), but I share… *[0 more]*	Commons

Figure 10.4 Speeches in Parliament 2019 referencing *Sybil*. Source: Hansard at Huddersfield, https://hansard.hud.ac.uk/site/site.php (accessed 17th July 2023)

The young Tony Blair (British prime minister 1997–2007) offers a good example of the rhetorical legacy of Young England in a speech he made in the House of Commons in 1984. Blair interprets Disraeli's most widely read novel *Sybil* as a warning not to take the institutional relationship between Parliament and wider society for granted:

> 'Sybil' was written against a background of Chartism and the industrial and social unrest of those times. Many of the young unemployed in my constituency, who see no future for them, do not simply say that they will not vote for the Labour party; they do not intend to vote at all. They regard Parliament as a process irrelevant to their lives. That is the danger that we face … it will eventually turn from quiescence to anger, and people will turn from Parliament to the streets (Hansard 1984).

In a limited way, Blair's New Labour resembled a late twentieth-century analogue of Disraeli's Young England – both were powerful political imaginaries grounded in political realities of the need to mobilise political support both inside and outside Parliament, to reshape public opinion and the terms of political debate. But Blair could not articulate his vision for New Labour through party-political marketing as Disraeli articulated Young England through his fiction. It seems unlikely that Blair's technocratic advocacy of the 'third way' between state socialism and un-regulated markets will enter into political discourse in the way that Disraeli's 'two nations' bequeathed the ideal of 'one-nation' conservatism to future generations.

It helped that Disraeli was able to articulate his fictional vision of Young England at a distance from the rhetorical conventions of parliamentary debates and the demands of modern media for specific policy initiatives. It was intended as living idea, a sensibility, a language rather than a codified political agenda. From a historical perspective, the dialogue of Disraeli's political life and the Young England novels reveals Parliament – the building and the institution it represents – less as a source of solace than as a vital *topos* for anchoring political imaginaries in the concrete realities of the routines, responsibilities and performances of power. Disraeli was not a democrat in the modern sense, but like the most gifted politicians, he forged political language that others want to share. It is the inevitable indeterminacy of such language and the communicative challenge of negotiating its meaning which makes parliamentary debate possible, indeed makes it imperative, in a democratic society.

Notes

1 For example, the front cover of the 1983 Penguin Classics edition uses a painting by Sir George Hayter of The Reformed House of Commons in St Stephen's Chapel 1833, while the Nonsuch Classics edition of 2007 uses a later painting of Barry and Pugin's House of Commons.

2 We use the freely available AntConc software (https://www.laurenceanthony.net/software /antconc) to do most of our corpus analysis, but we have also created customised software (see note 7).

3 DN includes Project Gutenberg editions of the following texts: *Vivian Grey* (1826), *Popanilla* (1828), *The Young Duke* (1831), *Ixion in Heaven* (1833), *The Wondrous Tale of Alroy* (1833), *The Rise of Iskander* (1833), *The Infernal Marriage* (1834), *Henrietta Temple* (1837), *Venetia* (1837), *Coningsby* (1844), *Sybil* (1845), *Tancred* (1847), *Lothair* (1870) and *Endymion* (1880). The novel *Contarini Fleming* (1832) was not included, as there was only a version on the Internet Archive, which unfortunately had too many OCR (Optical Character Recognition) errors in it to make it viable for this analysis.

4 *Pride and Prejudice* (Austen 1813), *Our Village* (Mitford 1824), *The Last Days of Pompeii* (Bulwer-Lytton 1834), *Mr Midshipman Easy* (Marryat 1836), *Oliver Twist, Hard Times, Great Expectations* (Dickens 1837–1839; 1854; 1861), *Agnes Grey* (A. Brontë 1847), *Jane Eyre* (C. Brontë 1847), *Wuthering Heights* (E. Brontë 1847), *Vanity Fair* (Thackeray 1847–1848), *Mary Barton* (Gaskell 1848), *Alton Locke* (Kingsley 1850), *The Heir of Redclyffe* (Yonge 1853), *Treasure Island* (Stevenson 1882), *The Warden* (Trollope 1855), *Adam Bede* (Eliot 1859), *The Picture of Dorian Gray* (Wilde 1890), *Jude the Obscure* (Hardy 1895), *The Hound of the Baskervilles* (Conan Doyle 1902).

5 'Raw' frequencies mean the mere count of words without setting them in relation to the total word count of a corpus, which would be the 'relative' or 'normalised' frequencies. The normalisation is achieved by calculating the frequency per million words.

6 *Endymion* is the last novel Disraeli completed and the only one other than the Young England trilogy to have a clear political focus. Unlike these novels, it is autobiographical in nature and written at the end, rather than the onset, of Disraeli's long political career. He lived just long enough to see it published in 1880.

7 A 'keyword' in corpus linguistics refers to a word that occurs more frequently in a 'target' corpus compared to a 'reference' corpus. The *keyness* of a word in a target corpus is evaluated by way of a statistical association metric. Several algorithms exist to compute the keyness; the advantages of each compared to others is an ongoing debate within corpus linguistics. For this chapter we used our own implementation of Kilgariff's (2009) 'simple math' algorithm used in the Sketch Engine corpus analysis software that is popular in the field. In this algorithm, a score below 10 usually indicates that the keyness is negligible. Only 34 words in YPS are above this score when using the YEN as reference corpus.

8 Although these include variants, such as 'yawn', 'yawned' and 'yawning'.

References

Blake, R. (1966) *Disraeli,* London: Eyre & Spottiswoode.

Disraeli, B. (1844) *Coningsby, or The New Generation,* 1982 edition, Oxford: Oxford University Press.

Disraeli, B. (1845) *Sybil, or The Two Nations,* 1954 edition, Harmondsworth: Penguin Books.

Disraeli, B. (1847) *Tancred, or The New Crusade,* 1918 edition, London: Longmans, Green and Co.

Disraeli, B. (1849) 'Preface to the Fifth Edition', in *Coningsby* (Oxford, 1931).

Disraeli, B. (1880) *Endymion,* London: Longmans, Green and Co.

Faber, R. (1987) *Young England,* London and Boston: Faber and Faber.

Fischer-Starcke, B. (2010) *Corpus Linguistics in Literary Analysis: Jane Austen and her Contemporaries,* London and New York: Continuum.

Hansard (16 February 1844) Hansard at Huddersfield. Available from: https://hansard.hud.ac .uk/site/site.php (accessed 15 January 2020).

Hansard (28 June 1984) Hansard at Huddersfield. Available from: https://hansard.hud.ac.uk/ site/site.php (accessed 15 January 2020).

Hill, R. (2007) *God's Architect: Pugin and the Building of Romantic Britain,* London: Penguin.

Kilgarriff, A. (2009) 'Simple maths for keywords', in M. Mahlberg, V. González-Díaz and C. Smith (eds), *Proceedings of Corpus Linguistics Conference CL2009,* University of Liverpool. Available from: https://ucrel.lancs.ac.uk/publications/cl2009/ (accessed 5 August 2023).

Mahlberg, M. (2010) 'Corpus linguistics and the study of nineteenth century fiction', *Journal of Victorian Culture,* 15(2), pp. 292–298. DOI: 10.1080/13555502.2010.491667.

Mahlberg, M., Wiegand, V., Stockwell, P. and Hennessey, A. (2019) 'Speech-bundles in the 19th-century English novel', *Language and Literature,* 28(4), pp. 326–353. DOI: 10.1177/09639 47019886754.

Maurois, A. (1931) *'Preface' to the World Classics edition of Coningsby by Benjamin Disraeli,* Oxford: Oxford University Press.

Moore, R.E. (2016) *Jane Austen and the Reformation: Remembering the Sacred Landscape,* London and New York: Routledge.

O'Kell, R.P. (2013) *Disraeli: The Romance of Politics,* Toronto: University of Toronto Press.

Watson, J.G. (1954) *'Introduction' to the Penguin edition of Sybil by Benjamin Disraeli,* Harmondsworth: Penguin.

Weeks, R.G. (1989) 'Disraeli as political egoist: a literary and historical investigation', *Journal of British Studies,* 28(4), pp. 387–410.

Williams, R. (1961) *Culture and Society 1780–1950,* Harmondsworth: Penguin.

Part III
The material structure of parliaments

11

The Palace of Westminster and the Reichstag building

Spatial form and political culture

Sophia Psarra and Gustavo Maldonado Gil

Introduction

Politics is one subject, architecture another; yet architects and design professionals recognised long ago that between one and the other there is a connection: there is politics in architecture, or more precisely, architecture is a political agent in its own right. But how is this so? Our natural intuition suggests that architecture is about patterns of spaces which reflect or embody patterns of political life. This intuition finds its most powerful expression in parliament. In the English language, the word 'parliament' means both a space of politics and a political institution. It signifies the place where the laws of the country and the processes of lawmaking take their shape. Yet, there is very little understanding within architecture, political science and related disciplines of how architecture influences politics and how architecture itself is affected by the political process. The main reason for this deficit is that architecture has both discursive and non-discursive dimensions. The former relate to how we organise space using language (labels, inscriptions, and so on), how we speak and communicate *in* space and how we speak and write *about* space. The latter concerns how we encounter space in everyday life, unconsciously, without thinking or speaking about it. The non-discursive dimension of space is difficult to address, requiring conceptual and analytical tools for describing patterns that are deeply embedded in the spatial organisation of buildings, rather than visibly manifested in their surface appearance.

How do the discursive and non-discursive dimensions of parliament buildings relate to the conduct of political life?

We explore this question in the context of the United Kingdom's Houses of Parliament (Palace of Westminster) and the German Bundestag in the Reichstag building (Figures 11.1 and 11.2). The two buildings are characterised different political systems and traditions, and different approaches to parliamentary architecture. Built in the nineteenth century, the Palace of Westminster is an early Victorian pastiche building designed by Charles Barry and E.W. Pugin to host and express a political system with a long constitutional history and incremental development based on what appears to be an informal, consensual and benign process (Hollis 2013) (for a history of the Palace of Westminster, see Melvin in this volume). Designed by Paul Wallot at the end of the nineteenth century to house the legislative body of the nascent German democracy, the Reichstag was remodelled at the end of the twentieth century according to a postwar ideal that likens an open society with a transparent one, and a democratically elected parliament with an accessible one, exemplified in its performance and architecture (Barnstone 2005) (for a history of the Reichstag, see Nelson in this volume). Designed by Foster and Partners, a British architectural firm, the remodelled building utilises transparent materials to indicate an honest, open and accessible parliament.

The second question we raise in this chapter is: how does the internal spatial organisation of the two buildings relate to their distinctive political cultures?

The questions addressed here have theoretical and practical implications. At the epistemological level, they are relevant to the spatial turn in the social sciences (Nieuwenhuis and Crouch 2017), accepting that *where* and *how* things happen in space is as critical as *why* they happen, and making the spatial dimension in different disciplines explicit. The argument we put forward through the study of the two parliaments is that buildings are instances of the transmission of culture by artefacts. At the performative level, this chapter looks at how parliaments 'work' or function as spaces shaping political culture, whether they are housed in historical structures, or in newly constructed buildings that need to evolve and adapt for a more sustainable future. At the level of architectural expression, the relationship between parliamentary space and political culture has to do with balancing contradictory performative and ideological requirements, such as manifesting historical continuity and responding to change; advocating accessibility and transparency while also ensuring control and security; expressing national identity and political ideals across diverse audiences (Markus and Cameron 2002).

These contradictory values are at the core of both buildings, particularly the UK Houses of Parliament, which has launched the

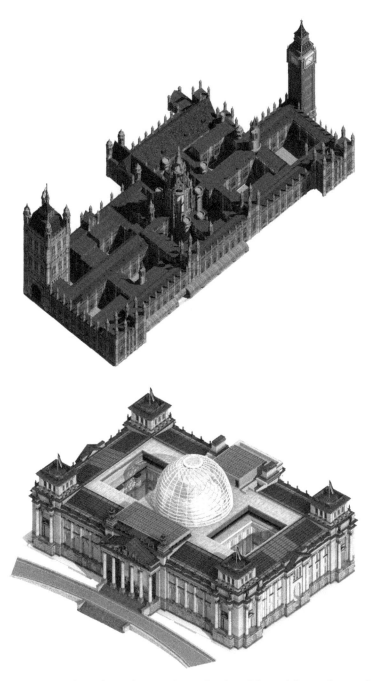

Figure 11.1 The Palace of Westminster (top) and the Reichstag (bottom).
© Matei Mitrache and Carlota Nuñez-Barranco Vallejo

Figure 11.2 The House of Commons (top) and the Reichstag (below) chambers. Top image © UK Parliament (2020). Photograph sourced from Flickr, reproduced on the basis of CC BY-ND 2.0 licence. Available at: https://www.flickr.com/photos/uk_parliament/50021458783/ (accessed 13 January 2023). Bottom image © Michael (2014). Photograph sourced from Flickr, reproduced on the basis of CC BY-ND 2.0 licence. Available at: https://www.flickr.com/photos/photo64/14622479697/ (accessed 13 January 2023).

Restoration and Renewal Programme (R&R) (October 2019), a programme of critical works in order to preserve and improve the building for the twenty-first century (Parliament 2020). The Palace of Westminster was designed and adorned to express political institutions that were rooted in historic tradition at a time of great technological innovation and imperial expansion (1840–1870). These institutions have adapted since then, but the stylistic and iconographic character of the Palace has largely remained the same, further accentuating the tensions between an imperial past and a contemporary society of diverse population (see Takayanagi in this volume). These tensions have come to the foreground in the context of the R&R, which has the challenging task to adapt an iconic World Heritage building to an architecturally, socially and politically sustainable future. The Reichstag, on the other hand, was remodelled in the postunification era in Germany, to express the need for various historical events to be brought into the present and be remembered simultaneously with current events, as history lessons for future generations (Barnstone 2005). Yet, as this study argues, the Reichstag building is not devoid of ideological symbolism embodied in its spatial structure through the particular agency of transparent materials.

Using a qualitative approach consisting of interviews with parliamentarians and a quantitative methodology (known as space syntax) for describing and visualising spatial characteristics of 'permeability' (how one moves inside a space) and 'visibility' (what one sees in a space), this study explores how the spatial configuration of the two buildings relates: first, to the political culture that takes place inside them, and second, to the contradictory needs related to political performance and ideological expression as described above. The chapter is organised in three parts. The first part discusses how parliamentary members perceive the relationship between spatial form and political life in the two buildings. The second one explores their spatial structures in terms of how they mediate spatial categories of power, control, knowledge and social interactions. The third part sets the findings of this study in the context of political history and ideology in Germany and the UK.

Political life and parliamentary space

Many studies suggest that the UK Houses of Parliament have a powerful impact on parliamentarians and staff who work inside the building (Meakin 2020; see also Meakin in this volume). Values and ideologies are not simply a matter of perceptions and beliefs, but also of spatial organisation being embedded into the ways in which buildings define boundaries between social categories (Markus and Cameron 2002). This is generally regarded as detectable in institutions which use architecture as a disciplining mechanism, embedding aspects of power and control through spatial practices (Foucault 1975). In order to understand how the spatial structure of the two parliament buildings affects the behaviour, experiences, social norms and expectations of their users, we conducted a series of pilot interviews with a diverse group of parliamentarians from the Palace of Westminster and the German Reichstag (Psarra and Riach 2020). The participants comprised current MPs, former MPs and peers. Interviews were conducted from July to September 2020 at a time of hybrid parliament, questioning nine parliamentarians. Three were current, two were former MPs and six were peers. Four were females and five were males. Discussing the relationship between spatial form and the style of the debate, two out of the nine parliamentarians referred to the opposite benches in the Commons chamber as facilitating an adversarial style of debate. However, there were counterviews to this idea. A German MP saw the difference between the debate style in the Commons and the Reichstag as being due to the difference between the two political systems (adversarial versus consensual). One particular interviewee from the House of Lords explained that the main reason for the debate style in the House of Commons is the impetus of communication, which is oriented towards argument and counterargument, as opposed to the horseshoe-shaped rooms of select committees where the aim is to reach consensus. Another interviewee from the House of Lords stated that the opposite-facing benches in the UK are based on an historical accident which has become entrenched and is difficult to reverse. In this, they referred to the ecclesiastical seating arrangement in St Stephen's Chapel in Westminster Palace, the first home of the House of Commons, where members would face one another like a monastic choir (Hollis 2013). An interesting explanation of the differences between chambers by one interviewee pointed to the spatial dynamics of visibility inside these spaces, a point to which we will return later in our analysis. Finally, a simple refutation of the determinism of spatial form influencing behaviour and vice versa was offered by a member of the House of Lords. This respondent contrasted sober reflection in the Lords with spontaneity in the Commons in spite of the similarity of their seating arrangements (with some cross benches added to the Lords). For comparative political economist Philip Manow, the idea that there is a straightforward correspondence between seating layout and political culture is unsustainable, as not all countries with the form of the British House of Commons chamber have a two-party system (see Canada), and not all countries with a two-party system have the British variant (see the USA) (Manow 2010). As to the view that the semicircle is better suited for 'speaking, seeing and hearing', Manow (2010) suggests that the symbolic display of political unity expressed by this shape has triumphed over functional demands for assembly. In architectural theory this debate is known as the form-function question, suggesting that buildings are shaped by the functions, cultures and behaviours they must satisfy. Both the pilot interviews and the literature on the relationship between form and function point to this relationship as being far more complex than functional, political or historical causality, requiring a shift of focus from architectural form as the agent of function to space and the ways in which it affords sociopoliti-cal relationships and power structures (Foucault 1975; Hillier 1996). We should, of course, examine the particularities of nation, political culture, system and context. But theory's role is to offer comparative forms of understanding that can explain a large set of occurrences beyond surface phenomena and the narration of events over time. In addition, when new parliament buildings are built or renovation programmes are under way, architects, theorists and political practitioners need more generalisable modes of knowledge regarding how parliamentary space influences and is influenced by political life. Further, there is more to parliament than the debating chamber. As many authors suggest, and as confirmed by the pilot interviews, legislatures perform a number of functions based on formal gatherings and informal, unplanned interactions (Norton 2019; see Norton, Crewe in this volume). This range of activities takes place in formal spaces, such as chambers and committee rooms, and informal spaces such as the tea rooms, bars, dining rooms, lobbies, corridors, sporting facilities and hair salons. Another principal function parliament buildings fulfil is interfacing the parliament with the public. The increasing importance of public accessibility can be seen in the Reichstag based on an elevated view into the chamber through a large circular window on its roof. This view is no longer possible as the views through the window are blocked, preventing images of documents and laptop screens in the plenary chamber from being widely circulated on social media. However, visitors can still reach a glass dome at the top level where two ramps spiral up to a viewing platform offering spectacular views of Berlin, conveying the citizens' 'ownership' of parliament. If a stable democracy requires a certain minimum level of public engagement with the political process, it is important to know how the two buildings we study here facilitate not only a range of parliamentary functions, but also public accessibility and engagement with the parliamentary process.

Describing and visualising spatial relations

Emblems and symbols in parliament buildings tangibly manifest political values and social norms. In contrast, the acting out of the social practices in space and time are intangible and difficult to describe through language. But together they form what we have come to know as the institution of parliament. In her work *How Institutions Think*, Mary Douglas explains that institutions 'make routine decisions, solve routine problems and do a lot of regular thinking on behalf of individuals' (Douglas 1987, p. 47). Studying the institutional power of space, Michel Foucault (1975) explains that spatial relationships permeate the ways in which people think in institutional settings. It is in the nature of these entities to become recognisable by people through frameworks that fall below the level of consciousness, structuring our thoughts and actions. We have no words to describe sociospatial relationships and norms of behaviour, but they form the apparatus we 'think with', guiding our actions (Hillier 1996). If language is inadequate in describing spatial and social patterns, we need a different medium to capture their logic. We use an approach developed by Hillier and Hanson (1984) and colleagues at UCL that describes sociospatial characteristics in relation to social activities and cultural meaning, in some respect addressing the shortcomings of language we mentioned above. This approach is built on two key ideas: first that space is an intrinsic aspect of human activity and how people relate to each other in buildings and cities, and second, that spatial configuration is about interrelationships of the spaces that make a layout as a whole. We can make this visually clear by taking three different layouts and drawing graphs in which each circle is a room and each line a door (Figure 11.3). We can place different spaces at the root of the graph to see how the layout is seen from these rooms. The graphs show that, despite similar geometries, the pattern of space looks different for each layout and from each room in these arrangements. To the degree that the graph from a space is 'shallow', which means that spaces cluster close to the root (the graphs at the bottom in Figure 11.3), we say it is 'integrated', and to the degree they stretch away from the root (the graph at the top right), we call it 'segregated'. Integrated spaces require fewer changes of direction to reach all possible destinations. In contrast, segregated spaces can be reached by complex paths requiring many directional turns. We can describe each space numerically in terms of how it relates to all the others. We use warm colours to express high levels of integration and cool colours to indicate segregation. In this study, these methods have

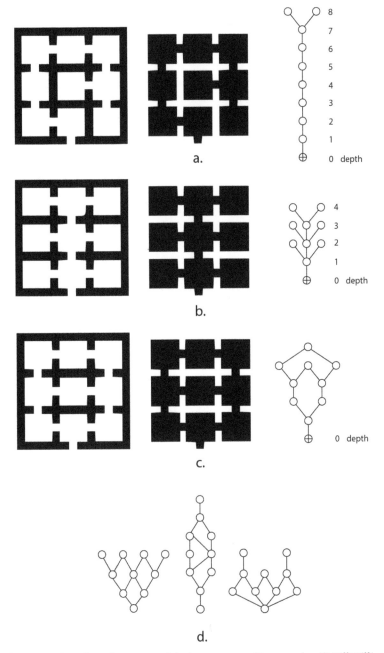

Figure 11.3 Three layouts and their corresponding graphs. © Bill Hillier 2022

been combined with customised computational scripts to capture spatial relationship in greater levels of detail. As previously mentioned, we use this approach to look at spatial connections of permeability capturing accessible spatial links, and visibility through elements such as glass and voids which enable vision to travel through them but restrict movement.

Permeability relations

The permeability analysis of the UK Houses of Parliament shows that the House of Lords is connected with the House of Commons through a highly integrated axial link extending along the length of the building and penetrating deeply into both chambers (Figure 11.4). A second integrated link, perpendicular to the first, joins the Central Lobby with Westminster Hall and the external area. Integration has a grid-like distribution covering the plan from east to west and north to south. In contrast, the Norman Porch, Robing Room, Royal Gallery and Prince's Chamber are segregated. Segregated spaces are spatially 'deep' from the centres of circulation which are characterised by high levels of integration. This means that segregated spaces require one to cover many rooms taking many directional changes in order to access them from any other location in the layout. The segregated nature of these rooms expresses the symbolic power of the monarchy and the State Opening ritual in which the monarch emerges from the deepest spaces of the building into the Lords' Chamber. The Central Lobby, on the other hand, is the most integrated space, where all-to-all routes meet, intersecting members of Parliament with each other and with the public. Thus, the structure of routes in the layout captures the interface between the key powers: the Commons, the Lords, and the monarch on the one hand, and between Parliament and the world of citizens, on the other.

Extensive research of different building types shows that the distribution of integration is closely related with high rates of movement of people, explaining why certain spaces are highly populated while others remain quiet, distant or private (Hillier 1996). There is significant evidence that people who move between specific familiar and unfamiliar locations are drawn to the most integrated spaces which lie on the simplest routes connecting all spaces to all others. Research findings also show that spatial integration stimulates informal interactions between different categories of users (Hillier 1996; Penn, Desyllas and Vaughan 1999). Further, there is evidence that stakeholders with key organisational roles tend to position themselves in spatially controlling locations (Hillier 1996).

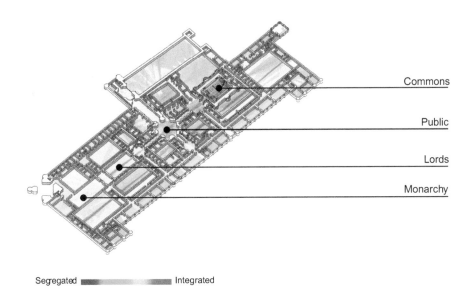

Commons

Public

Lords

Monarchy

Segregated ▬▬▬▬ Integrated

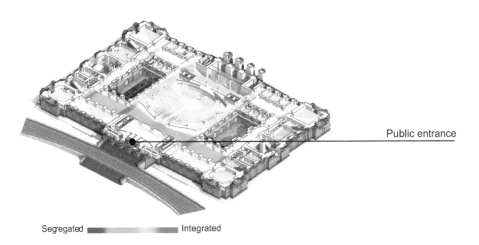

Public entrance

Segregated ▬▬▬▬ Integrated

Figure 11.4   Permeability integration in the Palace of Westminster (top) and the Reichstag (bottom). © Sophia Psarra and Gustavo Maldonado Gil

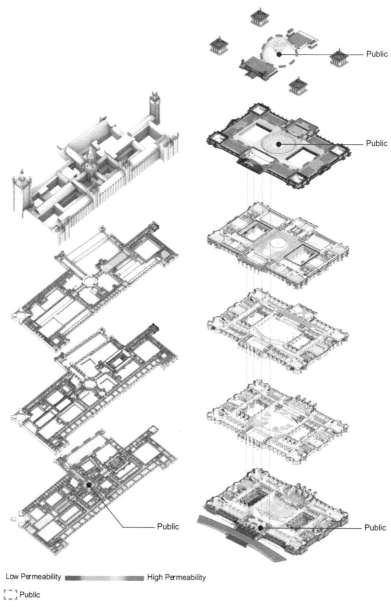

Low Permeability ▰▰▰▰▰▰▰▰▰ High Permeability

⌐ ¬ Public
⌊ ⌋

Figure 11.5 Permeability integration of entire buildings: the Palace of Westminster (left) and the Reichstag (right). © Sophia Psarra and Gustavo Maldonado Gil

It is of course important to take into account protocols, rules of behaviour and norms, as this analysis captures the natural movement patterns in the layout. Nevertheless, the results suggest that the constitutional configuration of the British Parliament as three powers is inscribed in the patterns of movement and accessibility. The analysis also captures our intuitive grasp of the Central Lobby, as the crossroads between different user groups, between Parliament and the public, when we visit the building (Psarra 2022). Moving to the Reichstag, we see that on the ground floor the highest values of integration are located at the front area next to the public entrance (Figure 11.4). When all floor levels are joined together and the building is analysed as a single system, integration shifts to the second and third floor levels, highlighting the parliamentary meeting room and the press conference room, respectively (Figure 11.5). In contrast, the analysis of joined floor levels in the UK Houses of Parliament shows that the ground floor is still the most integrated area in the entire building (Figure 11.5). The location of integration deep inside the Reichstag suggests that the building is inwardly oriented, and that the interface between visitors and Parliament is structured in two ways: it restricts access of visitors to the front lobby, the first floor galleries in the plenary chamber and the dome; it engages the press through the media space on the third floor.

Visibility relations

In her book *The Transparent State* (2005), Deborah Barnstone explains that transparency lies at the heart of the Federal Republic and has influenced the design of many federal buildings, including the renovation of the Reichstag. Examining 16 state parliaments and the Bundestag in Germany, Patrick Theiner and Julia Schwanholz (2020) argue that glass stands for transparency in these buildings whether they are new or modernised historical structures (see also Theiner and Schwanholz in this volume). Seen as a material, glass has demonstrable symbolic functions, expressing not only transparency, but also modernity, accessibility and public participation. Seen for the spatial properties it enables, it facilitates uninterrupted visibility through its surface. This allows immersive viewing where one is located within the scene viewed, and panoramic viewing where one is an observer outside the scene.

We explore the structure of visibility in the building – based on visual links that continue through glass and voids – and compare it with the structure of permeability discussed above, which captures only those

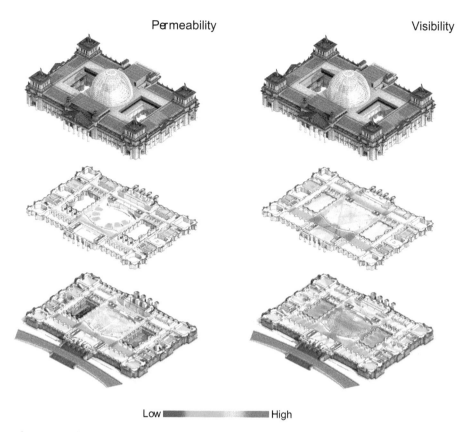

Permeability   Visibility

Low ▬▬▬▬▬▬▬▬▬ High

Figure 11.6 Permeability and visibility integration of the Reichstag. © Sophia Psarra and Gustavo Maldonado Gil

connections that are traversable by the human body. The visibility analysis reveals striking degrees of spatial interconnectivity in the Reichstag building (Figure 11.6). The wide spread of warm colours shows that the plenary chamber is visually interconnected with more than three-quarters of the ground floor area. The distribution of integration on the first floor is slightly less expansive than on the ground floor, but there is a clear emphasis on the front area through which visitors and the press enter the galleries. When the ground and first floor levels are joined by enabling vertical visual connections and analysed together as one system, we see a widely distributed pattern of integration that picks up the rostrum, the federal chancellor with their ministers, the members of the Bundestag, the two courts and the public entrance (see Nelson in this volume). Foster and Partners' team translated the idea of political transparency into internal spatial transparency, by making the plenary chamber visually integrated with the majority of the spaces in the building. The Reichstag's visibility structure stands in clear opposition to its permeability structure, which shows that the most integrated spaces are located on the parliamentary group level deeply inside the building.

The disjunction between visibility and permeability creates a contrast between seeing and going, allowing panoramic views to spaces that are not immediately accessible in one step logic. This phenomenon is common in institutions such as theatres, religious buildings and court rooms, the social functions of which require maximum visual integration and maximum spatial segregation. In these buildings, visual interconnectivity is maximised, but access is practically controlled, or ceremoniously denied. The disjunction between visibility and permeability in the Reichstag symbolises the central role of the plenary space in German democracy. The dominant message is that the political process is subject to visual scrutiny by the public, and that the public actually 'own' the building.

There is little scope in exploring the visibility structure of the UK Houses of Parliament as a separate system, as the windows are placed at high positions and there is no use of large, glazed surfaces in the building. However, a similar observation to that made about the disjunctive function of glass in the Reichstag can be made about the UK Houses of Parliament as the integrated permeable link traversing the Lords, the Commons and the Central Lobby implies unrestricted access, while in reality public access is highly controlled and the two houses 'speak to one another as little as they can' (Hollis 2013, p. 107).[1] At Westminster this reality relies on rules, protocols, rituals and norms of behaviour. In the Reichstag it is based on behavioural rules, symbolic centrality and transparent materials. For Manow (2010), democracy has no visual imagery. The medium that expresses the sovereignty of Parliament in the Palace of Westminster is the doors of the Commons chamber slammed shut in the face of the Black Rod in the State Opening of Parliament, an ancient ritual. In contrast, democracy in the Reichstag is expressed as popular authority. The medium that visualises and symbolises it is the architecture itself through the transparent surfaces and the visual interconnections they enable. The appearance of the monarch in the Lords chamber from the segregated spaces of the building at the State Opening of Parliament, or the presence of the throne when they are not there, interfaces the instrumental and symbolic requirements of constitutional monarchy. In the Reichstag, the plenary chamber carries the interface between the instrumental aspects of parliament and the symbolic expression of the body politic and the public.

The morphology of routes and formal-informal interactions

There are further marked differences between the two buildings related to the nature of their interconnections. In Figures 11.7 and 11.8 we see different types of spaces: dead-end spaces (blue, a spaces); spaces leading in a single sequence to a dead end with the same way back (yellow, b spaces); spaces in a ring of circulation offering an alternative way back (orange, c spaces); and spaces in the intersection of one or more rings (red, d spaces). The graph of the UK building has a complex structure, showing the interconnected areas of the MPs and the clear separation from the world of the public (Figure 11.7). The whips – the MPs responsible for party discipline – hold controlling positions on local rings extending off larger rings that pass through the chamber and the Central Lobby. In the House of Lords we see a higher number of orange-coloured spaces – those in a single sequence – than in the House of Commons, revealing the ritualistic nature of the House of Lords, with particular reference to the sequence of spaces the monarch crosses in the State Opening ritual (Psarra 2022).

The graph for the UK Parliament has a more complex structure and a higher number of d spaces than that for the Reichstag building (Figure 11.8). This is because the Reichstag consists of a single sequence distributing movement to a large number of dead-end spaces at the edges of the building. The UK Parliament, on the other hand, has a network of overlapping rings of circulation interfacing people who use local functional subcomplexes with those from other parts of the complex. Research shows that, the higher the number of d spaces (red), the more a building minimises depth and maximises the probability for incidental informal encounters (Hillier 1996). Various authors (Bold 2019; Norton 2019) and our interviews with MPs (Psarra 2023) confirmed that the corridor system in the UK Parliament facilitates informal interactions. A similar comment was made by two interviewees about the division lobbies in the Commons, which are part of a subcomplex of d spaces facilitating an elaborate voting system. MPs use the time spent in the division lobbies to informally exercise political influence. By contrast, in the Reichstag, as a German MP explained in the interviews, and as indicated by this analysis, there is not a spatial culture of informal interaction.

Inside the chamber

For the House of Commons and House of Lords, the spaces where the formal conduct of debate and ritual takes place are the respective chambers. Unlike the splendid decoration and sober atmosphere of the

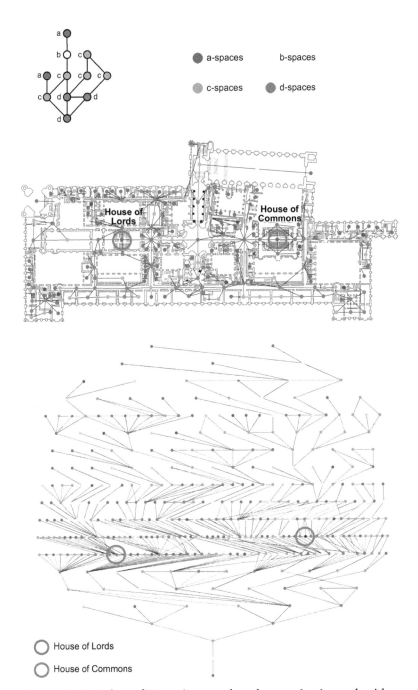

a-spaces   b-spaces

c-spaces   d-spaces

House of Lords

House of Commons

○ House of Lords

○ House of Commons

Figure 11.7   Palace of Westminster: a, b, c, d spaces (top); graph with a, b, c, d spaces superimposed on the ground floor plan (middle); graph justified from the entrance (bottom). © Sophia Psarra and Gustavo Maldonado Gil

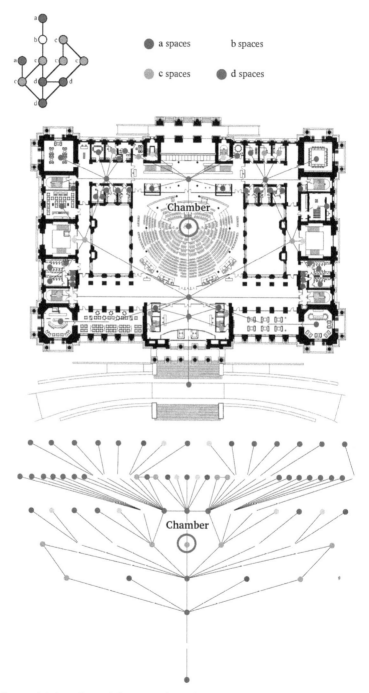

Figure 11.8 The Reichstag: a, b, c, d spaces (top); graph with a, b, c, d spaces superimposed on the ground floor plan (middle); graph justified from the entrance (bottom). © Sophia Psarra and Gustavo Maldonado Gil

Lords' Chamber, the Commons chamber is a 'galleried box' that is 'noisy and overcrowded' (Hollis 2013, p. 107). There are not enough seats for everyone, and the governing and opposition parties face each other in rows of benches notoriously two swords apart. In the interviews, one parliamentarian from the House of Lords explained that the dynamics of vision when seated in the chamber can offer an insight into relations of power and control quite different from the symbolic expression of a two-party system by the symmetrical form of this space. Using our analytical methods, we can define the area observed from the vantage point of a seat, and subsequently the most observed areas in the Commons and the Bundestag chambers by overlapping views from all seats (Figure 11.9a; see also Sailer in this volume). In spite of the current marked differences of political representation shown in Figure 11.11b, the number of seats and the area observed are broadly similar for all parties. There are very few MPs who are not covisible with other MPs in the Commons chamber (see Gibson et al. in this volume).

In the Reichstag, a combined proportional representation and a plurality system results in a wider and more even spread of parties and party representation, matching the even distribution of the number of seats and area visible from each party's position (Figure 11.9a). In the Reichstag, members mainly speak from a rostrum. A speaker facing parliament from this designated central place stands in clear distinction from a speaker addressing parliament from their own seat (Figure 11.9a). There is no such podium in the UK Commons. Rather, MPs speak from their unallocated seat only. MPs face the governing party or the opposition, depending on the party in power. Winston Churchill declined the provision of an enlarged parliament with a circular seating, for the inconvenience and the intimacy of a house that always feels full and at the edge of intense theatrical drama (see Gibson et al. and Melvin in this volume). The visual dynamics in the Commons chamber show that there is value given to the dialogue between the majority and the opposition. Speaking from one's place and the equally distributed views in the chamber give an almost equal spatial footing to the very unequal distribution of power.

Conclusion

The different configurational properties of the two buildings raise questions about the space of political debate, spatial-political practice, transparency, symbolism and heritage in two different parliament buildings with different historical, political and behavioural cultures.

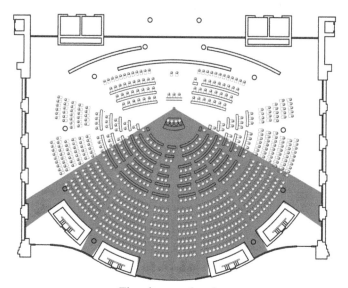

The plenary chamber

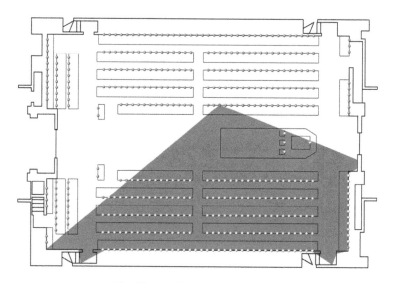

The House of Commons chamber

● Observer isovist

Member visible for the observer

Figure 11.9a View from the rostrum, Palace of Westminster (bottom) and the plenary chamber in the Reichstag (top). © Sophia Psarra and Gustavo Maldonado Gil

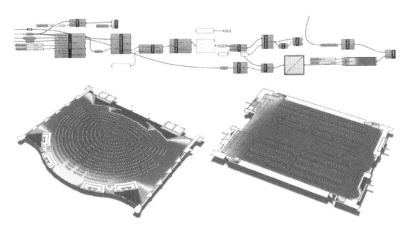

Figure 11.9b Computational script for calculating and visualising views from every seat and their overlaps highlighted in colour according to intensity from high (red) to low (blue). © Gustavo Maldonado Gil

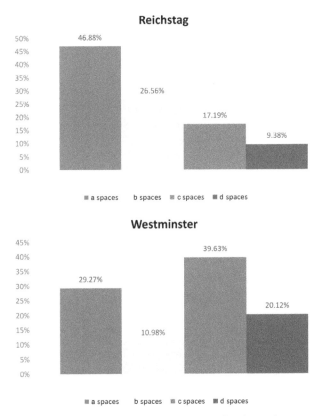

Figure 11.10 Proportional representation of a, b, c, d spaces at the Reichstag (top) and the Palace of Westminster (bottom). © Sophia Psarra and Gustavo Maldonado Gil

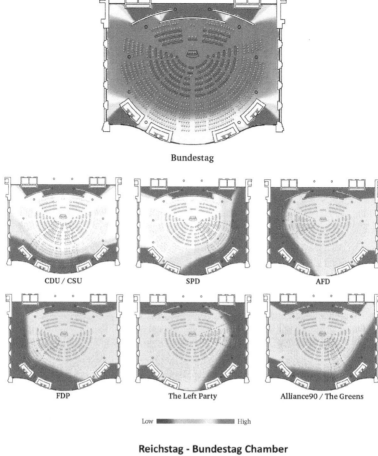

Bundestag

CDU / CSU

SPD

AFD

FDP

The Left Party

Alliance90 / The Greens

Low High

Reichstag - Bundestag Chamber

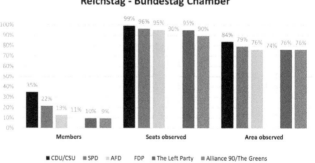

■ CDU/CSU ■ SPD ■ AFD FDP ■ The Left Party ■ Alliance 90/The Greens

Figure 11.11a The Reichstag, overlapping views from every seat (top) and proportional representation for each party (bottom). © Sophia Psarra and Gustavo Maldonado Gil

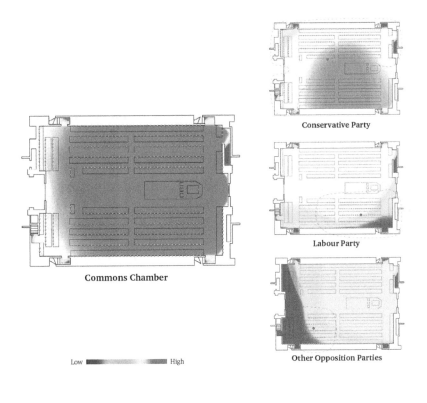

Commons Chamber

Conservative Party

Labour Party

Other Opposition Parties

Low ▰▰▰▰▰▰▰ High

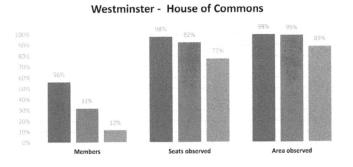

Westminster - House of Commons

■ Conservative Party   ■ Labour Party   ■ Other Opositions

Figure 11.11b   The House of Commons, overlapping views from every seat (top) and proportional representation for each party (bottom). © Sophia Psarra and Gustavo Maldonado Gil

The first contribution this study makes brings us back to the starting point in this chapter, that is, the intertwined significance of space and discourse in parliamentary contexts, and the limitations of language in capturing the role of space in shaping politics. Both space and words are important, as the word *transparency* in the context of the Reichstag illustrates, in the design of new buildings or the reshaping of existing ones. Language imposes order in the world, based on similarity and difference, concentration or distribution of power, permissible and non-permissible relations, including narratives of equality, accountability and nationhood. Language, however, is not capable of capturing complex spatial relationships and the spatial practices of the day-to-day communications in physical space. We need tools to account for the complex entanglements of space and language in political institutions and spatial settings.

The second contribution expands the discourse on transparency from the *symbolic function* of glass to *visual relations* enabled by glass. Is the drive towards political transparency in the Bundestag the same as the spatial transparency achieved in the building, or is it the expression of an ideal? Barnstone writes that this drive in Germany was a weapon against the past, intentionally incorporated into the West German constitution, the Basic Law, to militate against a potential relapse into totalitarianism, state-sponsored racism and a closed society (Barnstone 2005). Translated into architecture, this interest has evolved since the late 1940s into a dominant ideology for state buildings, especially the national parliaments, although neither the meaning intended by its proponents, nor the possible interpretations, have remained static over time (see Theiner and Schwanholz in this volume). As Barnstone writes: 'The competition brief for the Reichstag seemed to recognise the challenges, if not utter impossibility, of trying to implement architectural transparency in the existing stone structure by prescribing a transparent plenary chamber rather than a transparent building' (Barnstone 2005, p. 175). Visually integrated with all other spaces in two and three dimensions, the chamber expresses a transparent state when, in reality, it is not possible to see through a system of government (Dovey 1999; Markus and Cameron 2002). The public 'walks' over the heads of the elected representatives, reaching the dome at the top of the chamber to experience an 'imagined community' (Anderson 1983), sharing possession of the location, history and the institution. In contrast, the public in the UK Houses of Parliament has a more instrumental engagement with politics and the building. It does not reach a physically elevated position but is led to the Central Lobby, the crossroads in parliament. Architecture has agency not only through the symbolism of materials, figurative elements or architectural styles, but also through spatial configuration, affecting day-to-day interactions and the expression of ideals embedded in its very structure.

The third contribution of this work concerns the complex patterns of spatial-political practice at the Palace of Westminster. These are made possible through a highly interconnected spatial system of movement flows, and hence social encounters, intersecting diverse routes from each space to all others. It is interesting to ask how this spatial culture relates to the UK constitution. A constitution has two dimensions, constitution-as-form and constitution-as-function. Constitution-as-form is the written constitution. Constitution-as-function encompasses the larger constitutional order of a country, 'an order that might include "super-statutes, decisions of judges and agencies, and even informal institutions that make up some intersubjective consensus about what constitutes the fundamental laws of the land"' (UCL Constitution Unit). The UK constitution is constitution-as-function, where the limits of what Parliament can do are not codified in a single written document, but in constitutional leading statutes, conventions, judicial decisions, treaties as well as rules of practice. Written constitutions, argues Jonathan Sumption (2020), can have certain rigidities and act as a barrier to sociopolitical adjustment and resilience. While these written constitutions may be amended, an 'ancient' (Sumption 2020) culture which abides by an unwritten constitution, as Britain does, has embodied the practice of adjustment and negotiation, absorbing numerous internal shocks and elevating constitution to an uncodified mode of sociopolitical culture. The potential for probabilistic social encounters and informal communication in the building facilitates practices of socialisation, information exchange, influence and the mobilisation of political support, all of which are intrinsic parts of politics and parliamentary life (Norton 2019). It is possible to read this culture of political exchange in the building as akin to the capacity of the British state to adjust its policies and identity so as to respond to historical crises with short-term compromises (Psarra 2022). Within the UK Houses of Parliament some of the most radical changes, associated with human rights, the dissolution of the empire, the diversification of parliamentarians and Brexit, have been debated and legislated, enabled by a spatial system that facilitates negotiation and a culture of generative spatial encounters. In contradistinction to the adjustable constitutional settlement and the generative system of space, the iconographic narrative and symbolic references have a fixed presence being more resistant to social change (see Takayanagi in this volume). Tradition and continuity in the UK Parliament are not only expressed by the neo-Gothic style of the historical fabric, but also lived by spatial and cultural practices that moderate and mitigate potential shocks of real politics. As to the adversarial nature of the debate, it is not a matter of the shape of the chamber. It is rather a matter of spontaneity and informality moderating between the powers of the executive and Parliament, both at the level of the building as a whole and inside the chamber.

As the Palace of Westminster is preparing for a major renovation project that will affect the future of Parliament for the next hundred years, this study can make an important contribution to debates about its heritage in the context of historical and current discourses on architecture, politics, national identity and power. The Palace has previously experienced two debates about reconstruction: once after the fire of 1834 and the second time after the wartime bomb in 1941 (see also Melvin in this volume). In the nineteenth century it was caught in the discourse on the battle of styles, setting neo-Gothic English medieval against neo-Classical continental splendour. When, in 1941, the house had the opportunity to build a new Commons chamber in the form of a semicircular theatre, it opted for evolutionary order rather than a blank sheet of paper, maintaining the shape, intimacy and dimensions of the old chamber. The status of the Palace is currently being debated for the third time in its history, in committee rooms and chambers, interfacing space and discourse that is critical to the current challenges facing Parliament: the conflicting requirements of historical continuity and change, public engagement and control of access, and the significance of historical narratives in a house that 'remains unrepresentative', reflecting the 'traditions and preferences of Members who have historically populated it' (Childs 2016, p. 1). Capturing the spatial characteristics that define the mutable aspects of British politics based on a continuous generative process of socialisation and negotiation, this study argues that the spirit of the UK Parliament as revealed by this analysis should guide the aspirations of the R&R programme. The historical features of the building need to be preserved and the houses to be modernised. But the evolutionary capabilities of its spatial structure suggest that the R&R programme should enable the building to adapt and adjust rather than arrest and overwhelm its development by historicism and nostalgia.

Note

1 However, a new rule enables members of the two houses to mix with each other through some eating and drinking facilities that were previously exclusive to different houses.

References

Anderson, B. (1983) *Imagined Communities: Reflections on the Origin and Spread of Nationalism*, London: Verso.

Barnstone, D.A. (2005) *The Transparent State: Architecture and Politics in Postwar Germany*, London: Routledge.

Bold, J. (2019) 'Familiar Ordinary Things: The Corridor in English Architecture', *Transactions of the Ancient Monuments Society*, 63, pp. 41–78.

Childs, S. (2016) *The Good Parliament*. University of Bristol. Available from: https://www.bristol.ac.uk/media-library/sites/news/2016/july/20%20Jul%20Prof%20Sarah%20Childs%20The%20Good%20Parliament%20report.pdf (accessed 19 November 2021).

Douglas, M. (1987) *How Institutions Think*, London: Routledge and Kegan Paul Ltd.

Dovey, K. (1999) *Framing Places: Mediating Power in Built Form*, London: Routledge.

Foucault, M. (1975) *Discipline and Punish: The Birth of the Prison*, London: Allen Lane.

Hillier, B. (1996) *Space Is the Machine: A Configurational Theory of Architecture*, Cambridge: Cambridge University Press.

Hillier, B. and Hanson, J. (1984) *The Social Logic of Space*, Cambridge: Cambridge University Press.

Hollis, E. (2013) *The Memory Palace: A Book of Lost Interiors*, London: Portobello Books.

Manow, P. (2010) *In the King's Shadow: The Political Anatomy of Democratic Representation*, Malden, MA: Polity Press.

Markus, T. and Cameron, D. (2002) *The Words Between the Spaces*, London: Routledge.

Meakin, A. (2020) '"It was as though a spell has been cast on them": The relationship between the Palace of Westminster and the UK Parliament', *Parliament Buildings Conference*, UCL, 18–19 November. The Bartlett School of Architecture and UCL European Institute.

Nieuwenhuis, M. and Crouch, D. (2017) *The Question of Space: Interrogating the Spatial Turn between Disciplines – Place, Memory, Affect*, London: Rowman and Littlefield.

Norton, P. (2019) 'Power Behind the Scenes: The Importance of Informal Space in Legislatures', *Parliamentary Affairs*, 72(2), pp. 245–266. DOI: 10.1093/pa/gsy018.

Parliament (2020) Houses of Parliament: Restoration and Renewal. Available from: https://www.restorationandrenewal.uk/ (accessed 1 March 2022).

Penn, A., Desyllas, J. and Vaughan, L. (1999) 'The Space of Innovation: Interaction and Communication in the Work Environment', in *Environment and Planning B: Planning and Design*, 26(2), pp. 193–218. DOI: 10.1068/b4225.

Psarra, S. (2022) 'Instituting through Space and Text: How Institutions Materialise in Architecture, Cities and Language', in L. Gérald and C. Vandernoot (eds) *Institutions and the City: The Role of Architecture*, Zurich: Park Books, pp. 32–59.

Psarra, S. (forthcoming, 2023) 'The Embodied Competence of Institutions: Parliamentary Space and the UK Parliament', *Ardeth*, themed issue *Competency*.

Psarra, S. and Riach, G. (2020) *Inside Parliament: The Architecture of Democracy*, film created in collaboration with the UCL European Institute and G. Riach. Available from: https://www.parliamentbuildings.org.uk/video/inside-parliament-the-architecture-of-democracy/ (accessed 1 March 2022).

Sumption, J. (2020) *Trials of the State: Law and Decline of Politics*, London: Profile Books.

Theiner, P. and Schwanholz, J. (2020) 'Democracy by glass and concrete? The architecture of German State Parliaments', *Parliament Buildings Conference*, UCL, 18–19 November. The Bartlett School of Architecture and UCL European Institute.

UCL Constitution Unit (n.d.) Explainer: What is a constitution? Available from: https://www.ucl.ac.uk/constitution-unit/what-uk-constitution/what-constitution (accessed 18 November 2021).

12

Consensus democracy by glass and concrete?

The architecture of German state parliaments

Patrick Theiner and Julia Schwanholz

Introduction

Are symbolism and democracy systematically related? Is there a link between the architecture of political buildings and the essence of German democracy? Is architecture – as Klaus von Beyme observed – indeed 'the most political of all the arts' (von Beyme 1998, p. 22)?

Arend Lijphart (2012) classifies Germany as a *federalist consensus democracy*. Consensus democracy differs from majority democracies, which are characterised by the concentration of power. Instead, consensus democracies exhibit a dispersion of power, as political decisions often have to be negotiated or require qualified majorities. In contrast to majority democracies, Lijphart observes consensus democracies to be 'kinder and gentler' in social policy fields, and therefore more suitable for heterogeneous societies. Germany is also classified as one of the strongest exponents of a federalist state in Lijphart's *Patterns of Democracy* (1999). It is characterised by a division of legislative and executive power between the federal level and its 16 federal states (*Länder*), which results in a decentralised system of government. In this chapter we ask whether these characteristics of Germany's political system and culture can also be seen in its public buildings. What can we learn from the German case by looking at its political architecture, and is its type of federalist consensus democracy readily apparent in its buildings?

There are, of course, many empirical examples of how political power is expressed through buildings: Versailles in France and Buckingham Palace in the UK demonstrate how architecture can be used to project royal power. Europe's largest building, the colossal Palace of the Parliament in Bucharest (see Stătică and Bădescu in this volume), serves as a 'monstrous metaphor for [the] excessive tyranny' of the dictator who conceived it (Süddeutsche Zeitung 2010). At the other end of the spectrum, the Oscar-Niemeyer-designed modernist National Congress in Brasília or the stunning partially buried Parliament House in Canberra serve as confident expressions of modern democracies. States and their political elites demonstrate in political architecture how they see themselves or how they want to be seen (Wefing 1995).

Where should we look to better understand the German case? In parliamentary democracies, legislative assemblies provide good case studies because parliamentary buildings are often potent 'condensation symbols' (Edelman 1964, pp. 6–11) as the 'heart' of democracy. In this chapter, we explore the German political system and compare all 16 state parliaments (*Landtage*) and the federal parliament (Bundestag) to investigate to what degree German consensus democracy is truly reflected in its political architecture. Our analysis is based on an edited anthology published in 2020, which covers all German state parliaments in greater detail and thus facilitates a comparative perspective of the relationship between architecture of political buildings and the type and quality of democracy in the German context (Schwanholz and Theiner 2020).

Background: the case of Germany

Over the past century, Germany's history has been eventful, and its political systems have varied to an extreme (Fulbrook 2014; Hawes 2017). A nascent parliamentary democracy with vulnerable institutions was led into a first world war, which was followed by the doomed demo-cratic experiment of the Weimar Republic. This was replaced by a fascist dictatorship that used, subverted and eventually abolished the democratic process, embarking on a second world war, after which the German state collapsed. In 1945, large parts of the country were destroyed, leaving its physical and institutional architecture in ruins (Orlow 2002). The population's living space, as well as many public buildings, had to be rebuilt to enable the reconstruction of a democratic political infrastructure. St Paul's Church in Frankfurt may serve as a symbol of this process: seat of the first freely elected German parliament in 1848–49, and considered the cradle of German democracy, it was largely destroyed during the Second World War. It was boldly rebuilt immediately afterwards, preserving the historical exterior but keeping the interior strikingly simple – a physical representation of the rebuilding of democracy itself. But physical destruction was only one part of the postwar upheaval. When the allied powers split Germany in two, two diametrically opposed political systems emerged: one built on participatory democracy in the west, and the other based on one-party socialism in the east (McAdams 1993). The choice for West Germany to be organised as a federal republic with different territorial entities was driven by the hope that federalism would check possible excesses of centralised political power (Weber 2004). One of the major political tasks was, therefore, to select capital cities in West Germany's federal states and to elect parliaments. The necessary reconstruction or repurposing of buildings to house public infrastructure was accomplished at greatly varying speeds across the federal states.

After German reunification in 1990, the nation emerged as a well-functioning democratic state with a strong federalised structure, and many competences devolved to the state level. State parliaments are mostly directly elected through a system of personalised (or mixed-member) proportional representation and vary in size between 51 and 181 seats. The Bundestag – Germany's national parliament, assembling in the Reichstag building in Berlin – has 598 members who are also directly elected through a system of personalised proportional representation.[1]

Venues of political power – here exemplified by parliaments – have been studied extensively in different disciplines. Some contributions are interdisciplinary, such as social scientists collaborating with historians and architectural scholars to explore the development and design of urban centres of politics and power (Minkenberg 2014). From the political science perspective, the views from both the inside – such as the 'self-portrayal of democracy in buildings' (Wefing 1995) – and the outside – such as the 'Bundestag as an important building contractor in Berlin' (Galetti 2008) – are equally relevant. One interesting hypothesis in many such contributions is that the rebuilding of German democracy after 1945 was visualised chiefly through the medium of architectural transparency (Barnstone 2005, p. 213), although there is still debate about whether this is empirically the case, and what the advantages or disadvantages of this trend are. For example, Anthony Vidler (1992) argues that transparency can turn into obscurity if glass surfaces act like mirrors, reflecting views more than letting them pass (for further arguments, see Herzog and de Meuron 2016). Other authors – such as those writing on the Bundestag (Dörner 2000, p. 246) – find that most parliaments have been architecturally 'charismatised' and 'aestheticised' over time: they have become sources of charismatic power because they elevate the perceived importance of political institutions with their extraordinary physical appearance. The Reichstag in Berlin illustrates this not only through Sir Norman Foster's bold architectural alterations, but also through the massed use of contemporary works of art – both 'aesthetic' elements of interior and exterior design which communicate the importance of the building and, by extension, the parliament housed in it (Dörner 2000, pp. 238–240).

In contrast, some scholars caution that it might be difficult or even impossible to draw lessons about a political system from the architecture of its buildings (von Beyme 2004). Schirmer (1995) argues that political architecture is, in fact, influenced by the cultural dispositions of its time rather than political intent.

However, we believe that there is a middle ground between naive analogues of architectural and political themes, and the assertion that political buildings are created in a largely apolitical manner as mere reflections of the architectural *Zeitgeist*. Instead, we contend that while interpretative caution is necessary, we can generate important insights from a careful juxtaposition of political history and architecture, and especially from a comparative perspective. While they are not direct mirrors of each other, political culture and political architecture *are* linked, and learning about one can help understand the other. The following analysis is consequently based on a comparison of the 16 state parliaments and the Bundestag to analyse to what extent aspects of federalist consensus democracy are reflected in the physical properties of German state parliament buildings.

Architecture and federalist consensus democracy in Germany

What does the 'typical' German state parliament look like? Broadly speaking, we find two categories of buildings: *modern* or *modernised historical*. Baden-Württemberg, Bremen, North Rhine-Westphalia, Saxony and Thuringia can be classified in the first category with their twentieth-century buildings in concrete, steel and glass. Bavaria, Berlin, Hesse, Mecklenburg-Vorpommern, Lower Saxony, Rhineland-Palatinate, Saarland, Saxony-Anhalt and Schleswig-Holstein constitute the somewhat larger second category. The Bundestag at the federal level can also be sorted into the latter. Only two state parliaments do not adhere to these categories: Brandenburg and Hamburg. In Brandenburg, the decision was made in 2005 to reconstruct the historic City Palace from the eighteenth century, which had been demolished almost half a century earlier (Kolkmann 2020). In stark contrast to this stands Hamburg, whose legislative assembly has met in the almost unchanged city hall since the nineteenth century, which was only minimally adapted to modern requirements (Klinnert 2020).

Figure 12.1   Schwerin Castle, seat of the state parliament of Mecklenburg-Vorpommern in Schwerin. Built in the nineteenth century and situated on an island in the city's main lake, it became home to the Landtag in 1990, which shares the building with other public institutions. © Patrick Theiner

The typical German state parliament – this applies to 11 states – is located in a building with a historically significant role and architectural value. In some cases, pre-democratic stately residences and palaces were directly repurposed as parliamentary buildings, for example in Bavaria, Hesse, Mecklenburg-Vorpommern, Lower Saxony and Rhineland-Palatinate. These and other historic buildings, such as the Saarland's former casino and Schleswig-Holstein's former naval academy, have in common that despite their rich history they lack any connection to a genuinely *democratic* tradition (Klimmt 2020; Knelangen and Martin 2020). First, this is because Germany's democratic movements of the nineteenth and early twentieth centuries were tied to already existing pre- or proto-democratic places at the national level, such as Hambach Castle, St Paul's Church and the Reichstag. In contrast, similarly significant buildings were lacking at the state level, and the first dedicated state parliament was not built until 1961 in Stuttgart. The two exceptions to this rule are Berlin and Hamburg, which are the only parliaments housed in historic buildings that also possess historical connections to democratic decision-making. Second, German state parliaments had to embody a new beginning of democratic tradition after the end of the Second World War and the division of Germany. Parliamentarianism had to be relearned and reimagined. This is arguably easier when new parliaments meet in places that are not burdened by historical connections with autocratic or undemocratic regimes.

The interior of the typical German state parliament has a circular or oval plenary hall, which is a relatively recent development (Manow 2008, p. 323) that has spread quickly. Circular seating arrangements are meant to emphasise parliamentary cooperation and consensus-building in contrast to a Westminster-style configuration where government and opposition are facing each other as antagonists. A version of the latter can be found in Bavaria, the Saarland and Saxony-Anhalt, but even here parliamentarians sit in a semicircle instead of a more confrontational arrangement, such as the classroom-style former plenary in Mecklenburg-Vorpommern (Carstensen 2020).

Aesthetically, plenary halls are typically spartan – opulence in the style of a 'temple of democracy' is almost unheard of among state parliaments. Most of the rooms follow a sober design language: white surfaces, pale wood, clear lines, reduced colour pallets and few decorative elements. Some plenary halls, like those in Brandenburg (Figure 12.2) or Mecklenburg-Vorpommern, appear almost cloister-like in their aesthetic austerity.

The creation of architectural transparency is undoubtedly a postwar trend. In the last decades, all state parliaments' renovations or redecorations were guided by the idea that political processes should be made visible. New buildings in Baden-Württemberg, Bremen and Thuringia and modernised historic buildings in Berlin, Hesse, Lower Saxony, Saxony, Saxony-Anhalt and Schleswig-Holstein all attempt to create transparency through employing glass. But *how* this glass is used is quite varied. The plenary hall in Saxony-Anhalt features glass across its entire length, yet this opens onto an interior courtyard rather than a public space (Tullner 2020). The all-glass façade of Baden-Württemberg's state parliament allows a view into parliamentarians' offices, rather than the plenary hall (Siefken 2020). At the other end of the spectrum, Schleswig-Holstein's plenary hall is housed in an exposed all-glass cube that allows for an unobstructed view even from outside the building (Knelangen and Martin 2020). The only real exceptions to this transparency trend are state parliaments that have found historic homes and are bound by their buildings' status as listed historical structures. This often limits the use of modern materials such as glass. In Bavaria, Hamburg, Rhineland-Palatinate or the Saarland, glass walls or transparent roofs would fall foul of building conservation laws.

Figure 12.2 Plenary hall of the state parliament of Brandenburg, Potsdam. Inaugurated in 2013, its interior is modern, while externally the building is a faithful reconstruction of the eighteenth-century City Palace in the rococo style, which had been fully demolished in the 1950s. © Landtag Brandenburg

Despite all its openness, the typical German state parliament is primarily a legislative building and, therefore, intended for parliamentarians. *Politics as decision-making* can be made visible through the use of visitor galleries or windows, while *politics as administration* continues to take place behind the scenes (Mannheim 1929, pp. 71–73).

A notable pattern among all parliaments is the fact that they hardly feature any references to Germany's federal system, of which states are key members. Admittedly, federalism does not have an obvious architectural analogue: few of the parliaments include even Germany's national symbols

Figure 12.3 State parliament of Baden-Württemberg, Stuttgart. Completed in 1961, the uncompromisingly modernist structure was Germany's first custom-built parliamentary building. © Patrick Theiner

or flag. The most extreme exponents of this architectural trend are the parliaments in Dresden and Kiel, both of which feature enormous maps of their own state as the plenary's centrepiece. These, however, show neither neighbouring regions nor Germany as a whole (Schubert 2020; Knelangen and Martin 2020). This creates an impression of the state as a separate entity removed from its larger political and even cultural context. While it cannot always be conclusively established whether these choices are deliberate or incidental, federalism is, ironically, the political characteristic least translated into architecture.

Taken together, our exploration shows some clear across-case patterns, but such commonalities are limited to specific elements, rather than defining an overall model. Interestingly, we fail to find parliaments adhering to the established fault lines of German politics (Wehling 2006, p. 95). Typically, German political culture follows either a north-south divide between historically Protestant and Catholic areas, or an east-west divide due to the split of Germany after the Second World War. While research has found support for these cleavages in many areas of German politics, they are not present in our case, where all architectural trends we have identified – from pre-democratic buildings, to seating arrangements, to the use of glass – can vary widely even between immediate neighbours.

Parliamentary architecture as a mirror of political culture

Detailed case studies of German state parliaments show five main ways in which parliamentary architecture mirrors local politics and political culture (Schwanholz and Theiner 2020).

First, we find that the decision-making processes that lead to architectural choices come in two sharply divergent types, with no intermediate cases. In 'conflictual' instances of decision-making, parliamentary architecture is the result of long and sometimes bitter political disputes that can last for years and often involve the public. As an example, Bremen needed a decade and several bidding rounds to settle on a proposal for the renovation of its city hall (Fuchs 2020). In the Saarland, even decisions about chandeliers and seat upholstery were contentious (Klimmt 2020). In all other cases, we find 'harmonious' decision-making – here, parliamentary architecture is not contentious if it is debated at all, and conflicts are settled quickly. Berlin only needed three weeks to decide on its new parliament in 1990, and decision-making in North Rhine-Westphalia was highly consensual and pragmatic despite the resulting building's difficult location near a river and its high costs (Schacht and Minkenberg 2020; Kleinfeld 2020).

Second, and related to this apparent bipolarity, we find that decisions are often made behind closed doors to enhance consensus-building. Parliamentary architecture is frequently decided by estate committees, councils of elders, or similar organs separate from the plenary. In some cases, we even find nested layers of such bodies, such as in North Rhine-Westphalia, where a building commission reported to a council of elders (Kleinfeld 2020). While such non-plenary organs seem to lead to more efficient processes – they are present in all 'harmonious' cases – they also reduce transparency and public participation. The 'demos' is rarely involved in decision-making.

Third, all state parliaments seem eager to facilitate citizens' access to the political process. A visitor's gallery as the representation of the 'permanent presence of the sovereign' (Minkenberg 2020) is a universal feature. Nonetheless, there are few parliaments that allow for truly open – meaning spontaneous or unplanned – interactions between citizens and their parliament. Bremen with its laissez-faire approach to allowing citizens into all parts of its building is the closest approximation of this ideal, perhaps followed by the various parliamentary restaurants and cafeterias where politicians and their constituents can mix (Fuchs 2020). In most cases, citizens are clearly treated as visitors in 'their' representative building, many parts of which will be off limits.

Fourth, the previous finding emphasises that we must ask *for whom* state parliaments are built. If the primary goal is increased representation and transparency, then German state parliaments have indeed undergone dramatic changes since their beginnings in bunker-like plenary halls and temporary quarters, largely away from the public eye. However, in most cases at least the initial push for architectural revisions comes from those who work in parliament, with citizens' wishes for better access being a secondary driver at best.

Fifth, practically all cases show that both the public and political actors conceive of architecture as a literal mirror of politics. New builds are celebrated as representing new beginnings, historical buildings evoke a state's history, glass stands for transparency, circular seating for cooperation, and so on. When examining the wishes and justifications of political actors for specific architectural features, we largely find a superficial association of political ideals with a building's appearance, which is not driven by particularly deep readings of architectural history and theory or hidden motives. Nevertheless, parliaments clearly also follow architectural trends that make it hard to argue that only a political programme could have brought about their design: high, airy rooms dominated by glass, plenty of light, neutral colours and natural materials might be found just as easily in corporate headquarters, convention centres or universities.

Conclusion

Is German consensus democracy visible in parliament architecture? This chapter has briefly shown that baroque façades, renovation projects and new buildings all reflect some fundamental truths about German political culture. This includes an eagerness for new beginnings, confident demonstration of devolved power, rejection of opulence and desire for cooperation and transparency. However, we also find at times severe conflicts over architectural choices, private and corporatist decision-making, a carefully stage-managed integration of the public and few references to a larger federal system. Using Lijphart's characterisation, Germany's federalist consensus democracy is indeed reflected in its buildings, but its commitment to consensus has found much more architectural expression (such as in circular seating arrangements), while the system's federalist nature is rarely represented architecturally, and at times is seemingly actively obscured. There is also significant variation between individual cases in how well they adhere to the overall classification.

Table 12.1 Overview of German parliamentary buildings

State	City	Built	Style	Former use	Seating	Decision-making
Baden-Württemberg	Stuttgart	1961	Modern	–	Semicircle	Conflictual
Bavaria	Munich	1874	Historical	Civil service academy	Semicircle	Harmonious
Berlin	Berlin	1899	Historical	Prussian lower house	Circle	Harmonious
Brandenburg	Potsdam	1745/2013	'Modern'	Royal residence	Circle	Conflictual
Bremen	Bremen	1966	Modern	–	Semicircle	Conflictual
Hamburg	Hamburg	1897	Historical	City hall/council	Semicircle	Conflictual
Hesse	Wiesbaden	1841	Historical	Royal residence	Circle	Harmonious
Lower Saxony	Hanover	1844	Historical	Royal residence	Semicircle	Conflictual
Mecklenburg-Vorpommern	Schwerin	1850	Historical	Royal residence	Circle	Harmonious
North Rhine-Westphalia	Düsseldorf	1988	Modern	–	Circle	Harmonious
Rhineland-Palatinate	Mainz	1749	Historical	Ducal residence	Circle	Harmonious
Saarland	Saarbrücken	1898	Historical	Gentlemen's club	Semicircle	Conflictual
Saxony	Dresden	1928/1993	Modern	Public administration	Circle	Harmonious
Saxony-Anhalt	Magdeburg	1720	Historical	Bourgeois residence	Semicircle	Harmonious
Schleswig-Holstein	Kiel	1888	Historical	Naval academy	Circle	Conflictual
Thuringia	Erfurt	1936/2004	Modern	Public administration	Circle	Conflictual
Bundestag	Berlin	1894/1999	Historical	–	Semicircle	Conflictual

Empirically, the most surprising insight might be that German state parliaments' architecture is not that surprising. We could expect a nation with such a turbulent history to have equally varied political architecture; at the very least, we should see architecture reflecting established political fault lines. Yet, both modern and modernised historical buildings follow the same norms of architectural modernity, which leads to politically, economically and culturally different states sharing similar vocabularies of expression in federal parliaments. It is difficult even for informed observers to identify specific parliaments from ever similar pictures of circular plenaries, glass visitor galleries and angular white entrance halls. There is a final irony in this result: in their desire to showcase their modernity, independence and individuality, most state parliaments buy into the same symbolic language and thus demonstrate that they *do* belong to a larger polity.

Finally, a fruitful avenue for further research might be the exploration of physical *and* virtual parliamentary spaces. State parliaments in particular have recently begun to deploy digital technologies for democratic education of the public. This is expressed both in buildings and in virtual spaces (for example, guided online tours). As parliaments are often the only directly elected bodies in representative democracies, efforts to link them more closely to their citizens are well-invested – especially when democracy in Germany and elsewhere is under pressure from populist movements or wider societal challenges such as the COVID pandemic. Further research into the creation of virtual political spaces could augment our understanding of how parliaments and citizens conceive of and negotiate their relationships.

Note

1 So-called 'overhang mandates' increase the number of parliamentarians in practice; in 2022, the Bundestag has 736 members, making it one of the largest lower houses in the world.

References

Barnstone, D.A. (2005) *The Transparent State: Architecture and Politics in Postwar Germany*, London: Routledge.

Carstensen, F. (2020) 'Der Landtag von Mecklenburg-Vorpommern im Schweriner Schloss', in J. Schwanholz and P. Theiner (eds) *Die politische Architektur deutscher Parlamente: von Häusern, Schlössern und Palästen*, Wiesbaden: Springer, pp. 207–228.

Dörner, A. (2000) 'Der Bundestag im Reichstag. Zur Inszenierung einer politischen Institution in der, "Berliner Republik"', *Zeitschrift für Parlamentsfragen*, 31(2), S. 237–246.

Edelman, M. (1964) *The Symbolic Uses of Politics*, Champaign: University of Illinois Press.

Fuchs, S. (2020) 'Bremen: Das Haus der Bürgerschaft als zeitlos-moderner Ort der Demokratie', in J. Schwanholz and P. Theiner (eds) *Die politische Architektur deutscher Parlamente: von Häusern, Schlössern und Palästen*, Wiesbaden: Springer, pp. 147–168.

Fulbrook, M. (2014) *A History of Germany, 1918–2014: The Divided Nation*, Chichester: Wiley & Sons.

Galetti, N. (2008) *Der Bundestag als Bauherr in Berlin*, Düsseldorf: Droste Buchverlag.

Hawes, J. (2017) *The Shortest History of Germany*, Exeter: Old Street Publishing.

Herzog, J. and de Meuron, P. (2016) *Treacherous Transparencies*, Barcelona: Actar Publishers.

Kleinfeld, R. (2020) 'Am Ende gab es nur Gewinner – der lange Weg des nordrhein-westfälischen Landtags zu seinem Neubau am Rhein', in J. Schwanholz and P. Theiner (eds) *Die politische Architektur deutscher Parlamente: von Häusern, Schlössern und Palästen*, Wiesbaden: Springer, pp. 243–278.

Klimmt, R. (2020) 'Der Landtag des Saarlandes: Vom Casino zum Parlament', in J. Schwanholz and P. Theiner (eds) *Die politische Architektur deutscher Parlamente: von Häusern, Schlössern und Palästen*, Wiesbaden: Springer, pp. 297–318.

Klinnert, A. (2020) 'Das Hamburger Rathaus – Tempel der Bürger ?' in J. Schwanholz and P. Theiner (eds) *Die politische Architektur deutscher Parlamente: von Häusern, Schlössern und Palästen*, Wiesbaden: Springer, pp. 169–188.

Knelangen, W. and Martin, C. (2020) 'Der Landtag in Kiel: Parlamentsarchitektur in Schleswig-Holstein', in J. Schwanholz and P. Theiner (eds) *Die politische Architektur deutscher Parlamente: von Häusern, Schlössern und Palästen*, Wiesbaden: Springer, pp. 359–378.

Kolkmann, M. (2020) 'Der Landtag Brandenburg: moderne Infrastruktur in historischer Hülle', in J. Schwanholz and P. Theiner (eds) *Die politische Architektur deutscher Parlamente: von Häusern, Schlössern und Palästen*, Wiesbaden: Springer, pp. 125–146.

Lijphart, A. (1999) *Patterns of Democracy: Government Forms and Performance in Thirty-Six Countries*, New Haven, CT and London: Yale University Press.

Lijphart, A. (2012) *Patterns of Democracy: Government Forms and Performance in Thirty-Six Countries*, 2nd edition, New Haven, CT and London: Yale University Press.

Mannheim, K. (1929) *Ideologie und Utopie*, Bonn: Cohen.

Manow, P. (2008) *Im Schatten des Königs: Die politische Anatomie demokratischer Repräsentation*, Frankfurt: Suhrkamp.

McAdams, J. (1993) *Germany Divided: From the Wall to Reunification*, Princeton: Princeton University Press.

Minkenberg, M. (ed.) (2014) *Power and Architecture*, New York: Berghahn.

Minkenberg, M. (2020) 'Demokratische Architektur in demokratischen Hauptstädten: Aspekte der baulichen Symbolisierung und Verkörperung von Volkssouveränität', in J. Schwanholz and P. Theiner (eds) *Die politische Architektur deutscher Parlamente: von Häusern, Schlössern und Palästen*, Wiesbaden: Springer, pp. 13–39.

Orlow, D. (2002) *A History of Modern Germany: 1871 to Present*, London: Pearson.

Schacht, L. and Minkenberg, M. (2020) 'Das Abgeordnetenhaus von Berlin', in J. Schwanholz and P. Theiner (eds) *Die politische Architektur deutscher Parlamente: von Häusern, Schlössern und Palästen*, Wiesbaden: Springer, pp. 105–124.

Schirmer, D. (1995) 'Politik und Architektur: Ein Beitrag zur politischen Symbolanalyse am Beispiel Washingtons', in A. Dörner and L. Vogt (eds) *Sprache des Parlaments und Semiotik der Demokratie*, Berlin: Walter de Gruyter, pp. 309–339.

Schubert, T. (2020) 'Der Sächsische Landtag: Zeichen des demokratischen Neubeginns', in J. Schwanholz and P. Theiner (eds) *Die politische Architektur deutscher Parlamente: von Häusern, Schlössern und Palästen*, Wiesbaden: Springer, pp. 319–340.

Schwanholz, J. and Theiner, P. (eds) (2020) *Die politische Architektur deutscher Parlamente: von Häusern, Schlössern und Palästen*, Wiesbaden: Springer.

Siefken, S. (2020) 'Einigung, Arbeitsatmosphäre, Tageslicht: das Haus des Landtages von Baden-Württemberg und seine Symbolik', in J. Schwanholz and P. Theiner (eds) *Die politische Architektur deutscher Parlamente: von Häusern, Schlössern und Palästen*, Wiesbaden: Springer, pp. 67–86.

Süddeutsche Zeitung (2010) *Die Hausherrin*. Available from: https://www.jetzt.de/sz/die-hausherrin-494944 (accessed on 10 June 2022).

Tullner, M. (2020) 'Der Landtag von Sachsen-Anhalt: langer Weg zum modernen Parlament', in J. Schwanholz and P. Theiner (eds) *Die politische Architektur deutscher Parlamente: von Häusern, Schlössern und Palästen*, Wiesbaden: Springer, pp. 341–358.

Vidler, A. (1992) *The Architectural Uncanny: Essays in the Modern Unhomely*, Cambridge, MA: MIT Press.

von Beyme, K. (1998) 'Politische Ikonologie der Architektur', in H. Hipp and E. Seidl (eds) *Architektur als politische Kultur*, Berlin: Reimer Verlag, pp. 19–34.

von Beyme, K. (2004) 'Politische Ikonologie der modernen Architektur', in B. Schwelling (ed.) *Politikwissenschaft als Kulturwissenschaft*, Wiesbaden: Springer VS Verlag, pp. 351–372.

Weber, J. (2004) *Germany, 1945–1990*, Budapest: Central European University Press.

Wefing, H. (1995) *Parlamentsarchitektur: Zur Selbstdarstellung der Demokratie in ihren Bauwerken*, Berlin: Duncker & Humblot.

Wehling, H.-G. (2006) 'Föderalismus und politische Kultur in der Bundesrepublik Deutschland', in H. Schneider and H.-G.Wehling (eds) *Landespolitik in Deutschland: Grundlagen, Strukturen, Arbeitsfelder*, Wiesbaden: VS Verlag, pp. 87–107.

13

The architecture of political representation
A historiographical review
Remieg Aerts and Carla Hoetink

The cultural and spatial turns in political history

This chapter offers a historiographical survey of studies investigating the relationship between politics and the places in which it is mediated. In this it departs from the assumption that architecture has a sort of 'performative power' to shape political practice and political culture. The historical relationship between architecture and politics has been the subject of research for some time, albeit not in the mainstream study of political history. Yet since the 1990s, political history appears to have reinvented itself. In the preceding decades, the prevailing perspective of social and economic history and the French Annales school had effectively created the impression that politics was a mere epiphenomenon of deeper social and economic forces and relationships.

Three developments contributed to the renewal of political history. Perhaps the most important was the cultural turn, which inspired a much broader conception of politics. The concept of 'political culture' drew attention to the mental context and the language of politics, and to what Walter Bagehot (1867) once called the 'dignified parts' of the political system, such as the symbolic and ritual aspects, and its presentation forms, customs and practices. Tim Blanning and Peter Burke showed the relevance of both the power of culture and the culture of power in early modern politics (Burke 1991; Blanning 2002). The focus on political culture gave the study of the French Revolution an entirely new dimension (Baker 1987). Initially this innovative research focused on early modern politics, but the approach was subsequently extended to the nineteenth and twentieth centuries. The traditional understanding of 'politics' broadened to the study of 'the political'. In the German *Kulturgeschichte des Politischen* and the research programmes of the Bielefelder School, politics has come to be conceived as a form of communication, persuasion and rhetoric (Stollberg-Rilinger 2005; Frevert and Haupt 2005; Braungart 2012). Accordingly, regal representation, monumental architecture, parliamentary rituals, language and street manifestations are understood and studied as means of political expression and persuasion (Paulmann 2000; Andres, Geisthövel and Schwengelbeck 2001; Schwengelbeck 2007).

That approach was supported by the 'spatial turn' that occurred in the humanities and the social sciences more broadly from the 1990s onwards. In fact, historians have long known that 'public constructions are the material expression of political power, its exercise, and its form' (Minkenberg 2014, p. 3). The central assumption of the spatial turn is that all space is defined by politics, power and interest. This applies to the public sphere as well as to spatial planning and the use of and access to public spaces. Squares, boulevards and parks facilitate parades, protests, demonstrations and national commemorations. The location and distance between the seats and centres of political authority is relevant. From the time of monarchical absolutism and colonialism, architectural styles such as classicism and baroque have been the visual expression of power and authority (Mumford 1961; Schlögel 2003). Architecture is a language, and spaces and buildings 'can be read' (Alofsin 2006).

Apart from the important sociological analyses of Michel Foucault, Henri Lefebvre, Harold Lasswell and other authors on the relationship between power and the design of public space, historical research initially focused on the function and design of capital cities, as in Lawrence Vale's *Architecture, Power and National Identity* (1992; about the 'spatial turn': Rau 2013; Tally 2013; Kümin and Usborne 2013; Minkenberg 2014). Surprisingly, the consequences of the spatial turn for the interpretation of parliamentary architecture and other government buildings have been recognised quite tardily.

Interpreting the architecture of parliaments

The American social scientist and professor of public administration Charles Goodsell was a pioneer in the field of parliamentary architecture. Already in the 1980s he had made a start with the political interpretation of public space and government buildings. In his view, their shape and location manifest the permanency of a political system. Their architecture embodies political values, influences the behaviour of the politicians and officials, and conveys an ideal of government, authority and national sovereignty. Due to their design and layout, in particular of the plenary or assembly hall, they exert a major influence on the national political culture (Goodsell 1988a, 1988b, 2001). Although other social scientists or theoreticians of architecture showed some interest in related subjects, looking for a theoretical framework to systematise the relationship between architectural design and political practice, Goodsell's line of research did not meet with a wide following right away (Milne 1981; Seidel 1988; Mayo 1996).

Somewhat similar to Goodsell's work, though, is the type of research that has emerged in Germany. Problematic and ideologically charged as Germany's rich history is, it is no coincidence that German political scientists and historians even prior to Goodsell started to focus on the 'language' of political architecture. Some of the earliest reflections on the architectural effect and political meaning of parliament buildings can be found in German literature of the 1960s and 1970s (Götze 1960; Arndt 1961; von Beyme 1971; Münzing 1977; Warnke 1984). In the context of rebuilding democracy in West Germany after the Second World War, these first reflections were characterised by a normative stance on the interplay of architecture and politics. Up until today, the question of government and parliament buildings as embodiments of democratic values is at the heart of most German-language studies on the topic (Flagge and Stock 1992; Dörner and Vogt 1995; Lankes 1995; Wilhelm 2001; Brendger 2008; Paulus 2012). Apart from its common focus on the democratic and communicative aspect of architecture, the German body of litera-ture stands out because of its interdisciplinary approach, with a strong emphasis on iconography, semiotics and attention to parliamentary architecture as part of the public sphere (von Beyme 1991; Döring 1995; Schirmer 1995; Biefang 2002, 2003, 2009).

Whereas German research is foremost interested in the consequences of architecture and the use of space for political, and in particular demo-cratic, practice, the French- and English-language academic literature tends to take a more cultural and anthropological approach. In this type of research, parliamentary buildings are interpreted as architectural expressions of nationhood and the nation state, or of a conscious display of democratic values (Judge and Leston-Bandeira 2018; Leoussi and Brincker 2018; Leoussi, Payne and Sulak 2020). Political anthropologist Emma Crewe and political scientist Shirin Rai focus on parliament buildings as places of political performance or sites of work, debate and the image of the nation in miniature form. Another telling example of this approach offers the close reading of the French parliament building Palais Bourbon by sociologist and historian Delphine Gardey (Crewe 2005 and 2021, see also Crewe in this volume; Gardey 2015; Rai and Sparry 2018).

Besides this body of interpretive, analytical academic literature, there is also a pile of general interest publications on parliament buildings that should not be ignored. Richly illustrated publications of this kind usually appear on the occasion of the opening of new or renovated parliament buildings, on anniversaries, or as a catalogue accompanying an exhibition. In projects by architectural firms and in photo books, the shapes and layouts of parliament buildings around the world are being recorded, to gain insight into common models, or as a graphic work of art in its own right (Sudjic and Jones 2001; van Riet and van Bakel 2002; Kühn and Österreichische Gesellschaft für Architektur 2014; Mulder van der Vegt and Cohen de Lara/XML 2016; Bick 2019). Although these occasional publications and coffee table books usually have little academic pretensions, this rich body of literature is valuable for comparative research, and may contain scholarly contributions (exemplary is Riding and Riding 2000). The same is true for a number of biographical studies of nineteenth-century parliamentary architects and their networks, who designed a common 'European' style of political architecture (see Shimizu and Naraoka 2014).

Two lines of research: the exterior and the interior

For the type of study of political architecture advocated by Goodsell, it is relevant to distinguish between analysis of the exterior and of the interior. In fact, in the current state of the art, they constitute two different lines of research. Interpretations of the usual models of the plenary hall – the semicircular theatre form, the oppositional Westminster model and the authoritarian school-class model – and of the mutual positioning of the lower and upper chambers are usually mainly interested in the consequences for political practice, or the relationship between the political powers within the political system. Studies focusing on the location, the design or the reuse of parliament buildings and other centres of political authority appear to be more interested in political culture in the broader sense, or in the relationship between parliament, history and nation.

The *exterior* comprises everything connected to the setting of parliament, the architecture of its building and the decoration scheme. First, this concerns the 'politics of place', the site where parliament is located and its surroundings, particularly in relation to other centres of political authority such as the royal palace, the seat of government, the senate or government departments (Van der Wusten 2004; McNamara 2015; Gardey 2015). Second, of course, a study of the exterior deals with the architectural design: the style, shape and scale of the building. Third, exterior also includes decoration and ornamentation in terms of sculpture, paintings, texts, furniture, tapestry and more. This entails an analysis of invented traditions, the ideological programme of political, civic and national values that feeds the design of the building. After all, style, design conventions and location make the functions of public buildings immediately visible. Like nineteenth-century opera houses, theatres and universities, parliament buildings are a kind of *Gesamtkunstwerk* (an 'integral work of art'), a visual programme to place such institutions as the republic, democracy, law or science on a pedestal and to generate authority (see Aerts 2018; Aerts and van den Berg 2019).

In the nineteenth century, parliaments needed to create their own status and prestige. As an institution they were more or less new and faced the task of presenting themselves outwardly as the new high authority, next to or above the monarchy with its long tradition of majesty. To achieve this, they appealed to the tried and tested architectural rhetoric that had defined the face of the monarchy for so long. In order to boost their stature, the new parliaments provided themselves with a palace. In the first instance, these were former royal palaces or very substantial administrative buildings that were given a new use. The symbolic grasp of supreme power implied in a term like 'palace of the nation' alone was vividly felt by monarchists in the nineteenth century (see for instance, Krul 2011; Smit 2015). Many parliaments expressed their growing status in the second half of the nineteenth century with prestigious new buildings, when the old buildings were no longer adequate or had been damaged by fire. That was the moment to consciously express the representation of the nation, its history and its relationship with the executive and the head of state by choosing a location, a building style, a format, a layout and a decoration programme.

The allure of the parliament palaces was partly determined by their location. Both the older palaces or monasteries repurposed for parliamentary use and the newly constructed parliament buildings exploited the site's rhetoric to the extreme. They presented themselves visibly and grandly on a hill, on a wide square, in a historic location, on the main river of the capital and always above street level, visually elevated by a basement and stairs. The choice of locations was not only about the combination of visibility and size. Historical places, old strongholds of power or national *lieux de mémoire* were consciously chosen. In most cases the parliament buildings also sought a position next to or opposite the royal or presidential palace, the seat of government, or the senate or upper house, in a bicameral parliament (more extensively in Aerts 2018; Aerts and van den Berg 2019).

Unlike royal or presidential palaces, parliament buildings derive their status and public appeal as much from the main rooms at the heart of the building as from their façade. The study of the *interior* first and foremost regards the plenary hall, as its main assembly room and – certainly since the camera made its entrance into parliament – the central stage of national politics (Goodsell 1988a, p. 302). Particularly here, the internal and external effects of architecture come together and interact: the plenary hall shapes the practice and the (self)understanding of parliament – for example, the style, norms and values – and in the long run also reflects and becomes symbolic for a national political culture. Analysis of the interior should at least cover the shape, design and seating order of the plenary hall – and preferably also of the surrounding rooms.

Figure 13.1 Plenary hall of the French Assemblée Nationale, Paris. © Coucouoeuf, taken 3 July 2010. Source: Wikimedia Commons, reproduced on the basis of a CC BY-SA 3.0 licence. Available at https://commons.wikimedia.org/w/index.php?curid =21054979 (accessed 15 January 2023)

An intriguing intellectual-historical analysis of the shape of plenary halls as bearer of meaning comes from the German political scientist Philip Manow. In his *Im Schatten des Königs* (2008), Manow suggests that parliaments are an expression of a modern democratic mythology that grew directly out of the older monarchical mythology. After 1800, the traditional idea of the *body politic*, literally embodied by the monarch for centuries, gave way to the body of the sovereign people, the new *corpus morale*. The layout of modern democratic parliament rooms can still be seen as a schematic, symbolic representation, or deliberate replacement, of the aspects of the old body politic (Manow 2008, 2010).

With this, Manow introduces an important new perspective to explain why nation states all over the European continent after the French Revolution adopted a semicircular theatre arrangement for the plenary hall. While often explained by practical reasons and local circumstances, Manow points out that the adoption of the 'French model' on a deeper level refers to highly symbolic and fundamental thoughts on the new political order. The semicircle symbolised a post-monarchic order in which the 'body politic' of the monarch was replaced by parliament (Manow 2008, pp. 46–51 and chapter 2; Manow 2013; te Velde 2015).

Besides the basic layout of the plenary hall, the doings of parliament are reflected in and determined by other factors too. Careful reconstructions of parliamentary cultures and parliament as a working space, like those on the Weimar parliament by historian Thomas Mergel, and on the UK Houses of Parliament by political anthropologist Emma Crewe, provide us with evidence about a perceived influence of the physical surroundings of parliamentary debate on the style and form of the debate, as well as on constitutional and internal relations. Parliamentary cultures are likely to be swayed by circumstances such as the size, dimensions, design, arrangement and furnishing of the plenary hall (Mergel 2002; Crewe 2005; Hoetink 2018; see also Crewe in this volume).

Vice versa, certain norms of parliamentary debate, for example to what extent participants should reach out to the public, and ideals about the role of parliament as an institution, had an effect on the building itself and its use. Analysing the relation between political culture and parliamentary architecture means scrutinising a dynamic and interactive process, as Delphine Gardey argues in her stimulating microhistory of the French National Assembly in the long nineteenth century. Gardey demonstrates how fundamental political conceptions shaped the organisation of the National Assembly, which in turn had consequences for the building housing the Assembly, the design of which then structured the political and legislative processes taking place in it (Gardey 2015).

Less well studied, though not less telling, are the rooms surrounding the plenary hall. Yet histories of national parliaments offer abundant indication that a better understanding of the complex, including reception rooms and working plane, would add to our understanding of the role orientation and priorities of parliament. The spatial layout and the appearance of the entrance for example, the location of the committee rooms or the space reserved for restoration and informal gathering (Norton 2019), libraries or working space for officers, can reveal just as much about ideas on representation and governance as the spatial arrangement of the plenary hall. In this context, it is also important to recognise the narrative behind seemingly functionalist reorganisations of the parliament building. Which rooms and facilities are 'upgraded' and located close(r) to the plenary hall, at the cost of other facilities? Which facilities apparently need to be available and present in the building? Are the rooms open to all, or is access restricted to certain groups (defined, say, by gender, class, professional status or political affiliation)?

Interdisciplinary and comparative approach

If this overview of literature demonstrates one thing, it is that to really understand how parliamentary architecture 'works' – both internally and externally, in the short run and in the long term – a systematic interdisciplinary approach is invaluable. Only this will bring about a greater understanding of the architectural effect of parliament buildings, in the sense that it shapes and structures political practice and, at the same time, reflects and produces a specific political culture (Hoetink and Kaal 2018). Since parliament buildings are part of a *Gesamtkunstwerk* as previously defined, with a complex and layered narrative about the national past, the political system and the balance of powers, adopting such an integrated perspective would be a first step forward in the study of parliamentary architecture.

Although parliaments are, by political and historiographic tradition, strongly embedded in national histories, many similarities in their architectural style, layout and 'rhetoric' seem to point to transnational patterns. In fact, there is a historical, European-Atlantic design repertoire with several variants. This design tradition has spread globally through colonialism and, very concretely, through the British Commonwealth, so that parliaments as far as Sri Lanka and New Zealand could have been located in any European capital and contain numerous British furnishing elements that also influence the functioning of the order (Sudjic and Jones 2001, pp. 88–93; Roberts 2009). Goodsell only came as far as hinting to such transnational patterns. Other attempts to juxtapose several parliament buildings, such as the work of Minta and Nicolai, rather prove the point but fall short on explaining how ideas of parliamentary architecture spread the world (Minta and Nicolai 2014; Sablin and Bandeira 2021). Manow makes a convincing attempt to explain why the semicircle became the main seating plan for modern parliaments, but his study is also limited to that aspect.

A second important advancement in the study of parliamentary architecture, therefore, would be to adopt a systematic comparative approach. Or more precisely, to investigate parliament buildings along the lines of transfer and adaptation between different political cultures. In many ways this opens a whole new programme of research. The design, location and layout of the parliament buildings provide insight not only into the in-depth structure of national political cultures, but also into patterns of transnational imitation and exchange. Why do many parliament buildings look so similar, when in fact they are intended to represent the national political community and nationhood as such (Sudjic and Jones 2001, pp. 42–57; Aerts 2018, p. 109)?

Throughout time, culture, architecture and political power appear to be intertwined in all sorts of ways. The study of political culture, or of culture-specific aspects of politics, or of politics as culture, nowadays is considered an established paradigm within political history and political science. The spatial turn, which has manifested itself in many disciplines, has also given historians and political scientists a new angle for analysis and explanation. Now seems the time to start materialising this in the comparative and transnational study of parliament buildings.

References

Aerts, R. (2018) 'Architectuur en representatie: De cultuurgeschiedenis van politiek en ruimte', in R. Aerts, K. van Berkel and B. Hellemans (eds) *Alles is cultuur: vensters op moderne cultuurgeschiedenis*, Hilversum: Uitgeverij Verloren, pp. 94–109.

Aerts, R. and van den Berg, J.Th.J. (2019) 'The Ideal of Parliament in Europe Since 1800: Introduction', in R. Aerts, C. van Baalen, H. te Velde, M. van der Steen and M.-L. Recker. (eds) *The Ideal of Parliament in Europe Since 1800*, Cham: Palgrave Macmillan, pp. 1–22.

Alofsin, A. (2006) *When Buildings Speak: Architecture as Language in the Habsburg Empire and its Aftermath, 1867–1933*, Chicago: University of Chicago Press.

Andres, J., Geisthövel, A. and Schwengelbeck, M. (eds) (2001) *Die Sinnlichkeit der Macht: Herrschaft und Räpresentation seit den frühen Neuzeit*, Frankfurt: Campus Verlag.

Arndt, A. (1961) *Demokratie als Bauherr*, Berlin: Gebr. Mann.

Bagehot, W. (1867 [1963]) *The English Constitution*, Ithaca: Cornell University Press.

Baker, K.M. (ed.) (1987) *The French Revolution and the Creation of Modern Political Culture*, Oxford: Pergamon Press.

Bick, N. (2019) *Parliaments of the European Union*, Amsterdam: NAI Booksellers.

Biefang, A. (2002) *Bismarcks Reichstag: Das Parlament in der Leipziger Strasse*, Düsseldorf: Droste Verlag.

Biefang, A. (2003) 'Der Reichstag als Symbol der politischen Nation: Parlament und Öffentlichkeit 1867–1890', in L. Gall (ed.) *Regierung, Parlament und Öffentlichkeit im Zeitalter Bismarcks: Politikstile im Wandel*, Paderborn: F. Schöning, pp. 23–42.

Biefang, A. (2009) *Die andere Seite der Macht: Reichstag und Öffentlichkeit im 'System Bismark'*, Düsseldorf: Droste Verlag.

Blanning, T.C.W. (2002) *The Culture of Power and the Power of Culture: Old Regine Europe 1660–1789*, Oxford: Oxford University Press.

Braungart, W. (2012) *Ästhetik der Politik: Ästhetik des Politischen. Ein Versuch in Thesen*, Göttingen: De Gruyter.

Brendger, G. (2008) *Demokratisches Bauen: Eine architekturtheoretische Diskursanalyse zu Parlamentsbauten in der Bundesrepublik Deutschlands*, Dresden: Technische Universität Dresden.

Burke, P. (1991) *The Fabrication of Louis XIV*, New Haven, CT and London: Yale University Press.

Crewe, E. (2005) *Lords of Parliament: Manners, Rituals and Politics*, Manchester: Manchester University Press.

Crewe, E. (2021) *The Anthropology of Parliaments: Entanglements in Democratic Politics*, Abingdon and New York: Routledge.

Döring, H. (1995) 'Die Sitzordnung der Abgeordneten: Ausdruck kulturell divergierender Auffassungen von Demokratie?' in A. Dörner and L. Vogt (eds) *Sprache des Parlaments und Semiotik der Demokratie: Studien zur politischen Kommunikation in der Moderne*, Berlin and New York: De Gruyter, pp. 278–289.

Dörner, A. and Vogt, L. (eds) (1995) *Sprache des Parlaments und Semiotik der Demokratie: Studien zur politischen Kommunikation in der Moderne*, Berlin and New York: Walter de Gruyter.

Flagge, I. and Stock, W.J. (eds) (1992) *Architektur und Demokratie: Bauen für die Politik von der amerikanischen Revolution bis zur Gegenwart*, Stuttgart: Hatje.

Foucault, M. (1984) 'Space, knowledge and power', in P. Rabinow (ed.) *The Foucault Reader*, New York: Pantheon Books, pp. 239–252.

Frevert, U. and Haupt, H.-G. (eds) (2005) *Neue Politikgeschichte: Perspektiven einer historischen Politikforschung*, Frankfurt and New York: Campus Verlag.

Gardey, D. (2015) *Le Ligne du Palais-Bourbon: Corps, matérialité et genre du politique à l'ère démocratique*, Lormont: Le Bord de L'eau.

Goodsell, C. (1988a) 'The architecture of parliaments: legislative houses and political culture', *British Journal of Political Science*, 18(3), pp. 287–302. https://www.jstor.org/stable /193839.

Goodsell, C. (1988b) *The Social Meaning of Civic Space: Studying Political Authority through Architecture*, Lawrence: University Press of Kansas.

Goodsell, C. (2001) *The American Statehouse: Interpreting Democracy's Temples*, Lawrence: University Press of Kansas.

Götze, W. (1960) *Das Parlamentsgebäude: Historische und ikonologische Studien zu einer Bauaufgabe*, PhD thesis, Leipzig University.

Hoetink, C. (2018) *Macht der gewoonte: regels en rituelen in de Tweede Kamer na 1945*, Nijmegen: Van Tilt.

Hoetink, C. and Kaal, H. (2018) 'Designed to represent: parliamentary architecture, conceptions of democracy, and emotions in the postwar Netherlands architecture', in T. Grossmann and P. Nielsen (eds) *Architecture, Democracy, and Emotions: The Politics of Feeling since 1945*, London and New York: Routledge, pp. 18–38.

Judge, D. and Leston-Bandeira, C. (2018) 'The institutional representation of parliament', *Political Studies*, 66(1), pp. 154–172. DOI: 10.1177/0032321717706901.

Krul, W. (2011) 'Grote gebaren en een compromis: Bouwplannen op het Binnenhof (1848–1914)', in H. te Velde and D. Smit (eds) *Van Torentje tot Trêveszaal: De geschiedenis van de noordzijde van het Binnenhof*, The Hague: De Nieuwe Haagse, pp. 209–232.

Kühn, C. and Österreichische Gesellschaft für Architektur (2014) *Plenum: Orte der macht*. Sonderausgabe Biennale Venedig 2014, Basel: Birkhäuser.

Kümin, B. and Usborne, C. (2013), 'At home and in the workplace: a historical introduction to the "spatial turn"', *History and Theory*, 52(3), pp. 305–318. http://www.jstor.org/stable /24542988.

Lankes, C. (1995) *Politik und Architektur: Eine Studie zur Wirkung politischer Kommunikation auf Bauten staatlicher Repräsentation*, Münich: Tuduv.

Leoussi, A. and Brincker, B. (2018) 'Anthony D. Smith and the role of art, architecture and music in the growth of modern nations: a comparative study of national parliaments and classical music in Britain and Denmark', *Nations and Nationalism*, 24(2), pp. 312–326. DOI: 10.1111/ nana.12409.

Leoussi, A., Payne, G. and Sulak, D. (2020) 'The language of freedom: democracy, humanity, and nationality in the architecture and art of the modern European national parliament', in J. Stone, R.M. Dennis, P. Rizova and X. Hou (eds) *The Wiley Blackwell Companion to Race, Ethnicity, and Nationalism*, New Jersey: Wiley, pp. 245–276.

Manow, P. (2008) *Im Schatten des Königs*, Frankfurt: Suhrkamp.

Manow, P. (2010) *In the King's Shadow: The Political Anatomy of Democratic Representation*, Cambridge: Polity.

Manow, P. (2013) 'Kuppel, Rostra, Sitzordnung: Das architektonische Bilderprogramm moderner Parlamente', in J. Feuchter and J. Helmrath (eds) *In Parlamentarische Kulturen vom Mittelalter bis in die Moderne. Reden, Räume, Bilder*, Düsseldorf: Droste Verlag, pp. 115–129.

Mayo, J.M. (1996) 'The manifestation of politics in architectural practice', *Journal of Architectural Education*, 50(2), pp. 76–88. DOI: 10.2307/1425358.

McNamara, K. (2015) 'Building culture: the architecture and geography of governance in the European Union', in S. Börner and M. Eigmüller (eds) *European Integration, Processes of Change and the National Experience*, Basingstoke: Palgrave, pp. 100–117.

Mergel, T. (2002) *Parlamentarische Kultur in der Weimarer Republik: Politische Kommunikation, symbolische Politik und Öffentlichkeit im Reichstag*, Düsseldorf: Droste Verlag.

Milne, D. (1981) 'Architecture, politics, and the public realm', *Canadian Journal of Political and Social Theory*, 5(1–2), pp. 131–146.

Minkenberg, M. (2014) 'Power and architecture: the construction of capitals, the politics of space, and the space of politics', in M. Minkenberg (ed.) *Power and Architecture: The Construction of Capitals and the Politics of Space*, New York and Oxford: Berghahn Books, pp. 1–30.

Minta, A. and Nicolai, B. (eds) (2014) *Parlamentarische Repräsentationen: Das Bundeshaus in Bern im Kontext internationaler Parlamentsbauten und nationaler Strategien*, Bern et al.: Peter Lang.

Mulder van der Vegt, D. and Cohen de Lara, M. (2016) *Parliament*, Amsterdam: XML

Mumford, L. (1961) *The City in History: Its Origins, Its Transformations, and Its Prospects*, London: Harcourt, Brace & World.

Münzing, H.J. (1977) *Parlamentsgebäude: Geschichte, Funktion, Gestalt; Versuch einer Übersicht*, Stuttgart: University of Stuttgart (unpublished dissertation).

Norton, P. (2019) 'Power behind the scenes: the importance of informal space in legislatures', *Parliamentary Affairs*, 72(2), pp. 245–266. DOI: 10.1093/pa/gsy018.

Paulmann, J. (2000) *Pomp und Politik: Monarchenbegegnungen min Europa zwischen Ancien Régime und Erstem Weltkrieg*, Paderborn: F. Schöningh.

Paulus, S. (2012) '"Das baulige Herz der Demokratie": Parlamentsarchitektur im öffentlichen Raum', in A. Schulz and A. Wirsching (eds) *Das Parlament als Kommunikationsraum*, Düsseldorf: Droste Verlag, pp. 389–422.

Rai, S. and Sparry, C. (2018) *Performing Representation: Women Members in the Indian Parliament*, New Delhi and Oxford: Oxford University Press.

Rau, S. (2013) *Räume, Konzepte, Wahrnemungen, Nutzungen*, Frankfurt and New York: Fischer Taschenbuch Verlag.

Riding, C. and Riding, J. (2000) *The Houses of Parliament: History, Art and Architecture*, London: Merrel.

Roberts, N.S. (2009) 'Grand designs: parliamentary architecture, art, and accessibility', *Political Science*, 61(2), pp. 75–86. DOI: 10.1177/00323187090610020601.

Sablin, I. and Bandeira, E.M. (2021) *Planting Parliaments in Eurasia, 1850–1950: Concepts, Practices and Mythologies*, London and New York: Routledge.

Schirmer, D. (1995) 'Politik und Architektur: Ein Beitrag zur politischen Symbolanalyse am Beispiel Washingtons', in A. Dörner and L. Vogt (eds) *Sprache des Parlaments und Semiotik der Demokratie: Studien zur politischen Kommunikation in der Moderne*, Berlin and New York: De Gruyter, pp. 309–339.

Schlögel, K. (2003) *Im Raume lesen wir die Zeit: Über Zivilisationsgeschichte und Geopolitik*, Berlin: Hanser Verlag.

Schwengelbeck, M. (2007) *Die Politik des Zeremoniells: Huldigungsfeiern im langen 19. Jahrhundert*, Frankfurt: Campus Verlag.

Seidel, A. (1988) 'Political behavior and physical design: an introduction', *Environment and Behavior*, 20(5), pp. 531–536. DOI: 10.1177/0013916588205001.

Shimizu, Y. and Naraoka, S. (2014) 'Shaping the diet: competing architectural designs for Japan's Diet building', *Legislative Architectures and Processes in Asia*, CP11. Sydney: Australian Political Studies Association. DOI: 10.2139/ssrn.2490873.

Smit, D. (2015) *Het belang van het Binnenhof: Twee eeuwen Haagse politiek, huisvesting en herinnering*, Amsterdam: Wereldbibliotheek.

Stollberg-Rilinger, B. (ed.) (2005) *Was heisst Kulturgeschichte des Politischen?* Berlin: Zeitschrift für Historische Forschung. Beihefte.

Sudjic, D. and Jones, H. (2001) *Architecture and Democracy*, London and Glasgow: Laurence King Publishing.

Tally, R.T. (2013) *Spatiality*, London and New York: Routledge.

te Velde, H. (2015) *Sprekende politiek: Redenaars en hun publiek in de Gouden Eeuw*, Amsterdam: Prometheus.

Vale, L. (1992) *Architecture, Power and National Identity*, London: Routledge.

Van der Wusten, H. (2004) 'Public authority in European capitals: a map of governance, an album with symbols', *European Review*, 12, pp. 143–158.

van Riet, M. and Van Bakel, G. (2002) *Architectuur en democratie: Bouwen voor de volksvertegenwoordiging*, Den Haag: Tweede Kamer der Staten-Generaal.

von Beyme, K. (1971) '"Politische Kultur" und "Politischer Stil": Zur Rezeption Zweier Begriffe aus den Kulturwissenschaften', in K. von Beyme (ed.) *Theory and Politics/Theorie und Politik. Festschrift zum 70. Geburtstag für Carl Joachim Friedrich*, The Hague: Martinus Nijhoff, pp. 352–374.

von Beyme, K. (1991) 'Architecture and democracy in the Federal Republic of Germany', *International Political Science Review*, 12(2), pp. 137–147.

Warnke, M. (1984) *Politische Architektur in Europa (vom Mittelalter bis heute Repräsentation und Gemeinschaft*, Cologne: Dumont.

Wilhelm, K. (2001) 'Demokratie als Bauherr: Überlegungen zum Charakter der Berliner politischen repräsentationsbauten', *Aus Politik und Zeitgeschichte*, 34–35, pp. 7–15.

Part IV

Political transitions and constructions of legitimacy

14

Architectures of power and the Romanian transition

From the House of the Republic to the Palace of the Parliament

Gruia Bădescu and Iulia Stătică[1]

Introduction

What is the burden for a small, young democracy of having the world's largest parliament building, and one that was erected by a recent dictator, no less? Romania's parliament is an embodiment of both the aspirations of an authoritarian regime to shape the material-architectural apparatus of power as well as of the challenges of a tumultuous political transition. Therefore, we ask: in what manner can architectures of power be associated with both totalitarian regimes *and* democracy? We address the case of the Romanian Palace of the Parliament through a genealogy of its space, and through its impact on present displays of civic engagement. As such, the chapter opens the discussion on political transitions and constructions of legitimacy by exploring three questions: how an authoritarian regime has shaped its parliament; how such spaces are reshaped during transitional periods and by aspirations of reflecting democracy; and how protest and civic engagement challenge architectures that supposedly express the power of the people. We will see how the relationship between architecture and power becomes essential in building not only specific aspirations of a dictator, but also how symbols associated with them within a democracy interfere with forms of civic practices. When it comes to the monumental expression of power, the Romanian parliament building in Bucharest is unparalleled in Europe: the world's heaviest building, and among the largest and most expensive to run on the planet. Central point of Nicolae Ceaușescu's *Victory of Socialism* Boulevard and of the *Civic Centre* urban project of the 1980s, it has been often described in the literature as a megalomaniac structure to embody power, reorient space and fulfil the political vision of a 'new city' for the 'new human' of Romanian socialism (Barris 2001; Iosa 2006, 2011; Ioan 2007; Light and Young 2013). However, less has been written about how this monolithic architectural form has been adapted to become the Parliament of Romania after the 1989 fall of Ceauşescu's regime, and what is its symbolic role within the rich topography of protests from the recent years. By focusing on continuities and frictions between different spatial visions, this chapter explores the spatial construction of political practice in the Romanian democracy. Through developing a genealogy of this space, the chapter enquires into the relationship between explicit representations of power and the transformation and reappropriation of architecture and the urban fabric still carrying material, political and ethical traces of a contested past.

Genealogies of power

Part of the extensive programme of transformation of Bucharest during Nicolae Ceauşescu's dictatorship, the then-called House of the Republic marked a turning point in the constitution of a new urbanism, one that related to a territorial scale through vast demolitions of the historical fabric and that was closely linked to the construction of the Civic Centre. The project was presented as celebrating the fortieth anniversary of the 'revolution of social and national liberation', and made public in 1984 as the national expression of socialism (Zahariade 2011). Seen as the future kernel of Bucharest, the project was imagined to be the symbolic and representative centre of the city, around which the rest of the city – a homogeneous periphery – would develop as an urban and architectural model easily constructible and above all reproducible (Racolta 2010). The final project consisted of two main elements: the central axis, the Victory of Socialism Avenue – 120 metres wide and 4.5 kilometres long – and its ending point, the House of the Republic (Figures 14.1 and 14.2).

Starting in the mid-1970s, the systematisation of Bucharest initiated an intense construction of mass housing, and aimed at discarding the idea of the city as an archipelago formed of isolated *cvartals* – comparatively small urban housing projects – and *microrayons* – larger residential districts – instituted in the 1950s, following the USSR model. While the 1950s and the 1960s had witnessed the expansion of the city through mass housing construction, the Law of Systematisation of 1974 marked a shift in the urban development. The new regulations proposed to create a scientifically organised city, one that not only developed in the peripheries, but that incorporated the centre, including the historical

Figure 14.1   View (1989) towards the House of the Republic, today the Romanian Palace of the Parliament. © Sorin Vasilescu

Figure 14.2   View (1989) from the balcony of the House of the Republic, today the Romanian Palace of the Parliament, towards the Victory of Socialism Avenue, today Union Boulevard. © Sorin Vasilescu

fabric of the city. Urban elements that had been abandoned in the preceding communist decades – such as the street and the monument – were rescued during Ceauşescu's regime in the endeavour to reimagine the city. On the one hand, the street again became significant in the urban structure insofar as it is delimited by housing blocks. On the other hand, while heritage was being dismantled – with the dissolution of the Commission for Historical Monuments in 1977 – the idea of the monument was recovered. A new type of monument replaced the early socialist pseudo-modernist approach of a city with no landmarks as an attempt to detach the city from associations with tradition. With its volume and dominance over the urban landscape, and recognisability, the architecture of the House of the Republic epitomises the idea of the monument in a very literal sense, the same way in which the so-called Victory of Socialism Avenue epitomises the idea of the street. The destruction produced during the great earthquake of 1977 was seen as an opportunity by Ceauşescu to impose his own political agenda through the process of the reconstruction of the city, and a means of legitimising an entire campaign of demolitions (Ghyka and Călin 2018). While entire districts were demolished to make room for the new project of the Civic Centre, private homeowners were relocated in new apartment blocks spread all over the city (Giurescu 1989). The construction of the Civic Centre, which marks the climax of an urban modernity (Althabe 1996), involved the demolition of a fifth of historic Bucharest – an area of more than 500 hectares – and included the relocation of over 40,000 people (Iosa 2006).

Following a multistage national competition, in 1981, Anca Petrescu was chosen to head the project. It is important to emphasise the choice of Petrescu, a 27-year-old woman, as its principal architect in connection to the political articulation of gender in late socialist Romania. One might argue that the question of scale is generally politicised and often gendered, insofar as women have historically been identified with the intimate scale of the domestic space, while men were usually the main figures of the public, political sphere (Gieseking 2018; Steiner and Veel 2020). In our specific case, associating women with a massive scale that represents the political becomes a way of reaffirming their desired – at least in the official discourse – emancipation. The gesture of choosing a young woman as the leader of the colossal project has to be read as a statement to reaffirm her significance as a public figure, and in this way as an essential aspect in the literal construction of socialism. While generally Anca Petrescu was the subject of harsh criticism among her architect colleagues, we argue that her position within the project is more nuanced and her choice in leading the project was deeply embedded in the political rhetoric. She should not be seen as the mere sole author of the House – the position she herself claimed after 1990 (Vais 2017) – but rather as instrumental to the political project, and more specifically to Ceauşescu's vision. We might also note here that this needs to be seen against a general contested background whereby women's intimate agency was undermined by a restrictive legal framework that emphasised both their productive and reproductive duties (Kligman 2000). At the same time, bringing a woman to the forefront as the architect of the monument of socialist power symbolises its association with notions of maternity and thus of a creative agency capable of, and charged with the creation of the *new socialist person*. Anca Petrescu herself, as a young architect leading the vast project, became the very symbol of the *new socialist woman*: modern, educated and a mother. Situated on the Spirii Hill – the highest topography of the city – and occupying more than 330,000 square metres,[2] the House of the Republic was to embody the image of socialist power, and to centralise all the governing institutions of the state: the headquarters and committee of the Communist party, the government and the ministerial headquarters, as well as the republic's presidency (Panaitescu 2012). Its envisioning as a landscape rather than as a building – which violently replaced a significant part of the historical fabric of Bucharest – aimed to create not just a physical object, but a symbolic site for the projection of specific political and cultural ideals. Nature – in the form of the highest topography of the city – becomes integral to the architectural project, and functions as a pedestal for the monument. The House of the Republic thus embodies the excessive scale of power, along with ideas of growth and progress, while expressing contradictory affects and motivations such as surveillance, inequality or megalomania. The state's totalising role that has been explicit in the production of mass housing construction throughout the socialist regime is now replaced by the figural role of the monument of power.

Transitioning back to origin

In December 1989, Nicolae Ceauşescu was deposed during a violent uprising, understood at the time and in the post-socialist culture of remembrance as a revolution (Siani-Davies 2007). Nevertheless, the transition of the 1990s was marked by continuities of elites, including the conversion of the former Communist party and the Securitate (secret police) into main actors of the political scene and the privatisation processes (Gallagher 2005). The communist past, while decried by intellectual circles, was not scrutinised by state actors until the 2000s, when it was criminalised through a presidential commission (Tănăsoiu 2007; Stan 2013). The fate of the House of the Republic mirrored this political evolution. While there were calls from the public in 1990 to demolish the building, still unfinished, as a symbol of authoritarianism, the state resumed the works interrupted by the uprising and completed the building well into the 1990s. A shift in public opinion occurred when the site was briefly opened for visits in 1990: many of the Bucharest residents who queued and visited the palace became aware of the great amount of labour and materials put into the site and were convinced that it was too late to demolish. Symbolically, the House of the Republic had become the House of the People (*Casa Poporului*), which has remained its most common informal name among the population. Alternative proposals for its makeover came from artists and businessmen in Romania and abroad: the largest casino in the world, a hotel, a new stock exchange to match the new capitalist economy or a museum of communism (Light and Young 2013; Duijzings 2018).

Yet the building became what it was intended to be. The House of the Republic was remade into the Palace of the Parliament. As such, the structure which materialised the aspirations of Ceauşescu's political project was re-metabolised as the representative building for democracy. In March 1993, the Romanian parliament decided that the Chamber of Deputies, the lower house of the parliament, would be moved to the House of the People. The Senate, the upper house, was also relocated to the building in 2005. The two chambers moved from two buildings with distinctive historical-political meaning. The Chamber of Deputies was previously located in a palace built in 1907 in the French Beaux-Arts style prevalent in Bucharest on the Patriarchate Hill, next door to the headquarters of the Romanian Orthodox Church. The palace had been the seat of the National Assembly in Romania during both the kingdom years and the socialist period. The Senate was moved to the House of the Republic from the building that housed, until 1989, the Central Committee of the Communist party, featuring the balcony from where Ceauşescu gave his last speech.[3] The 1989 Revolution began in front of that building, which has in fact a longer history of association with authoritarianism. The construction of what was originally intended as a Ministry of Internal Affairs began in 1938, just as King Carol II installed a royal dictatorship to respond to the growth of the far-right Iron Guard movement and to what he saw as the weaknesses of democracy. The building was erected in a severe neoclassical style typical of the political buildings sponsored by the king in the city, intended to evoke authority during times of political upheaval. The post-1989 Romanian democracy thus originally housed its two parliament chambers in buildings that have rather distinctive pasts, one related to a longer tradition of democracy and the other to two authoritarian regimes. The two chambers came to coexist in the House of the Republic, thus realising Ceauşescu's intention for the building to be the administrative centre of Romania. As Augustin Ioan (2007) pointed out, the one thing missing from fulfilling Ceauşescu's dream was the relocation of the presidential headquarters, which in post-socialist Romania has been housed in the nineteenth-century Cotroceni Palace, not far away from the Palace of the Parliament.

In 1995–1996, the area around the House of the Republic became the subject of a large international architectural competition. The initiative of the Union of Architects of Romania was supported by the Ministry of Public Works and Territorial Planning and the competition was organised by the City Hall of Bucharest under the patronage of the president of Romania. As such, it looked at the time to be a project of national priority. Entitled Bucharest 2000, it aimed to give a new vision to the site and to address the 'urban wounds' that the 1980s operation created (Barris 2001; Ghyka 2015). While the competition called for the House of the Republic to be left in place, multiple projects suggested its symbolic destruction (Barris 2001). Nevertheless, one entry, surprisingly awarded fourth place, included three additional classical parade courts on the north, south and west sides of the palace, catering to the Versailles metaphor of the 1980s (Ioan 2007). The winning solution, focused on reducing the impact of the palace on the cityscape by inserting office buildings on all sides, never materialised, as the City Hall shelved the project by 2000 (Iosa 2006; Ioan 2007).

Two significant modifications did occur to the site. First, there was the insertion of the National Museum of Contemporary Art (MNAC) in a wing of the building. This was intended to revamp the site, but was contested by Anca Petrescu as an unacceptable alteration of her vision (Jurnalul 2006). The main supporter of the MNAC project was Adrian Năstase, the prime minister from the Social Democratic party, seen as the party created by former communists. It was realised between 2003 and 2004, thus a mere six years from the completion of the palace. According to Adrian Spirescu, one of its architects, the design team debated whether to have an intervention based on rupture and resignification or one of dialogue with the existing structure. The final approach came from the decision to favour the conversation with the building and the cohabitation of the museum with the palace. This was seen as a response to the aggressive nature of the 1980s intervention, with the conciliatory gesture understood as a way to move forward without repeating the mistakes of the past.[4] One change was made, namely a glass annex and two lifts on each side. This brought critique from Anca Petrescu, who called the additions 'a ringworm on the façade of the Palace of the Parliament' (Jurnalul 2006) and opened legal action for a breach of copyright. Nevertheless, critics such as architect Ștefan Ghenciulescu (2006) pointed to the irony of the lawsuit for a small intervention on a building that itself was the result of a 'frightening destruction'. Anca Petrescu was in fact a member of the parliament at that time, representing the nationalist Greater Romania party. The MNAC stayed on the site, and several contemporary artists refused to even come to the space. Moreover, in time, the museum's presence in the parliament building became a hot issue for the two chambers of parliament, with claims that it constituted a possible breach of security. As such, sources indicated that there had been continuous pressure to relocate the museum elsewhere, including the refusal to pay for the repair of the access road and various security regulations. Initiated with the desire to reactivate the space, its relatively isolated location and the security hurdles have hurt the MNAC.

The second significant change on the premises was the construction of the People's Salvation Cathedral in the large empty space behind the palace (Tateo 2020). Religion joined secular politics in an urban ensemble, mirroring the old arrangement on the Patriarchate Hill, but expanded to gargantuan proportions. Indeed, the dimensions of the new cathedral are voluminous; it appears on one side of the Palace of the Parliament as a taller structure, disrupting the symmetric front view achieved in the 1980s. As such, instead of the mitigating effects of the Bucharest 2000 winning solution, the cityscape remained faithful to Ceaușescu's vision, yet with an iconoclastic addition to the socialist project: a gigantic church, marking the renewed importance of the Orthodox Church in post-1989 Romania.

Moreover, the former House of the Republic saw another symbolic reshaping moment in 2008, when it housed the twentieth summit of NATO, the organisation which opposed the Warsaw Pact of which Ceaușescu's Romania was a member.

The wall of democracy

In the Romanian public sphere, the debate on the relationship between the architecture of power and the new Romanian democracy has been focused on the exterior wall of the complex. Almost three kilometres long, it separates the parliament compound from the city streets and squares of what was intended to be the Civic Centre. A number of public figures have pointed out that the wall is incompatible with the transparency of democracy, keeping the Romanian parliament as a fortress that excludes citizens, and as such echoing its dictatorial past rather than its allegedly open present. Architects were at the forefront of the campaign to remove the wall. For instance, architect and cultural entrepreneur Teodor Frolu, one of the artisans of the Integrated Urban Development Plan for Central Bucharest which advocated for the wall's removal, stated that:

> The problem is that public space is not used by residents of the Capital. It was conceived as a buffer space by the *Securitate*. Although Parliament seems to be well installed in this particular framework, we insisted on giving it back to the citizens through the creation of a large park (DC News 2012).

A number of politicians supported the idea of tearing down the wall and creating an open park, including a minister of tourism, a head of the Chamber of Deputies, and one district mayor. In August 2013, as Pink Floyd gave a concert in Bucharest, the president of the Chamber of Deputies and the band's lead Roger Waters hit the wall with a sledgehammer. Capitalising on the band's famous song 'The Wall', the Romanian politician gave Waters a piece of the wall, underlining the symbolic gesture that would have broken the barrier between the parliament of a democratic Romania and its citizens.

The Chamber of Deputies launched a competition for the area around the parliament. The winning project proposed a relandscaping centred on Romanian identity, by suggesting seven thematic gardens corresponding to Romanian landscapes, including mountains and the Danube Delta. Yet the wall remained. The opposition to these projects came from the political class mainly with regards to 'security concerns' and for the costs of the demolition. A former prime minister pointed out that the demolition of the wall would cost around 6 million euros, which would be a luxury for the struggling Romanian budget.

The most recent attempt to tear it down came from an architect-led project, supported by a new political movement. A team of architects from Bucharest and Copenhagen submitted a proposal in 2018 to remove the wall to create a large urban park. Connecting it with the Izvor Park – a large green area replacing a historic neighbourhood demolished in the 1980s – and the unused urban void behind the 1980s Romanian Academy, this new Uranus Park would be one of the city's largest and would 'bring the area back to the people'. The examples of Berlin, Ottawa and Oslo came to the forefront – the argument was that most parliaments in Europe are spatially connected with citizens. Architecture and landscaping were seen as central to redemocratising the public sphere. This project was supported by the Save Romania Union, a party created by former NGO activists with the intent to renew Romanian democracy, and quickly entered parliament, capitalising on the disgruntlement of young voters with the political establishment shaped by the Romanian transition. While not yet adopted, the debate erupts time and again, highlighting both the view associating spatial openness with democracy, and the opposing platform of the politics of security.

Spaces of contestation: reshaping symbolic topographies of protest

If the question of openness of the Palace of the Parliament within the broader landscape has been discussed among architects, urban planners and NGOs for the past two decades, the issue has become a constitutive feature of recent rebellions against various instances of power. Taking the case of two of the most recent sets of protests, we may note both resonances and contrasts with established symbolic topographies within the city.

First, we refer to the vast protests sparked by the deaths of 64 people in a fire at Colectiv Club in Bucharest at the end of October 2015 and the subsequent deaths in state hospitals, all seen as symptomatic of state collapse (Mucci 2015). Tens of thousands of protesters took to the square in front of the parliament, with 'corruption kills' as the main slogan (Cretan and O'Brien 2020). Second, a number of significantly larger protests, also centred on an anti-corruption platform, took place in Bucharest between 2017 and 2019. Peaking at half a million protesters in early February 2017, they assembled against the emergency decree of the government to grant amnesty for a wide array of corruption acts, as well as to amend the penal code in a way that would have led to the acquittal of numerous politicians convicted for non-violent crimes (Păun 2017).

Both the protests around Colectiv and the anti-corruption protests between 2017 and 2019 started in University Square and marched towards Victoriei Square, in front of the government building, or towards the Palace of the Parliament, depending on what political body was supposed to take decisions. The place of departure – University Square – was a key symbolic space for the 1989 Revolution, and thus carried an important value in the symbolic topography of the city. Victoriei Square became a symbol of the fight against corruption, with images of the filled

Figure 14.3 Anti-corruption protest in front of the Palace of the Parliament, January 2018. © Gruia Bădescu

square becoming emblematic, as did those of police brutality during a large protest in August 2019. The space around the parliament, while also the stage of protests, became less viral, with the exception of images of protests in front of the wall (see Figure 14.3).

However, more recent protests have produced a shift in this symbolic topography of rebellion. In December 2021, protesters gathered to oppose the measures negotiated by the government to pass a new bill that would introduce mandatory vaccination against COVID for most workers. Thousands of supporters of the right-wing populist and nationalist Alliance for the Union of Romanians (Alianța pentru Uniunea Românilor) gathered in front of the parliament building.[5] Hundreds of rioters forced their way into the parliament, vandalising cars and trying to enter the building.

It is interesting to observe that this protest started at the Palace of the Parliament, generically still remembered in the collective imaginary as the House of the People. From this perspective, we may also note that it marks a new language of rebellion that acts on a new symbolic ground, reclaiming new urban symbols for the populist, nationalist discourse. Nevertheless, the resurrection of the Palace of the Parliament in the revolutionary configurations of Bucharest is significant insofar as it brings to light a new discourse: the symbolic crossing of the wall around the building of the parliament becomes a symbolic way of speaking about the popular power over a potential democratic crisis. Emerging as an act of violence against the building itself – and in this way paralleling the violence of the *tabula rasa* generated by the very building of this complex during socialism – the December riots at the Palace of the Parliament reinforced 'the stereotypical representation of the revolution' and the confluence of its initiators, mostly men, towards a new symbolic site of democracy (Cherstich, Holbraad and Tassi 2020, p. 14).

In articulating a divergent topography of rebellion, these protests contribute both to a centralisation of specific civic encounters, as well as to a hierarchisation of the symbolic structures of the city. In doing so, they emphasise ruptures not only with the past, but also within the present, and make clear the limits of transitions from authoritarian regimes themselves to clear away the ghosts of radical national projects. In contrast to a desire for designed transparency, in EU member Romania, the wall which was part of the initial 1980s' vision for the state building has endured decades after. It has become a symbol of opposition from architects and NGOs, as well as for disenchanted protesters.

Conclusion

This chapter has highlighted, on the one hand, continuities in the treatment of space beyond the mere survival of the architectural monolith of the Romanian parliament building. On the other hand, it showed how its wall – despite its relative fragility when compared to the building itself – has remained a symbol of both power and transgression, and its continued presence has eliminated any possibility for public appropriation apart from violence. We have addressed the House of the Republic through a genealogy of becoming the Palace of the Parliament, and have seen how, rather than fading away, the symbolic distinction still resurfaces with vigour into tensioned practices. While in the case of the official institutional reappropriation the process has been rather straightforward, in the political unconscious of the city, its presence has stirred at once rebellious and disobedient attitudes. Nevertheless, the post-communist reappropriations of the space reside in the ability of contemporary imaginaries to highlight unexpected interpretations and re-significations, and at the same time to multiply its understandings as radical visions of civic engagement.

Notes

1 While writing this article Iulia Stătică received funding from the European Union's Horizon 2020 research and innovation programme under the Marie Skłodowska-Curie Postdoctoral Individual Fellowship grant agreement no. 840633.
2 As a comparison in terms of dimension, it is worth remembering that the proposed project for the Palace of Soviets occupied an area of 36,800 square metres (Racolta 2010, p. 165).
3 The Romanian Senate, created in 1866, was dissolved in 1940 and did not exist throughout the entire socialist period, when the National Assembly acted as the sole legislative body.
4 https://www.adrianspirescu.ro/proiecte/mnac (accessed on 15 October 2020).
5 Founded in September 2019, AUR gained wide popularity within a short time, and obtained almost 50 seats in the parliament during the June 2020 elections.

References

Althabe, G. (1996) 'Le Centre Civique De Bucarest', Éditions Parenthèses, pp. 147–151. DOI: 10.4000/enquete.823.

Barris, R. (2001) 'Contested Mythologies: The Architectural Deconstruction of a Totalitarian Culture', Journal of Architectural Education, 54(4), pp. 229–237. DOI: 10.1162/104648 80152474547.

Cherstich, I., Holbraad, M. and Tassi, N. (2020) Anthropologies of Revolution: Forging Time, People, and Worlds, Berkeley: University of California Press.

Crețan, R. and O'Brien, T. (2020) 'Corruption and Conflagration: (In)justice and Protest in Bucharest after the Colectiv Fire', Urban Geography, 41(3), pp. 368–388. DOI: 10.1080/02723638.2019.1664252.

DC News (2012) 'Zidul lui Ceaușescu, demolat. Centrul Istoric, legat cu un pod de Palatul Parlamentului', 27 November. Available from: https://www.dcnews.ro/zidul-lui-ceausescu -demolat-centrul-istoric-legat-cu-un-pod-de-palatul-parlamentului_253608.html

Duijzings, G. (2018) 'Transforming a Totalitarian Edifice: Artistic and Ethnographic Engagements with the House of the People in Bucharest', in C. Raudvere (ed.) Nostalgia, Loss and Creativity in South-East Europe, Cham: Palgrave Macmillan, pp. 11–36. DOI: 10.1007/978-3 -319-71252-9_2.

Gallagher, T. (2005) Modern Romania: The End of Communism, the Failure of Democratic Reform, and the Theft of a Nation, New York: New York University Press.

Ghenciulescu, S. (2006) 'Editorial: Copyright la Casa Poporului', Arhitectura, No. 46. Available from: https://e-zeppelin.ro/editorial-copyright-la-casa-poporului/.

Ghyka, C. (2015) 'Defining Spatial Violence: Bucharest as a Study Case', Diversité et identité culturelle en Europe, 12, p. 37.

Ghyka, C. and Călin, D. (2018) 'Reverse-engineering Political Architecture: The House of the People and Its Hidden Social Effects', Studies in History and Theory of Architecture: Politics. Too Much or Not Enough, 6, pp. 108–125.

Gieseking, J.J. (2018) 'Size Matters to Lesbians, Too: Queer Feminist Interventions into the Scale of Big Data', The Professional Geographer, 70(1), pp. 150–156. DOI: 10.1080/00330124 .2017.1326084.

Giurescu, D. (1989) The Razing of Romania's Past, International Preservation Report.

Ioan, A. (2007) 'The Peculiar History of (Post) Communist Public Places and Spaces: Bucharest as a Case Study', in K. Stanilov (ed.) The Post-Socialist City, New York: Springer, pp. 301–312.

Iosa, I. (2006) L'Héritage Urbain de Ceaușescu: Fardeau Ou Saut En Avant? Paris: L'Harmattan.

Iosa, I. (2011) Bucarest: L'emblème D'une Nation, Rennes: Presses Universitaires De Rennes.

Jurnalul. (2006) 'Anca Petrescu Despre MNAC', 17 June. Available from: https://jurnalul.ro/stiri /observator/precizari-anca-petrescu-despre-mnac-18903.html.

Kligman, G. (2000) Politica duplicității: Controlul reproducerii în România lui Ceaușescu, Bucharest: Humanitas.

Light, D. and Young, C. (2013) 'Urban Space, Political Identity and the Unwanted Legacies of State Socialism: Bucharest's Problematic Centru Civic in the Post-Socialist Era', Nationalities Papers, 41(4), pp. 515–535. DOI: 10.1080/00905992.2012.743512.

Mucci, A. (2015) '"Corruption kills" protests won't stop with Ponta', *Politico*, 6 November. Available from: https://www.politico.eu/article/corruption-kills-protests-ponta-romania-resignation / (accessed 10 May 2022).

Panaitescu, A. (2012) *De la Casa Scânteii la Casa Poporului: Patru decenii de arhitectură în Bucureşti 1945–1989*, Bucharest: Simetria.

Păun, C. (2017) 'Romanians protest government plan to commute sentences', *Politico*, 22 January. Available from: https://www.politico.eu/article/romanians-protest-government-plan-to -commute-sentences/ (accessed 10 May 2022).

Racolta, R.P. (2010) *L'architecture totalitaire: Un monographie du Centre civique de Bucarest*, Saint-Étienne: Université Jean Monnet.

Siani-Davies, P. (2007) *The Romanian Revolution of December 1989*, Ithaca: Cornell University Press.

Stan, L. (2013) *Transitional Justice in Post-Communist Romania: The Politics of Memory*, Cambridge: Cambridge University Press.

Steiner, H. and Veel, K. (2020) *Tower to Tower: Gigantism in Architecture and Digital Culture*, Boston: The MIT Press.

Tănăsoiu, C. (2007) 'The Tismaneanu Report: Romania Revisits Its Past', *Problems of Post-Communism*, 54(4), pp. 60–69. DOI: 10.2753/PPC1075-8216540405.

Tateo, G. (2020) *Under the Sign of the Cross: The People's Salvation Cathedral and the Church-Building Industry in Postsocialist Romania*, Space and Place, Vol. 18, New York: Berghahn Books.

Vais, D. (2017) 'The (In)famous Anca Petrescu: Authorship and Authority in Romanian Communist Architecture 1977–1987', in M. Pepchinski and M. Simon (eds) *Ideological Equals: Women Architects in Socialist Europe 1945–1989*, Abingdon: Routledge, pp. 139–154.

Zahariade, A.M. (2011) *Arhitectura în Proiectul Comunist: România 1944–1989/Architecture in the Communist Project: Romania 1944–1989*, Bucharest: Simetria.

15

'Make it look more democratic, Mikhail Mikhailovich!'

Potemkin parliamentarism and the project to redesign the Russian State Duma

Michał Murawski and Ben Noble

Introduction

The Russian State Duma – the lower chamber of the country's national legislature – is often dismissed as an inconsequential body. Statements abound of it being a mere 'rubber stamp', entirely controlled by the Russian executive to realise the policy agenda of the government and the president (Noble and Schulmann 2018; Noble 2020). This accords with characterisations of Russia's political system as a form of non-democracy – and one decreasingly tolerant of dissent and increasingly reliant on coercion as a mode of governance (Dollbaum, Lallouet and Noble 2021).[1]

Despite its peripheral political role, the State Duma is *geographically* situated in the heart of Moscow, adjacent to Red Square and the Kremlin. The legislative body occupies a sprawling, haphazard complex in a 1930s post-constructivist building – formerly the headquarters of the all-powerful Soviet State Planning Committee (Gosplan) (Figure 15.1). The State Duma began operating in this building in 1994, following the shelling (and subsequent closure) of the previous Russian legislature – the Supreme Soviet – by President Boris Yeltsin in October 1993 (Figure 15.2). Around three decades since the Duma's opening, the building's increasingly bedraggled interiors – the work of veteran architectural grandee Mikhail Posokhin and the enormous 'Mosproekt-2' design studio that he has headed since 1993 – are still clad in the official style of the era: a hybrid of 1970s Soviet stagnation chic and 1990s restrained bureaucratic bling.

Figure 15.1 The current headquarters of the State Duma, adjacent to Manezh Square in the centre of Moscow. Architect: Arkady Langman. Originally built in 1932–1935 as the seat of the Council of Labour and Defence. © Dmitry Ivanov, 9 July 2016. Source: Wikimedia Commons, reproduced on the basis of a CC BY-SA 4.0 licence. Available at: https://commons.wikimedia.org/wiki/File:Building_of_Council_of_Labor_and_Defense,_Moscow.jpg (accessed 25 July 2023)

This chapter provides an analysis of the politics, aesthetics and morphology – the procedures, styles and shapes – of the State Duma during the post-Soviet period. It surveys the (failed) projects to build a new, permanent, purpose-built home for the Duma, and focuses, in particular, on recent – so far inconclusive – discussions for the redesign of the existing Duma's plenary chamber. In telling this story, we also provide a case study of reflexivity – between political form and content – highlighting the remarkably pivotal role played in the recent design debates by the book *Parliament* (XML 2017).

The political morphology of Posokhin's parliaments

Since the early 1990s, Mikhail Posokhin's Mosproekt-2 has been responsible for the creation of dozens of structures throughout the Russian capital: from churches (and one cathedral) to stadiums and neo-Stalinist

Figure 15.2   A view of the fire-damaged 'White House', the headquarters of the predecessor to the State Duma – the Supreme Soviet of the Russian Federation, located on Krasnopresnenskaya Embankment, Moscow – following shelling by tanks ordered by Russia's President, Boris Yeltsin, on 4 October 1993. Architects: Dmitry Chechulin and Pavel Shteller. Built 1965–1981. © Bergmann. Source: Wikimedia Commons, reproduced on the basis of a GNU Free Documentation licence. https://commons.wikimedia.org/wiki/File:%E3%83%99%E3%83%BC%E3%83%AB%E3%82%A4%E3%83%89%E3%83%BC%E3%83%A0.jpg (accessed 25 July 2023)

skyscrapers. In the knowledge that a brand new parliament building would necessarily one day be built – a decision to this effect had been made by Yeltsin in 1998 (Kozichev 2012) – Posokhin made sure to render himself indispensable for this project. Dozens of locations were considered – among them the (now disused) eighteenth-century Foundling House on the banks of the Moscow River, and the adjacent, Red-Square-abutting Zaryadye district (Bocharov and Sirenko 2015). And Posokhin played a prominent role in the design work on each of these locations (Bocharov and Sirenko 2015; Ivanov, Aminov and Pushkarskaya 2018).

Posokhin's career suffered a slump, however, following then-President Dmitry Medvedev's dismissal of the architect's patron, Yury Luzhkov, as mayor of Moscow in 2010. Mosproekt-2 had no discernible part to play in the 2012 competition for the replanning of Moscow, which followed the Medvedev-decreed annexation of an enormous chunk of the neighbouring Moscow Oblast (region) and its incorporation into the city limits. Shortlisted concept designs for a new Russian 'Federal Centre' – incorporating both houses of parliament and parts of the federal government – in Kommunarka, at the heart of the annexed territory, included those by numerous global superstar bureaus, among them Rem Koolhaas's OMA and Ricardo Bofill Taller de Arquitectura (Chubukova 2016; Argenbright 2018). In summer 2014, however, an announcement was made that Russia's legislative chambers would finally have purpose-built homes (Interfax 2014). A grandiose (350,000 square metre) new parliamentary centre – bringing the State Duma and the Federation Council together in new, proximate buildings – would be built in the north-western suburbs of Moscow (Revzin 2015).

A closed-door competition was held (in apparent violation of new rules governing such processes passed in the Moscow City Duma in 2013 by the then-new chief architect, Sergey Kuznetsov); and the results were announced during a secretive press conference in July 2015, to which few journalists were invited (Revzin 2015). Surreptitiously snapped phone images of the shortlisted designs were leaked by a few of those present at the announcement (Belov 2015). Only three projects were admitted to the (never concluded) second round: a pastiche of the Capitol in Washington DC by the St Petersburg veteran Evgeniy Gerasimov; another Capitol replica by Lanfranco Cirillo (architect of the so-called 'Putin's Palace' in Gelendzhik on southern Russia's Black Sea coast); and – no prizes for guessing – a submission by Posokhin's Mosproekt-2. The latter took the form of a multi-winged hybrid of the Berlin Reichstag and a Brezhnev-era ministry building, with an inverted pyramid appended to it. Posokhin won the most votes among all the entries (Revzin 2015).

Critics were up in arms. 'Luzhkov is back', cried the influential urban blogger Ilya Varlamov (2015). Mocking the scale of the complex, leading architecture critic Grigoriy Revzin pointed out that the proposed edifice would be big enough to fit the Palace of Westminster – built at the height of the British empire's global reach – 19 times over:

> [T]he situation of conducting a competition for the main public building of the country in a closed regime, via the non-transparent procedure of inviting architects to participate, is simply sickening and shameful … it's like conducting a closed presidential election. Our parliamentarians are revealing their disgracefully low qualifications in mastering the basics of 'managed democracy' – even comrade Stalin, designing the Palace of the Soviets, was capable of simulating the procedures of an open international competition (Revzin 2015).

Over the coming months and years, Posokhin's '19 Westminsters' project – and the very idea of creating a parliamentary centre on the fringes of Moscow – was delayed and, eventually (by October 2018), quietly abandoned (Surnacheva et al. 2016; Kuznetsova 2018). But the desire to redesign the Duma was not dead.

The state of the Duma, personalism and the power of the book

Quite independently of these processes, two Dutch architects – Max Cohen de Lara and David Mulder van der Vegt, founders of the Amsterdam-based architecture office XML – were also thinking about the design of legislatures. Their 2017 book *Parliament* presents plenary hall floorplans for all 193 United Nations member states. Not only do they find that the design of these chambers can be categorised into five basic types – 'opposing benches', 'semicircle', 'horseshoe', 'circle' and 'classroom' – but they also suggest that there is a relationship between these types and the level of democracy in particular states. According to their typology, Russia provides a textbook example of legislative architecture expected in non-democracies: the State Duma's plenary hall has a classroom design (XML 2017: 308) (Figure 15.3).

The Duma's leadership became aware of *Parliament* – and drew on its findings in their project to redesign the chamber, planning to move from a classroom to a semicircle configuration, which they regarded to be more democratic, in line with the patterns reported by XML (2017). In other words, parliamentary leaders hoped by means of architectural fiat to imply democratic substance through democratic form; and a book noting a possible relationship between democracy and design looked likely, itself, to shape part of the reality it described.

We can reconstruct an unbroken chain from the book's publication to the Duma redesign plan. Following *Parliament*'s publication, David Mulder published a blog post on 7 February 2017 on the book's central findings for the Hansard Society – a research organisation focused on the Westminster Parliament (Mulder 2017). On reading this post, one of this chapter's authors (Noble) posted a link to the blog entry on Facebook on 22 February (Noble 2017a). This Facebook post was seen by Ekaterina Schulmann – a Russian political scientist, expert on legislative politics and prominent public intellectual – who commented 'Aah! What a beauty!', and then posted a YouTube video on the topic on 23 February (Schulmann 2017a). After receiving a copy of *Parliament* from a benefactor who had seen the video, Schulmann then made a second

Figure 15.3 Plenary hall of the State Duma, consistent with the 'classroom' type noted in *XML* (2017). © XML Architecture Research Urbanism

video about the book (Schulmann 2017b).[2] And this second video was, in turn, seen by a senior official of the State Duma.[3]

The Duma's leadership was at this moment particularly receptive to redesign and renovation ideas for the plenary hall for at least three reasons. First, the long-running plan to build a parliamentary centre had stalled, as noted above. Second, the Duma plenary hall was showing its age. According to various reports, hazardous voids were discovered underneath the building, the offices were cramped and the roof was leaking (Golovanov 2017; BBC News Russian 2017; *Kommersant* 2019; News.ru 2020). In June 2017, a debate was held in the Duma's plenary chamber concerning the planned so-called 'renovation' of Moscow's Khrushchev-era mass housing, considered by many Muscovites – and especially by Moscow property developers – to be substandard and in need of replacing (Gunko et al. 2018; Mizrokhi 2021). Following the conclusion of the debate, the (now deceased) veteran Duma deputy and leader of the Liberal Democratic Party of Russia (LDPR), Vladimir Zhirinovsky, brought up the pitiful state of the plenary hall. That same day, another LDPR deputy had seen

Екатерина Шульман: Книга о парламентах пришла от дарителя

PARL
I AM
EN
T

▶ ▶| ◀ 0:01 / 8:21   ⊟ ◔ ⇆ ᴎ ᴎ

Figure 15.4 A screenshot from Ekaterina Schulmann's 14 March 2017 video.
© Ekaterina Schulmann. Source: YouTube, reproduced under YouTube's fair use
policy and with the permission of Schulmann. https://www.youtube.com/watch?v
=qbcBoRVIAaA (accessed 17th July 2023)

his own chair collapse beneath him during a debate in the chamber.
Zhirinovsky said:

> [E]ven our own chairs cannot bear the weight of our tireless work!
> When will the renovation of the State Duma happen? … We are
> sitting in the worst building in the world. This is a room for the
> cleaners and security guards of Gosplan, this is where they had
> movies put on for them, the cleaners. So, let's also do a renovation
> of the State Duma, finally. We've been here for 26 years, we've
> been helping the country, but we ourselves are in this here building
> (Kochetkov 2017).

Zhirinovsky's appeal was responded to by the Duma's speaker, Vyacheslav
Volodin:

> You're quite right to say this, we are working for the country, but
> we're not making our own conditions any better. And that's why
> you're elected. If you were to improve your own conditions, they
> wouldn't elect you (Kochetkov 2017).

In fact, the third reason senior Duma officials were keen to explore renovation options for the chamber relates to Volodin himself. Elected in October 2016, Volodin had previously held a much more powerful position in the Presidential Administration, as its first deputy chief of staff. Deciding to make the most out of what many regarded as a demotion, Volodin set about transforming the State Duma into his own fiefdom (Noble 2017b). Redesigning the Duma's main hall fitted nicely, therefore, into this broader and intensely ambitious 'empire-building' plan.

In December 2017, Volodin convened a closed-door meeting in the Duma complex at which Posokhin presented his designs for a restored Duma chamber, which saw the classroom-shaped layout replaced by a semi-circular amphitheatre. Some of those present gushed over Posokhin's design, which was described (to Murawski in a personal communication) as a 'bad attempt at a copy paste' of the assembly chamber at St Petersburg's Tauride Palace – the meeting place of the Tsarist-era Imperial State Duma.[4] Volodin was, however, less impressed. Clutching a copy of XML's *Parliament*, Volodin berated the veteran architect: 'Can't you make it look more modern, more democratic, Mikhail Mikhailovich?' And, by early 2018, a decision had been made by the parliamentary leadership to redesign the plenary hall in the shape of a 'forum', on the basis of the 'experience of other countries' (Ivanov et al. 2018).

Following Volodin's intervention, Posokhin retained only nominal control over the project; the design work itself was handed to two younger architects, one of those being Moscow's chief architect, Sergey Kuznetsov. Following a tussle over symbolism – Kuznetsov was allegedly fixated on an unworkable ambition to install a giant replica of Norman Foster's Reichstag dome above the debating chamber – the project appeared to stall. Some concept drawings, however, were made by Kuznetsov and submitted to Volodin. These drawings were described by Kuznetsov as representing the 'spirit of openness' which the Russian Duma should exude.

In December 2018, however, it transpired that Posokhin somehow *was* still in the running. Although the first tender with Mosproekt-2 (on the strength of which Posokhin had made his initial drawings) was torn up, a new one – for an even more wide-ranging or 'global' reconstruction of the Duma – was drawn up instead, again on the basis of a secret internal procedure rather than an open architectural competition (Interfax 2018). The Duma speaker was photographed displaying printouts of Posokhin's new designs, which appeared to draw heavily on the concept drawings made by Kuznetsov some months before (Pozdeeva 2019). Even the layout of the page and placement of the logos mimicked that of the portfolio submitted by Kuznetsov. Volodin announced that the renovation of the Duma would be completed by spring 2020 – but the project appeared to stall yet again (Gazeta.ru 2020).

As one Moscow architect told Murawski, whatever form the Duma ends up taking, it may have little to do with any of the above-discussed visions:

> [F]irst they wanted to move the Duma somewhere else … and then they wanted to inscribe into this rectangle all that they wanted from democracy; but what they will get … will be the result of all sorts of compromises. It will only really be interesting to see … what happens after the project is completed. To see what manages to squeeze its way into this box, that is the Duma. And I think this is the sense, the meaning, of Russian democracy, too.

Vertical intimacy, architectural design and the determinants of democratisation

This has been a tale of complex reflexivity – of how commentary on architectural design and its relationship with democracy can itself become part of the story and influence design choices. By drawing out patterns suggestive of the ways in which politics shapes, and is shaped by, architecture, XML's book *Parliament* became an actor in its own right in the project to redesign the Russian State Duma, seized upon by an ambitious new speaker to raise the prestige of his new domain. More broadly, the story provides an opportunity to reflect on the relationship between politics (including the difference between the procedures of parliamentary democracy and of architectural competitions) and aesthetics or morphology (understood to refer to the style, shape and appearance, not only of buildings or their representations, but also of procedures themselves).[5]

The case also provides insights into the nature of politics in modern-day Russia. The links in the chain between the publication of *Parliament* and the Russian State Duma's redesign debate speak to what we might call the 'intimacy' of authoritarian power in Russia – that is, of a system in which a Facebook post by a foreign academic about a book by Dutch architects, amplified by two YouTube videos filmed by an influential Russian intellectual from her kitchen, could end up influencing the choices of senior politicians. Indeed, this resonates with a perennial theme in analysis of Russian politics: that personal connections and the attitudes of well-placed actors can sometimes (apparently) easily outweigh the effects of formal institutions and rules – but that these effects are sometimes unintended, unexpected and their precise trajectories difficult to predict.

The perils of 'personalism' are well known and much analysed (see, for example, Wright 2010). But, perhaps converging with insights provided by ethnographic studies of informal governance and its aesthetic and material manifestations (Ledeneva 2013), the ongoing saga of the Russian Duma's redesign might help us to conceive of some of its unintended *potentials*. Does the informal, unpredictable and intimate operation of power also possess within itself some capacity to subvert the operations of the 'power vertical' – that is, the supposed direct line of command from Putin to all lower levels of the state and society – which it is ordinarily seen to undergird?[6] In contrast to naive images of authoritarian top-down control, there is ample space for uncertainty, messiness and serendipity – dynamics that pervert or readjust our scholarly (and popular) perceptions of a seemingly well-oiled, pyramidal machinery of governance and decision-making, where power and decisions flow from top to bottom (Noble and Schulmann 2021).

The details of the story we have told are also relevant to critiques of Russian politics implying that any suggestion of democracy or demo-cratisation is merely rhetorical, a sham or 'virtual' (Wilson 2005). There is more to 'Potemkin parliamentarism' than mere falsehood. Political personalism – and informal, ad hoc processes – may end up having democratic effects, whether intentional or unintentional. However, the experiences of other experiments in what might be called architectural 'vertical horizontalism' realised recently in Russia do not bode well on this front (Murawski 2019b). Most notable among these are the Kremlin-abutting Zaryadye Park or the numerous exercises in the transformation (*blagoustroistvo*) of public space in Moscow in recent years (Murawski 2022). The procedures by which these spaces are brought into being and managed are (often brazenly) top-down and vertical; the spaces themselves are saturated with surveillance cameras and security personnel and with more subtle mechanisms of disciplining their users. Notwithstanding the obsessively overstated rhetorical emphasis on their 'unscripted' nature, 'wildness' or their potential for 'desacralising power' and 'enabling freedom', spaces like Zaryadye are, in fact, much more regimented, controlled, commodified and exclusive than 'traditional' parks and public spaces (Lähteenmäki and Murawski 2023).

We are not suggesting, then, that the State Duma's new plenary chamber – if it is ever realised – will transform Russia's deputies into earnest practitioners of democracy. It would be naive and even dangerous to assume that a mere redesign of the Duma's plenary chamber could bring about democratisation in Russia. There are other, far more plausible – even if not currently likely – routes to liberalisation, including changes to the formal rules and informal practices shaping elections. And yet, in line with the idea that democratic form can nurture democratic content – however obliquely or minutely – could it be that an initiative apparently driven by Vyacheslav Volodin's concern for the *optics* of democracy might, perhaps, increase the chances of greater pluralism in parliamentary debate?

In Russia, however, the legislature is as much – if not more so – a space of *exclusion* as of representation. The political opposition is divided between the 'systemic' and the 'non-systemic': the former co-opted by the Kremlin and allowed to take part in elections (and win legislative seats); the latter facing repression and formidable hurdles when trying to take part in traditional forms of politics. Unscripted, autonomous, 'real' politics involving the non-systemic opposition takes place, therefore, *outside* of the State Duma's walls – in the streets, in courtrooms and online, although the space for dissent continues to shrink (Dollbaum et al. 2021). As long as democratic rights are trampled on in Russia, questions about democratic parliamentary design – albeit interesting – will remain of peripheral practical importance.

Notes

1 This chapter was originally submitted on 23 February 2022 – that is, the day before Russia's full-scale invasion of Ukraine.
2 The benefactor has not given their consent to be named.
3 The senior official has not given their consent to be named.
4 The individuals cited in this section have consented to being cited but not to being named.
5 For a theorisation of political morphology, see Murawski (2019a) and Bach and Murawski (2020).
6 For more on the 'power vertical', see Monaghan (2012) – and for more on perversions of the 'power vertical', see Maksimov et al. (2022).

References

Argenbright, R. (2018) 'The Evolution of New Moscow: From Panacea to Polycentricity', *Eurasian Geography and Economics*, 59(3–4), pp. 408–435. DOI: 10.1080/15387216.2019.1573693.
Bach, J. and Murawski, M. (2020) 'Introduction: Notes towards a Political Morphology of Undead Urban Forms', in J. Bach and M. Murawski (eds) *Re-Centring the City: Global Mutations of Socialist Modernity*. London: UCL Press, pp. 1–14.
BBC News Russian (2017) 'V rossiyskoy Gosdume protekla krysha [The roof of the Russian State Duma leaked]', 14 July. Available from: https://www.bbc.com/russian/news-40611973 (accessed on 16 February 2022).
Belov, A. (2015) 'Vnimanie vsem … [Attention, all …]', Restricted Facebook post, 14 May.
Bocharov, Y. and Sirenko, E. (2015) 'Parlament Rossii na okraine stolitsy [The parliament of Russia on the outskirts of the capital]', *Academia. Arkhitektura i stroitel'stvo*, 3, pp. 108–111.
Chubukova, M. (ed.) (2016) *Kak Postroit' Novuyu Moskvu? [How to Build New Moscow?]*. Moscow: KB Strelka.

Dollbaum, J.M., Lallouet, M. and Noble, B. (2021) 'Alexei Navalny was poisoned one year ago. His fate tells us a lot about Putin's Russia', *The Washington Post 'Monkey Cage'*, 20 August. Available from: https://www.washingtonpost.com/politics/2021/08/20/alexei-navalny -was-poisoned-one-year-ago-his-fate-tells-us-lot-about-putins-russia/ (accessed on 16 February 2022).

Gazeta.ru. (2020) 'Gosduma otkazalas' ot remonta i sekonomlennye 700 mln rubley napravila biznesmenam [The State Duma has given up on its renovation and sent the saved 700 million roubles to businessmen]', Gazeta.ru, 21 April. Available from: https://www.gazeta.ru/busi ness/news/2020/04/21/n_14322877.shtml (accessed on 19 February 2022).

Golovanov, R. (2017) 'Pod deputatami zatreshchali kresla [Chairs cracked under the deputies]', *Komsomol'skaya Pravda*, 19 June. Available from: https://www.kp.ru/daily/26693/3717677/ (accessed on 23 February 2022).

Gunko, M., Bogacheva, P., Medvedev, A. and Kashnitsky, I. (2018) 'Path-dependent Development of Mass Housing in Moscow, Russia', in D. Baldwin Hess, T. Tammaru and M. van Ham (eds) *Housing Estates in Europe*. The Urban Book Series. Cham: Springer, pp. 289–311.

Interfax (2014) 'Gosduma i Sovet Federatsii pereedut v Nizhnie Mnevniki [The State Duma and Federation Council will move to Nizhnie Mnevniki]', 29 August. Available from: https:// interfax.ru/394048 (accessed on 19 February 2022).

Interfax (2018) 'Gosdumu rekonstruiruyut za 2 mlrd rubley [The State Duma will be renovated for 2 billion roubles]', 18 December. Available from: https://www.interfax.ru/russia/642837 (accessed on 19 February 2022).

Ivanov, M., Aminov, K. and Pushkarskaya, A. (2018) 'Kryshu Gosdumy prikroyut kypolom [The roof of the State Duma will be covered with a dome]', *Kommersant*, 6 February. Available from: https://www.kommersant.ru/doc/3540597 (accessed on 16 February 2022).

Kochetkov, D. (2017) 'Zakonoproekt o renovatsii prinyat Gosudarstvennoy Dumoy s uchetom vsekh mneniy v okonchatel'nom chtenii', [Bill on renovation taking into account all opinions adopted by the State Duma in final reading], 1TV.ru, 14 June. Available from: https://www.1tv.ru/news/2017-06-14/327035-zakonoproekt_o_renovatsii_prinyat _gosudarstvennoy_dumoy_s_uchetom_vseh_mneniy_v_okonchatelnom_chtenii (accessed on 23 February 2022).

Kommersant (2019) 'Zdanie Gosdumy mogut priznat' avaryinym [The State Duma building might be declared to be in a critical condition]', 21 May. Available from: https://www.kommersant .ru/doc/3975624 (accessed on 23 February 2022).

Kozichev, E. (2012) 'Trudnaya sud'ba parlamentskogo tsentra [The difficult fate of the parliamentary centre]', *Kommersant*, 19 April. Available from: https://www.kommersant.ru /doc/1918633 (accessed on 19 February 2022).

Kuznetsova, E. (2018) 'Vlasti okonchatel'no otkazalis' pereselyat' Dumu i Sovfed v Mnyovniki [The authorities have ultimately decided against moving the Duma and Federation Council to Mnevniki]', *RBK*, 29 October. Available from: https://www.rbc.ru/politics/29/10/2018 /5bd31bf59a794719066b0702 (accessed on 19 February 2022).

Lähteenmäki, M. and Murawski, M. (2023) 'Blagoustroistvo: infrastructure, determinism, (re-) coloniality, and social engineering in Moscow, 1917–2022', *Comparative Studies in Society and History*, pp. 1–29. DOI: 10.1017/S0010417523000063.

Ledeneva, A. (2013) *Can Russia Modernise? Sistema, Power Networks and Informal Governance*. Cambridge: Cambridge University Press.

Maksimov, D., Mileeva, M., Murawski, M. and Roberts, D. (2020) 'Making Pyramids Disappear: Faux Horizontalism and Wild Capitalist Topologies of Speculation', In M. Vishmidt (ed.) *Speculation: Documents in Contemporary Art*. Cambridge, Mass: MIT Press/The Whitechapel Gallery.

Mizrokhi, E. (2021) 'Living in Anachronistic Space: Temporalities of Displacement in Moscow's Soviet-era Standardised Housing', *Political Geography*, 91(November). DOI: 10.1016/j. polgeo.2021.102495.

Monaghan, A. (2012) 'The *Vertikal*: Power and Authority in Russia', *International Affairs*, 88(1), pp. 1–16. DOI: 10.1111/j.1468-2346.2012.01053.x.

Mulder, D. (2017) 'Parliaments around the world: What can architecture teach us about democracy?', Hansard Society Blog, 7 February. Available from: https://www.hansardsociety .org.uk/blog/parliaments-around-the-world-what-can-architecture-teach-us-about -democracy (accessed on 16 February 2022).

Murawski, M. (2019a) 'Radical Centres: The Politics of Monumentality in 21st Century Warsaw and Johannesburg', *Third Text*, 33(1), pp. 26–42. DOI: 10.1080/09528822.2016.127 5188.

Murawski, M. (2019b) 'Vertical Horizontalism and Green Revolution in Tatarstan', *Calvert Journal*, 8 August. Available from: https://www.new-east-archive.org/features/show/11314/the-inside-story-of-tatarstans-remarkable-controversial-green-urban-revolution (accessed on 3 August 2023).

Murawski, M. (2022) 'Falshfasad: Infrastructure, Materialism and Realism in Wild Capitalist Moscow', *American Ethnologist*, 49(4), pp. 461–477. DOI: 10.1111/amet.13104.

News.ru. (2020) 'Slishkom tesno: Zhirinovskiy pozhalovalsya Putinu na zdanie Gosdumy [Too crowded: Zhirinovsky complained to Putin about the State Duma building]', News.ru, 6 October. Available from: https://news.ru/politics/zhirinovskij-pozhalovalsya-putinu-na-zdanie-gosdumy/ (accessed on 23 February 2022).

Noble, B. (2017a) 'I need this book in my life …', Facebook post, 22 February. Available from: https://www.facebook.com/ben.noble.92/posts/10101978194674179 (accessed on 16 February 2022).

Noble, B. (2017b) 'The State Duma, the "Crimean Consensus," and Volodin's Reforms', in O. Irisova, A. Barbashin, F. Burkhardt and E. Wyciszkiewicz (eds) *A Successful Failure: Russia After Crime(a)*. Warsaw: Centre for Polish-Russian Dialogue and Understanding, pp. 103–117.

Noble, B. (2020) 'Authoritarian amendments: Legislative institutions as intraexecutive constraints in post-Soviet Russia', *Comparative Political Studies*, 53(9), pp. 1417–1454. DOI: 10.1177/0010 414018797941.

Noble, B. and Schulmann, E. (2018) 'Not Just a Rubber Stamp: Parliament and Lawmaking', in D. Treisman (ed.) *The New Autocracy: Information, Politics, and Policy in Putin's Russia*. Washington, DC: Brookings Institution Press, pp. 49–82.

Noble, B. and Schulmann, E. (2021) 'Myth 15: "It's all about Putin – Russia is a Manually Run, Centralized Autocracy"', in J. Nixey (ed.) *Myths and Misconceptions in the Debate on Russia: How they Affect Western Policy, and What Can Be Done*. London: Chatham House, pp. 91–95.

Pozdeeva, M. (2019) 'Predstavleny eskizy novogo zala zasedaniy Gosdumy [Sketches of the new meeting chamber of the Gosduma have been presented]', *Daily Storm*, 7 March. Available from: https://dailystorm.ru/news/predstavleny-eskizy-novogo-zala-zasedaniy-gosdumy (accessed on 20 February 2022).

Revzin, G. (2015) '19 Vestminsterov. Dazhe Bol'she. Grigory Revzin o Parlamentarizme v Osobo Krupnykh Masshtabakh [19 Westminsters. Even more. Grigoriy Revzin on parliamentarism in especially large dimensions]', *Kommersant Weekend*, 5 June. Available from: https://www.kommersant.ru/doc/2735359 (accessed on 20 February 2022).

Schulmann, E. (2017a) 'Ekaterina Shul'man: Parlamentarizm: Pravila rassadki [Ekaterina Schulmann: Parliamentarism: Seating rules]', YouTube video, 23 February. Available from: https://www.youtube.com/watch?v=UYGtoxF0MUg (accessed on 16 February 2022).

Schulmann, E. (2017b) 'Ekaterina Shul'man: Kniga o parlamentakh prishla ot daritelya [Ekaterina Schulmann: Book about parliaments has arrived from a donor]', YouTube video, 14 March. Available from: https://www.youtube.com/watch?v=qbcBoRVIAaA (accessed on 16 February 2022).

Surnacheva, E., Antonova, E., Bocharova, S., Rustamova, F., Reyter, S. and Deryabina, A. (2016) 'Pereezd Gosdumy v Mnevniki otlozhili po esteticheskim soobrazheniyam [The move of the State Duma to Mnevniki has been postponed for aesthetic reasons]', *RBK*, 1 February. Available from: https://www.rbc.ru/politics/01/02/2016/569d00c69a79475b06215be3 (accessed on 19 February 2022).

Varlamov, I. (2015) 'Moskva budet luzhkovskoy [Moscow will be Luzhkovite]', Varlamov.ru, 16 June. Available from: https://varlamov.ru/1370502.html (accessed on 25 May 2022).

Wilson, A. (2005) *Virtual Politics: Faking Democracy in the Post-Soviet World*. New Haven, CT, and London: Yale University Press.

Wright, J. (2010) 'Aid effectiveness and the politics of personalism', *Comparative Political Studies*, 43(6), pp. 735–762. DOI: 10.1177/0010414009358674.

XML (2017) *Parliament*. Amsterdam: XML.

16

Absorbing Cold War heritage

From a Stalinist skyscraper to a seat of EU democracy?

Aneta Vasileva and Emilia Kaleva

Introduction

September 2020 was the month when the Bulgarian parliament relocated. Relocation by itself is not that intriguing in this case – at least not in comparison with the choice of a new destination. At some point it had become clear that the existing neoclassical building, completed in 1928, was too small for its active occupants and their growing number of staff. It was decided that the National Assembly should be moved, and the new building to be occupied should be none other than the former Bulgarian Communist party headquarters in Sofia, a mini Stalinist skyscraper and one of the starkest architectural symbols of the failed communist regime in the country.

Coincidentally, in 2020 Bulgaria was experiencing the biggest antigovernment protest wave since 2013–2014. For more than 100 days, starting in mid-July, a series of ongoing demonstrations were held mainly in the capital, Sofia, and less regularly in some bigger Bulgarian cities and places with large Bulgarian diaspora abroad. Protesters demanded the resignation of the centre-right pro-European government of Boyko Borisov[1] and of chief prosecutor Ivan Geshev, accusing them of corruption, backroom connections with the mafia and the mismanagement of EU funds.

Rallies reached a climax on 2 September 2020, with thousands of people gathering for the so-called 'Grand National Uprising'. This protest aimed to block access to the new Bulgarian parliament building and to coincide with the day Bulgarian lawmakers returned for their first working day after the summer break. It ended late at night with violence, pepper spray and tens of people and policemen injured (Todorov 2020). No less badly hit was the new parliament building.

The Largo of Sofia

All rallies in the capital, Sofia, usually start from one place, the Largo or the so-called 'Triangle of Power': an elongated square between the buildings of the Council of Ministers, the presidency and the former headquarters of the Bulgarian Communist party, which together form an eclectic, socialist-realist architectural ensemble, completed between 1948 and 1955 (Figure 16.1).

The building of the former Bulgarian Communist party headquarters is part of this bigger architectural complex. The creation of the Largo was the most serious twentieth-century urban intervention in the heart of a Bulgarian historical city. It was a direct ideological and architectural import from the political centre of Moscow during times of orthodox socialist realism – and a strong propaganda symbol for the whole period of state socialism in Bulgaria. The ensemble consists of three six-storey blocks (two rectangular and one trapezoid) forming a rectangular public space, open to the west. It replaced the small-scale and fragmented urban tissue of prewar Sofia, taking advantage of the fact that the area was seriously hit by allied bombing. Nevertheless, a number of well-preserved multistoreyed, prewar buildings were cleared in addition to provide a proper *tabula rasa* for the new development. In those early postwar years of ideological battles, the introduction of a completely new urban scale was regarded as indispensable – corresponding to the changed priorities and large ambitions of the brand new socialist People's Republic of Bulgaria (officially announced as such in 1948).

At first sight, the Largo is indeed a sudden and deliberate urban gesture, completely alien to the existing historical layers of the city. Yet alongside its destructive effect, the ensemble can be interpreted as historically enriching and adding new identities. Situated in the ancient centre of Sofia, overlapping the Roman city of Serdica and the medieval city of Sredets, the Largo's construction both destructed and uncovered a plethora of historical layers, consequently integrated into one organism. The prewar religious and commercial identity of the place was completely transformed by simultaneously adding new Stalinist structures and, in the process, revealing the hidden ancient layers of the place.

One distinct feature of urban development in Bulgaria during Stalinism is that the newly introduced totalitarian model was never fully completed. Many competitions, projects and plans were prepared,

Figure 16.1 The Largo of Sofia in the 1970s. © project ATRIUM archive

discussed and presented, but none of them was finalised in its totality. Thus, the centre of Sofia and the area of the Largo were spared a complete reconstruction according to the preliminary approved plan. The royal palace and churches within the area were preserved (despite their unwanted symbolism) and the general historical structure and spatial relationships within the zone had also remained traceable (Krestev 1996; Krastev 1998). Thus, the seemingly rigid ensemble of the Largo seems almost properly integrated in a rich historical context within its structural constraints. The main boulevards and the square of the Largo overlap with and can be interpreted as contemporary transformations of the main vectors from the Roman period – *cardo maximus, decumanus maximus* and the Roman forum of Ulpia Serdica (first century AD).

Thanks to the construction of the Largo, large-scale archaeological research was performed. Many of the uncovered structures were subsequently destroyed, but an important part of them is preserved and integrated in situ – the eastern gate of Serdica (dated sixth century AD), the rotunda of St George church (fourth century AD), the medieval Church of St Petka of the Saddlers (eleventh century AD). Today, especially after recent archaeological works completed in the context of the construction of a new metro line in the area, the Largo acts as a richly hybridised and multilayered urban space – in fact an asset to any aspiring global city. The historical and archaeological reserve 'Serdica–Sredets' is listed as national heritage, and for several years the Largo was included in the Council of Europe's network of cultural routes within the ATRIUM (Architecture of Totalitarian Regimes of the 20th Century in Europe's Urban Memory) route. At present there is a municipal initiative for the Largo complex to be listed in the national register of cultural heritage as well.

The building of the former Bulgarian Communist party headquarters

An indisputable visual, architectural and ideological dominant feature of the Largo ensemble is the building of the former Communist party headquarters (1954, architect Petso Zlatev et al.) (Figure 16.2). After the political changes in 1989 and the subsequent dissolution of the Eastern Bloc, the building was unsurprisingly subject to anticommunist counter reactions. It was stripped of all communist decorations (including the hammer and sickle stone detailing and the red star on top) and was finally set on fire in August 1990 after days of violent demonstrations. Nobody knows who lit the matchstick, but the general suspicion is that the destruction of important communist archives housed in the building was the main goal (Darik News 2006). Yet, the building survived, only to become once again the central location of mass rallies during the political and economic crisis in 1996–1997, and the customary place of antigovernment protests in the following years.

This turbulent background is in sharp contrast with the idea to relocate the parliament there, which emerged quite unexpectedly a couple of years after the arson attack in 1990.

The relocation

The proposal to relocate the Bulgarian parliament to the building of the former Communist party headquarters was met with surprising political consensus. As early as 1992, when the president of the National Assembly was Stefan Savov (Democratic party), some parliamentary activities were moved there. Four hundred million leva of the state budget were spent on repair works, the MPs' offices were moved from the old building and a number of halls were reconstructed to house meetings of the parliamentary commissions. Thus, the former Communist party headquarters officially became the second building of the National Assembly.

Figure 16.2 The Bulgarian Communist party headquarters in the 1960s–70s.
© project ATRIUM archive

PARLIAMENT BUILDINGS

In 1996 the then president of the National Assembly Blagovest Sendov (Bulgarian Socialist Party) announced the first architecture competition for the former grand hall of the party headquarters – 'Georgi Kirkov' hall,[2] subsequently renamed to 'St Sofia' – to be transformed into a new plenary hall.

The main argument in favour of all relocation activities was that the original old building on National Assembly Square was too small to house all contemporary parliamentary functions – the seats were old and uncomfortable, there were not enough meeting rooms for all parliamentary commissions and, last but not least, the MPs had to travel daily between the old building and the former party headquarters, given that their offices had already been moved into the latter. It seemed completely logical for the three powers – presidency, Council of Ministers and National Assembly – to gather together in the 'Triangle of Power', saving time and space.

It is worth noting that the old building of the National Assembly of Bulgaria was one of the first public buildings to be completed in the first years of Bulgarian independence from the Ottoman empire. The new Bulgarian state was constituted in 1878 and Sofia declared its capital. The building was designed specifically for a national assembly by the Serbian architect of Bulgarian origin, Konstantin Yovanovich, and was consecrated in 1885. Its eclectic, regionalised neoclassical and neo-Renaissance style was the result of several additions to the original project by the Bulgarian architects Yordan Milanov (addition during 1896–1899) and Pencho Koychev (addition in 1925). The building is now listed as a national (historical, architectural and artistic) cultural heritage and has a central location in the composition of the National Assembly Square.

All motivations for the present relocation seem perfectly pragmatic and devoid of any political or ideological message. But any parliament building is a symbol, and their every change is always also a political act – whether deliberate or accidental. Therefore, it seems strange that the new plenary hall of the Bulgarian parliament is simply pragmatic: 'We have lots of square metres of unused state property in a massive building in the centre of the capital. Why not use them?'

Four architecture competitions

A series of architectural competitions followed in 1996, 2003–2004, 2008–2009 and 2011. All revealed a captivating development of the idea of what the parliamentary seat of an EU democracy should look like when placed in the old Communist party headquarters' assembly hall.

Figure 16.3 The building of the Bulgarian parliament until 2020 and then from 2021 onwards. © Aneta Vasileva

Every time, despite different prevailing party majorities, relocation was reasoned purely pragmatically – and never as a political message. The architectural results of all competitions were peculiar in themselves, as to reconstruct the former 'Georgi Kirkov' grand hall was both a complicated and an easy task. Easy, because it was not too difficult to turn an 800-delegate hall into a hall for 240 MPs. And complicated, because the former Communist party headquarters was a building of compelling aesthetics, situated in a complex ensemble with rather specific interiors of grand spaces and intricate detailing.

The first competition (1996) was won by a project which draped the former party headquarters in a transparent 'curtain' – thus 'hiding the past' behind glass (Klisurova 2004). The same architect – Boris Kamilarov, a prolific author of public buildings in the period of late socialism – was announced winner of the second (2004) competition as well (Popov 2004). That competition attracted only three entries, with the notable presence of the Swiss 'starchitect' Mario Botta in a team with the Bulgarian-based and practising architect of Italian origin, Raimondo Flaccomio. Botta's project was ranked last, but it was the one project which made the most dramatic changes to the Stalinist mastodon out of all competitions to come (Figure 16.4). The western façade of the socialist-realist palace was completely removed and replaced by an inclined prism with a grove of trees on top and a glass entrance, open to the square. In fact, Botta and his team crashed the uniformity of the whole Largo ensemble and presented a totally different building – a revolutionary proposal which caused much commotion in Bulgarian professional circles (Popov 2004). But Ognyan Gerdzhikov, then president of the National Assembly, did not come to an agreement with Botta (Gerdzhikov liked Botta's project best, but it was rather too expensive) (Dimov 2004). In the end, none of the projects were realised, as shortly after the end of the competition, its winner Boris Kamilarov died.

This was the period when all parliamentary parties supported the relocation, and even the most openly anticommunist of them, the Union of the Democratic Forces, insisted that a move to the former party headquarters would be a symbolic act of regained democracy and victory over totalitarianism in Bulgaria (Dnevnik 2003).

After a third competition intermezzo in 2008, when Georgi Pirinski (president of the National Assembly, Bulgarian Socialist party) attempted to place a brand new parliamentary hall in the inner courtyard of the former headquarters, thus both preserving the 'Georgi Kirkov' hall intact (Figure 16.5) and allowing for a copy of Norman Foster's Reichstag glass cupola, the final architecture competition was announced in 2011. The ruling majority party at the time was the centre-right and pro-European GERB (Citizens for European Development of Bulgaria), member of EPP, and president of the National Assembly was Tsetska Tsatcheva. This time the competition brief specifically precluded the deconstruction of any part of the building (perhaps trying to counter any attempts like Botta's) and placed a requirement to preserve the artistic value of the existing architecture.

The competition attracted 11 entries, all from Bulgaria. Some preserved the existing stone and marble colonnade of the hall, trying to warm up the atmosphere with wood cladding and new furniture. Others removed all decorative columns. Some preserved the strikingly ornate existing ceiling of the hall, others replaced it with a light ceiling. Some projects preserved the 'classroom' orientation of the hall towards the former scene, others reversed it or suggested a round plenary hall. There were projects which again directly copied some visual characteristics of the new Berlin Reichstag. The project which was ranked second (Tilev

Figure 16.4 Sketch of Mario Botta's competition entry for the parliament in Sofia.
© Emilia Kaleva

Architects; Figure 16.6) preserved much of the existing architecture –
materials, overall appearance, the ceiling, the grand glass chandelier,
all finishings and the general atmosphere. It was more a project for
restoration than for reconstruction of the hall. The winning architects,
Niconsult, however, were not that delicate. They changed the slope and
the proportion of the hall and placed an additional press room beneath.
They also removed the entirety of the existing ceiling and replaced it with
a glass roof (Figure 16.7).

This is by and large the project which, with minor amendments, was
realised in the subsequent years. Initially, the reconstruction was planned
to be finalised in 2018, for the Bulgarian presidency of the Council of the
EU, but construction works were behind schedule, and it was decided
to postpone relocation to 2020. The total sum of the reconstruction
amounted to 44 million Bulgarian leva (about 22 million euro) and a
number of roof, installations and façade repairs are still ongoing even at
present (Cherneva 2020).

Figure 16.5 The original interior of the 'Georgi Kirkov' hall in 2011. © Nikola Mihov for project ATRIUM

Two questions

Both the relocation saga and the reconstruction project raise a number of interesting questions, architectural and political at the same time.

First, is there a political message when a fresh democratic state decides to move its parliament into the architectural icon of a former totalitarian regime? Because we could have received such a message, even several. If the building of the former Communist party headquarters had been drastically changed by total reconstruction, it would have demonstrated cutting any links to the near past – thus radically clearing all traumatic memory. If the ex-'Georgi Kirkov' hall had been treated as a cultural heritage, preserving much of its features intact, this would have signalled a desire to live in peace with our own history. The realised project does neither of the above.

Second, what should be done with the old National Assembly building? Presently it is an empty shell, listed as national cultural heritage yet devoid of its original function. There are plans to turn the building into a museum, but this would be a banal and quite retroactive preservationist attitude towards a living and, until recently, fully functioning cultural monument.

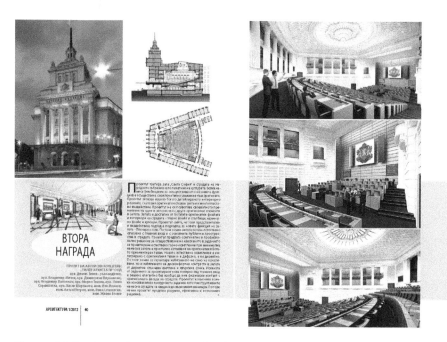

Figure 16.6 Second prize entry of 'Tilev Architects' in the 2011 competition.
© *Architecture* magazine 1/2012, p. 41

Figure 16.7 First prize entry of 'Niconsult' in the 2011 competition.
© *Architecture* magazine 1/2012, pp. 38, 40

Dissonant heritage

When the newly completed plenary hall was revealed to the press and the public, it was met with general and almost total disapproval. Both experts (Vasileva 2020) and ordinary citizens, in the official press and especially on social media, criticised its proportions, colours, the painted stone and marble columns, cheap detailing, the lack of a visual connection between MPs and the press, the loss of the original ceiling and its remarkable chandelier. People commented on the unusually good acoustic for a plenary hall, posing the question why this relocation was needed at all and why the former Georgi Kirkov hall was not used for a concert hall instead. Most reactions coincided with the escalating political tensions in the country and the ongoing antigovernment rallies, which started to physically attack buildings of the state: the new parliament was attacked with firecrackers, self-made bombs, stones, pieces of pavement, dust bins, plastic chairs and tables on 2 September 2020, the Sofia municipality building was symbolically pelted with eggs on 25 September, eggs and tomatoes were thrown at the Ministry of Defence on 19 October, and at the Ministry of Finance on 22 October, and so on.

It turns out that in contemporary Bulgaria, one building has always been a contested symbol of power and dissonant heritage par excellence, the building of the former Communist party headquarters. It is a symbol of a long-gone era and the target of any subsequent civil disapproval of the state. In a post-1989 world, from the point of view of a post-socialist European country, the quickest and easiest example of contested architectural heritage to come to mind in our society is the legacy of the grand construction efforts of the former socialist People's Republic of Bulgaria. Most politically burdened of all are exactly those public places that had been used to demonstrate the power of the one-party state: monuments and memorial places (of the Soviet Army, of Stalin, Lenin and local communist leaders), commemorative places, the Communist party headquarters, and others. After November 1989, they were the ones most severely subjected to the perfectly understandable destructive impulses of the crowds. The anticommunist demonstrations in 1990 and subsequently were vocally demanding the removal of all communist and Soviet symbols from government buildings and the urban public space, and this gradually happened. Yet the buildings remained – without stars, hammers and sickles, but preserving their representative state functions.

The former headquarters of the Bulgarian Communist party in Sofia is a symbol of all those conflicts. And this is the place to which the

Bulgarian parliament decided to relocate exactly in the turmoil of 2020. Undeniably, this will be an ongoing saga.

In 2021, following the 2020 antigovernment protests, Bulgaria held a series of parliamentary elections. A government, formed of a wide coalition, was formed only at the third attempt – after the November 2021 elections. In the meantime, still in the spring of 2021, after the first round of elections, the Bulgarian parliament was relocated back to the old building of the National Assembly and the freshly reconstructed former Communist party headquarters remains serving only administrative, but not representative functions. The grand ex-'Georgi Kirkov' hall remains empty.

Notes

1 Party affiliation GERB, member of the European People's Party (ENP).
2 Georgi Kirkov was a socialist and party and trade union activist before the Second World War.

References

Cherneva, M. (2020) 'Narodnoto sabranie dava 19 miliona za remont na bivshia Partien dom [The National Assembly to Give 19 Mln for the Repairs of the Former Communist Party Headquarters]'. *Capital*, 15 July. Available from: https://www.capital.bg/politika_i _ikonomika/infrastructure/2020/07/15/4091329_narodnoto_subranie_dava_19_mln_lv _za_remont_na/ (accessed on 5 January 2022).

Darik News (2006) 'The secrets of the party archive of the BKP', 9 June. Available from: https:// dariknews.bg/novini/afera/tajnite-na-partijniq-arhiv-na-bkp-67810 (accessed on 5 January 2022).

Dimov, P. (2004) 'Davat 4 miliona za novia parlament [Over 4 Mln BGN for the New Parliament]', *Trud*, 10 January 2004, p. 5.

Dnevnik (2003) 'Sinite deputati podkrepiat premestvaneto na parlamenta [Blue MPs back relocation of parliament]', 4 December. Available from: https://www.dnevnik.bg/bulgaria /2003/12/04/61630_sinite_deputati_podkrepiat_premestvaneto_na_parlamenta/ (accessed on 5 January 2022).

Klisurova, L. (2004) 'Staklena zavesa shte pazi deputatite [Glass curtain will guard MPs]', *24 Hours*, 2 February 2004, p. 16.

Krastev, T. (1998) 'Auf der Suche nach Toleranz', *Der Architekt*, 1 January, pp. 47–50. Berlin: Ernst & Sohn.

Krestev, T. (1996) 'L'architecture stalinienne en Bulgarie. Stalinistische Architektur unter Denkmalschutz?', *Eine Tagung des Deutschen Nationalkomitees von ICOMOS und der Senatsverwaltung für Stadtentwicklung und Umweltschutz in Berlin*, 6–9 September 1995.

Popov, P. (2004) 'Targat za zala Sv. Sofia [The competition for St. Sofia Hall]', *Kultura*, 13 February, 6 (2573).

Todorov, S. (2020) 'Protest tension grows in Bulgaria amid standoff in parliament', *Balkan Insight*, 2 September. Available from: https://balkaninsight.com/2020/09/02/protest-tension -grows-in-bulgaria-amid-standoff-in-parliament/ (accessed on 5 January 2022).

Vasileva, A. (2020) 'Noviyat star Partien Dom [The new old Communist party headquarters]', *Toest*, 12 September. Available from: https://toest.bg/noviyat-star-partien-dom/ (accessed on 5 January 2022).

17

Barra (Get Out!)

Agency for public resistance at the parliament of Malta

Andrew Borg Wirth and Michael Zerafa

Introduction

Architecture is a call to action. It is an invitation for the confrontation between a building and its users. Architecture does not solely lie within a physical enclosure, but in the event of direct negotiation, or conflict, between user and space. Bernard Tschumi's assertion that 'there is no architecture without violence' (Tschumi 1996, p. 121) introduces the important dual nature of the architectural object: its status as the event, and the relevance of its violent character.

Parliament buildings play a vital role in democracies, not solely because of the decision-making role of those they host on the inside, but also because of what they represent for others on the outside. In deciding on how a parliament operates and looks, architects effectively participate in the way democracy functions in that place. With the parliament building in the Maltese capital Valletta, designed by Renzo Piano Building Workshop in collaboration with AP Valletta, there are cues and notes throughout that show the intention for healthy democratic activity and a contemporary interface between representatives and the represented. Five years since its opening, the building has seen Malta dive deep into political turmoil (Stancati 2019), fast becoming the scene against which much confrontation took place.

This chapter seeks to investigate the parliament of Malta and a series of events which happened around it in light of revelations surrounding the assassination by car bomb of Daphne Caruana Galizia. The underlying effort is to understand how the intentions of an architect can enable democratic action even if they are resisted through interference from governing powers.

Figure 17.1 Photos posted on Instagram. © Andrew Borg Wirth and Michael Zerafa. @aborgwirth and @mikezerafa, 2019

Caruana Galizia was an independent investigative journalist whose murder in 2017 sent shockwaves way beyond the shores of Malta, the European Union's smallest state (Garside 2017). A public inquiry into her assassination was made public in 2020. In a report that was released by the inquiry's board, the state of Malta is held directly responsible for the conditions within which Caruana Galizia's murder was allowed to happen. It also called out the creation of 'an atmosphere of impunity, generated from the highest echelons of the administration inside Castille [the office of the prime minister of Malta], the tentacles of which then spread to other institutions, such as the police and regulatory authorities, leading to a collapse in the rule of law' (Borg 2021). Yorgen Fenech, a businessman whose corrupt dealings had been investigated by Caruana Galizia, is currently accused of having been the mastermind behind the assassination (Vella 2019). Proof of close relationships between Fenech and several high-ranking members of Malta's political class have been brought to light.

On 16 October 2017, the political situation on the island, which Daphne Caruana Galizia had called 'desperate' in her last blog post (Caruana Galizia 2017), escalated when a rental car she was using was blown up minutes away from her home. Caruana Galizia was a critic of both the governing party, at the time enjoying approval rates of 55 per cent and a seven-seat majority in a parliament of 67 (Politico 2022) – unprecedented in Maltese politics – and of the leader of the opposition. She had insisted both were unfit for their respective positions.

A growing group of activists chose to express their grief for the assassination of the journalist at a site which quickly turned into a makeshift memorial in front of the law courts of Malta, a seven-minute walk down the road from the city gate of Valletta. Government workers would clear out the memorial every night on orders from the justice and culture minister (Agius 2018), but activists upheld a daily commitment to bring flowers, candles and photos of Caruana Galizia, to never leave the place empty of her memory. This continuous show of collective grief was complemented by a monthly vigil in front of the memorial (Farrugia 2021; Times of Malta 2021).

On 20 November 2019, more than two years after her assassination, a major shift occurred in the unfolding unrest of the political situation in Malta. New revelations into how actors at the very apex of the political structure were connected to the main suspected mastermind of her assassination had begun to surface (Vella 2019). On the day itself, a turning point within the crisis, the quiet vigil at the makeshift memorial abruptly doubled back to the feet of the new parliament building, at the door to the city, and became a violent protest (Figure 17.2).

The general feeling among protesters that evening was that the political situation had deteriorated to a point where every member of cabinet had become complicit in this state of affairs. The silent group turned into a loud mob as it spontaneously made its way to the parliament building, where a session was ongoing. Chants, most noticeably 'barra' ('get out'), were repeatedly hurled at the building. This was a simultaneous call for the resignation of the guilty, and a demand for a direct confrontation with those currently within the chambers and considered complicit. As the justice and culture minister attempted to make his way out of the parliament building, his car was immobilised by the impromptu mob, who exhibited anger through hurled insults and physical force upon the vehicle. This violent confrontation took place because at that moment, the minister personified (to the protesters) the injustice and impunity that they were there to contest. Other government ministers (including the prime minister) escaped through passageways and side roads to which the architects had connected the building. The mob, familiar with the fabric of the city, moved to each entrance and exit, blocking any further dispersal.

The movement from the memorial to the parliament was instrumental in displaying the change in tone communicated by the protesters. Grief

Figure 17.2 Direct confrontation between protesters and the considerable police presence at the protest in front of the parliament building in Valletta, Malta. © Joanna Demarco, 2022

had turned into anger, reaching unseen levels, and the parliament, to them, housed the characters at whom their anger was directed.

The following days saw groups of unprecedented size assemble daily outside the parliament. They also saw increased security measures and performative exercise on state power with barriers increasing throughout the main thoroughfare, completely cutting off all access to the open zones under the parliament's envelope (Figure 17.3). This series of events would become, arguably, one of the most reinforced performances of power, democracy, public space and politics in recent Maltese history.

The protests can be theorised as a chaotic disruption to a desired 'efficiency' (Žižek 2015) within the public realm in Valletta. They blocked the main entrance and exit to the city, disrupted commerce during the Christmas season and voiced loud cries of protest challenging the message of the government. It was this disruption to the daily routine of the city that gave more attention to the protesters. The bigger the protests got, the greater the inefficiency caused; the greater the inefficiency caused, the stricter the security measures became. This led the border between

Figure 17.3 Crowds encircled by barriers and police presence in front of the parliament building, 2019. © Joanna Demarco, 2022

the parliament and the public realm – which the architect had designed to be permeable through a simple penetrable glass – to transform into an impermeable boundary (ArchDaily 2015). The intense police presence and abundance of metal barriers (Fleri Soler and Darmanin n.d.) sent in by politicians grew as the anger escalated. Here, each of the parties effectively staged the approach of the other. Richard Sennett (2013) argues that the healthiest of interactions within the public realm happen on permeable borders where two different groups of people confront each other.

On the tenth day of protests, 2 December 2019, the crowd responded to the resistance which the political class were showing to confronting them. While the parliament was in session in the building, people conspired, through the use of WhatsApp group chats and megaphones, to lock the parliamentarians inside. Informed by both the transparency of the parliament building and its superimposition on the city map, the crowd mobilised spatially. It spread from City Gate Square and the beginning of Republic Street to other avenues which can be used as exits of the city: Castille Square first and then Ordinance Street, followed by both sides of the ditch under the parliament building (Figure 17.4).

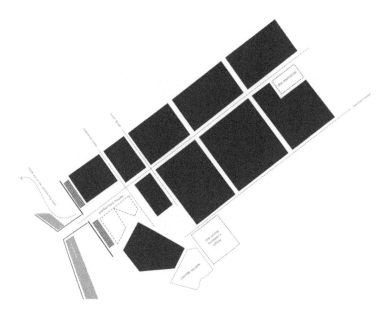

Figure 17.4 Schematic map of the gridiron complex in which the parliament is placed and where the protests took place. © Andrew Borg Wirth and Michael Zerafa

The parliamentarians were trapped in the glass-cladded ground floor of the parliament building. Barricades intended to overrule the architect's intention to promote political transparency through its permeability now showcased disgraced parliamentarians waiting helplessly for the mob to calm down and unable to avoid listening to what the people had to say.

Jürgen Habermas writes of the horizontal governance which is essential for healthy democracies to flourish. He argues that democratic politics should be governed not through the undermining of top-down governance, but through an informed understanding of the bottom-up moralities within a republic (Habermas 1962, p. 15). In the case of Malta, the revolt around the parliament unfolded not in opposition to top-down governance. Rather, it can be read as defiance to a perceived disregard of bottom-up moralities.

Relatedly, we posit that the built envelope of a parliament building plays an active role in embodying, and projecting, a value structure as an intrinsic characteristic of the archetype. In the case of the Maltese parliament building, it seems that Renzo Piano aimed for it to be a piece of communicative infrastructure between parliamentarian and pedestrian, to foster, in Habermas's words, a horizontal political setup by designing a number of architectural cues for confrontation (Habermas 1962, p. 53).

The politician's role in a society is to distil the opinion of many and act as the negotiator for a collective morality (Billiard 2014, p. 3), whereby the status quo is relatable to a large enough group of the population. In this case, a large enough group of the republic did not see this role being fulfilled – and used the parliament building to voice this.

The resistant group (the protesters) were unwilling to allow for borders and restraint to be imposed on a building designed to be permeable to its exterior. In negotiating the nature of the building's boundaries, they found agency. This was made possible through fundamental architectural decisions taken by the architect. The violence that Tschumi (1996) speaks of manifests within the momentary intrusion of an architectural space by a public, which, he says, is 'implicit' to the building's design.

Three main design decisions in particular provided for the horizontal democratic setup for the Maltese parliament building, enabling confrontation:

1 the big void in front of the parliament;
2 the layers of transparency of the parliament building; and
3 its superimposition on the city map.

The main square is far more than an extension of the main Republic Street. Offering a space of that scale can be considered an opportunity for people to gather and hence for events to manifest. It is also beneficial that the space is void, meaning that it does not contain cues which suggest how the pedestrian should act. Moreover, because of the recessed ground floor of the parliament, it feels like the void is penetrating the building rather than vice versa, making approaching the building less intimidating to a public (Figure 17.5).

The ground floor of the parliament is effectively a glass box, which continues to reinforce the architect's ambition to make the parliament more accessible. Right of access to the ground floor was intended to offer the public opportunities for chance encounters with politicians on their way to parliamentary sessions. This transparency exposes the politicians to confrontations with the general public. It acts as what Sennett (2013) calls a border, 'an edge where different groups interact', rather than a boundary, or 'an edge where things end', thus making the idea of politics more accessible to the general public.

The superimposition of the parliament complex upon the gridiron network of the city map exposes why this building has contributed to

Figure 17.5 The growing presence of physical barriers and police presence in Valletta, against the backdrop of the visibly permeable ground floor of the parliament building, 2019. © Joanna Demarco, 2022

the intentions of the protesters. To design in Valletta is to understand that Valletta has always been home to a people under siege, who require the flexibility to defend themselves through it, if and when it is required of them. To embed this mindset within architecture is to understand the role that was required of this building at this point in history. The parliament building built on the familiarity that users of the city have become accustomed to: whereby there is never any 'one' exit; where routes are long but intuitive; where there is a logic and geometry one can familiarise oneself with.

The political infancy and latent postcolonial attitudes of Malta as a young democracy, which became independent from British rule in 1964, are well documented (Baldacchino 2002), as is the unavoidable nature of its island status (Baldacchino 2004). It was Caruana Galizia herself who said that 'those who wish to understand how Maltese society functions have no choice but to read up on amoral familism' (2013) – a family-centric way of doing politics, where the idea of 'public good' is often in conflict with benefits of oneself and those of their innermost circles (Veenendaal

2019). The parliament building was just one of a number of disputes in Malta that typically take on a partisan nature, with public opinion swaying in line with partisan propaganda (Vassallo 2010).

Once more, the comparison to the hierarchical systems considered by Habermas in his discussions on the fundamentals for a healthily democratic society is illuminating. The vertical structures that dictate political activity in Malta can seem to be in direct conflict with Habermas's ideals of a functioning democracy. Political polarisation seems endemic in Malta (Baldacchino 2002; Veenendaal 2019). Children are accustomed to party paraphernalia (party-owned media, mass political demonstrations and abundant proximity to partisan political players) at a young age. They learn of history through particularly tinted lenses, and there is a general expectation that party loyalty makes one deserving of benefits when one's supported party is in power. Discontent with this entrenched political culture contributed to the slowly brewing anger which erupted that November evening. After months of quiet grief, and a slow realisation of the desperate state of affairs, a collective group found the parliament building to be the most suitable space on which to perform their insistence and a revitalisation of horizontal democracy.

To conclude, this chapter has married events within the Maltese contemporary context with theoretical investigations into architecture as event (Tschumi 1996), and of ways in which architecture performs most violently when interacting with the public it was designed for. Renzo Piano's design of the Maltese parliament building in Valletta has been used as a paradigm case to explore and illustrate what architecture can give rise to, and how this is where the role of the architect really lies.

Democracy and power reflect, and are reflected in, the built form. Architecture is an implicit performance of realities and cultures that are bred and shared by a people. In analysing the treatment of public space and the symbols of power and leadership on the island, one can better understand the respect and admiration that politicians enjoy within the Maltese anthropological cross-section (Veenendaal 2019), and why the events of late 2019 hold important reflections of the society the building had to be equipped for.

In particular, the events which were enabled by the architecture of the parliament building managed to displace this relationship between politician and civilian to become one which is less hierarchical and more confrontational. A vertical democratic setup in which the parliamentarians are higher in the system, and have greater influence than the general public, does not imply a state of impunity. When this

Figure 17.6 Large protests around the parliament building in Valletta, Malta, in reaction to revelations around the murder of Daphne Caruana Galizia, 2019. © Jeremy Debattista, 2022

needed to be disrupted, it was the architecture that permitted it. From the political crisis in 2019 in Malta and its relevance to the parliament building, one can further comprehend how, in the words of Tschumi, architecture 'ceases to be a backdrop for actions, becoming the action itself' (1996).

The symbiotic relationship of architecture with its public continues to be contested through the building in Malta, while the role of the architect as enabler in this process is reinforced. In Malta, the architect had to work within a complex historical narrative, while pre-empting what has become a complicated time in the Maltese political timeline. As the parliament building became the stage for this conflict, it performed its democratic role particularly because of the agency it gave its public. Rather than focusing solely on the chamber for its parliamentarians, the building offered a place for resistance to an imposed efficiency (Žižek 2015). It does this through the symbiosis between its symbolic value within the urban fabric, and its utilitarian function within the chamber's walls. The facilitation of the protests happened because of architectural decisions that will continue to manifest as performative action. While designing the building, the architect effectively assembled the event (Figure 17.6). Therefore, the architecture of the parliament building was central to the paralysis of the country that November. It remains a tool for public agency for Malta's future.

References

Agius, M. (2018) 'Justice minister gave orders to have Daphne Caruana Galizia memorial cleared, court told'. MaltaToday.com.mt. Available from: https://www.maltatoday.com.mt/news/court_and_police/90859/justice_minister_gave_orders_to_have_daphne_caruana_galizia_memorial_cleared_court_told (accessed on 16 October 2020).

ArchDaily (2015) 'Valletta City Gate/Renzo Piano Building Workshop'. Available from: https://www.archdaily.com/632066/valletta-city-gate-renzo-piano (accessed on 16 October 2020).

Baldacchino, G. (2002) 'A Nationless State? Malta, National Identity and the EU', *West European Politics*, 25(4), pp. 191–206. DOI: 10.1080/713601632.

Baldacchino, G. (2004) 'The Coming of Age of Island Studies', *Tijdschrift voor Economische en Sociale Geografie*, 95(3), pp. 272–283. DOI: 10.1111/j.1467-9663.2004.00307.x.

Billiard, E. (2014) *When the dark night rises. The morality of public space*. Available from: https://www.academia.edu/8025417/When_the_dark_night_rises_The_morality_of_public_space (accessed on 19 July 2021).

Borg, J. (2021) 'State should "shoulder responsibility" for Daphne assassination – inquiry'. *Times of Malta*. Available from: https://timesofmalta.com/articles/view/state-should-be-held-responsible-for-journalists-assassination.889936 (accessed on 29 July 2021).

Caruana Galizia, D. (2013) 'Amoral familism', *Daphne Caruana Galizia*. Available from: https://daphnecaruanagalizia.com/2013/03/amoral-familism/ (accessed on 16 August 2021).

Caruana Galizia, D. (2017) 'That crook Schembri was in court today, pleading that he is not a crook'. *Daphne Caruana Galizia's Notebook, Running Commentary*. Available from: https://daphnecaruanagalizia.com/2017/10/crook-schembri-court-today-pleading-not-crook/ (accessed on 16 October 2020).

Farrugia, C. (2021) '"I am genuinely sorry" – Owen Bonnici on clearing Daphne memorial'. *Times of Malta*. Available from: https://timesofmalta.com/articles/view/i-am-genuinely-sorry-owen-bonnici-on-clearing-daphne-memorial.922447 (accessed on 31 December 2021).

Fleri Soler, E. and Darmanin, A. (n.d.) 'Drawing the line – a Pavlovian experiment'. *Textcatalogue.com*. Available from: https://textcatalogue.com/portfolio/drawing-the-line-a-pavlovian-experiment-parliament-building-valletta/ (accessed on 9 January 2022).

Garside, J. (2017) 'Malta car bomb kills Panama Papers journalist'. *The Guardian*. Available from: https://www.theguardian.com/world/2017/oct/16/malta-car-bomb-kills-panama-papers-journalist (accessed on 9 January 2022).

Habermas, J. (1962) *The Structural Transformation of the Public Sphere*, 6th ed. Cambridge, MA: The MIT Press.

Politico (2022) *Malta — National parliament voting intention*. Available from: https://www.politico.eu/europe-poll-of-polls/malta/ (accessed on 28 January 2023).

Sennett, R. (2013) The Open City. Available from: https://www.youtube.com/watch?v=0uyHey4QuUE (accessed on 12 December 2021).

Stancati, M. (2019) 'Malta's prime minister hit by growing political crisis over journalist's assassination'. *Wall Street Journal*. Available from: https://www.wsj.com/articles/maltas-prime-minister-hit-by-growing-political-crisis-over-journalists-assassination-11575071155 (accessed on 16 October 2020).

Times of Malta (2021) 'Activists demand "Justice for Daphne" in monthly vigil'. *Times of Malta*. Available from: https://timesofmalta.com/articles/view/activists-demand-justice-for-daphne-in-monthly-vigil.887179 (accessed on 12 December 2021).

Tschumi, B. (1996) *Architecture and Disjunction*, Cambridge, MA: The MIT Press.

Vassallo, B. (2010) 'Renzo Piano's plans are a flop'. *Times of Malta*. Available from: https://timesofmalta.com/articles/view/renzo-pianos-plans-are-a-flop.302196 (accessed on 8 January 2022).

Veenendaal, W. (2019) 'How Smallness Fosters Clientelism: A Case Study of Malta', *Political Studies*, 67(4), pp. 1034–1052. DOI: 10.1177/0032321719828275.

Vella, M. (2019) 'Yorgen Fenech was guest at Girgenti Party in 2019, gifted Muscat three bottles of Petrus'. *MaltaToday*. Available from: https://www.maltatoday.com.mt/news/national/99440/yorgen_fenech_was_guest_at_girgenti_party_in_2019_gifted_muscat_three_bottles_of_petrus#.Yds9cmjMK3A (accessed on 9 January 2022).

Žižek, S. (2015) *Democracy and Capitalism Are Destined to Split Up*. BigThink [Online video]. Available from: https://youtu.be/AXVEnxtZe_w (acccessed on 4 August 2023)..

Part V

Mediated parliament and digital interactions

18

Mediating politics and architecture

The European Parliament from television to the digital age

Pol Esteve Castelló and Dennis Pohl

Introduction

In recent years, the use of digital communication platforms has affected all aspects of our lives – politics is not an exception. The digital era has drastically transformed the forms of engagement between citizens and institutional politics. Generalised internet access has changed the place and pace of political discussion; social media deeply impacts the tone of political debate while portable technologies have made the user a content generator and a dataset at the same time. When television turned politics into a reality show decades ago, information was distributed unidirectionally to a passive audience. However, the digital provides a means of interactive communication where each agent is both sender and receiver. The consequences of such paradigmatic change in the circulation of information are still being evaluated. But how do they relate to the architecture of politics – both physically and digitally? The European Parliament (EP), the only political body directly elected by 447 million European Union (EU) citizens, provides an exemplary case study to explore the potentials and risks brought by the digital era in relation to architecture, institutional politics and democracy.

Based on historical and field research conducted in the EP in 2016, this chapter questions what agency architecture has in shaping democracy between physical and digital space. We look at the media history of the EU to understand how politics and 'the political' meet in the institutional space of parliament and foster a democratic culture in the digital era. By politics we mean the regulated institutional speech and spatial setting that covers a broad set of activities related to government, political parties and politicians. Politics aims for consensus and involves citizens in different ways, from being passive spectators to becoming active interlocutors. By 'the political' we understand the negotiations in political debate beyond institutionally regulated speech. With Chantal Mouffe, we consider 'the political' as creating, 'agonistically', a heterogeneous public sphere (Mouffe 2005). This is conceived as a space where (political) adversaries do not become 'antagonistic', nor enemies. In fact, agonism is 'the very condition for a vibrant democracy' (Mouffe 2013, p. 7), and the necessary condition under which we see democratic culture developing in the coming years.

In this context, the EU and its parliament are paradigmatic of how new forms of remote and distributed participation through media allow for an agonistic expression of differentiated political voices. New media technologies are being incorporated into institutional politics, thus defining new patterns of regulated speech. Yet difficulties in bridging politics and 'the political' remain. This chapter addresses the tensions and opportunities emerging from the encounter between politics and 'the political' as it is reified in the relationship between physical space and mediated space. On one hand, we analyse how broadcasting and digital communications restructure political debate and citizen participation, creating new forms of speech. On the other hand, we recognise that new media platforms also produce inequalities and can even interfere with democratic processes.

Arranging speech between the *agora* and the *pnyx*

For architectural historians and political scientists, parliament is a legislative and representative institution. The parliament building in particular is considered both instrumental to regulating political speech and a symbol of democracy. In addition, political debate happens informally – or at least not regulated by institutional rules – in the street, the bar, the family living room and so on. The separation of these two differentiated spaces has been present in western culture at least since ancient Greece (Arendt 1958). Although this dichotomy might seem heuristic, as the distinction between public and private crosses these spaces (Habermas 1992), it reveals two distinct principles of regulated and informal speech. As the sociologist Richard Sennett argued, the complementarity between the *pnyx* as a space for orderly speech and the *agora* as a space to experience diversity with informal debates essentially equilibrated Greek political life (Sennett 1998). Heirs to the principles of the *pnyx*, western parliaments have spatially arranged a bipolar position between speaker and audience to organise political speech. Seating was designed to face either a principal orator or other parliamentary members. Parliamentary chambers are not built for distributed or multifocal political debate.

Even when television acquired a central role for political communication during the second half of the twentieth century, parliament remained the main physical site and symbol for political speech regulated by institutional rules. Following Sennett, parliament remained a *pnyx* while television enlarged the *agora*. Despite mass media accelerating the circulation of information, a gap remained between the parliament as a physical space for institutionally regulated speech and the outside as a physical space for informal forms of political debate regulated through social and informal norms, understandings and expectations. This is reflected in the fact that, until the digital era, scholars mainly addressed the space of parliament, and particularly the semicircle, focusing on their physical agency. Political scientists have considered how the ideology of political systems was reflected in architectural forms and the spatial disposition of the parliament (von Beyme 2004). Architects engaging with parliaments worldwide assumed that democratic or authoritarian notions were shaped by spatial settings (XML 2017). The form of a plenary hall, they argue, is not only explained by functional necessities such as acoustics or visual aspects, but an expression of political culture (Döring 1995; Sennett 1998).

Yet it became evident with the arrival of the digital that political debate inside and outside parliament might never have been quite as separated as Sennett suggests. Parliamentary debate already spilled over into television debate formats and social interactions, which in turn did not go unnoticed by parliamentarians. For instance, when the UK Parliament's sessions started to be broadcasted, parliamentarians feared politics would become a 'theatre' (Franklin 1992). But with the digital, Baudrillard's hypothesis of television drawing people into a play of images, blurring all boundaries between reality and simulation (Baudrillard 1983), seems to have been confirmed. At least partially, digital technologies blur the separation between these two allegedly differentiated physical spaces: parliament as the realm of politics and the space beyond it as the realm of 'the political'. Although television broadcasted parliamentary debates into living rooms and therefore directly inserted political speech into public debate, as much as radio and journalism formerly did, no interaction was possible. Parliament and the living room were unidirectionally connected until the digital era brought public interaction and informal debate closer to political institutions. With that, the logics of the public square, the bar and the living room, transformed democratic culture in unpredictable ways.

Televising the European Parliament

To understand the challenges brought by the digital, it is pertinent to look at how the advent of television changed the political setting in the EP. Contrary to digital media, adopted in reaction to its ubiquitous and fast development outside the institution, television has a pioneering history within the EP. The EP was the first parliament in history to broadcast its plenary sessions and implemented policies to distribute 'objective' news transnationally. Almost half a century ago, the EP adapted television protocols to transmit political speeches to an audience outside the chamber. It adopted media policies that regulated satellite transmission for a common market (Collins 1998; Holtz-Bacha 2006), and collaborated in setting up the TV channels Eurovision, Europa TV and Euronews to foster what it conceived as a new European *demos* in the first European elections of 1979. In a pioneering move, the Parliament introduced cameras to the semicircle and adapted its own plenary sessions to be publicly broadcast on television, at a time when national parliaments were still reluctant to do so.

The EP's proactive policies towards mass media – adapting its semicircle to camera positions, broadcasting parliamentary debates and standardising television technology throughout Europe – contrasted with politicians still following Winston Churchill's belief that parliament would need to be protected 'against the mass and against the machine'. By 'machine', Churchill was referring to television; for him it was 'a shocking thing to have the debates of Parliament forestalled by this new robot organisation of television and BBC broadcasting' (quoted in Cockerell 1988, p. 41; Franklin 1992). We hypothesise then not only that the EP has a history of media networks (television and radio) and formats (news, parliamentary debates, TV studio debates and so on) that have shaped public notions of a European democracy to date, but in the same fashion, we argue, the digital has the power to determine a future notion of European democracy.

Not coincidentally, the first step was taken when Denmark, the UK and Ireland joined the European Community in 1973. After the parliament had outgrown the physical capacity of the first parliament building, the Maison de l'Europe in Strasbourg, the semicircle in the new building, Palais d'Europe, was designed twice the size (Monnet et al. 1951; Dassler 1951). However, the main difference between these two buildings was that the visitor galleries in the former building were replaced by television facilities in the plenary hall. In other words, the new Palais d'Europe kept the audience at a televised distance. Furthermore, to improve the image quality of plenary sessions, the new TV cameras were operated with a remote-controlled robotic pan and tilt system by Vinten, a fast and precise mechanical device initially developed for military purposes (Figure 18.1). While this enhanced the video transmission, and thereby the viewer experience, it removed the cameramen as a human factor when broadcasting from the plenary hall.

From an adjunct television studio, operators were able to dial a camera position according to the seat of a member of the European Parliament (MEP) in order to record the speaker without disturbing the plenary session (Figure 18.2).

This period of the 1970s was marked by a general scepticism from the public, challenging the legitimacy of European integration. Consequently, the European Community sought to improve its public image and include citizens (Sternberg 2013, pp. 78–102). In this regard, television can be seen as an instrumental medium for the attempt to change what was perceived as a "'Europe of bureaucrats" into a "Europe of people"' – and to promote direct universal suffrage (European Parliament 1975, p. 69). The EP launched a large institutional television information campaign and directed advertising agencies in every member state to explain the

Figure 18.1 Remote Vinten television camera in the Plenary Hall. © European Communities, 1988

Figure 18.2 Audiovisual facilities in Strasbourg, 1994. © European Communities, 1994

elections in a 'neutral' way, to raise public awareness without political bias – at least in theory. In practice, no campaign, no speech, nor any TV camera is free of bias, as a closer look to the role of television in the Parliament will reveal.

Using technical standards for political reach

At the turn of the 1980s, the European Community was convinced that 'radio and television are today the chief media for informing and shaping public opinion'. For this reason, it supported the European Broadcasting Union (EBU)[1] and national television companies in turning the Eurovision network – which was established in the 1950s – into 'a European television channel' that promotes objective information and European culture as 'diversity in unity' (European Community 1982, pp. 110–112; Fickers and Lommers 2010).

The territorial coverage of Eurovision transmissions followed a clear geopolitical strategy. In order to reach its European target audience, Eurovision adopted specific technical standards so that the signal was received in western Europe – but not beyond the iron curtain.

To broadcast live content from the European parliamentary sessions, Eurovision operated with EBU transmission standards, called PAL and SECAM-L. The standards were not immediately compatible with the standards of the so-called Eastern Bloc, which had a different radio frequency spacing. Technically, black-and-white images could be received on both sides of the iron curtain; however, the east could not receive both image and sound simultaneously, but only one or the other (Simmering 1989, p. 3; Fickers 2007). Format and content thus reveal the political power of communication technologies. The use of technical standards predetermines the medium and the reach of the message: European politics would be televised only to western Europeans. Marshall McLuhan's 'global village', to whom the EP referred in TV-policy reports, was a western, Europeanised village framed by the EBU standards (European Commission 1983, p. 9).

During the 1980s, the EP not only adapted its own architecture with audiovisual equipment for broadcasting, but it also actively backed policies that saw in satellite television a means to counter Euroscepticism (Collins 1998; Holtz-Bacha 2006). Specifically, the EP believed that opening up its own proceedings for live television, and creating a common European News channel and a film organisation, could be beneficial in building up a common audience and a common image of Europe. The idea of a European television consortium took shape in autumn 1985. Four European broadcasters – the German ARD, the Dutch NOS, the Italian RAI and the Irish RTE, with the later addition of the Portuguese television RTP, joined forces to launch a new experimental programme, *Europa TV*. This aimed for a declared 'non-national perspective' to promote impartial and unbiased information but was rather short-lived. It closed after one year, revealing the limits of such an endeavour (European Parliament 1984a, p. 7; European Parliament 1984b, pp. 147–150).

Indeed, the extent to which a 'non-national perspective' can presume to be unbiased, and how the political shaping of parliamentary sessions affects the viewers' perceptions, became evident with events such as Ronald Reagan's address to the EP on 8 May 1985, the fortieth anniversary of the end of the Second World War. That day, his speech was interrupted by Left-wing and Green parliamentary members who protested from their seats against the proliferation of nuclear arms and the US intervention in Nicaragua (O'Donnell 1992). It cannot be attributed to the inattentiveness of the remote cameramen that the worldwide live coverage filmed by the official cameras from the centre of the semicircle entirely omits images of the protesters and any audience reactions. Contrastingly, footage by independent broadcaster cameras filming the

Figure 18.3 Protests in the background of Ronald Reagan's speech in the EP in Strasbourg on 8 May 1985. © European Communities 1985

same event from the journalist tribune show the antiwar message boards brought into the semicircle (Figure 18.3).[2]

Institutional and independent camera lenses thus offered two entirely different (political) perspectives. If muting public opinion was the price for objectivism, it was arguably the opposite of what the EP had intended – it was not 'adequately' informing European citizens. Quite the contrary: the audience does not know what the audience does not see. This episode made evident how the construction of institutional narratives depended on the spatial setting of broadcasting technologies. The position and framing of the camera is both a design and a political question: it determines what and who reaches the audience and thus shapes public debate.

In addition to the power to frame the view and control the message, television gave independent broadcasters the power to quantify TV quota, to process viewer data and calculate popularity. Even if broadcasting parliamentary sessions across the world have disappointing ratings, analysing viewer quota foreshadows a form of data economy for broadcasters, that becomes decisive for politics in the digital age. But beyond that, it confirmed Churchill's fears of turning politics into reality

TV shows, sustained by the fact that politicians could receive immediate feedback about the success and impact of their broadcasting footage in terms of audience parameters. This makes the media-technical condition of politics so problematic. Analysing, predicting and targeting the audience become as relevant as the content of debate: a media-based form of politics that would be decisive for later media strategies of populism. TV quota are the predigital statistical forms of what metadata means today for politics in the digital age (Pohl 2022). Consequently, it is only a question of computation power until these are strategically used as a weapon in politics. In other words, television was an efficient medium for the Parliament to distribute the principles of directed and regulated speech to the European public, but it bore risks for the institution which would only become explicit in the digital era.

Programming the European user-electorate

Following the introduction of television as a quantifiable medium in parliamentary activities, it is not surprising that the EU has also rapidly incorporated digital resources into its communication infrastructures. Its geographical scale together with its vast and diverse citizenry are reason enough to get a grip on the newest media technologies with the aim to foster citizen engagement. In the last years, EU institutions have become not only testing grounds for new narratives on power linked to media representation, but also a battleground to fight the disruptive impact that digital media can have on democratic processes. In recent years the Commission and the EP have been active in creating digital policies, such as the General Data Protection Regulation (GDPR) (European Union 2012). The arrival of social media and big data have accentuated a growing crisis of institutional disaffection, that was made particularly evident after the 2008 debt crisis divided Europe. In this context, the EP, like national parliaments, has had to confront the increasing presence and power of independent media platforms. Since the turn of the century, the EP – both as an instrument for the regulation of political speech and as a symbol of democracy – has developed a conflictual relationship with the faster and interactive forms of communication enabled by digital platforms.

In the last decades, the omnipresence and continuous information feed provided by digital platforms have considerably displaced political debate into the digital space. This is exemplified by political movements that made intensive use of social media, such as the Arab Spring (Wolfsfeld, Segev and Sheafer 2013) and the EuroMaidan (MacDuffee Metzger and

Tucker 2017) as well as the popularity of some politicians' private accounts on social media, such as the French president, Emmanuel Macron, with more than 4 million followers on Twitter or Italy's Deputy Prime Minister Matteo Salvini, with almost 1.5 million followers on Twitter. In this context, where new media has expanded the diversity and volume of politically relevant information (Schroeder 2018), certain parliamentary logics and principles of speech have been disrupted and substituted by a distributed field of online exchanges between political institutions and citizens, humans and bots. The unidirectionality of the orator speaking towards a defined audience in the plenary hall has been displaced by the constant real-time exchange of posts and comments between the public, which nurtures feeds and infinite scrolls and turns every user into a speaker.

If we look back at the distinction between spaces of orderly debate and of informal discussion signified by the *pnyx* and the *agora*, and we compare them with digital space and the logics of communication on digital platforms, the digital appears closer to the *agora* than the *pnyx*. While the debating practices of parliaments have been slow to adapt, digital media have brought informal debating principles of the public square closer to the parliament's semicircle. Or rather, perhaps, digital technologies have merged all spaces into one. It could be argued that a new representational topology emerged, in which several public spaces and private spaces overlap with each other. Departing from Gilles Deleuze's and Félix Guattari's understanding of the rhizomatic (Deleuze and Guattari 1987) as non-hierarchical, decentred and heterogeneous, we could argue that the digital is deployed in a rhizomatic space that opposes the logics of the Euclidean space of the physical parliament and semicircle. In other words, while the semicircle constitutes a topology that relies on objects and points – the relative position of the speaker and listener, the dais and so on – digital space constitutes a smooth topology that relies on sets of relations between multiple actors or users. This new topology is not predominantly visual, like the semicircle privileging the view towards the speaker or even television, but also tactile – the finger touches the screen or the keyboard to interact. Thus emerges a new representational topology for politics, one which is based not on the univocality of the parliamentarian speaker but on the polyvocality of digital users simultaneously interacting with the screens. The symbolic character of the parliament has been distributed into several platforms crossing the entire political spectrum, which are taken as representative for the interests of potential electoral groups.

The role of digital platforms in European politics became most evident during the process of the UK's referendum on European membership in

2016. In a context where European politics was contrasted to national politics, public interest in the referendum went hand in hand with the popularisation of social media, which rivalled television. Although this phenomenon was particularly acute in the UK, it also impacted European politics at large. At a national level, political debate was increasingly occurring outside institutional frameworks. Personal social media accounts of popular politicians and media personalities often had a stronger impact on national audiences than established television channels and press or institutional communications. Particularly in the UK, Facebook and Twitter contributed significantly to the politicisation of public debate (Brändle, Galpin and Trenz 2021; Šimunjak 2022). Contrastingly, on a European level, political actors like MEPs often lacked sufficient individual presence on social platforms to generate debate and public engagement.

Not long before the Brexit debate took over European politics, a technologically advanced television studio was erected inside the EP building in Brussels (Figure 18.4). With the intention to introduce more interactive forms of communication, the EP intuitively anticipated the role social media would acquire around the time of the referendum.[3]

This studio exceeded in scale and ambition those already existing in the Brussels and Strasbourg parliamentary complexes. The most advanced digital broadcasting equipment was installed in order to facilitate online live and interactive political discussions with the citizens through digital platforms. Independent journalists, analysts, specialists and parliamentarians themselves could use the set to engage in a conversation with a digital public. The new TV studio, along with institutional social media accounts – which generally had more followers than the personal accounts of MEPs – offered an institutional framework of a space and camera equipment for the MEPs to address the European public on social media, both through their own channels and the EP Facebook account. With this operation, the parliament building intended to become a more transparent space for debate, embracing the interactivity of digital platforms and breaking with the unidirectionality of the plenary sessions and broadcasting protocols still in place. The set was meant to operate as a sort of digital *agora* to produce political discourse. Participatory politics were enacted by Facebook Live discussions with politicians, where citizens were able to interact and ask direct questions. The new TV set facilitated the production of a stream of interactive content that, to an extent, could be institutionally curated – establishing live interaction, filtering the questions and allowing the speaker to prepare the conversation beforehand – and purposefully used to distribute an institutional narrative through social networks.

Figure 18.4　TV set in the interior of the European Parliament. © Esteve and Pohl 2019

This new operational format implied a shift from the passive televiewer-electorate towards a newly constituted user-electorate, addressed by interactive interfaces between the institution and citizens. It also revealed the need for other representational broadcasting spaces connected to the digital. The 'Brexit TV studio' – as we would name it after the relevance it acquired during Brexit discussion – is located in the central axis of the parliament building and has views over the main central hall and the public square in front of the building, significantly called Agora Simone Veil. The interactive set rivalled the semicircle in its privileged position within the building and in providing a representative space for (digital) political debate. In this set, the physical encountered the digital to create a representative space for interactive political debate and thus bring 'the political' to 'politics'.

However, despite these efforts, the results have been rather discrete in terms of popularity. For instance, when Antonio Tajani, at the time EP president, participated in a Facebook Live discussion, only around 700

Figure 18.5   Screenshot of Antonio Tajani, President of the European Parliament, in a Facebook Live discussion with citizens, 1 June 2019. © Esteve and Pohl 2019

out of 446 million inhabitants in the EU were connected (Tajani 2019; Figure 18.5).

In October 2021, similar results were obtained when Jytte Guteland, a member of the EP's committee for the environment, discussed on Facebook Live the European Climate Law,[4] affecting environmental policies until 2050 – which was going to be voted on the day after in the semicircle. Furthermore, the presence of the EP on social networks is residual, and direct citizen participation in political debate through digital platforms is almost negligible. As an example, the EP president Roberta Metsola has only 57,000 followers on Instagram and 61,000 on Twitter; the EP's Facebook page has around 2.6 million followers, its Instagram account 330,000. Taking into consideration that Europe has around 400 million active Facebook users, more than 100 million on Instagram and around 120 million on Twitter, the engagement with the EP's institutional and MEPs' personal accounts is low. There are surely multiple reasons behind citizens' disengagement, but we suggest that exchanges such as Facebook Live are seen as impactless events, which are instrumentalised by the institution to create an *image* of openness, rather than being an effective tool for public participation.

Participation versus representation

In recent years, participatory politics has been on the agenda of European institutions to further engage with citizens, advance democratic strategies and counteract misuses of media platforms. Like television, social media is quantifiable, polls can be generated equally by viewer and user data. The data generated by clicks, likes and comments can be used purposefully to better understand citizens' political stances and expose users to certain content, shaping opinions with the very form of the digital space people navigate in. This can also be misused, when platforms such as Facebook are instrumentalised to interfere in the public debate with partisan purposes – as we have seen with the Cambridge Analytica affair (Cadwalladr 2017; Brändle et al. 2021).

Motivated by the EU's decade-long efforts of institutional legitimacy, participation was seen as key for setting up a less hierarchical 'good governance', according to the EC white paper from 2001 (European Commission 2001, p. 10; Sternberg 2013, pp. 128–152). In 2019, the EU's chief Brexit negotiator Michel Barnier set out three principles for a more participative democracy: transparency (making as many documents as possible public), cooperation (with all key decision-makers, notably member state governments and the EP) and consultation (with business representatives, think tanks, civil society and other interest groups). These principles had already been introduced by the Lisbon Treaty as transparency, civil society dialogue and participation in Article 8 (European Union 2007), and were consolidated on the Treaty on European Union revision in Title II Articles 9 to 11, which affirm the right of every citizen to 'participate in the democratic life of the Union' (European Union 2012).

Barnier did not speak for the EP and the examples above were not direct EP initiatives, yet they reflected an overall ambition of EU institutions to bring politics closer to citizens. But with Brexit looming, the EP adapted its architecture with the TV studio and its media politics with the aim to expand democratic participation – also digitally. Building on the European Citizens Initiative,[5] the European Network of Ombudsmen,[6] or the European Parliament Committee on Petitions,[7] the institutions seek to further engage with private actors and platforms – such as Change.org. Most recently, the Conference on the Future of Europe was designed as a hybrid forum, to include online interaction and physical participation (Figure 18.6). In partnership with the Commission and the Council, the EP launched a website, where citizens could interactively discuss and register their opinions, and co-hosted a series of live events, organised by independent entities across Europe. The objective was to engage with citizens across EU territories and, in their words, to listen 'from all walks of life and corners of the Union'.[8] First assessments, however, criticised the conference as being a blend between bottom-up participatory democracy and top-down elite decision-making, in which the constitutional mandate and institutional organisation remain uncertain (Fabbrini 2020).

In parallel, as the EP in Brussels outgrows its own building, it continues to expand physically, most recently in 2008 with the addition of the

Figure 18.6   Inaugural event of the Conference on the Future of Europe in the EP in Strasbourg on 9 May 2021. © European Union 2021

Figure 18.7 View of an editing room in the EP in Brussels. On the screens can be seen several of the meeting rooms in the complex. © Esteve and Pohl 2021

József Antall building and its five large conference rooms (Figure 18.7). Hundreds of political discussions hosted by the parliamentarians, 27 committees and subcommittees and 39 delegations, which happen across the parliamentary buildings, are still inaccessible to citizens. The general public cannot access the building without special permission, meetings and discussions can only partially be followed online in a non-interactive manner. Architecture continues to act as a filter mechanism.

With the EP announcing a new architectural competition for the redesign of its plenary building in Brussels on 26 May 2020, public access and transparency may now be reconsidered – but equally, it may not. Although the competition brief insisted on the symbolic relevance of the EP as the 'home of European democracy', the relation to digital media remained underdeveloped. Instead, the brief stated that 'democratic heritage' should be 'preserved and further developed as a strong symbol of our modern history'. For the Parliament, this meant that it 'seeks a paradigm of architecture and strong visual identity for the building and the Chamber. This design should […] resonate with the European citizens as a representation of the power of their voice' (European Parliament 2020). Representation instead of participation was also the guiding principle in the antiquated media concepts in the brief, meticulously explaining the arrangement of journalists and camera crews. Consequently, it remains up to the design team to find creative solutions to address the role of digital media in relation to the physical spaces of the parliament.

Conclusion: designing policies, protocols and architecture for a *phygital* parliament

Despite the undeniable disruptive impact the digital space has had on representative democracy in recent years, such as misinformation, surveillance abuse, and troll farms, it is still unclear how the digital space can be shaped according to principles of representative democracy. We have observed how the EU adapted to the rise of digital media through new policies, such as the GDPR, and through physical interventions in the working of its parliament, such as the Brexit TV studio. The physical space of the parliament could provide valuable insight into this problem, as designing policies and architecture becomes a collaborative task for politicians and architects alike, that has a particular history within the EP.

Doubtless, the efforts of participatory democracy over the course of European integration cannot only be assigned to the EP. Euroscepticism has been a challenge for the entire European Community at least since the 1970s. However, the EP has probably been the most affected institution.

As the history of television shows, the EP broadcasted its plenary sessions, adapted its plenary hall to TV cameras, and advocated for several TV programmes to promote the first European elections in the late 1970s. In other words, television became instrumental for the EP, literally mediating representative democracy. But while television reached the targeted audience, it excluded any form of interaction.

Even if new digital media may promise participatory democracy, and the EP made efforts to be present on social media platforms, they come along with the pitfall of risking manipulation, capture and access inequality. In a recent article in *The Economist*, the founder of *Renew Democracy*, Garry Kasparov (Kasparov 2020), advocated for further integration between technology and politics. The initiative's aim was to avoid market forces and interests conflicting with democratic principles to take control of the media complex, instead enabling social communication and political discussion. If the EP were to redesign its media politics, it should start by questioning the normativity and structure of hegemonic digital platforms. Instead of taking these for granted, the EU has the legislative power to redesign Europe's communication channels, while the EP could apply such legislation in favour of public interest, integrating its own plenary procedures with *agoraic* political debate.

Nevertheless, representative democracy has something to offer that social media cannot replace. It provides clear procedural principles of speech, allowing different factions of society to be heard through their representatives. Even if not all citizens feel fully represented, at least the regulatory practices of speech offer a space of discussion that avoids the negative implications of political debate in social media. Often, the attention economy of social media reduces information to emotional content, prioritises popular feeds, and creates intellectual isolation by personalised information selectivity according to the ideological frame of user groups. In the Greek *agora* it meant only those who shouted their opinion the loudest were heard. Representative democracy, on the contrary, mediates information in a regulated manner, ideally considering manifold informed perspectives to arrive at a public judgement and deep deliberation. In the Greek *pnyx* it meant regulated speech of elected representatives, facilitated by a specific type of parliamentary architecture. So how could architecture help to mediate between the two?

The challenge is to link digital infrastructures to physical space, supporting participation by embracing both the capacity of social platforms to generate interest in politics and the human affects generated in physical encounters. Or even more importantly, to constitute a new participatory architecture between digital and physical that includes representative democratic principles. For the participatory dynamics of social media, this means to learn from the orderly principles of the *pnyx*, the semicircle and the parliament, by including productive strategies to articulate speech into the digital, stemming from the tradition of institutional representative democracy. Institutional architecture could also challenge its traditional configurations, by considering the form of the parliament and expanding its activities beyond its current limits by embracing the potentials of remote interaction. This could provide the necessary equilibrium for democracy between spaces for regulated speech and informal debate, integrating them in one. The future of democracy needs to overcome the duality of the *agora* and the *pnyx* while seeking the construction of an agonistic public sphere. It needs to imagine a new smooth topology that also contains objects and points. It is in the capacity of the EU and the EP to design and build this *phygital* in-between – between digital and physical – that opens the possibility of politics meeting 'the political' in unforeseen ways, and yet fosters new forms of agonistic speech on which democracy could keep growing.

Notes

1 The European Broadcasting Union is an organisation of public service media founded in 1950. It is unrelated to the EU but has broadcast debates between candidates to the European Commission presidency and parliamentary elections.

2 Compare President Reagan's Address to the European Parliament in Strasbourg, France, 8 May 1985, https://www.youtube.com/watch?v=Dysv5ozSj5w (accessed on 8 May 2020) and President Reagan's Trip to Strasbourg, France, on 8 May 1985, https://www.youtube.com/watch?v=BBrRbOh92LI (accessed on 8 May 2020).

3 The information regarding the installation of the new TV set has been gathered from an interview with Johanna Den Hertog and Wilfried Kumeling, both members of the Directorate-General for Communication, Directorate for Media, and Audiovisual Unit of the European Parliament. The interview was conducted on 18 November 2021 in the European Parliament in Brussels.

4 Regulation (EU) 2021/1119 of the European Parliament and of the Council of 30 June 2021 establishing the framework for achieving climate neutrality and amending Regulations (EC) No. 401/2009 and (EU) 2018/1999.

5 The European Citizens' Initiative, introduced in the Treaty of Lisbon, is an EU mechanism providing a direct path for citizens to propose new laws. Its aim is to enable EU citizens to participate directly in the development of EU policies. Any initiative reaching 1 million signatures will be considered by the European Commission. Further information can be found here: https://europa.eu/citizens-initiative/_en (accessed on 29 February 2022).

6 The European Network of Ombudsmen, established in 1996, links together national and regional ombudsmen in Europe, and similar bodies of the EU member states, candidate countries, and other European Economic Area countries, as well as the European Ombudsman and the Committee on Petitions of the European Parliament, to address citizens' complaints at the right levels.

7 The European Parliament Committee on Petitions is a body ensuring that all citizens' petitions are provided with a response: https://www.europarl.europa.eu/petitions/en/home (accessed on 29 February 2022).

8 See: What is the Conference on the Future of Europe? https://futureu.europa.eu/pages/about?locale=en (accessed on 3 March 2022).

References

Arendt, H. (1958) *The Human Condition*, Chicago: University of Chicago Press.

Baudrillard, J. (1983) 'The Ecstasy of Communication', in H. Foster (ed.), *The Anti-Aesthetic: Essays on Postmodern Culture*, Port Townsend, WA: Bay Press, pp. 126–134.

Brändle, V.K., Galpin, C. and Trenz, H. (2021) 'Brexit as "politics of division": social media campaigning after the referendum', *Social Movement Studies*, 21(1–2), pp. 234–253. DOI: 10.1080/14742837.2021.1928484.

Cadwalladr, C. (2017) 'The great British Brexit robbery: how our democracy was hijacked', *The Guardian*, 7 May. Available from: https://www.theguardian.com/technology/2017/may/07/the-great-british-brexit-robbery-hijacked-democracy.

Cockerell, M. (1988) *Live from Number 10: The Inside Story of Prime Ministers and Television*, London: Faber.

Collins, R. (1998) *From Satellite to Single Market: New Communication Technology and European Public Service Television*, London: Routledge.

Dassler, E. (1951) 'Haus des Europa-Rates in Strassburg', in *Die neue Stadt: Zeitschrift für die Gestaltung von Stadt und Land*, vol. 5, pp. 22–26.

Deleuze, G. and Guattari, F. (1987) *A Thousand Plateaus*, Minneapolis: University of Minnesota Press.

Döring, H. (1995) 'Die Sitzordnung des Parlaments als Ausdruck unterschiedlicher Leitprinzipien von Demokratie', in A. Dörner and L. Vogt (eds), *Sprache des Parlaments und Semiotik der Demokratie*, Berlin: de Gruyter, pp. 278–289.

European Commission (1983) *Interim Report: Realities and Tendencies in European Television: Perspectives and Options*, 25 May, HAEC, COM (83) 229.

European Commission (2001) *European Governance: A White Paper* (COM (2001) 428).

European Community (1982) *Official Journal of the European Communities* (OJ), C 87 (5 April).

European Parliament (1975) 'Institutions and organs of the Communities', in *Bulletin of the European Communities*, no. 1.

European Parliament (1984a) 'Minutes of Proceedings of the Sitting on Monday', 13 February, in OJ, C 77 (19 March).

European Parliament (1984b) 'Resolution on Broadcast Communication in the European Community (The Threat to Diversity of Opinion Posed by Commercialization of the New Media)', [The Hutton Resolution], in OJ, C 127 (14 May).

European Parliament (2020) *International Design Competition of the Paul-Henri Spaak Building in Brussels*. Available from: https://www.european-parliament-design-competition.eu/projects_european-parliament-design-competition_information_e.htm (accessed on 1 November 2020).

European Parliament and Council of the European Union (2016) 'Regulation (EU) 2016/679 of 27 April 2016 on the Protection of Natural Persons with Regard to the Processing of Personal Data and on the Free Movement of such Data, and Repealing Directive 95/46/EC (General Data Protection Regulation), in OJ, L 119/1 (4 May 2016). Available from: http://data.europa.eu/eli/reg/2016/679/oj

European Union (2007) 'Treaty of Lisbon amending the Treaty on European Union and the Treaty establishing the European Community', signed at Lisbon, 13 December. OJ C 306, (17 December). Available from: https://eur-lex.europa.eu/legal-content/EN/TXT/?uri=CELEX:12007L/TXT.

European Union (2012) 'Consolidated Version of the Treaty on European Union', OJ 326/13, 26.10.2012. Available from: https://eur-lex.europa.eu/resource.html?uri=cellar:2bf140bf-a3f8-4ab2-b506-fd71826e6da6.0023.02/DOC_1&format=PDF.

Fabbrini, F. (2020) 'The Conference on the Future of Europe: process and prospects', *European Law Journal*, 26(5–6), pp. 401–414. DOI: 10.1111/eulj.12401.

Fickers, A. (2007) *"Politique de la grandeur" versus "Made in Germany"*, Munich: R. Oldenburg Verlag, pp. 82–98.

Fickers, A. and Lommers, S. (2010) 'Eventing Europe: Broadcasting and the Mediated Performances of Europe', in A. Badenoch and A. Fickers (eds), *Materializing Europe: Transnational Infrastructures and the Project of Europe*, Basingstoke: Palgrave MacMillan, pp. 225–252.

Franklin, B. (ed.) (1992) *Televising Democracies*, London; New York: Routledge.

Habermas, J. (1992) *The Structural Transformation of the Public Sphere: An Inquiry into a Category of Bourgeois Society*, Cambridge, MA: Polity Press.

Holtz-Bacha, C. (2006) *Medienpolitik für Europa*, Wiesbaden: VS Verlag für Sozialwissenschaften.

Kasparov, G. (2020) 'Garry Kasparov on the need to improve our politics with technology', *The Economist*, 12 October. Available from: https://www.economist.com/by-invitation/2020/10/12/garry-kasparov-on-the-need-to-improve-our-politics-with-technology.

MacDuffee Metzger, M. and Tucker, J.A. (2017) 'Social media and EuroMaidan: a review essay', *Slavic Review*, 76(1), pp. 169–191. DOI: 10.1017/slr.2017.16.

Monnet, B., Cromback, L., Guri, F. and Schirrer, V. (1951) 'Les bâtiments semi-permanents du Conseil de l'Europe à Strasbourg', *L'Architecture d'aujourd'hui*, 22, p. 86.

Mouffe, C. (2005) *On the Political*, Abingdon, New York: Routledge.

Mouffe, C. (2013) *Agonistics: Thinking the World Politically*, London: Verso.

O'Donnell, T. (1992) 'Europe on the Move: The Traveling Parliament Roadshow', in B. Franklin (ed.), *Televising Democracies*, London: Routledge, pp. 262–263.

Pohl, D. (2022) 'Cedric Price's pop-up parliament: a role model for media architecture and data politics', *Footprint*, 15(2), pp. 93–106. DOI: 10.7480/footprint.15.2.6115.

Schroeder, R. (2018) *Social Theory After the Internet: Media, Technology and Globalization*, London: UCL Press.

Sennett, R. (1998) *The Spaces of Democracy*, Ann Arbor: University of Michigan College of Ann Arbor.

Simmering, K. (1989) *HDTV – High Definition Television. Technische, ökonomische und programmliche Aspekte einer neuen Fernsehtechnik*, Bochum: Studienverlag Brockmeyer.

Šimunjak, M. (2022) *Tweeting Brexit: Social Media and the Aftermath of the EU Referendum*, London: Routledge.

Sternberg, C. (2013) *The Struggle of EU Legitimacy*, London: Palgrave Macmillan.

Tajani, A. (2019) 'Discuss live with Antonio Tajani. President of the European Parliament', Facebook Live, 1 June (accessed on 1 June 2019).

von Beyme, K. (2004) 'Politische Ikonologie der modernen Architektur', in B. Schwelling (ed.), *Politikwissenschaft als Kulturwissenschaft: Theorien, Methoden, Problemstellungen*, Leverkusen: Leske+Budrich, pp. 351–372.

Wolfsfeld, G., Segev, E. and Sheafer, T. (2013) 'Social media and the Arab Spring: politics come first', *The International Journal of Press/Politics*, 18(2), pp. 115–137. DOI: 10.1177/1940161212471716.

XML (2017) *Parliaments*, Amsterdam: XML.

19

Knife edge

Abingdon Street Gardens and its field of vision

James Benedict Brown

Abingdon Street Gardens and the mediated space of British politics

The statutory devolution of self-government to Scotland, Wales and Northern Ireland has led to the commissioning of two modern parliamentary buildings that were deliberately designed to include television cameras and to consider the needs of political journalists and commentators. The buildings housing the Scottish Parliament in Holyrood, Edinburgh (Enric Miralles, 1999–2004), and the National Assembly for Wales, the Senedd, in Cardiff (Richard Rogers Partnership, 2001–2006), feature not only broadcast-ready debating chambers (designed with camera positions and fields of view in mind). They also offer offices for journalists to work from, and comfortable and generous interior spaces for on-camera interviews.[1] But like many European legislatures, the building housing the UK Parliament, the nineteenth-century Palace of Westminster, predates the television age.

Building on previous work on mediated spaces (Brown 2018, 2019), which examined the relationship of the television camera to architecture and urban spaces *designed* for broadcast TV, this chapter is a critical exploration of the mediated image of an *existing* building. It will first discuss the Palace itself, and its exterior, with reference to a set of cultural and political values which have historically framed it, and as a shorthand for British democracy today. Then it will look at how the conditions affecting media access to the Houses of Parliament and their location in central London frame the Palace of Westminster, above all, from the point of a view of one particular public park, Abingdon Street Gardens. The significance of this park, the field of vision it established and the Henry Moore sculpture *Knife Edge Two Piece* which it houses, became particularly apparent in the months leading up to and following the United Kingdom's referendum on European Union membership, held on 23 June 2016.

The Palace of Westminster

The design of the Palace of Westminster (1840–1876) is jointly attributed to Charles Barry (1795–1860) and Augustus Welby Pugin (1812–1852), although Pugin's contribution was not initially acknowledged to the extent that it is today. Fazio, Moffett and Wodehouse ascribe the overall arrangement of the building to Barry, but the 'profusion of lively and historically correct detail, inside and out, was Pugin's' (Fazio, Moffett and Wodehouse 2013, p. 421). Having converted to Catholicism in 1834, Pugin had earlier been denied commissions on the grounds of his faith. He was obliged to submit his designs for the Palace of Westminster in the names of the architects Gillespie-Graham and Charles Barry. Barry omitted to give any credit to Pugin for his huge contribution to the design (Hill 2007, p. 480). Pugin's son Edward published a short pamphlet entitled *Who Was the Art Architect of the Houses of Parliament, a statement of facts* (Pugin 1867) which sought to correct the presumption that Pugin had not contributed to the design of the building.

Pugin's father was a draughtsman who had emigrated from France during the Revolution. During his youth, his father published multiple volumes of drawings including *Specimens of Gothic Architecture* and *Examples of Gothic Architecture* (Pugin and Wilson 1825), which became the standard references for Gothic architecture for a century or more. In addition to being apprenticed in all aspects of the Gothic, Pugin the younger, in turn, published two editions of *Contrasts* (1836 and 1841), a polemic in favour of the Gothic style that made a number of famously biased comparisons between examples of Gothic and classical architecture, as well as *The True Principles of Pointed or Christian Architecture* (1841), which was premised on his two fundamental principles of Christian architecture. The Palace of Westminster is regarded as the greatest achievement of Pugin's architectural career, a building that lived up to his aspiration to demonstrate that 'not only was late Gothic much superior to anything built in the modern period, it was so because late Gothic society outshined the contemporary industrial world in its humaneness and faith' (Kostof 2010, p. 589).

With Barry and Pugin's winning design for the Palace, the Gothic revival was in the ascendency for public commissions in England. By the

1860s, Lord Palmerston blocked George Gilbert Scott's classicist proposal for the Foreign Office and War Office, demanding a redesign. The Palace of Westminster remains a landmark not only of British society but also for what Pugin called 'pointed' architecture, with its asymmetrical massing on a large but awkwardly shaped site, its varied silhouette and plasticity of form. Through the Palace of Westminster, we can read not only an argument for the decline of the classical style and the ascension of the Gothic, but also the intersection of an idiomatic nationalism and the celebration of craftsmanship at a time of increasing mass production and industrialisation (Kostof 2010, pp. 592–594).

Indeed, Pugin regarded the Gothic revival as an embodiment of the moral and religious values that were threatened by the emerging industrial era. The building could not have been realised without modern materials, but apart from certain interior details, these were generally hidden behind hand-carved limestone from the Anston Quarry in Yorkshire. The 98-metre-tall Victoria Tower (the world's tallest square tower at the time of its completion), the 18-metre-tall royal entrance at its base and the fire-proofed Parliamentary Archives were only conceivable thanks to a sophisticated structural system of cast iron columns and girders. Yet the building's stone façades are richly and densely decorated with references to a pre-industrial Britain: below the windows are heraldic symbols, often a crown and shield or a floral motif. The carved symbol of a portcullis gate appears repeatedly, referring to what Christopher Jones describes as Barry's intention that the building 'was to be a legislative castle [and] the King's Tower its keep' (Jones 1984, p. 113). Indeed, the portcullis is now the official logo of the British Parliament, appearing on its website and stationery as a symbol of the solidity of British democracy.

The Palace and its exterior

Whereas the decoration of the Palace of Westminster can be interpreted in its historical context as a manifestation of a set of cultural and political values, today the exterior of the Palace of Westminster has also become a visual shorthand for British government, democracy and the country. We are familiar with the exterior of the Palace of Westminster in film and television precisely because media access to the interior is so strictly controlled. The interior of the building has very different conditions, affecting its representation in the media. It took several decades of debate before fixed television cameras were installed in the House of Commons in 1989 to provide news broadcasters with footage of speeches and debates. In terms of the one-to-one interviewing of individuals, strict rules govern the rights of journalists to interview politicians and civil servants within the complex (Serjeant at Arms and Black Rod 2017). Only accredited reporters are permitted to conduct interviews and only in carefully designated interior spaces of the Palace, such as the Central Lobby. The privilege of journalistic access to politicians in the Central Lobby leads to the moniker of *lobby correspondent*, namely senior member of the press with direct but often unattributable access to members of Parliament. To facilitate broader media access to conduct interviews with peers and MPs, interviews by a wider range of journalists and outlets must take place outside the building.

The prominent location of the Palace of Westminster beside the River Thames places it in a wide number of public fields of vision. These include the public right of way along the South Bank between Westminster and Lambeth bridges, the latter being a favourite of solo videographers or foreign correspondents, and from office buildings across the river on the Albert Embankment, where at least one independent production company rents out by the hour or day a small studio in a corner suite facing the parliament buildings. However, these locations, separated from the Palace of Westminster by the breadth of the river, are not so amendable to the immediacy of journalism responding to rapidly unfolding political events. What they gain in wide angle views of the Palace they lose in proximity to members of Parliament. Given these constraints, and restricted from interviewing politicians within the grounds of the Palace, many broadcasters have established (albeit temporary) footholds in a small park to the south-west: Abingdon Street Gardens.

Abingdon Street Gardens is a park with a relatively short but telegenic history. In the title sequence of Patrick McGoohan's enigmatic television series *The Prisoner* (1967), a secret agent drives into an underground car park adjacent to the Palace of Westminster in London (Figures 19.1 and 19.2). Passing via an underground corridor into an adjacent building, presumably in or close to the Palace itself, he storms into an office and delivers his resignation, triggering his abduction and interrogation. That two-storey car park lies beneath Abingdon Street Gardens. We never discover why the agent, known only as Number Six, resigns, nor do we discover what information he might still possess about the activities of the British state. But we are reminded at the beginning of each episode, in which a new Number Two attempts fruitlessly to interrogate Number Six, that the import of his position and knowledge is great. His shadowy employers operated from a location so secret it needed hiding underground and so important that it had to be adjacent to the legislature, closer even than the Security Service MI5 or the Secret Intelligence Service MI6.

Figure 19.1 Still from the title sequence of *The Prisoner* (dir. Patrick McGoohan and others, © ITC Entertainment, 1968)

Figure 19.2 Still from the title sequence of *The Prisoner* (dir. Patrick McGoohan and others, © ITC Entertainment, 1968)

Designed by Eric Bedford (1909–2001; best known for his design of the BT Tower, 1961–1964), Abingdon Street Gardens and its car park were created after Luftwaffe bombing in the Second World War damaged the eighteenth-century terraces of houses on Abingdon Street and College Mews (Collins 2019). Today, the car park is managed by a commercial operator but is closed to members of the public. At street level, Abingdon Street Gardens are part of the parliamentary estate and open to the public except in times of heightened political activity when they are closed to provide television and radio broadcasters space for outside broadcasts with a visual backdrop of the Palace of Westminster. In the last decade, the park has witnessed an ever-increasing number of days of media occupation per annum, covering four general elections, 12 budgets and two referendums, Scotland's membership of the UK and the UK's membership of the EU.

In fact, media use of Abingdon Street Gardens has become so extensive that, in 2020, an application was made to Westminster City Council to redesign the southern perimeter of the park to facilitate extended periods of closure, including the erection of temporary structures, tents and gazebos in the park from which television broadcasters can conduct interviews. Public protests for and against the outcome of the EU referendum have caused Parliament, City of London police and broadcasters to change how they use Abingdon Gardens too (Wheeler 2019). With the intensification of public interest in the referendum on the UK's membership of the EU, for instance, more substantial fencing was constructed and police protection of the Abingdon Street Gardens media village was heightened. Within the densely populated temporary city of television and radio studios, modular mesh fencing was also constructed to protect the park's only public artwork, *Knife Edge Two Piece* by Henry Moore, 1962–1965 (Figures 19.3 and 19.4).

Knife Edge Two Piece

Knife Edge Two Piece was unveiled in the presence of the minister for the arts, Jennie Lee, the minister of works, Robert Mellish, and Sir Kenneth Clark on 1 November 1967,[2] the same year that our unnamed spy drove into Abingdon Street to deliver his resignation. The era of Moore's work which *Knife Edge Two Piece* represents was a turning point in Moore's practice (Moore 2002), being one of his earliest abstract works cast in two pieces. As Moore shifted his focus from exploring the human figure to abstract forms, the Knife Edge series introduced a new abstraction to the human form and a new subjectivity to the viewer's gaze. Different

Figure 19.3 Abingdon Street Gardens, Westminster. © Magnus Manske, CC BY-SA 2.0

from his series of reclining figures, many of which he would cast in more than one part, *Knife Edge Two Piece* is an enigmatic arrangement of two monumental forms.

Whereas earlier fragmented reclining forms can be interpreted by the viewer as parts of a single figure, *Knife Edge Two Piece* and the works that followed it explore a new kind of plasticity, one in which the tension of the two pieces is articulated by the space between them. The twisting forms of bronze recall both geological forms but also animal bones. A ravine emerges as the viewer moves around the sculpture, inviting them to look through the smooth bronze surfaces upon the richly carved stone façade of the Palace of Westminster. The contrast between Moore's bronze and Barry's stonework was heightened by coinciding with the completion of a four-decade project (1928–1960) of restoration works at the Palace of Westminster, which replaced pieces decaying due to air pollution.

Knife Edge Two Piece is not unique. The cast in Abingdon Street Gardens is one of four made between 1962 and 1965. One other is in England, at Henry Moore's former home and studio, Perry Green, in Hertfordshire. The others were exported across the Atlantic: one stands in Queen Elizabeth Park in Vancouver, British Columbia, while the other is

Figure 19.4 *Knife Edge Two Piece* by Henry Moore. © James Benedict Brown

in the gardens of Kykuit, the house of the Rockefeller family in Tarrytown, New York. The cast in Abingdon Street Gardens is by far the most publicly accessible work in this series, and the only one adjacent to a historically significant building. Implicit in the relationship of *Knife Edge Two Piece* to the Palace of Westminster is the tension between two interdependent parties, suggestive of the historically oppositional nature of two-party politics and the axial debating chamber in the House of Commons. It is significant that the sculpture was initially positioned several metres to the south of where it now stands, but with Moore's involvement it was moved and rotated 180 degrees in 1970. Over the first three years of its installation in Abingdon Street Gardens, it is apparent that Moore visited the work often, reconsidering its relationship to its broader context and ultimately proposing its repositioning.

The Gothic revivalist architecture of the Palace of Westminster represents an embodiment of the values that were being threatened by an emerging industrial revolution. Set against this backdrop, Moore's sculpture represents a similar shift. Composed in the 'white heat' (Wilson 1963) of Britain's cultural and economic renaissance in the 1960s, *Knife*

Edge Two Piece is the most prominent example of Moore's dramatic turn towards abstraction. It is reductive to imply an analogy between the two pieces of the sculpture and the oppositional nature of two-party British politics, but Moore's precise selection of the site, the sculpture's relocation and rotation strongly suggest that he maintained a critical relationship with the piece. The fact that Moore revisited Abingdon Street Gardens to recommend the repositioning of *Knife Edge Two Piece* relative to the Palace of Westminster suggests that he was keenly aware of its relationship to its context.

Abingdon Street Gardens and its field of vision

Just as the Palace of Westminster was a considered backdrop for Moore's sculpture, the strict rules that determine the activities of journalists inside the Palace have inadvertently contributed to the heightened importance of the building's elevations. Captured from a range of obtuse angles, depending on the implied importance of the media outlet producing the imagery, the architecture of the Palace has become less an enclosure for political debate and more a backdrop for political argument. The trend for politicians to announce policy or make important statements via press conferences or interviews instead of in parliamentary session reflects not only the limited access of journalists to question politicians but also the limitations on politicians to promote policy, reactions and opinions directly to the media (Curtis 2011).

At the height of its temporary use by journalists and technical crew, Abingdon Street Gardens becomes a largely autonomous media village, one of the most digitally connected and mediated spaces in the world. The only permanent elements are modest wall boxes that house connections to telecommunications networks, providing broadcasters with high-speed data connections. On the adjacent streets, parking spaces are reserved for the trucks containing satellite uplink hardware. A city of temporary structures, including waterproof garden gazebos, tents and enclosed temporary studio spaces, is erected for permitted durations of time. Their position on the park is determined by an unwritten code of journalistic superiority, with Britain's three primary television news producers (BBC, ITN and Sky) occupying the plots with the greatest space and the most unhindered view of the Palace of Westminster. A dozen or more smaller temporary structures are assigned to agencies and overseas broadcasters, each arranged to create a curving auditorium of journalistic witness that overlooks the Palace's west façade.

As a result of the hive of media activity occurring in Abingdon Street Gardens, the consequential views over the Palace of Westminster have become a magnet for public protest. Journalists and members of Parliament reported that they perceived a heightened sense of insecurity when walking to and from the park and participating in interviews while pro- and anti-Brexit campaigners competed for prominence in the background of television footage (Wheeler 2019). Whereas Moore's *Knife Edge Two Piece* was previously the only part of the park to be fenced in to protect it from accidental damage, Abingdon Street Gardens is now patrolled and protected by police officers during these periods. In February 2020, an application was made to Westminster City Council to redesign the wall and gate along Abingdon Street to better secure the site during periods of temporary public closure (Westminster City Council 2020).

Whereas Parliament Square Garden, slightly to the north and opposite the Elizabeth Tower, has historically been a more frequent site of collective gathering and protest, the location, position and field of vision from Abingdon Street Gardens now gives it a new importance. Abingdon Street Gardens once provided a convenient locale for impromptu broadcast interviews between parliamentarians and roving journalists who were excluded from the lobbies, but the heightened national and international interest in British politics in recent years has led to the establishment of a small village of semipermanent buildings. During the months leading up to and following the Brexit referendum, a small city of tents, rostrums and gazebos had become a fixture of Westminster's streetscape, formalised by the planning permission sought by the British government. The once privileged access afforded to journalists in the lobbies, inside the Palace of Westminster, was eclipsed by the more frenzied activity between a wider section of parliamentarians and journalists outside. Within the small area of the park itself, organised by the parliamentary estate, the media conurbation was organised around implicit media hierarchies, with Britain's most prominent broadcasters afforded two-storey structures and the most uninterrupted view of the Palace of Westminster. Just as in any town or city, lower value properties were arranged around its periphery. The intermediate spaces of this mediated *polis* have the effect of a town square, albeit one which is organised around exclusionary rights of access.

Conclusion

Abingdon Street Gardens is not a public park, in the sense that right of access is always guaranteed. It is part of the parliamentary estate, and the heightened demand for media coverage of activities in a building which has limited provision of such inside has consequently led to the creation of a new kind of mediated relationship between the television viewer and

Figure 19.5 A journalist prepares for a live outside broadcast from Abingdon Street Gardens, with *Knife Edge Two Piece* and the Victoria Tower of the Palace of Westminster beyond. © James Benedict Brown, 2022

the building. In *Mediated Space* (2018), I explored how the field of view of a television camera could conceal, heighten or imply relationships. In *The Production Sites and Production Sights of New Broadcasting House* (2019), I was particularly interested in how the lengthy and complicated redevelopment of BBC Broadcasting House in London was shaped by the desire to demonstrate public accountability through visibility of the corporation's activities. But in both of those works, I neglected to consider the liminal nature of those impromptu places of media production which disappear in the act of broadcasting. Abingdon Street Gardens itself is barely visible to viewers of television broadcasts produced there: the arrangement of broadcast positions and the framing of journalists and interviewees on camera is designed in such a way as to exploit the south and west façades of the Palace of Westminster as a backdrop (Figure 19.5). The intricately carved stonework of the building cannot be seen in such a view, but its presence (in focus or not) serves as a code that symbolises the proximity of the events unfolding on camera to the seat of British democracy.

In *The Prisoner*, we did not need to see anything more than the arrival of a secret agent into a car park next to the Palace of Westminster to understand his position of privileged trust and security. In daily television news broadcasts, we do not need to see the heraldic carvings of the Palace to understand the position of proximity to unfolding events. The building has always communicated its position in British society and relationship to democracy, only now it does so via a small grassy corner of the parliamentary estate. The poignant contrast between Barry and Pugin's Gothic revival architecture and Henry Moore's *Knife Edge Two Piece* captures the inviolable rhythm of British history: cultural paradigms that now seem incontestable yet were revolutionary at the time of their appearance. Here, in Abingdon Street Gardens, is the confluence of and tension between the image and reality of one of Europe's most recognisable parliament buildings.

Notes

1 The parliament buildings in Stormont, Northern Ireland (Arnold Thornely, 1928–1932) are the exception, designed on the cusp of the modern television age.
2 Moore believed he had donated the sculpture, via the Contemporary Art Society, to the nation – but actual ownership and responsibility for its upkeep was unknown for many years. It was restored in 2013 after being described as 'the most damaged Henry Moore on public view' (Bailey 2011, 2013). It was granted Grade II listing in January 2016 (Historic England 2016).

References

Bailey, M. (2011) 'Who owns this damaged masterpiece by Henry Moore?', *The Art Newspaper*, October.
Bailey, M. (2013) 'Long-neglected Moore sculpture to be conserved', *The Art Newspaper*, 11 February.
Brown, J.B. (2018) *Mediated Space*, London: RIBA Publishing.

Brown, J.B. (2019) 'The Production Sites and Production Sights of New Broadcasting House', in S. Psarra (ed.) *The Production Sites of Architecture*, Abingdon: Routledge, pp. 129–144.

Collins, M. (2019) *Abingdon Street Gardens ('College Green')*, London: UK Parliament.

Curtis, P. (2011) 'Ministers could face censure for leaking policy announcements to media', *The Guardian*, 2 February. Available from: https://www.theguardian.com/politics/2011/feb/02/ministers-face-censure-leaking-policy-announcements (accessed on 27 March 2022).

Fazio, M., Moffett, M. and Wodehouse, L. (2013) *A World History of Architecture*, 3rd edition, London: Laurence King.

Hill, R. (2007) *God's Architect: Pugin and the Building of Romantic Britain*, London: Allen Lane.

Historic England (2016) Knife Edge Two Piece Sculpture. Available from: https://historicengland.org.uk/listing/the-list/list-entry/1430343 (accessed on 26 September 2020).

Houses of Parliament (2019) Application for Planning Permission to Westminster City Council, reference 19-09366. 2 December.

Jones, C. (1984) *The Great Palace: The Story of Parliament*, London: BBC.

Kostof, S. (2010) *A History of Architecture: Settings and Rituals*, international second edition, Oxford: Oxford University Press.

Moore, H. (2002) *Henry Moore: Writings and Conversations*, Berkeley: University of California Press.

Pugin, E.W. (1867) *Who Was the Art Architect of the Houses of Parliament?* London: Longmans, Green & Co.

Pugin, A. and Wilson, E.J. (1825) *Specimens of Gothic architecture: selected from various ancient edifices in England: consisting of plans, elevations, sections, and parts at large, calculated to exemplify the various styles, and the practical construction of this admired class of architecture*, London: M.A. Nattali.

Serjeant at Arms and Black Rod (2017) 'Photography, filming, sound recording, painting, sketching, mobile telephones and pagers in the Palace of Westminster', London: UK Parliament. Available from: https://www.parliament.uk/globalassets/documents/CPA/CPC2011/Photography-Leaflet.pdf.

Westminster City Council (2020) Planning Application 20-00725. London: Westminster City Council.

Wheeler, B. (2019) 'Why do broadcasters use College Green?' *BBC News*, 8 January. Available from: https://www.bbc.com/news/uk-politics-46795958 (accessed on 13 June 2020).

Wilson, H. (1963) *Labour's Plans for Science*, Labour Party Conference, 1 October, Scarborough.

20

Continuous virtual surveillance in a new space?

Monitory democracy at Westminster

Ben Worthy and Stefani Langehennig

Introduction

The arrival of new digital tools and sources to 'watch' politicians has helped to create a new virtual 'monitory' space that exists, sometimes uneasily, alongside the 'physical' space of Westminster (Edwards, de Kool and Van Ooijen 2015). There now exists a 'datafied', or virtual, Westminster made up of data on events and behaviour within the legislature, over voting, expenses and interests, as well as around wider issues of the makeup and work of the institution itself. The data allows the public to see more about what happens within the physical building, creating heuristics and standards while, to an extent, allowing the public to participate in and 'remix' democracy. In this sense, the new 'monitory' space appears more democratic, fluid and open than the concrete buildings. However, transparency of institutions only extends so far, and the new space raises questions of misrepresentation and privacy for those being watched (Strathern 2000).

This chapter draws on the theory of 'monitory democracy', which argues that democracy, a system of government in which power is held by elected representatives, is not only about voting but also, increasingly, about the continuous surveillance of politicians, parties and government by the public and non-parliamentary bodies. A rolling series of transparency mechanisms constantly opens up new areas of public life to scrutiny and challenge, often outside more traditional channels and institutional spaces.[1] Monitory ideas, developed by thinkers such as Michael Schudson (1998) and John Keane (2018), sit alongside other 'conflictual' theories of democracy, such as Rosanvallon and Goldhammer's (2008) conception of

Figure 20.1   View of Big Ben. © Bruce Mars CC0-1.0. Source: StockSnap. Available at: https://stocksnap.io/photo/clock-tower-SX34RMWRMH (accessed on 13 January 2023)

'counter-democracy', or Mouffe's 'agonistic pluralism' (2017). They merge with ideas around democracy and democratic mobilisation as a form of conflict over what is publicly exposed or kept secret (Schnattschneider 1960). Monitoring offers to make public much of the 'backstage' of the UK's most important political institution (Goffman 1959).

In what follows, we argue that such a 'virtual monitory space' offers more democratic potential for access and participation than the often forbidding and exclusive physical environments of parliaments (Puwar 2004). Despite its openness, however, monitoring can only do so much to 'open up' Westminster. Julia Strathern (2000) argues that 'visibility conceals', and while it exposes some issues, it throws others into darkness. Making an institution more transparent can further obscure the 'real facts' of how it functions, hiding the relationships, networks, skills and 'invisible processes' through which it actually operates (Strathern 2000, p. 314). However, while access enables scrutiny and democratic accountability, it too is skewed and biased in important ways. Much depends on what or who is being observed, and the behaviour of those being watched, with assumptions over how politicians act in public or private, or how records are kept (see Prat 2005; Stasavage 2006; Novack and Hillebrandt 2020).

Monitoring Parliament and the virtual space

The history of the Palace of Westminster has been, from one viewpoint, a series of attempts to make the institution more visible to the public (Coleman 2017). This can be seen across a series of crises and junctures, from the public recording of debates from the 1680s, to the reporting of proceedings by newspapers in the 1800s and televising of proceedings in the late 1980s (Rix 2014). Just as the physical space of Parliament creates a 'backstage' and 'frontstage' (Goffman 1959), so does the virtual world, with boundaries altering over time. The physical frontstage includes the performance of members in debates or committee hearings, while the closed backstage involves party meetings, the working of the whips and so on. Similarly, the virtual space allows us to see voting records and expenses but keeps in the dark dataless activities such as MPs' constituency work or lobbying meetings.

This virtual space is created and defined by a wide array of ever changing and expanding tools and sources, labelled parliamentary monitoring organisations (see Edwards et al 2015). For any curious citizen in the twenty-first century, a raft of tools and mechanisms are available, which potentially at least allow for continuous scrutiny. Open data on how members vote, the expenses they file and the register of interests they declare is easily available; it is compiled and made searchable by Parliament and by non-parliamentary sites such as *They Work For You* and *Public Whip*.[2] The data is available via user-driven instruments such as Freedom of Information (FOI) requests, or via self-reporting mechanisms such as Registers of Financial Interests. A series of innovations has been developed, from postcode look-ups, where you can find which way your MP voted in key divisions to new sites which analyse and update the registers of interests. Data from one FOI request led to the creation of a Twitter bot, Parliament Wiki Edits, which tweets out to highlight whenever a computer with a Parliament IP address has made changes to a Wikipedia entry.

Most famously, at the centre of these transparency ecosystems stands *They Work For You* (TWFY), which monitors MPs' voting and other activities. It was created by volunteers in 2004 and since 2005 has been run by mySociety, a not-for-profit group pioneering the use of online technologies to empower citizens to take their first steps towards greater civic participation (mySociety 2003). TWFY allows us to see individual members of the House of Commons' (MPs') and members of the House of Lords' (peers') voting records far more easily than in the past. For each MP it offers up, as the website describes, 'a summary of their stances on important policy areas, such as combating climate change or reforming the NHS', described with phrases such as 'generally voted for', 'always voted against' and 'never voted for'. Elsewhere it lists their full record, appearances and declarations on the register of interests. It averages around 200,000 to 300,000 monthly visits, though this jumps amid elections or scandals, as well as longer critical events, such as Brexit (Escher 2011; Hogge 2016).

Much depends on who looks at this data. There can be a very different impact depending on whether the person conducting the search is a curious member of the public on a fact-finding mission, a journalist hunting a story, a voter making up their mind or an aggrieved local party member looking to cause trouble. The data also reaches the outside world through various routes – the 'hybrid media system', national and local press, campaign groups or social media networks (Chadwick 2017, p. 4).

In some sense, the 'spaces' this transparency ecosystem creates are modern, compared with the physical space of Westminster. But they are also chaotic. Nirmal Puwar called Parliament a mixture of 'museum, mausoleum, political pantomime, palace, cathedral and club': 'British parliament reveals several layers of life; palace, law ... Parliament is both a memorial to a selected history of politics and the nation and a working environment court, church, debating chamber and club' (Puwar 2004, p. 234).

By contrast, Parliament as 'virtual space' is a seemingly 'free and unlimited space' compared with the fixed, and forbidding, physical environment (Jungherr, Rivero and Gayo-Avello 2020). It is potentially more democratic and accessible, with a set of different power relations. Most significantly perhaps, the audience can themselves become participants in e-expression, by instantly circulating, interposing, disrupting and offering views and expression (Jungherr et al 2020). There is also some evidence that data is linked to wider campaigns and activities such as online petitions. The data itself is subject to refinement, reinterpretation and change, and, on its darker side, subject to misinforming and manipulation (see Graves 2017). The process and outcome of monitoring could well open up a parliament whose physical surroundings are heavily traditional and can be imbued with a patriarchal atmosphere. Yet it is potentially more disruptive, more conflictual and more invasive.

Patterns of use in the virtual space

Exactly what happens in the new space is driven by users. Monitoring data in the new virtual space can be unbundled or analysed in various ways, whether circulated as isolated bits of information about an individual or aggregated to create a set of benchmarks and measures. This is driven by who does the monitoring, which can vary according to interests and expertise (Dommett 2019). Data are often used individually as a shortcut or heuristic, and to get a sense of where MPs or peers stand, or stood, on various issues – or *who* they are if they are unknown. Certain controversial or 'moral' votes, from same-sex couples to military action, can be seen as benchmarks or identifiers of politicians. The data also create a permanent record – and thus a trail of accountability that can come to haunt politicians (Hogge 2016).

Beyond the individual, data also opens up the group dynamics of blocs of MPs and peers and can tell us, for example, who blocked Brexit or the link between expenses and attendance in the Lords (Russell 2019a; Radford, Mell and Thevoz 2020). It can reveal an institution-wide picture and has been used to examine how representative Parliament is, in terms of members or staff, or how widespread bullying or prejudice are, or even the connection between historical art and Britain's role in the slave trade (Syal 2020).

However, despite the seeming 'openness' of this space, other aspects of what MPs do remain hidden or very difficult to quantify (Strathern 2000). While data on voting records, expenses and allowances is easily available, there is no comparable data, for example, on how many constituency surgeries MPs hold. We can see only on social media or the local press what they do in their communities. Even in Westminster, valuable work in committees is necessarily out of sight. Institution-wide systems that are essential to making the Palace of Westminster work also remain hidden, such as the 'usual channels' (Crewe 2015). The extent and impact of lobbying in both houses remains almost wholly hidden, except when exposed (McKay and Wozniak 2020; Solaiman 2021).

Just as the spaces of Parliament shape who is important and reinforce hierarchies, so does the virtual space, which can recreate them. Normally, transparency policies in legislatures focus on individuals rather than institutions as a whole (Hazell, Bourke and Worthy 2012). An analysis of users of the TWFY website found a tendency to focus on certain key MPs (such as the prime minister or leader of the opposition), members connected with controversy or certain high-profile debates, such as on the NHS (Escher 2011; Hogge 2016). It is, moreover, skewed in terms of gender, and monitory scandals such as the MPs' expenses scandal which punished female MPs disproportionately (Waylen and Southern 2019).

What impact has the new space had?

The arrival of digital media enables both easier diffusion of information and more rapid creation of groups (Jungherr et al 2020). It creates a continuous kind of 'spirit of the hustings' across a range of MPs' activities, from voting to expenses and attendance (Lawrence 2009, p. 24). Away from any grand narratives of technology driving transformation, monitoring has had a series of complex, 'everyday' effects (Jungherr et al 2020). The impact appears different between the House of Commons, where surveillance is continuous and intense, and has lesser interest in the Lords, which peaks around certain activities (appointments, votes and semi-regular exposés over expenses and attendance) or controversy. This is, at least in part, because the House of Lords evokes less public interest and critical scrutiny than the House of Commons.

Monitoring has opened up the 'backstage' of political activity in Parliament and blurred boundaries between what is exposed or hidden, public or private: issues that were previously harder to access or were covered up are now, at least partially, open to scrutiny. As Keane (2018) argued, monitoring is continuous and expansive pressure atop the existing system, generating measures and yardsticks of what a 'good politician' and 'good representation' should look like. Such a process creates new lines of conflict over what can be opened up and, when it is, further political conflict over meaning and accountability (Schnattschneider 1960).

The biggest impact has been in shaping 'everyday' discussions of what happens in the House of Commons (Schudson 1998; Bakardjieva 2012). The data and numbers help the public to know and understand more, and make it easier to hold politicians to account outside of the traditional spaces and routes. While there are few formal mechanisms to hold MPs or peers accountable between elections in the UK, the data can help fuel either 'affective' criticism on social media and the press or, more rarely, campaigns and organised pressure. Diverse groups mobilise to use the data, from political parties or candidates to campaigners for electoral reform (Schnattschneider 1960).

Unbundled data has become an everyday tool for understanding and judging politicians, with voting records or even expenses used, repeated in the mainstream and social media, and rapidly becoming a yardstick and heuristic. A regular feature of public discussion, this data is now greater and easier to find (Rix 2014) and provides a set means of assessing groups of politicians. Objective numbers can then lead to subjective judgement (Beer 2016; Mau 2019). Just as the physical space of Parliament is defined, above all, by partisanship, so it shapes the virtual space. Any benchmark risks slipping from describing something to making a moral judgement about it (Beer 2016). Data on expenses can tell us who is the 'worst abuser' or who claimed the least, but the *Sun's* 2010 list of 'lazy' MPs included several female MPs on maternity leave.

There has been some behavioural change of those being monitored, though the data can only tell us so much. It raises the question of how those being monitored respond and if data, and internalised experience of ordering and measuring behaviour, has become an 'engine of anxiety' for those being monitored, who then react accordingly (Sauder and Espeland 2016). MP Nick De Bois pointed out how speaking in the Commons was done:

> Sometimes … so you can enlighten constituents on your position on any given issue. Either that, or because it's not a good thing to have against your name, 'below-average number of speeches in the House of Commons' on that pesky 'They Work for You' website, which relentlessly measures how active you are in the chamber (De Bois 2018).

As per the Independent Parliamentary Standards Authority (IPSA), there is evidence that some MPs have been reluctant to claim expenses for fear of criticism (see IPSA 2017). The data may have led to a small number of MPs seeking to 'game' attendance or, at least initially, ask more questions to appear higher in aggregate rankings (Hogge 2016). Here the uncertainty matches, for example, the contradictory effects of publicity in the nineteenth century, or televising Parliament in the 1980s and 1990s. The regular publication of debates and what was said after 1832 meant some members became more verbose, while the creation of two physical lobbies led to some members avoiding votes, with others seeking to celebrate their voting records to show their loyalty to their electoral promises (Rix 2014). Television impacted on some everyday behaviour in seeking attention, and arguably made and broke a few careers, but was accepted and absorbed by the institution (see Franklin 1992).

In terms of concrete change and accountability, voting record data has played a part in attempts at deselection over Brexit by local party associations and the national party (Alexandre-Collier 2020). FOI led to not only wholesale change with IPSA, but also to a change of peers' tax status in 2010. Perhaps most importantly, erroneous lists of 'lazy' MPs helped make the case for proxy voting in 2019, which came of age during the COVID-19 pandemic. Semi-regular data exposés in the House of Lords around allowances or attendance of peers often feed a sense that the Lords is a remote, elite and dysfunctional institution (Russell 2019b). The House of Lords has experienced an ongoing data-driven allowances scandal, with regular exposés of what peers do and how much they cost, triggering waves of criticism and calls for reform (Russell 2013).

It is less certain that data leads to direct effects on voters. In theory, such data could aid decision-making, feed retrospective assessments of performance or help voters understand whether they share issues and social identities with candidates (Achen and Bartels 2017). Data required to influence voters are highly context-dependent and often short-term, requiring constant reinforcement (Achen and Bartels 2017; Jungherr et al 2020). For instance, MPs' positions on Brexit had little impact on their constituency votes, even where constituency and MP were opposed (Hanretty, Mellon and English 2021). Nor did the largest monitory scandal, the MPs' expenses scandal of 2009, have a significant effect on vote outcome, being mitigated by partisanship and a lack of public awareness (Eggers 2014).

Despite the doubts, in the US and UK, research has shown how most voters have a rough sense of where lawmakers stand, picking up 'clues and scraps' from the media, politicians themselves and opponents, and the nature of the new data fits with how voters already absorb information and make decisions (Valgarðsson et al 2021). The data can also support, reinforce or even create narratives about Parliament (Ruppert and Savage 2011). The danger is that much of this may accord with what the public dislikes about politics already, from partisanship and slowness to the sense that representatives are a 'captured elite' (Hibbing and Theiss-Morse 1995). The question is whether monitoring strengthens democratic links and responsiveness or merely 'fans the flames' of disapproval (Hibbing and Theiss-Morse 1995). For example, while individual MPs' voting records on Brexit have surprisingly little effect, Brexit also fed a narrative around the House of Commons. Despite the fact that it was pro-Brexit MPs helped stop Brexit legislation, both (Conservative) politicians and the supporting media were happy to portray 'remainers' as 'blocking Brexit' – a theme that then percolated through to public views (Russell 2019a).

Conclusion

Some have compared the effects of transparency with architectural alterations, pointing to Norman Foster's famous glass roof of the Bundestag, which allows those outside to see the activity within (Hood and Heald 2006). Monitory data is driven by a similar desire to 'open' the hidden democratic activity within the UK's older and more forbidding space. To an extent it has done so, forcing greater accountability from those within and even, occasionally, driving changes that alter the space itself. The reform to proxy voting in 2019 meant that, for the first time, MPs did not have to be present to vote, a symbolic and practical gesture that made for greater access and more diversity. The 'virtual space' is more fluid, more democratic and more amenable to citizens and others to 'remix' or reorder the democracy they wish to see on an everyday level on social media or elsewhere – where anyone can find the data they want and, to an extent, interpret it how they wish.

However, it falls short of the true 'openness' of a glass roof. Data highlights certain activities but obscures others, and are skewed and hierarchical, containing inequalities just as the physical institution does. While we see more of what MPs and peers do in Westminster, we see even less of what they do in their constituencies. Vital areas such as lobbying remain in a kind of dataless darkness in the virtual world, as they do in the physical. As seen in stories about expenses or interests, data often creates narratives that serve to reinforce age-old assumptions rather than alter views.

Notes

1 The authors' Leverhulme Trust project (RPG-2019-124) looked at how new data sources and web platforms have made it easier to monitor Parliament and its members outside of the traditional physical spaces of parliament. The project combines analysis of media and social media with case studies and surveys to map out who is using this data and what impact it is having, both on those being watched and those doing the watching.
2 The two sites can be found at www.TheyWorkForYou.com and www.publicwhip.org.uk.

References

Achen, C.H. and Bartels, L.M. (2017) *Democracy for Realists: Why Elections Do not Produce Responsive Government* (Vol. 4), Princeton: Princeton University Press.
Alexandre-Collier, A. (2020) 'From rebellion to extinction: where have all the Tory remainer MPs gone?' *The Political Quarterly*, 91(1), pp. 24–30. DOI: 10.1111/1467-923X.12824.
Bakardjieva, M. (2012) 'Mundane citizenship: new media and civil society in Bulgaria', *Europe-Asia Studies*, 64(8), pp. 1356–1374. DOI: 10.1080/09668136.2012.712247.
Beer, D. (2016) *Metric Power*, London: Palgrave Macmillan.

De Bois, N. (2018) *Confessions of a Recovering MP*, London: Biteback.

Chadwick, A. (2017) *The Hybrid Media System: Politics and Power*, Oxford: Oxford University Press.

Coleman, S. (2017) *Can the Internet Strengthen Democracy?* London: John Wiley & Sons.

Crewe, E. (2015) *The House of Commons: An Anthropology of MPs at Work*, London: Bloomsbury Publishing.

Dommett, K. (2019) 'Data-driven political campaigns in practice: understanding and regulating diverse data-driven campaigns', *Internet Policy Review*, 8(4). DOI: 10.14763/2019.4.1432.

Edwards, A., de Kool, D., and Van Ooijen, C. (2015) 'The information ecology of parliamentary monitoring websites: pathways towards strengthening democracy', *Information Polity*, 20(4), pp. 253–268.

Eggers, A.C. (2014) 'Partisanship and electoral accountability: evidence from the UK expenses scandal', *Quarterly Journal of Political Science*, 9(4), pp. 441–472. DOI: 10.1561/100.00013140.

Escher, T. (2011) *Analysis of Users and Usage for UK Citizens Online Democracy. They Work For You*. London: mySociety/UK Citizens Online Democracy.

Franklin, B. (1992) *Televising Democracies*, London: Routledge.

Goffman, E. (1959) *The Presentation of Self in Everyday Life*, New York: Garden Books.

Graves, L. (2017) 'The monitorial citizen in the "democratic recession"', *Journalism Studies*, 18(10), pp. 1239–1250. DOI: 10.1080/1461670X.2017.1338153.

Hanretty, C., Mellon, J. and English, P. (2021) 'Members of parliament are minimally accountable for their issue stances (and they know it)', *American Political Science Review*, 115(4), pp. 1275–1291. DOI: 10.1017/S0003055421000514.

Hazell, R., Bourke, G. and Worthy, B. (2012) 'Open house? Freedom of information and its impact on the UK parliament', *Public Administration*, 90(4), pp. 901–921.

Hibbing, J.R. and Theiss-Morse, E. (1995) *Congress as Public Enemy: Public Attitudes toward American Political Institutions*, Cambridge: Cambridge University Press.

Hogge, B. (2016) 'Open data's impact, TheyWorkForYou, taking the long view', *Odimpact*. Available from: http://odimpact.org/files/case-study-they-work-for-you.pdf (accessed on 10 October 2018).

Hood, C. and Heald, D. (2006) *Transparency: The Key to Better Governance?* (Vol. 135), Oxford University Press for The British Academy.

IPSA (2017) *Findings from the Annual Survey of MPs and their Staff 2016*, London: IPSA.

Jungherr, A., Rivero, G. and Gayo-Avello, D. (2020) *Retooling Politics: How Digital Media Are Shaping Democracy*, Cambridge: Cambridge University Press.

Keane, J. (2018) *Power and Humility: The Future of Monitory Democracy*, Cambridge: Cambridge University Press.

Lawrence, J. (2009) *Electing Our Masters: The Hustings in British Politics from Hogarth to Blair*, Oxford: Oxford University Press.

Mau, S. (2019) *The Metric Society: On the Quantification of the Social*, London: John Wiley & Sons.

McKay, A.M. and Wozniak, A. (2020) 'Opaque: an empirical evaluation of lobbying transparency in the UK', *Interest Groups & Advocacy*, 9(1), pp. 102–118. DOI: 10.1057/s41309-019 -00074-9.

Mouffe, C. (2017) 'Democracy as agonistic pluralism', in E. Ermarth (ed.), *Rewriting Democracy*, London: Routledge, pp. 35–45.

mySociety (2003) Available from: https://www.mysociety.org/about.

Novak, S. and Hillebrandt, M. (2020) 'Analysing the trade-off between transparency and efficiency in the Council of the European Union', *Journal of European Public Policy*, 27(1), pp. 141–159.

Prat, A. (2005) 'The wrong kind of transparency', *American Economic Review*, 95(3), pp. 862–877. DOI: 10.1257/0002828054201297.

Puwar, N. (2004) 'Thinking about making a difference', *The British Journal of Politics and International Relations*, 6(1), pp. 65–80. DOI: 10.1111/j.1467-856X.2004.00127.x.

Radford, S., Mell, A. and Thevoz, S.A. (2020) '"Lordy Me!" Can donations buy you a British peerage? A study in the link between party political funding and peerage nominations, 2005–2014', *British Politics*, 15(2), pp. 135–159. DOI: 10.1057/s41293-019-00109-4.

Rix, K. (2014) '"Whatever passed in parliament ought to be communicated to the public": reporting the proceedings of the reformed commons, 1833–50', *Parliamentary History*, 33(3), pp. 453–474. DOI: 10.1111/1750-0206.12106.

Rosanvallon, P. and Goldhammer, A. (2008) *Counter-democracy: Politics in an Age of Distrust* (Vol. 7), Cambridge: Cambridge University Press.

Ruppert, E. and Savage, M. (2011) 'Transactional politics', *The Sociological Review*, 59, pp. 73–92.

Russell, M. (2013) *The Contemporary House of Lords: Westminster Bicameralism Revived*, Oxford: Oxford University Press.

Russell, M. (2019a) 'Which MPs are responsible for failing to "get Brexit done"?' *UK In A Changing Europe Blog*, 2 October. Available from: https://constitution-unit.com/2019/10/02/which-mps-are-responsible-for-failing-to-get-brexit-done/.

Russell, M. (2019b) 'Foreword: bicameralism in an age of populism', in R. Albert, A. Baraggia and C. Fasone (eds), *Constitutional Reform of National Legislatures: Bicameralism Under Pressure*, Cheltenham, UK and Northampton, MA, USA: Edward Elgar Publishing, pp. ix–xix.

Sauder, M. and Espeland, W. (2016) *Engines of Anxiety: Academic Rankings, Reputation, and Accountability*, New York: Russell Sage Foundation.

Schnattschneider, E.E. (1960) *The Semi-sovereign People*, New York: Holt, Reinhart, and Winston.

Schudson, M. (1998) *The Good Citizen: A History of American Civic Life*, New York: Martin Kessler Books.

Solaiman, B. (2021) 'Lobbying in the UK: towards robust regulation', *Parliamentary Affairs*. DOI: 10.1093/pa/gsab051.

Stasavage, D. (2006) 'Does transparency make a difference? The example of the European Council of Ministers', in C. Hood and D. Heald (eds), *Transparency: The Key to Better Governance?* Proceedings of the British Academy, British Academy Scholarship Online. DOI: 10.5871/bacad/9780197263839.003.0010.

Strathern, M. (2000) 'The tyranny of transparency', *British Educational Research Journal*, 26(3), pp. 309–321.

Syal, R. (2020) 'Westminster's links to Britain's slave trade revealed in art survey', *The Guardian*, 30 September. Available from: https://www.theguardian.com/politics/2020/sep/30/westminsters-links-to-britains-slave-trade-revealed-in-art-survey.

Valgarðsson, V.O., Clarke, N., Jennings, W. and Stoker, G. (2021) 'The good politician and political trust: an authenticity gap in British politics?', *Political Studies*, 69(4), pp. 858–880. DOI: 10.1177/0032321720928257.

Waylen, G. and Southern, R. (2019) 'When are women as corrupt as men? Gender, corruption, and accountability in the UK parliamentary expenses scandal', *Social Politics: International Studies in Gender, State & Society*, 28(1), pp. 119–142. DOI: 10.1093/sp/jxz045.

Part VI

The spatial production of assemblies

21

Shaping and expressing politics

A comparative study of national parliament buildings in the European Union

Naomi Gibson, Sophia Psarra and
Gustavo Maldonado Gil

Introduction

A parliament building is a living thing; it speaks to and expresses a nation's history, stages the exercise of politics and defines political cultures. Like theatres, parliaments are places of memory, oration and performance (Yates 1984; Goodsell 1988), shaping a nation's idea of itself in both its present and future. The practices of politics and the representational role of parliaments extend far beyond the physical boundaries of their buildings. The storming of the US Capitol by protesters in 2021, for example, has drawn worldwide attention to the role of parliaments as places and processes of history, legitimacy and power in concentrated form. These qualities are often typified by the plenary hall, the space where the performances of debating, speaking and voting take place. Political decision-making increasingly transpires in a range of parliamentary spaces, yet the plenary hall remains the space where democracy is 'seen to be done'.

Within Europe, controversies related to rising inequalities and nationalism as well as the 2008 economic crisis have drawn attention to democratic structures and narratives of European integration. The withdrawal of the UK from the European Union (EU) has led to divisions within Britain about identity and sovereignty, and generated broader questions about the disparate yet connected histories and cultures of nations within larger political structures. Over centuries, neighbouring European countries have geographically shifted, been absorbed by empires, affected by political ideologies and broken away in search of independence. They have been to war, controlled and culturally influenced each other. If parliament buildings embody and express the trajectories of their nations, a comparative study of European parliament buildings can provide a first step in understanding the interlaced threads of European cultures, the values these buildings embody and the stories they tell.

In this chapter we explore the diversity and interlocking dimensions of parliamentary space and political cultures through the comparative study of 28 European national parliament buildings and plenary halls. Looking at parliaments as built spaces, spatial practices and lived experiences, we ask: how are the political cultures and histories of these 28 nations interwoven with their parliament buildings? Then, in addition, how do their plenary halls shape the political cultures, power dynamics and processes that are acted out within? To do so, we will explore the evolution of these 28 parliament buildings, interpretations of plenary hall typologies and government–legislative relations. We will also examine relationships between spatial configurations, visibility, density and power within a subset of six plenary halls. We will close with an examination of the exercise of power through speaking and voting practices in the Belgian and UK parliaments.

In this chapter we will not debate the processes and values of the EU, but rather examine the national parliament buildings of EU countries in relation to the political cultures they shape and represent. We have included the UK due to its former membership of the EU and the particularity of its political traditions. While all European countries have distinct political cultures, the UK and British Commonwealth countries in Europe, Cyprus and Malta, have followed a separate path. This is not to make a case for UK exceptionalism; rather, our purpose is to understand the differences between, and intertwined trajectories of these European nations who, following Enlightenment reason, post-revolutionary France, the political upheavals of revolutions and the world wars, emerged as democratic states. We do not claim authority over the political history and governance of these countries, nor an in-depth understanding of all parliamentary spaces. Our aim is to lay the groundwork for future research by presenting the first comparative study of the relationship between parliamentary spaces, the exercise of power and political culture within European countries. As 15 of the 28 nations examined have unicameral legislatures, the focus of the research in the case of bicameral legislatures is restricted to the lower chambers and their buildings.

Interpreting the plenary hall

Architectural studies of plenary halls have typically been records of typologies and forms. Traditionally, five types of plenary halls have been identified based on the shape of the legislature: opposing benches, semicircles, horseshoes, circles and classrooms. Of these typologies, opposing benches are associated with medieval, aristocratic systems of rule, the semicircle with classical antiquity and European democratic assembly, while the horseshoe is regarded as a hybrid of the two forms. The classroom is associated with authoritarian regimes. These types are present in parliaments worldwide, as demonstrated by TU Vienna's 2014 national parliament database[1] and XML architect's 2016 study. However, this classification system tells us little about how these spaces are performed by politicians. Using XML's classification, the 28 European parliaments present a mix of all chamber typologies, with the semicircle the dominant type, characterising 14 of the chambers (Figure 21.1). However, the spatial form of some parliamentary chambers in Europe remains ambiguous.

In his book *In the King's Shadow* (2010), Philip Manow questions this classification, suggesting that there are just two types of plenary hall: opposing benches and the semicircle. Other types are simply variations on the semicircle. Tracing the symbolism and history behind these two typologies, Manow presents the notion of the 'body politic' in two forms: the medieval king figurehead with members along opposing benches, and the post-revolutionary 'unified body' of the French semicircle. With the shift from opposing benches to semicircle there was a shift in political culture. Without the king, the body politic in post-revolutionary France found expression in the unity of the semicircle, and ended 'the ceremonial, spectacular or theatrical side of rule that was so characteristic of the *Ancien Régime*' (Manow 2010, p. 2). However, the unity and stagecraft of the theatre ensured it remained relevant for parliamentary settings. Following the work of Charles Goodsell and Herbert Döring, Manow points out that the differences in seating arrangements cannot be explained functionally, for example, to better see or hear a member speaking. Rather, they are 'the expression of a political culture that they themselves partly help to shape' (Manow 2010, p. 8).

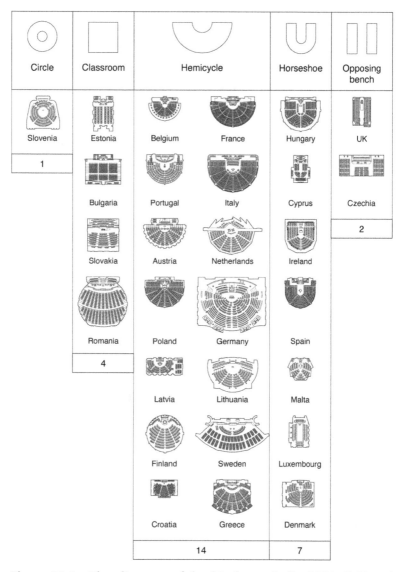

Figure 21.1 Plan diagrams of the 28 plenary halls, 2021. © Naomi Gibson

The UK Parliament has a history of slow evolution, unlike other nations which have experienced abrupt changes. The old chapel of St Stephen was the first room of the House of Commons which perished, but its model for furniture arrangement has outlived fire, revolution and war (Hollis 2013). The Second World War gave the Commons an opportunity to build a new chamber, whereby Winston Churchill argued that 'its shape should be oblong and not semi-circular' and 'should not be big enough to contain all its members at once without overcrowding' (HC Deb 28 October 1943). He insisted on a small chamber to create an urgent, crowded atmosphere. The rational, classical theatres 'had, in the opinion of one MP, been the "death warrant of democracy on the continent"' (Hollis 2013, p. 109). Another MP sitting on the Commons' rebuilding committee insisted that a semicircle was best if members spoke from a rostrum, but not when members spoke from their places (Port 1976, p. 13). Manow also challenges the received wisdom that opposing benches are naturally adversarial while the semicircle is more appropriate for cooperation and proportional representation. In a series of interviews we conducted, parliamentarians in the UK and Germany voiced the same opinion, discussed by Sophia Psarra and Gustavo Maldonado Gil in this volume.

While established typologies for plenary halls may speak to symbolic political gestures and lineages, they provide a simple, sometimes misleading picture. They do not articulate how seats within the legislature are allocated, nor the relationship of the government to the legislature, rostrum or presidium. They tell us little about the dynamics of speaking, debating and voting, the rules of behaviour or culture in the spaces, or the invisible power relationships embedded in the sightlines of members from their seats. In addition, a careful examination of political and architectural histories is required in order to be able to understand the nuances of meaning in the architecture of parliament buildings and their spaces, both in their configuration and how they are performed. It is these absences in the architectural understanding of parliaments that we wish to address in this chapter, and which are also examined by the authors in this section on the spatial production of assemblies. Employing the motion-form of bodies in political gatherings as a point of departure, Harald Trapp in this volume explores the evolution and steady enclosure of political assemblies from pre-civilised society through to the French Revolution. Concerned instead with the spatial structuring of chambers in relation to the culture of political debate and the drives to consensus or dissensus, Gordana Korolija in this volume offers an interpretation of the Palace of Westminster's edifice as a salve and steadying force for a fractious political system without the grounding of a written constitution. Finally, Kerstin Sailer in this volume employs space syntax methods in her study of the German, UK and EU parliaments in order to analyse the dynamics of 'visibility, proximity and group solidarities' in the built space of these assemblies.

Reading inhabitation and government²–legislative relationships

In his study of executive–legislative relations, Anthony King (1976) noted hierarchies and tensions present within parliaments that went beyond a simple executive–legislative split. He identified dynamics ranging from intraparty tensions, frontbench and backbench dynamics, government–opposition relations, to the executive versus the legislature. To understand how such political dynamics materialise and are spatially embedded, our study involved making broad classifications based on the shape of the chamber and position of the executive, chair, rostrum and MPs.

Among 24 of the 28 parliaments, where members sit is determined by political party and bears no relation to which parties constitute the government. In the UK, Ireland and Malta, the parties change location depending on which party is in power. Sweden is alone in its seating arrangement being determined by geography, with each seat belonging to a particular constituency. Whether seats are designated to an individual also varies between parliaments. In illustration, within the Belgian chamber, MPs are designated a seat, whereas in the UK, where an MP sits is not permanent or allocated but results from an organic process of social negotiation. Michel Foucault (1995, pp. 145–146) writes of keeping individuals in set spaces, of organising individuals by 'places' and 'ranks' as a means for guaranteeing their obedience. In the context of parliaments, the predetermination of seats and the manner in which they are determined has the ability to establish, at the outset of a parliamentary term, hierarchies within the chamber, from the power of the chair and bureau members in maintaining order in the chamber, the power differentials between large and small political parties and the power structures internal to a political party.

When the locations of the government, legislature, chair and rostrum are mapped, detailed readings of the chambers expose emerging spatial typologies (Figure 21.2). There is a split between arrangements where the government seats are integrated with the legislature, as is the case in the UK and France, and those where the government is separate and faces the legislature, the situation in Germany. Where the government sits within the same block as the legislature, parliaments fall onto a spectrum from those where the government sits along one side with the chair in their peripheral vision, see Denmark, and those who face the chair directly, see Luxembourg. Those chambers where the government is spatially separated from the legislature divide into parliaments where

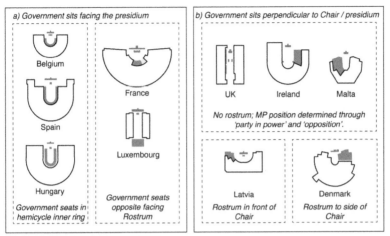

a) Government sits facing the presidium

Belgium

Spain

Hungary

Government seats in hemicycle inner ring

France

Luxembourg

Government seats opposite facing Rostrum

b) Government sits perpendicular to Chair / presidium

UK   Ireland   Malta

No rostrum; MP position determined through 'party in power' and 'opposition'.

Latvia

Rostrum in front of Chair

Denmark

Rostrum to side of Chair

Government sits alongside the legislature
Government sits separate to the legislature

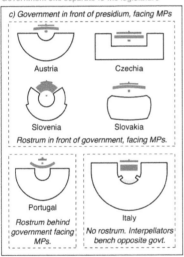

c) Government in front of presidium, facing MPs.

Austria

Slovenia

Czechia

Slovakia

Rostrum in front of government, facing MPs.

Portugal

Rostrum behind government facing MPs.

Italy

No rostrum. Interpellators bench opposite govt.

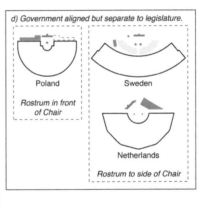

d) Government aligned but separate to legislature.

Poland

Rostrum in front of Chair

Sweden

Netherlands

Rostrum to side of Chair

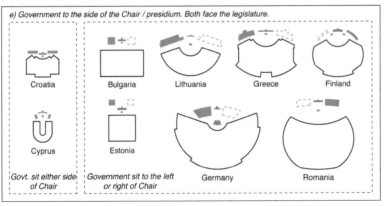

e) Government to the side of the Chair / presidium. Both face the legislature.

Croatia   Bulgaria   Lithuania   Greece   Finland

Cyprus   Estonia   Germany   Romania

Govt. sit either side of Chair

Government sit to the left or right of Chair

Figure 21.2 Government–legislature relationships: a diagram of emerging spatial typologies, 2021. © Naomi Gibson

the government sits in front of the chair, thus cannot see the chair, and those where the government sits to one or both sides of the chair. In the case of Poland, Sweden and the Netherlands, the government does not fall neatly into either type. The positions of the main powers in these chambers show that they are not always a single entity as implied by the semicircle and other chamber types. Their variations reveal a rich fabric of places and ranks that can reveal much about the hierarchies, conflicts, rituals and rules in these nations.

Locating each of these diagrams geographically (Figure 21.3), it is possible to see similarities between neighbouring countries where patterns of executive–legislative relationships cluster together, as well as vestiges of former empires. Within a group of countries that formed part of the Austrian Empire, followed by the Austro-Hungarian Empire (Slovenia, Austria, Czechia, Slovakia), both the government bench and presidium face the legislature, where the government occupies a row in front of the presidium, and so is unable to see the presidium. In many eastern European countries which were formerly under Soviet or Communist rule, the government bench sits to one or both sides of the presidium. Ireland and Malta contain echoes of the British Empire in their government–legislature relationships. The horseshoe legislature of these two nations is an act of hybridity, a crossing of the UK's opposing benches and the semicircle – a trait seen in Commonwealth countries globally (Manow 2010, pp. 11–14). What this mapping of plenary halls begins to capture is the fluidity of national borders and nation states over history, gesturing to the existence of political maps beyond the familiar territorial map of Europe. In addition, it points to the historical-cultural hybridity of these chambers and their parliaments.

How did these parliament buildings evolve?

Beyond the lineages and types of government–legislature relationships we have described, there are other patterns of historical-cultural hybridity and past–present tensions in the fabric of the parliament buildings and their interiors. Next, through a selection of cases we will review how national political trajectories are reflected in current parliament buildings.

Our review of the 28 parliament buildings revealed many of these buildings were not purpose-built as parliaments but chosen and adapted for the purpose. More particularly, six of the 28 buildings (21 per cent) were first built as aristocratic palaces, with more placed within originally aristocratic complexes and sites. Ten of these structures (36 per cent) are

Figure 21.3 Government–legislature relationships across Europe, 2021.
© Naomi Gibson

repurposed buildings. All but one of these buildings were constructed or converted to parliaments after 1800, a phenomenon coinciding with the emergence of nation states in the nineteenth century, the dissolution of empires and recovery of sovereignty for countries such as Ireland and Greece.

Markus and Cameron (2002, p. 123) state that 'reappropriating old buildings for new uses … is not just a practical solution … it is a clear and powerful ideological statement about the nature and principles of the new regime'. However, we are cautious about asserting this. For every France, whereby the coopting of an aristocratic palace after the revolution could be interpreted as a powerful ideological statement, there are countries such as Ireland where the choice of premises had practical concerns. The building chosen to house the Irish parliament was set back from the road, reducing bomb risk, while the lecture theatre installed by the Royal Dublin Society offered a space that could be easily adapted for use as a plenary hall. There is also the case of Cyprus – a nation with a parliament building viewed as a temporary solution in the 1960s, where decades-long delays to the construction of a new parliament has meant the need to continue adapting their existing building.

Among the 28 nations we examined, 17 (61 per cent) underwent dramatic constitutional change from the 1950s onwards, gaining independence or shifting from military and communist republics to western liberal democracies at the end of the twentieth century. We wondered whether the establishment of these democracies entailed changes to their parliament buildings in order to reflect their new status and political ideology. There has been no universal response. While there are countries such as Slovakia and Romania (see Stătică and Bădescu in this volume) which have not made changes to their buildings and halls, others have built anew. Finally, there have been acts of adaptation which have taken place, examples of which we outline next.

In 2015, a new parliament building was completed in Valletta, Malta (see Borg Wirth and Zerafa in this volume). It is a contemporary building of glass and stone which speaks to modern notions of transparent democracy, but some traditions from the UK remain. Members speak from their seat and there is no central rostrum; the side of the chamber on which members sit depends on which party is in power; the voting procedure is called 'division', after which the 'speaker' will state the number of 'ayes' and 'noes'.

In 2000, Slovenia refurbished their plenary hall, replacing their classroom-shaped legislature from their era as part of the Republic of Yugoslavia with a circle. Dressed with clean lines, polished granite and cherry wood, the circle harks back to the Slovenian archetype of community elders gathering. The executive–legislative seating relationship, however, aligns with the pattern of other former nations of the Austrian Empire, while the central rostrum follows the tradition of the French semicircle.

Between 2001 and 2005, the Lithuanian parliament was extended to build a semicircle, in a move away from the classroom chamber built while part of the former USSR. The old plenary hall has been retained for ceremonial purposes, while the new hall retains some of the spatial traditions of the former. The layout also follows several other eastern European nations: the government sits to one side of the rostrum and the chair, facing the legislature.

Through this review of the 28 parliaments and the approaches to building adoption and adaptation we have outlined, it is noticeable, but unsurprising, that the response to parliament buildings and the cultures underpinning them has typically not been one of *tabula rasa*, but of 'make do and mend'. Consensus is difficult to achieve and takes a long time. Making buildings is expensive and laborious, and each country has its own set of circumstances to navigate. Relationships between nations and national parliament buildings are complicated and may just as importantly remind citizens of more sombre historical moments. As Hollis (2013) observes, buildings outlive the purposes for which they were built, mutating over time. These parliament buildings are no different, the alterations of old structures a 'retelling' of political evolutions and events.

While adaptation has partly been a response to practical and functional matters, there have also been processes of ideological and symbolic adaptation, negotiating an idealised version of history with contemporary pragmatic concerns. In *Collage City*, Colin Rowe and Fred Koetter (1983, pp. 144–145) observe the negotiation between the concepts of tradition and utopia, proposing the notion of 'collage' as a means for societies to deal with the problems both concepts inspire, as 'collage accommodates both hybrid display and the requirements of self-determination'. We can see this tension between tradition and utopia within parliaments, in both buildings and political processes. This tendency towards collage is sometimes visible in the need to legitimise a political present and future by rooting it deeply in the past, as in the combination of Pugin's preference for the Gothic and Barry's commitment to a classical plan at the Palace of Westminster. At other times collage operates by borrowing the systems, forms and emblems of established parliaments and powers, as seen in Hungary's echoing of the UK's neo-Gothic architecture and adoption of a horseshoe legislature, while incorporating an array of Renaissance and baroque ornamental details alongside national iconography and imagery to create something unique to Hungary. The tradition–utopia dialogue is also present in recent parliament buildings and chambers which may look contemporary, but still contain elements of 'what came before', as demonstrated in Malta, Slovenia and Lithuania.

Understanding plenary halls as dynamic spaces and processes

But what of the spatial practices and lived experience of these plenary halls? Plenary chambers are spaces of performance and ritual acted out in space and time. Here, we examine the relationship between spatial configuration, visibility and power; spatial density and procedural intensity; the performance of following the rules of procedure written for a particular parliament and chamber. This analysis represents an initial foray into the subject. The intent is to illustrate the value of understanding plenary halls as dynamic spaces and processes, and therefore the value of combining architectural, historical and social science research in the study of parliament buildings as institutions of knowledge and power.

Visibility and power

For Foucault (1995), the form of modern disciplinary power was Jeremy Bentham's panopticon, which articulated not the fact but the possibility of observation. We studied six plenary halls to examine the visual connectivity at play within (Figures 21.4 and 21.5). These dynamics refer to embodied vision: what one sees when seated at different positions within the chamber – a dynamic also interrogated by Kerstin Sailer in this volume. We used 'isovists' (Benedikt 1979) to draw visual polygons representing what each person sees, and subsequently the areas of overlap of these polygons define the most and least observed areas in each chamber. Each of the six plenary halls represents a different executive–legislative spatial typology, and includes representatives of several typologies: three semicircles, one circle, one classroom and one opposing bench.

With Belgium, one can see strong visual interconnectivity for the presidium, rostrum and government. Within the legislature, those towards the rear edge of the semicircle are least seen but have the longest views. The Netherlands and Germany have similar results. For the Netherlands, the shape of the semicircle is more 'open', so the outer ring of seats is more strongly visually interconnected compared to Belgium.

For Estonia there is substantial variation in the level of visibility among the government. Those at the front of the government seats are in everyone's field of view, and those at the back more segregated. MPs seated towards the rear of the classroom are least seen. For Slovenia, the rostrum, government and much of the legislature are strongly visually interconnected due to the circular arrangement of the space. However, the chair presiding over sittings is less visually prominent and pushed to the periphery, thus conversely benefiting from long views. Although the government sits apart from the legislature, visibility relationships in the circular form provide a level of parity among those within the chamber.

Finally, the UK, as discussed by Psarra and Maldonado Gil and Korolija in this volume, shows the strong visual integration of the speaker, front benches, dispatch boxes and much of the legislature. Parties pushed on the opposition benches the furthest end from the speaker are less visually interconnected. When the UK chamber is compared to the other chambers, Churchill's view of what constitutes an assembly culture reveals itself. There are few MPs who are not covisible with other MPs in the Commons chamber.

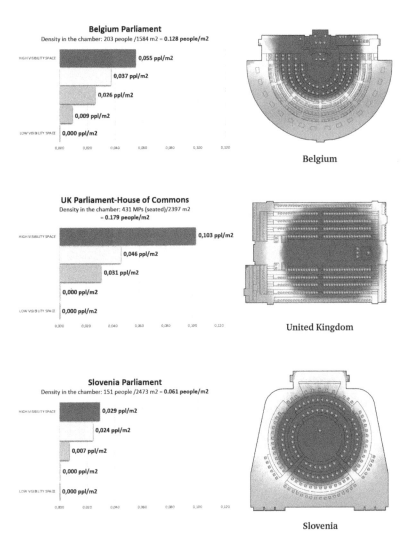

Figure 21.4   Visual connectivity within the plenary halls of Belgium, the UK and Slovenia, alongside density of high- and low-visibility areas within the plenary halls, 2021. © Gustavo Maldonado Gil

Intensity, density and power

With Churchill's comment that 'a small chamber and a sense of intimacy are indispensable' in mind (Goodsell 1988, p. 298), we examined the seating density of all six chambers, dividing the number of people by the chamber area (Figures 21.4 and 21.5). We also examined the distribution

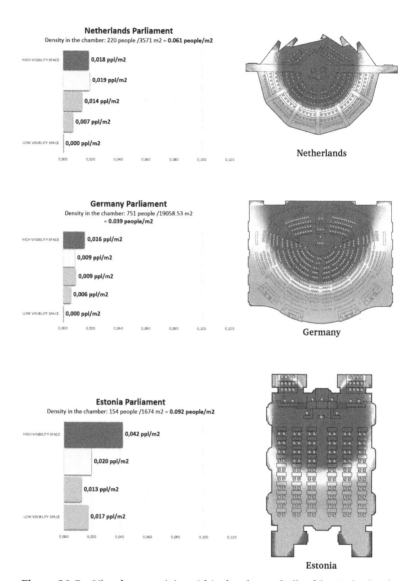

Figure 21.5 Visual connectivity within the plenary halls of the Netherlands, Germany and Estonia, alongside density of high- and low-visibility areas within the plenary halls, 2021. © Gustavo Maldonado Gil

between high- and low-visibility areas. The UK's House of Commons chamber is the densest as a whole, and has the highest density within its high-visibility zone, with Belgium's Chamber of Representatives a distant second. Germany's Bundestag is the least dense and thus most spacious by both measures.

As a caveat, these density figures are calculated assuming a full chamber. The UK plenary hall can exceed capacity as there are not enough seats for all MPs, which would push the density higher. In addition, plenary hall business takes place once a quorum is reached, the figure for a quorum varying by nation, but in all cases not all members need to be present.

The sense of intimacy and level of density has also, since 2020, been affected by the COVID pandemic, as parliaments have moved to hybrid digital-physical sessions and employed strategies to enable members to keep their distance from each other. The spatial and cultural impact this is having upon parliaments has been noted. In 2021 the UK's Hansard Society raised concerns about the erosion of parliamentary control due to virtual participation methods and other changes put in place to permit the safe functioning of Parliament (Fox et al. 2021). These developments demonstrate the power of physical presence in the chambers in holding the government to account.

Exercise of power

To examine the exercise of power within plenary halls, we looked at two parliaments and their rules of procedure: Belgium and the UK (Figures 21.6 and 21.7). The aim was to explore how the performance of the space, from individual behaviours to the movement of members to the rostrum to speak, add to our picture of the spatial power dynamics in the chambers. Belgium and the UK are both constitutional monarchies and bicameral parliaments, but this is where the similarities end. We argue that they exemplify the differences observed by Manow between the structures and cultures of opposing bench and semicircle parliaments.

We examined these parliaments in relation to their behavioural codes, though one should remain conscious that not all rules are written but are learnt through the practice of being an MP. At Westminster, as Kari Palonen (2018) writes, unlike Francophone parliaments, the precedents and practices beyond the standing orders form the rules of procedure which are developed through continued use across centuries.

A general principle for rules is given by Hillier and Hanson (1984), where the longer the description of the rules governing an event, the more likely the event is formal, and the shorter the rules, the more likely the event is informal and open to negotiation, contingency and probability. For

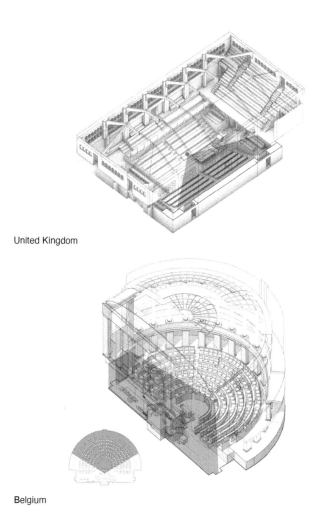

United Kingdom

Belgium

Figure 21.6   Comparing the views of speaking members in the UK and Belgian chambers, 2021. © Carlota Nuñez-Barranco Vallejo

parliamentary rules, Emma Crewe (2021, p. 7) adds 'the more serious the decision is viewed by those who control the rules, and the more it might be difficult to reach agreement, the more it tends to be ritualised'. Compared to Belgium, the UK rules give more space to informality, though the UK Parliament involves some prominent rituals, particularly in the acts of voting, appointing the speaker and the State Opening of Parliament. For day-to-day business, the UK has fewer rules relating to time limits on speaking and who speaks when, whereas Belgium has granular rules on this issue.

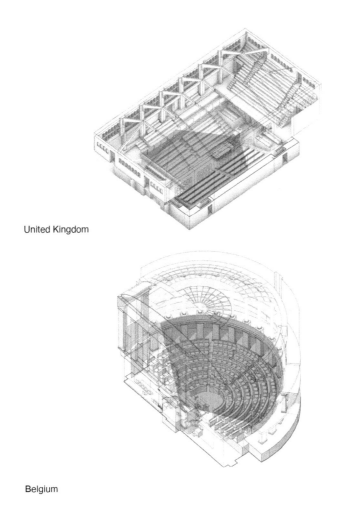

United Kingdom

Belgium

Figure 21.7 Comparing the views of the chair in the UK and Belgian chambers, 2021. © Carlota Nuñez-Barranco Vallejo

Speaking

In the UK, MPs speak from their seat unless they are a government minister or shadow minister, in which case they are able to speak from a dispatch box. In Belgium, members speak from their seat or from the rostrum (Figure 21.6).[3] In the UK, when speaking, those in your party are not facing you, but sit behind you or would need to twist to see you. Instead, as you speak you look across to the chair and opposite parties. MPs and the chair are covisible, which is indicated in the chamber's parlance: 'Mr Speaker and honourable member …'.

In Belgium, there is a difference in dynamic whether speaking from the rostrum or from your seat. From the rostrum the chair is not visible; you speak to the semicircle, which includes both the government and the legislature. From your seat you look towards the chair and may catch glimpses of other members.

View of the chair

Belgian members can request to speak via their console during the course of a debate, but protocol is to inform the chair in advance of a sitting of an intent to speak. The chair will pre-plan the speaking order and will aim to arrange for opposition and majority speakers to speak alternately, as well as ensuring Flemish and French speakers have their turn.

In the UK, MPs catch the eye of the speaker on the floor of the chamber (Figure 21.7). MPs are also encouraged to inform the speaker's office if they wish to speak. In this more ad hoc system, it is essential that MPs and the chair are covisible as the sequencing rules of speaking rely on the chair's discretion and a sign-based behavioural language, whereby MPs rise from their seats to indicate their wish to speak.

Voting

In Belgium, voting is usually undertaken from the member's seat. In the UK, members exit the chamber and pass through one of two division lobbies. The act of voting through division lobbies and the time given over to this activity, as Goodsell (1988), Philip Norton (2019) and our interviews note, gives time and space to last minute negotiations and lobbying. Electronic voting methods do not permit such interactions.

The interplay of spatial configuration and behavioural rules

Permanent visibility and the accompanying state of mind ensures the automatic functioning of power (Foucault 1995). But power and control, in parliamentary deliberation at least, are neither static nor merely physical, but dynamic processes open to negotiation. They define, as Palonen (2018) writes, theories of knowledge, different modes of acting and thinking politically. To better understand the distribution of power and principles of social control in relation to space, we turned to Basil Bernstein's work in education settings. Bernstein identified a typology of social relationships based on the notions of 'strong' or 'weak' classification, and 'strong' or 'weak' framing (Bernstein 1977). Applying these concepts to spatial arrangements, he defined classification as the strength of the boundary between contents in space, and framing as the structure of communication and social relationships in time.[4]

Classification in our study is interpreted within plenary halls as the strength of differentiation in visibility relationships: within the legislature; between the legislature and the government; among the legislature, the government and the chair. Framing translates to the degree of control the legislature, government and chair possess over the selection, organisation, pacing and timing of knowledge transmitted in parliamentary debate.

Our analysis indicates that Belgium is strongly classified, as there are strong differences between the visibility relationships among the legislature, government and chair. Conversely, the UK is weakly classified, due to greater levels of visibility parity among these powers and a correspondence between seating and speaking positions. The UK is also weakly framed as there is less explicit control over the selection, organisation, pacing and timing of communication. The stronger the classification and framing, the more the parliamentary debate tends to be formalised and ritualised. The weaker the classification and framing, the more tacit the principles of debate, permitting 'a large range of combinations and re-combinations based on intensified forms of interaction' (Bernstein 1977, p. 155).

If, as Palonen writes, the dissensus between perspectives defines parliamentary debate as a parliamentary theory of knowledge, weak classification and weak framing have the potential to create a vast range of possibilities, 'provoking the political imagination of parliamentarians to introduce perspectives that reshape the terms of the debate' (Palonen 2019, p. 49). It will be valuable to investigate whether the underlying legal systems, one based on prescriptive civil law (Belgium), and the other on a more discretionary common law system (UK), play a role in creating these differences, and if these differences remain consistent throughout parliaments that follow one of these two legal systems – a notion that Korolija explores in this volume.

Conclusion

It is pointless to study the spatial-social dynamics of a parliament building without considering the cultures, histories and diversity of opinions among the people it represents. The intertwined trajectories, colonial influences, adaptations and reconstructions caused by wars, fires and political rifts collectively shape each nation's sociopolitical system. Our investigation suggests that buildings and spatial morphologies are more permanent and resistant to change than political ideologies, but power relations, rituals and behaviours outlive both.

While traditional plenary hall typologies have a symbolic-historical function, they do not automatically provide a means for understanding the differences within executive–legislative relationships. Nor do they explain deliberative assemblies and how they are characterised by their *pro et contra* parliamentary debates. Informed by Foucault, King, Bernstein, Markus and Cameron, we show that there is no easy division of parliamentarians into 'the powerful' and 'the powerless', but that there are varied typologies based on seating arrangements, visual interconnectivity, rules of procedure and rhetoric.

Further, if 'parliament should reflect the entire anatomy of society' (Rosanvallon 1998, p. 22), the study of parliaments as an eclectic mix of buildings, chambers and social microcosms opens a window to understanding political issues such as the diverging cultures of the UK's devolved parliaments, and navigating, as well as recognising, the diverse historical and social realities of European nations as part of the EU project. Europe arises as a reflection of the tension between the common destiny of parliamentary democracy and the pragmatics of diverse political cultures.

Our study generates more questions and research directions than answers. There is not a single narrative of parliament buildings, either seen together or individually, but multiple narratives based on assorted histories, political systems and other dimensions that are beyond the scope of this study. As an untapped subject of architectural research, however, the study introduces lines of enquiry that can enrich the understanding not only of parliaments, but also of buildings dedicated to governance, knowledge and justice. Understanding these buildings is as much a matter of interdisciplinary study as historical or morphological research. There is more to learn about the time-bound processes of social interaction within institutional settings, and how this both manifests within and is shaped by the buildings themselves.

With the current urgent questioning of institutional structures and need for a multiformity of people within our institutions, it is important to understand the complexities of social and institutional cultures alongside the ways in which the buildings themselves perpetuate, both visibly and invisibly, inequalities and structures of power. In some cases, as shown in the case of the UK chamber, institutions can place unequal categories face-to-face, rebalancing the unequal distribution of power.

Notes

1 See website *Plenum: Places of Power*, available at: https://www.labiennale.at/2014/aus
stellung.html (acessed 1 August 2023).).

2 By 'government' we refer generally to the dedicated seating for cabinet ministers/council
of ministers and prime minister. In some cases, such as Lithuania and Latvia, the President
of the Republic also sits with the government. In the case of France, the *Bancs des
Commissions* (benches for committee chairs and their appointed rapporteurs) are situated
with the *Bancs des Ministres* (cabinet ministers' benches) within the semicircle.

3 In *The Rules of Procedure of the Belgian House of Representatives* (English translation)
(2020) it is simply stated under rule 44 point 4 that 'The speaker may only address the
President or the House. MPs must stand and speak from their place or from the rostrum'
(p. 38). What governs when an MP speaks from their place or from the rostrum is not
further defined in the written rules of procedure. However, there are other parliaments –
such as in Austria – who have further granularity on this issue, stating within their rules
of procedure when members speak from their seats, from the rostrum or from a third
location.

4 In this chapter we are not, of course, seeking to underplay the factor of political parties in
structuring power within a parliament and the major role they have in determining voting
and speaking behaviour. Rather, we are seeking to look at the structure of communication
within the chamber as it happens in real time, within an already structured system of
knowledge and power.

References

Benedikt, M. (1979) 'To take hold of space: isovists and isovist fields', *Environment and Planning
B*, 6(1), pp. 47–65. DOI: 10.1068/b060047.

Bernstein, B. (1977) *Class Codes and Control: Volume 3 Towards a Theory of Educational
Transmissions*, London: Routledge and Kegan Paul.

Crewe, E. (2021) *The Anthropology of Parliaments: Entanglements in Democratic Politics*, London:
Routledge.

Döring, H. (1995) 'Die Sitzordnung der Abgeordneten: Ausdruck kulturell divergierender
Auffassungen von Demokratie?' in A. Dörner and L. Vogt (eds) *Sprache des Parlaments und
Semiotik der Demokratie*, Berlin: de Gruyter, pp. 278–289.

Foucault, M. (1995) *Discipline and Punish: The Birth of the Prison*, translated by Alan Sheridan,
2nd edition, New York: Vintage Books.

Fox, R., Russell, M., Cormacain, R. and Tomlison, J. (2021) 'The marginalisation of the House of
Commons under Covid has been shocking: a year on Parliament's role must be restored',
Hansard Society, 21 April. Available from: https://www.hansardsociety.org.uk/publications
/briefings/the-marginalisation-of-the-house-of-commons-under-covid-has-been-shocking
-a (accessed on 26 January 2022).

Goodsell, C. (1988) 'The architecture of parliaments, legislative houses and political culture',
British Journal of Political Science, 18(3), pp. 287–302. DOI: 10.1017/S00071234000
05135.

HC Deb (28 October 1943) vol. 393, cols. 403–406. Available from: https://api.parliament.uk
/historic-hansard/commons/1943/oct/28/house-of-commons-rebuilding (accessed on 26
January 2022).

Hillier, B. and Hanson, J. (1984) *The Social Logic of Space*, Cambridge: Cambridge University
Press.

Hollis, E. (2013) *The Memory Palace: A Book of Lost Interiors*, London: Portobello Books.

King, A. (1976) 'Modes of executive–legislative relations: Great Britain, France, and West
Germany', *Legislative Studies Quarterly*, 1(1), pp. 11–36. DOI: 10.2307/439626.

Manow, P. (2010) *In the King's Shadow: The Political Anatomy of Democratic Representation*,
Malden MA: Polity Press.

Markus, T. and Cameron, D. (2002) *The Words Between the Spaces: Buildings and Language*,
London: Routledge.

Norton, P. (2019) 'Power behind the scenes: the importance of informal space in legislatures',
Parliamentary Affairs, 72, pp. 245–266. DOI: 10.1093/pa/gsy018.

Palonen, K. (2018) 'A comparison between three ideal types of parliamentary politics: representation, legislation and deliberation', *Parliaments, Estates and Representation*, 38(1), pp. 6–20. DOI: 10.1080/02606755.2018.1427325.

Palonen, K. (2019) *Parliamentary Thinking: Rhetoric, Poetics and Society*, London: Palgrave Macmillan.

Port, M.H. (1976) *The Houses of Parliament*, New Haven, CT and London: Yale University Press.

Rosanvallon, P. (1998) *Le Peuple introuvable: Histoire de le representation démocratique en France*, Paris: Gallimard.

Rowe, C. and Koetter, F. (1983) *Collage City*, Cambridge, MA: MIT Press.

TU Vienna (2014) Plenum, Places of Power [online database]. Available from: https://web.archive.org/web/20210928182815/https://www.places-of-power.org/wiki/index.php?title=Main_Page.

XML Architects (2016) *Parliaments*, Amsterdam: XML.

Yates, F.A. (1984) *Volume III The Art of Memory*, Abingdon: Ark Paperbacks (Routledge).

22

From *Thing* to revolutionary assembly
Architectural systems of gathering

Harald Trapp

Introduction

The architecture of assemblies is still often reduced to its representative aspect. But from its very beginning, as the 'Thing' of the Teutons bears in its name, gatherings are interactions between bodies, issues to be discussed and physical settings, increasingly developing into complex architectural systems. This becomes especially evident during the early stages of the French Revolution, which referred to classical references in its attempt to redefine the spatial production of political decisions.

The name of the juridical and political gatherings of the Teutons was Thing. Originally this encompassed the totality of the assembled warriors, their weapons, the place, its marking, the topics at issue and the process of their negotiation and decision. The Thing as the *Urform* of gathering, is reflected, says Heidegger, in the example of the jug. The jug is a thing as a vessel only because it can hold something:

> Sides and bottom are, to be sure, what is impermeable in the vessel. But what is impermeable is not yet what does the holding. ... The emptiness, the void, is what does the vessel's holding. The empty space, this nothing of the jug, is what the jug is as the holding vessel (Heidegger 1971, pp. 166–167).

In Luhmann's distinction between medium, or the loose coupling of elements, and form, or the strict coupling of elements, space is a medium and an object is a form in the medium space. A form in social communication is an operation, a distinction. Spatially, individuals are bodies, a special type of object, as they are endogenously restless, equipped with perception and move as long as they exist. Any gathering of bodies must hence configure a spatial form based on the restriction of this urge to move. Such a restriction on the movement of bodies leads to what we call a motion-form. Motion, because even people standing still, through their perception are in motion, form, because a gathering of bodies distinguishes an object in space. Interpreted in this way, the Teutonic meeting Thing begins as a restriction on the physical and perceptual mobility of free warriors. In *Germania*, Tacitus explicitly describes the hesitation of those who come together and thus refers to the resistance that such a coordination of independent movements has to overcome (Tacitus 2011, p. 18).

If the form object is moved in space or its shape is changed, we speak of a form-motion, which is what happens in the case of the Thing: the space of the gathering is delimited by a circle of stones or hazel shrubs.

Thus, the motion-form of the warriors is connected to a form-motion of stones and shrubs to create a spatial system. The gathered warriors distinguish themselves from the rest of the tribe not only by forming a circle, but also through the handling of objects connecting to it. But the gathering Thing is not yet architecture, as its system is based on discipline and not yet on isolation, the restriction of social communication through objects. The stones and shrubs are marking a space rather than isolating bodies through a wall. The ring of objects, which connects to the motion-form of the warriors, produces a spatial, not yet an architectural distinction.

Like the Teutons, the Greeks and Romans chose open-air circles for their gatherings, but their *Ecclesiasterion* and *Comitium* were designed to install an assembly. Following the example of the theatre, the form-motion of the gathering connecting to the motion-form of the seating arrangement became more effective and, with that, its agency is intensified. The sustained attention needed for the more complex decisions in a city-state rather than a tribe demanded exposure of the speaker and an immobilisation of the listeners.

> The audience for this political theater sat around the bowl in assigned places ... The citizens watched each other's reactions as intently as the orator at the bema [the podium]. People sat or stood in this relation for a long time, as long as the sunlight lasted. The theatrical space thus functioned as a detection mechanism, its focus and duration meant to get beneath the surface of momentary impressions (Sennett 1998, p. 17).

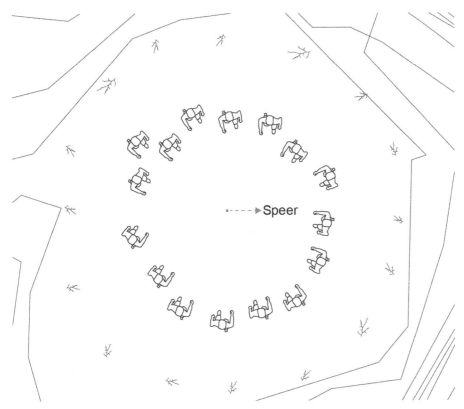

Figure 22.1 Diagrammatic reconstruction of a Teutonic Thing. © Harald Trapp

The discipline of the warriors was now augmented by the fixing of bodies in places, thus producing an assembly, a sociospatial 'device' guiding 'eye, voice, and body' to 'hold citizens responsible for their words' (Sennett 1998, p. 17).

But the theatrical element of these commonly accessible assemblies made them increasingly ineffective in supporting public consensus. In the Roman *Comitium*, Ann Vasaly writes, a magistrate:

> could no longer depend on respect for his *auctoritas* to bend the masses to his desires, for the demagogues of the late Republic had accustomed their audiences to expect the orators who addressed them here to define all issues in terms of the libertarian catchwords and slogans of the day. In the best of times, the best of orators might

successfully induce his audience to equate their own interests with the welfare of the state; in the worst of times, all persuasion yielded to violence (Vasaly 1993, p. 74).

The necessary reorganisation required a more complex spatial system than the open amphitheatre. By consequence, Greek city-states and the Roman Republic differentiated their rule between popular assembly and council (the *bouleuterion* and the *curia*), the latter holding the authority for making decisions. Representation through deputies was preferred over direct participation of all citizens. The assembly since then had to actively pull together a common will, replacing the amalgamation of particular opinions of citizens who were no longer present. The *bouleuterion* and the *curia* were houses, as they were not primarily built for protection against adverse conditions or for symbolic representation, but to spatially isolate the assembly from the citizens. After surrounding and placing, a new level of form-motion of the assembly was reached: the discipline of distance and immobilisation had turned into isolation.

Motion-form and form-motion are complementary objective operations, alternately connecting to one another to create a sociospatial system. The gathering of warriors is a motion-form and connects to the form-motion of the circle of shrubs and vice versa. The forms have to be objectively complementary (the circle of the warriors has to fit into the circle of shrubs) and as long as one can connect to the other, the system continues to operate. Once this system, as in the case of the *curia* and the *bouleuterium*, distinguishes between an interior and an exterior space, architecture comes into operation. Only when the restricted movement of bodies is enclosed by the restricted movement of objects and vice versa does an architectural system develop. This does not negate the process of symbolisation intrinsic to any social communication, but denies its primacy. In architecture, signs are one aspect of forms, as the process of signification accompanies its objective operations.

The societies of Greece and Rome turned out to be vulnerable. In the course of history, they overwhelmed the available physical and social structures due to an increase in complexity, which ultimately led to their dissolution. Over the following centuries, in Europe, rule became condensed into the sacral figure of the king. One body was all that remained of the gathering:

It is the body of the monarch, which has to be considered and not his decision-making, because only the body (not the decisions) of the monarch can be recognised as a *sacrum*. The killing of the monarch in the French Revolution is therefore to be understood as one of the great historical amputations that makes decisions necessary (Luhmann 2002, p. 326, author's translation).

For this reason, the French Revolution radically reinvented the legislative assembly, based on popular sovereignty. The last meeting of the General Estates in the Salle des Menus Plaisirs in May 1789 clearly demonstrated what had to be overcome, as it was designed to allow only the physical presence and no exchange between its 1,200 deputies, arranged before Louis XVI. After the king's attempt to exclude the Third Estate from the next

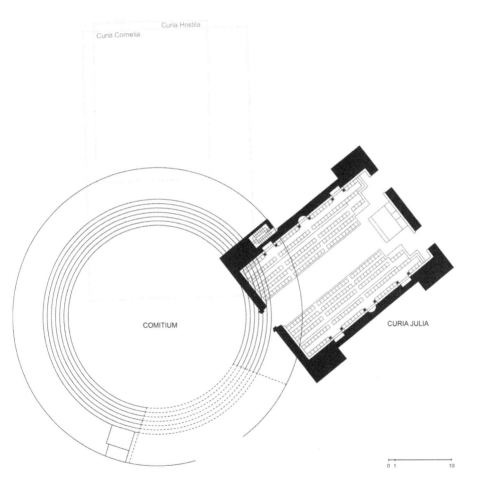

Figure 22.2 Site plan of Comitium and Curia Julia (44–29 BC), Rome. © Harold Trapp

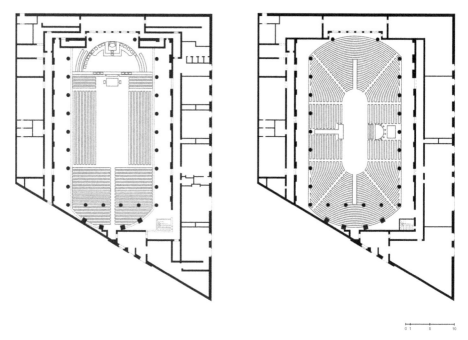

Figure 22.3   Salle des Menus Plaisirs, Versailles, on 5 May 1789 and on 23 June 1789.
© Harald Trapp

meeting had failed and the bourgeoisie pressed for reforms, carpenters hurriedly replaced the hierarchical furnishings with an oval amphitheatre.

The circle as a spatial system promised to answer all revolutionary requirements, as it seemed capable of producing accord and order, to counter antagonistic behaviour by deputies and support the diffusion of speech.

> This space gathers together distinct individuals, separated by divergent interests that distinguish them from one another, while holding them, as Etienne Tassin points out, 'in an exteriority of some toward others and in an exteriority of each to the assembly as a whole,' but which can nevertheless bring them closer and unite them (Heurtin 2005, p. 766; Tassin 1992).

The circle supported the expression of a common will that would speak directly to the heart of the assembly and promise unity, transparency and immediacy – and brought the nation to appear. 'Reified forms of life' (motion-forms) respond to 'grammars of action in the solid state' (form-motions), adds Heurtin (2005, p. 764), but they remain at the level of spatial systems, embedded into the interior of the hall and amplified by its enclosure.

If building a nation demanded a communion, devising a constitution required representation. A constitution can only be worked out through representatives, who have to establish a common will by working on a text. The work of the constituent assembly thus follows the model of the division of labour, led by the impossibility of distilling a common will from the sum of individual opinions of all citizens. This can only be achieved through debates and deliberation by their representatives, as Heurtin explains, quoting Sieyès:

'Representation, and nothing before it, is a sovereignty limited by the common good. That is how the social body gives itself a head, a common reason, to organize itself.' Representation is a task – and, in this respect, it is integrated into the social division of labour – a task of production of the third common, and then of turning that common into a public issue (Heurtin 2005, p. 766).

Compared to its classical precedents, the architectural system of the Revolution expands representation to production and adds division to isolation. The moving of the revolutionary assemblies through five different places and six different configurations between 1789 and 1798 gives evidence of the importance of space for this process and the difficulties entailed.

Until the move to the Salle des Machines in 1793, the circular seating arrangement for the assemblies was retained, even when the structural conditions in the Salle du Manège deformed it into an oval.

Although the closed circle was suitable to allow the nation to appear through embodiment and collective eye contact, the actual power was now increasingly expressed through the voice of the deputies. As François Furet notes:

Since it is the people who alone have the right to govern, or who must at least in the lack of power to do so, re-institute public authority ceaselessly, power is in the hands of those who speak in its name. Which means that speech, since the word, which is by its nature public, is the instrument that discloses what would like to remain hidden, hence evil (Heurtin 2005, p. 768).

The Revolution demanded a culture of scrutiny towards the opinions presented, similar to the empirical observation evolving in the sciences

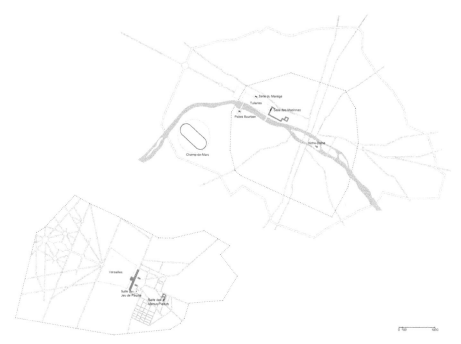

Figure 22.4 Venues of Assembly, Versailles and Paris, 1789–1798, site plan.
© Harald Trapp

at the same time. Despite popular belief, the final layout of the assembly, therefore, is not derived from the amphitheatre, but the anatomical theatre, recently perfected in the École de Chirurgie (1764). In the assembly, the epistemology through spatialisation and verbalisation cited by Foucault (1973) was transferred to the dissection of speeches. The opposition between speaker and assembly additionally favoured the semicircular configuration of the anatomical theatre. No wonder that Victor Hugo, writes Vidler, saw in the Salle des Machines 'a direct transcription of the Revolution in architecture: "The whole ensemble was violent, savage, regular. The correct in the wild." … By its "hard rectilinear angles, cold and cutting as steel", its severity contrasted with the riot of decoration common to ancien regime theaters' (Vidler 1991, p. 206).

But the rational power of spatial configuration does not foster the emotional bond of a nation. As much as the motion-form of the festival – the organisation of the movement of bodies, the elements of spectacle, liturgy and procession – contradicted the requirements for the production of common decisions, the motion-form of the house and the closure of its interior was irreconcilable with the idea of unanimity and equality.

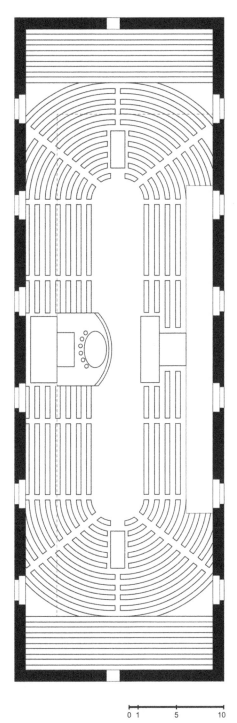

Figure 22.5 Salle du Manège, Paris, on 9 November 1789, floor plan. © Harald Trapp

0 1   5   10

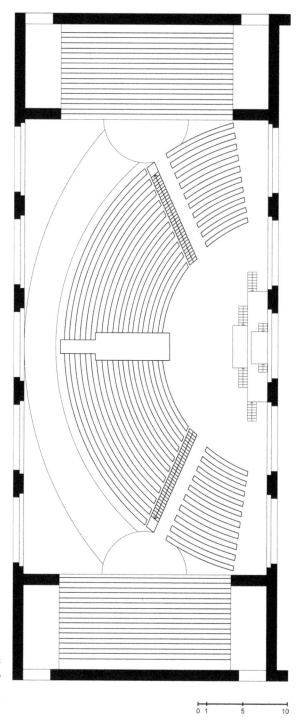

Figure 22.6 Salle des Machines, Paris, May 1793, floor plan. © Harald Trappr

Based on the tradition of religious, pastoral and ceremonial festivals, the French Revolution therefore reanimated a type of gathering which had become outmoded during the Enlightenment. It was precisely the barely controllable affective aspects of these festivals which provided the necessary complement to the cold rationality of politics. The spatial system employed to produce the revolutionary festival was radically different from the architectural system of the assembly. The festival thus was essentially non-architectural or even anti-architectural, as it only accepted the roof of the sky above it and the boundlessness of territory beneath. The assembly's interiority and structured debates stood in stark contrast to the outdoor spectacle of the festive space, where:

> once the procession has reached its goal, there is no additional indication to the celebrants as to what they should do next. It is as if the monument and even the temple itself provided sufficient emotional satisfaction simply by virtue of being seen. What, then, was the point of going inside? (Ozouf 1988, p. 136).

The festival expanded horizontally in contrast to the verticality of the house of the assembly and with it the locked-in world of despotism disappeared:

> What was needed was a festive space that could contain an endless, irrepressible, and peaceful movement like the rise of tidal waters. ... For Fichte, the dazzling flood was that of Revolutionary truth; for the festival organizers, it was that of Revolutionary joy. But both sensed an identical expansion: 'Democracy is the happy, unimpeded extension of happiness'; 'holy equality hovers over the whole earth,' said the official reports (Ozouf, 1988, p. 127).

This festive space found its culmination on the first anniversary of the storming of the Bastille in 1790, when over half a million people gathered on the Champ de Mars in Paris. The Fête de la Fédération (Festival of the Federation) celebrated the democratic paradox of the unity of the ruler and the ruled, and with it 'the passage from the private to the public, extending to all the feeling of each individual "as by a kind of electrical charge." It allowed "that which despotism had never allowed" ... The gathering in the Champ de Mars seemed to everybody to be the reverse of that partitioned world' (Ozouf 1988, p. 54).

The revolutionary festivals did not hinder the evolution of the political assembly, which could be interpreted as an increasing architecturalisation:

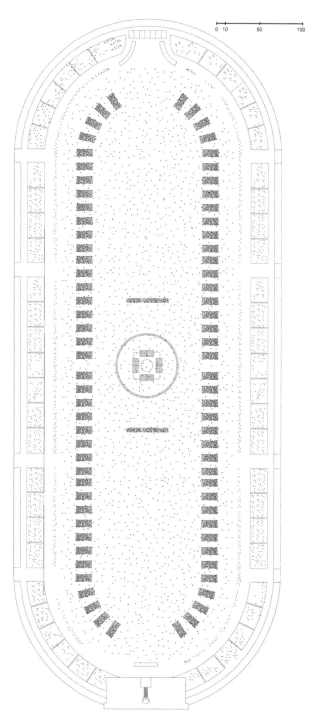

Figure 22.7
Champ des Mars,
Paris, on 14 July
1790, floor plan.
© Harald Trapp

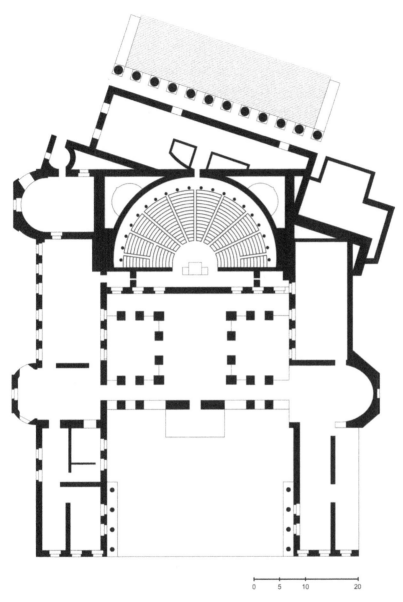

Figure 22.8 Palais Bourbon, Paris, 1798, floor plan. © Harald Trapp

from the Thing through the *curia* to the Salle d'Assemblée. Whereas
in the spatial system of the Thing, warriors do not represent, but present themselves and their issues to one another, the architectural system
of the *curia* embodies representation through the separation of deputies
from the people they represent. The *Assemblée* developed this prototype

of the rational machine to define a common will in the competition of particular interests in the assembly.

Returning to Heidegger and his statement that 'the jug is a thing as a vessel' (Heidegger 1971, p. 166), and that it is a vessel through the empty space it gathers, Michelet perfectly described the symbol of the revolutionary assembly: '"while the Empire had its columns and the Royalty had the Louvre, the Revolution had for its monument ... only the void"'(quoted in Vidler 1991, p. 207).

References

Foucault, M. (1973) *The Birth of the Clinic: An Archaeology of Medical Perception*, London: Tavistock Publications.

Heidegger, M. (1971) *Poetry, Language, Thought*, New York: Harper & Row.

Heurtin, J.-P. (2005) 'The Circle of Discussion and the Semicircle of Criticism', in B. Latour and P. Weibel (eds) *Making Things Public: Atmospheres of Democracy*, Cambridge, MA and London: ZKM, Center for Art and Media Karlsruhe, pp. 754–769.

Luhmann, N. (2002) *Die Politik der Gesellschaft*, Frankfurt a.M.: Suhrkamp.

Ozouf, M. (1988) *Festivals and the French Revolution*, Cambridge, MA: Harvard University Press.

Sennett, R. (1988) *The Spaces of Democracy*, Chicago: The University of Michigan College of Architcture and Urban Planning.

Tacitus, P.C. (2011) *Germania, De origine et situ Germanorum liber*, Stuttgart: Reclam.

Tassin, E. (1992) 'Espace commun ou espace public? L'antagonisme de la communauté et de la publicité', *Hermès, La Revue*, 1992/1 (no. 10), pp. 23–37. DOI: 10.4267/2042/15351.

Vasaly, A. (1993) *Representations: Images of the World in Ciceronian Oratory*, Berkeley, Los Angeles and Oxford: University of California Press.

Vidler, A. (1991) 'Researching revolutionary architecture', *Journal of Architectural Education*, 44(4), pp. 206–210. DOI: 10.1080/10464883.1991.11102696.

23

Dynamics of an architectural framing, parliamentary debates and the Palace of Westminster

Gordana Korolija

Introduction

Tackling politics and architecture is always highly relevant and profoundly challenging. By grasping the nature and the conditions of parliamentary debates, this chapter theorises the nature and the role of parliamentary architecture and its spaces in governmental debates. It analyses the ways in which spatial relations have been formed, designed and interpreted by architects and various agents of power to instil and maintain a set of procedures, related values and a hierarchy of state order.

The theoretical background to this chapter is my previous research related to the works of: (1) Michel Foucault, who had importantly and dynamically attended to the subject of space and architecture, most poignantly in *Discipline and Punish* (Foucault 1975); (2) Lewis Mumford, who had grappled with these questions when discussing the city in history, its transformations from antiquity to modern times (Mumford 1961); and (3) canonical architectural treatise writers such as Vitruvius (first century BC [1960]), Leon Battista Alberti (1452 [1989]) and Sebastiano Serlio (1611 [1983]) who had raised and set up many pertinent aspects of this discourse. The more recent work of political theorist Stuart Elden (2014) on politics and space is also considered, including his theory of the territory of a nation as being not simply an empty container of sovereignty, or a product of practising territorialisation, but a space where historically contextualised sets of ideas and practices had been used at different junctures to stabilise the complex ways in which the relationship between place, space and power was forged. In the case of parliamentary buildings this set of ideas and practices is voiced and materialised through the workings of parliament and its central action – the parliamentary debates.

Due to architecture's focus on the formal values of an architectural object, more conjectural and speculative aspects related to the spatiality and spatial effects of buildings have achieved less prominence until what came to be known as 'the spatial turn' exemplified in the works by Foucault, Derrida (1962), Deleuze and Guattari (1988), Virilio (1997) and others who are related to the work of these theorists.

In this context, parliamentary buildings provide a particular typology of edifices containing special significance for their respective nations due to their all-encompassing role and emblematic status. Their symbolic aura is constantly reinforced and disseminated via a proliferation of statements, images, films, television programmes and other forms of digital media spinning the appearances of the national edifice ad infinitum.

How can we begin to address the spatiality of the parliament, its implicated logic and the effects of the structure that is the symbolic home for the nation?

This is an important question of an underrepresented area of architectural knowledge that deserves further scrutiny even if we remain aware that the political agency of architecture is limited, non-direct and non-explicit, yet relevant and graspable. Indeed, the works of writers and conceptual artists from Kafka (1915 [2009]) via Christo and Jeanne-Claude's *Wrapped Reichstag* (1995), to Langlands and Bell's *UN Security Council* (1991) have put forward the concerns, apprehensions, fears and the perplexities of institutional spaces of this kind.

In this chapter, I shall focus on the following two aspects: (1) the origins and status of the 'parliamentary debate' as a philosophical category with reference to the work of Immanuel Kant, and (2) the nature of the perceived need for specific architectural provision for parliamentary deliberations primarily centred on the Palace of Westminster and its Commons chamber, noting its differences to European parliaments. Based on the discussion of these two aspects, I shall draw conclusions about the relationship between the nature of a debate and its architectural framing in parliamentary edifices.

'Parliamentary debate' as a philosophical category

Where does parliamentary debate come from? What is going on in this debate and related procedural motions? Agreements, disagreements or a range of disagreements? Conflict, or attempts to resolve it and achieve consensus? Given that the ideas that had underlined eighteenth-century political thinking also came to underpin the emergence of parliaments and subsequently relate to their edifices built predominantly in the nineteenth century, I begin by addressing Kant's work on political philosophy, focusing on his *Perpetual Peace: A Philosophical Essay* (Kant 1795). This work considers the central question of good state governance. I shall also mention other texts by this philosopher, such as *The Ground Work for the Metaphysics of Morals* (Kant 1785) and *Metaphysics of Morals* (Kant 1797). *Metaphysics of Morals* is further divided into two parts: *Doctrine of Rights* and *Doctrine of Virtue*. There are also several other relevant essays such as 'An Answer to the Question: What is Enlightenment?' (1784) and 'Theory and Practice' (1793) on the role of the state.

In his political philosophy, Kant championed the Enlightenment[1] and the idea of freedom by addressing both natural law and the tradition of social contract as the basis for politics (Kant 1784). Inspired by the French Revolution, he argued that every rational being had an innate right to freedom and a duty to enter a civil society governed by social contract (Rauscher 2017).

His 1795 philosophical sketch concentrates on the necessary rules for nations to achieve lasting peace, by arguing that nations can be brought into federation with one another without a loss of sovereignty, according to certain rules. These rules include:

1. No treaty of peace shall be regarded as valid, if made with the secret reservation of material for a future war. 2. No state having an independent existence – whether it be great or small – shall be acquired by another through inheritance, exchange, purchase or donation. 3. Standing armies (*miles perpetuus*) shall be abolished in course of time. 4. No national debts shall be contracted in connection with the external affairs of the state. 5. No state shall violently interfere with the constitution and administration of another. 6. No state at war with another shall countenance such modes of hostility as would make mutual confidence impossible in a subsequent state of peace: such are the employment of assassins (*percussores*) or of poisoners (*venefici*), breaches of capitulation, the instigating and making use of treachery (*perduellio*) in the hostile state (Kant 1795).

Kant argues that although nature makes use of conflict and war, in the end, it impels us towards peace. In that respect, the philosopher from Königsberg (Kaliningrad) sought to examine whether these ideas are merely theoretical, or whether they bear translation into practice. He made a distinction between the moral politician and the political moralist, pointing out that practical considerations of theoretical ideas can bring conflict by concealing and excusing behaviour that can lead to discord and, ultimately, war.

As argued by many Kantian scholars including Palmquist (2005), Ellis (2012) and Rauscher (2017), dichotomy and conflict have been crucial concepts in Kant's critical philosophy on several levels. Without conflict, he argued, the human mind could not function, as knowledge would be impossible if the realms of the senses and of understanding did not stand in opposition to each other. This conflict (opposition) Kant famously endeavoured to resolve in his 'third critique', *The Critique of Judgement [Kritik der Urteilskraft]* (Kant 1790), that has subsequently become a major philosophical reference point for any theory of judgement. Reason itself, Kant maintains, does not free us from conflict; it only raises the stakes. In our attempts to think about objects and contemplate beyond the realm of the senses, we often find ourselves giving two opposite yet equally reasonable answers to the most fundamental questions human beings can ask themselves about the nature of their life and death (Palmquist 2005). Given the complex nature of this reasoning that reflects the tension between our faculties, and since this tension fuels the debate, a stabilisation that leads to a possible (re)solution of any debate, including the parliamentary, is required. It is required in all kinds of parliaments but even more so where there is no written constitution. We can thus detect how Kant's philosophy is relevant for arguments about the nature of the parliamentary space of debate. The conflict as understood by Kant is the human condition into which we are born and into which we stay, balancing our own act on both personal and societal levels.

This metaphysical condition is a science in itself, most recently systematically explored by the psychoanalyst and neuroscientist Iain McGilchrist in his *The Master and his Emissary* (2009). Within the context of developments in neuroscience, McGilchrist argues that the two brain hemispheres are different in their nature and that this distinction can give us a clue about two different types of human personalities that are either predominantly a left-hemisphere (more inclined to logical, rational thinking) or right-hemisphere type (more prone to intuitive thinking). To an extent these two types of personalities in McGilchrist correspond to the two types in Kant's *Perpetual Peace*. The two different roles our separate brain hemispheres have will always be in some kind of opposition, even if not in conflict.

To think about Kant's position further, we need to consider the key political and philosophical concept of *Rechtsstaat*. *Rechtsstaat* is defined as the constitutional right of a citizen (Schmitt 1928 [2008]) and is commonly referred to as 'the rule of law' within the Anglo-American context. It has not been defined or used by Kant. This notion was first introduced by Carl Theodor Welcker in 1813 and was popularised by Robert von Mohl in his discussion on German policy science according to the principles of the constitutional state (von Mohl 1833). The term literally means 'state of rights' and is a part of the doctrine in continental Europe's jurisprudence based on German – predominantly Kant's – philosophy. It is often translated into English as 'rule of law' notifying 'state based on justice and integrity'.[2] According to Carl Schmitt, *Rechtsstaat* refers to a 'constitutional state' in which the exercise of governmental executive power is constrained by the state of law (Schmitt 1928 [2008]).

However, *Rechtsstaat* significantly differs from the Anglo-American 'rule of law' not only because it indicates 'the state of rights' as opposed to 'the rule of law', but also because it specifies what is just – it signifies moral righteousness founded on ethics, rationality, religion, natural law and equity for all. In this way, it is different from a parliamentary situation such as in the UK, where the constitutional rights are not at all times guaranteed as it were a priori, due to the lack of a written constitution that would specify and guarantee them. Here the rights are at times subject to the will of the parliament and its majority. This majority rule can prevail over minority and thus it can sometimes (not always) override what would be considered just. There are, of course, mechanisms to prevent this as the opposite sides can argue their cases in parliament and refer to the all-important precedents. There are also parliamentary committees that examine the relevant details and procedures. In a sense one can argue that there is certain openness to this kind of debate that can generate excitement by demonstrating and exercising arguments for various new situations. At the same time the continental followers of the doctrine of *Rechtsstaat* can potentially see this as 'arbitrary use of power' claimed by the parliamentary majority exercising its supremacy according to the agreed rules of common law as understood in this country. Importantly, Kant disagreed with the rule of majority, which for him always leaves the minority at a loss, crucially in situations when they could be righteous.

Although Kant is associated with the concept of *Rechtsstaat*, he did not use the term itself. He contrasted an existing state (*staat*) with an ideal, constitutional, just state (*republik*). In that sense Kant has addressed the concept of justice and the state similar to the way in which the concept of just city is discussed in Plato's *Republic* (Plato 385 BC [2008]) or the way in which St Augustine addresses the ideal city of God, *civitas dei* as opposed to *civitas terrena* in *The City of God* Books XI–XIV (St Augustine fifth century AD [2006]).

Kant's specific contribution to political theory is in the introduction of the supremacy of a country's written constitution that guarantees the implementation of a central idea: a permanent peace for all. By stating and fixing the importance of equity for all through written constitution, Kant introduces a certain stability to his political and philosophical discourse on justice and the state. The idea of permanent, peaceful life is understood as a basic condition for the happiness and prosperity of all people. It is just and guaranteed by a constitution agreed by all people and maintained by parliaments and governments.

Overall Kant's political doctrine could be summed up as twofold: (1) a republican government (based on law – later *Rechtsstaat*), and (2) an international organisation as guarantors of peace (based on perpetual peace). Crucially, Kant's political philosophy and his legal doctrine reject the opposition between moral education based on religious doctrine, and the play of passions as alternate opposing foundations for social life as it was previously understood within monarchical courts. Instead, the state is constituted by laws that are rational and necessary a priori because they come from the very concept of law – Kant's categorical imperative.

This is Kant's a priori stating that a regime can be judged by no other criteria nor be assigned any other functions than those proper to the lawful order as such (Strauss and Cropsey 1987, pp. 581–582 and 603). The place where these arguments are presented, contested, recorded and framed for posterity is the parliament. What kind of place is the parliament?

The space and the architectural provision for parliamentary debates

What are the spatial conditions that underpin the parliamentary debate? (See Figure 23.1.) What is the nature of the debate and its outcome? Is it all, as Kant wanted it to be, a reasonable consideration between parties that follows the logic, rationality and the moral a priori made for the purpose of world peace? Kant's discourse was orderly and stable, reflecting his life that was reigned by regular routine. We are told that the citizens of his native Königsberg could check their watches according to the professor's routine (Kuehn 2009).[3] He lived in East Prussia, the country that reportedly

Figure 23.1 The Frankfurt parliament in Frankfurt's Paulskirche in 1848/49. Coloured, contemporary engraving. View at the president's table, over which the portrait *Germania* by Philipp Veit emerges. Contemporary lithograph after a drawing by Leo von Elliott; original is at the Prussian Picture Archive, copyright expired

from 1763 became an 'enlightened absolutism' under Frederick the Great (1712–1786), where some legal reforms, the development of education and economic activities took place (Frederick II 1789).

We can sense the complexity of the response to Kant's ideas given the European history in the nineteenth and twentieth centuries that has followed but also challenged Kant-based doctrine. At the same time, the early twenty-first century marks the moment when 27 European nations have approached a state of union based on debates and consensus (even if the union does not include all European nations just yet). Contemporary theorists of debate such as Chantal Mouffe argue that a democracy relies on dissensus as much as on consensus, in her discussion on pluralism, dissensus and democratic citizenship (Mouffe 2004), and on concepts such as agonism and agonistic pluralism (Mouffe 2013).

The late twentieth-century philosopher Jean-François Lyotard went further, stating that there are points when it is impossible to achieve consensus at all, or at any time in the future (Lyotard 1988). Lyotard introduced the concept of the '*differend*' – as a wrong or injustice that arises because of the prevalence of hegemonic discourse that actively precludes the possibility of an injustice (real or perceived) being expressed. For Lyotard, such injustices are exemplified in the experiences of Nazi concentration camps, as the victims are never going to be able to communicate the full horror as experienced (Lyotard 1988).[4]

This argument by Lyotard contrasts and relates to what has been known as Kant's 'transcendental illusion' – a belief that the realm of understanding can account for all areas of reason. Lyotard radically questioned this rationalist supposition in Kantian debate, attacking the claim that understanding can dominate the entire field of reason. Lyotard states that it is in the nature of political debates and aspirations to be linked to such an illusion; treating ideas of reason as if they were the concepts of understanding.

Be it a 'dissensus', 'agonistic pluralism' (Mouffe 2013) or '*differend*', what has been argued is that there are, and always will be, debates where consensus cannot be reached and where debates cannot produce rational arguments for agreement. In parliamentary democracies such as in the UK, voting and the rule of majority applies in these situations. However, this is not always the case everywhere. For example, within the European Union, all heads of member states sitting around the circular table must agree a policy to become a law by means of consensus. Similarly, the parliamentary representatives must sit in circular-shaped European Parliament to debate

Figure 23.2   The circular shape of the European Parliament where parties spread and link radially from left-wing to the right-wing parties, all converging to one centre. Plenary hall, 2012. © Cherry X Wikimedia Commons. reproduced on the basis of CC BY-SA 3.0 licence

and vote for a policy (see Figure 23.2). We could argue that this marks their indebtedness to Kant and his ideas of consensus and perpetual peace.

The UK Parliament and its context

In the context of the UK, we have witnessed how many people often had problems with the shared sovereignty and the consensual governing of the EU, as the British style of apparently sovereign government and parliamentary life is based on a majority vote rule that thrives on debates, the dynamics of opposition and dissensus. This phenomenon appears to be based on the British tradition of social lifestyle, sense of identity and (I would add) theatre culture. Even if the disregard for consensus might be in many respects detrimental to the nation, the proponents of dissensus have been more comfortable with it and with the ideological framework of Brexit, preferring not to consider or contemplate consensus.[5] Opposition, parliamentary confrontation, fractions and majority voting are celebrated in the UK Parliament, which is not underpinned by written constitution as the guarantor of equal rights for each citizen. Instead, parliamentary majority, common law and its doctrine of precedent together with the government, cabinet and the governing party have exceptional powers to shape political outcomes in Westminster (Lijphart 2012). This model determines the important political outcomes and acts of Parliament as the system never fully broke away from its previous monarchical model based on religious doctrine, where the head of the Church is also the monarch. We see instances of tension between the two opposing parliamentary congregations facing each other head on, as the ensuing strain between the opposing sides is often palpable. We have observed this in the process of exiting the EU and the 2019 controversy concerning the prorogation of Parliament. This was turned down by the UK Supreme Court, established in 2009 to address complex parliamentary cases for which there were no precedents.

The party opposition is spatially expressed in parliamentary seating, where the governing majority faces adversely the opposition (see Figure 23.3).

Intriguingly, during the moments of difficult debates and parliamentary crises, the nation focuses on the ritual of the parliamentary motions where procedures are enabled, framed and guided by tradition, including the spatiality of the parliamentary architectural decorum. The opposing parliamentarian parties and factions debate, fight, hold on to power (or fall from it) through these debates but also rituals, voting processions, vote counting and result proclamations according to rehearsed choreography set on the stage of the parliament building's interior. The

Figure 23.3 The oppositional arrangement of parliamentary seating where governmental majority and opposition minority parties sit confrontationally, Chamber of the House of Commons, 2012, London. © UK Parliament. Wikimedia Commons, reproduced on the basis of CC BY-3.0 Unported licence. Available at: https://commons.wikimedia.org/wiki/File:House_of_Commons_Chamber_1.png (accessed 17th July 2023)

procedural courses of action capture the attention of observers as the members of Parliament obey traditional rules of the parliamentary fixture as they must, because procedure, choreography and spatiality are the law, or at least part of it. The lack of a written constitution and related regulations means sticking to the inherited spatial mores that have never been replaced by fixed constitutional (and moral) a priori for all citizens, as is the case in most European constitutional democracies. This indicates a lack of agreement about implementing the conceptually different rule of law (*Rechtsstaat*) that includes aspiration in defining righteousness and calls for equity, as originally defined by Kant's Enlightenment-based philosophy. This difference and specificity of the UK political context could be seen as one of the contributing factors for the persistency as well as the product of the class system. Although abolishing the class system might not be achieved by proclamation in law alone, stating the equality unequivocally in the form of a written state constitution could nevertheless help in identifying societal aims and aspirations. Any ambiguity is being discriminatory in nature, and that is why the phenomenon concerning equity in front of the law has always lacked clarity. This opacity needs to be hidden and masked to the point of non-recognition, which is why at the crucial, delicate points of parliamentary deliberations there is excess of pomp, lustre and ceremony instead of strife for clarity, equality and fairness.

Consensual, Europe-wide political agreements, forged in and symbolised by the EU's circular table in the Europa Building, the home of the European Council, the thirteenth-floor oval meeting room of the European Commission Berlaymont Building (both in Brussels), and the semicircle of the EU Parliament in Strasbourg, have therefore been (consciously or unconsciously) resisted and perceived inappropriate for the majority of people in the UK, where political agreements are made in the parliamentary chamber of Westminster with its straight-linear and opposing geometry.[6]

The origins of this could be traced back to the opposing seating arrangements in the seventeenth- and early eighteenth-century Protestant churches such as those built by Christopher Wren, including St James's Piccadilly, that were based on medieval precedents, as opposed to the ones built by his apprentice Nicholas Hawksmoor (such as St George's Bloomsbury) that had more of a proscenium and theatre-like seating arrangement.[7]

It is almost as if the dominant spatial model of public debate determined by the opposed seating arrangement of MPs interferes and spatially guides the members to speak and act in opposition to each other. There is no angle or a radial curve to round up and bring the diverse voices closer to each other to reach a consensus. Instead, the rule of opposing, ostentatious majority is confirmed through shouting (sometimes humour) – a practice more reminiscent of the passions of Jacobian theatre than Kantian debate.

The uneasiness of critical parliamentary events is therefore managed by the traditional ritual and its spatiality. Within this spatial context the instability and apprehension caused by divided public opinions are toned down and alleviated, the decisions are reached and agreed through procedural moves within the spaces bursting with architectural decorum bearing the insignia of the sovereign power. Internal logic being that the process of parliamentary procedural choreography comes down to the inner working of the ornate spatiality of the building's interior and its *chora*. Standing for (and acting in) the name of the sovereign, the purpose of the parliamentary configuration and rituals is first to keep the government accountable, but second, when required, to steady the ship-of-state, prevent friction and stop any potentially intimidating events from exploding into uncertainty of painful reasoning and undesirable questions regarding equity for all subjects.

In parallel, from the outside, the building's perpendicular, neo-Gothic guise provides the intended language of all-important tradition and continuity. The parliamentary aura is stylistically and spatially maintained, made recognisable to the nation and visitors alike. The parliamentary building, thus, successfully frames debates of all kinds by being the omnipresent inner fixity of quotidian parliamentary business, while maintaining a symbolic, historical façade externally. By being firmly anchored on the banks of the Thames, the parliament building gains additional significance due to its proximity and connectedness to the water and the seas that made the nation flourish.

By moving through and experiencing the physical spaces of the Palace of Westminster internally and externally, members of Parliament and the visiting public sense the walls of power and their effects. Through the physicality and symbolism of the building, they expose themselves to feel and grasp (consciously and unconsciously) the medium of architecture that transports them back to the nation's history and the original acts of parliament-formation with its significant and often violent happenings that determined the trajectory of its power. The fear, related to the forcefulness of past junctural events including the nearby site of decapitation of one ambitious king that led to monarchy's subsequent submission to the parliament, re-emerges. It is repeatedly invoked through the ritual of the Black Rod and the opening of Parliament.[8]

Conclusion

All states have protective symbolism often embedded in their parliamentary insignia to keep unity and peace, help them through crises or through situations of unsolvable differences in the absence of consensual judgements. In all these situations, a parliamentary building is not simply a container, but a very complex space where parliamentary acts, bills and other stately documents are written, power is negotiated and relations of authority, control and supremacy are established. By virtue of providing a protected, secure and safe space where an agreement can be forged, the parliamentary building can potentially, if needed, work as a recompense for the lack of agreement among parties.

However, there are limits to the power of parliamentary architecture and its spatiality. Parliaments can become places of more violence and conflict, such as instances where the buildings were set on fire, as in the Nazi burning of the Reichstag in Berlin on 27 February 1933, four weeks after Adolf Hitler was sworn into power as the chancellor of Germany (see Nelson in this volume). The arson was blamed on the communists, while the Nazi leadership claimed that emergency legislation was needed to prevent the leftist uprising. The resulting act, commonly known as the Reichstag Fire Decree, abolished constitutional protections and paved the way for Nazi dictatorship. In this case we can observe how the act of burning the building that provided space for parliamentary life and democracy was both real and symbolic destruction.

It is therefore possible to conclude that making, providing and maintaining parliamentary spaces and spatiality for the rituals of parliamentary life in honour and dignity are significant activities inextricably linked to the tradition of democracy. More recently, they seem to have acquired an unappealing and unsavoury pathos. In the absence of rigorous argument this pathos is producing rhetorical effects and acts as a supplement for the failure of exact and thorough acts and reasoning. The role of space and architecture can thus become empty and gestural for the sensitive situations when the rational argument is absent.

Acknowledgements

I am indebted to Geoffrey Bennington and Julian Roberts, whose lectures at the AA in the 1980s initially inspired me to write this paper.

Notes

1 Kant's essay 'An Answer to the Question: What Is Enlightenment?' (1784) addresses this notion directly by using the very term.
2 The 'rule of law' is defined as 'the authority and influence of law in society, especially when viewed as a constraint on individual and institutional behaviour; hence, the principle whereby all members of a society (including those in government) are considered equally subject to publicly disclosed legal codes and processes' (OED online, accessed on 13 September 2020).
3 On this subject Kant's biographer, Manfred Kuehn, argues that the legendary punctuality relates to mature Kant, while his early years had been more colourful.
4 This could also refer to some unresolved and potentially unresolvable issues that haunt the European Union, such as those concerning the states of former Yugoslavia that have not all been included in the European political home. In fact, the signing of the Maastricht Treaty, the foundation of the EU, on 7 February 1992, coincided with the full blown civil war in former Yugoslavia. In addition, 2016 Brexit itself could also be seen as a *differend* that supports Lyotard's argument.
5 The Brexit Party and its ideology for example.
6 It is important to note that Scottish and Welsh parliament buildings, completed in 2004 and 2006, respectively, do not have the opposing sets of seats. The long-term spatial effects of these two assemblies are still to be seen as they are both relatively new.
7 For this observation I am indebted to Julian Roberts, who has argued and lectured about this at the Architectural Association, London, during the late 1980s.
8 Or, indeed, any other symbolic weapons in the case of other nations.

References

Alberti, L.B. (1452 [1989]) *De re aedificatoria; The Art of Architecture in Ten Books*, Cambridge, MA: MIT Press.
Bennington, G. (1990) 'The Rationality of Postmodern Relativity', *Journal of Philosophy and Visual Arts*, 'Philosophy and Architecture', pp. 23–31.
Christo and Jeanne-Claude (1995) *Wrapped Reichstag*, Christo and Jeanne-Claude Foundation, https://christojeanneclaude.net/artworks/wrapped-reichstag/ (accessed on 10 February 2023).
Deleuze, G. and Guattari, F. (1988) *A Thousand Plateaus: Capitalism and Schizophrenia*, London: The Athlone Press.

Derrida, J. (1962) *Edmund Husserl's 'Origin of Geometry' An Introduction*, Lincoln, NE and London: University of Nebraska Press.

Elden, S. (2014) *The Birth of the Territory*, Chicago: University of Chicago Press.

Ellis, E. (ed.) (2012) *Kant's Political Theory: Interpretations and Applications*, University Park, PA: The Pennsylvania State University Press.

Fontana-Giusti, G. (2013) *Foucault for Architects*, London: Routledge.

Foucault, M. (1975) *Discipline and Punish: The Birth of the Prison*, New York: Vintage Books.

Frederick II, King of Prussia (1789) *Posthumous Works of Frederic II. King of Prussia*, translated by Thomas Holcroft, London: Printed for G.G.J. and J. Robinson.

Kafka, F. (1915 [2009]) *The Trial*, translated by D. Wyllie, New York: Dover Publications.

Kant, I. (1784) 'An Answer to the Question: What Is Enlightenment?' Available from: http://web.cn.edu/KWHEELER/documents/What_is_Enlightenment.pdf.

Kant, I. (1785) *The Ground Work for the Metaphysics of Morals*. Available from: https://www.earlymoderntexts.com/assets/pdfs/kant1785.pdf.

Kant, I. (1790) *The Critique of Judgement [Kritik der Urteilskraft]*. Available from: https://www.gutenberg.org/files/48433/48433-h/48433-h.htm (accessed on 20 January 2022).

Kant, I. (1793) 'Theory and Practice'. Available from: http://users.sussex.ac.uk/~sefd0/tx/tp2.htm.

Kant, I. (1795) 'Perpetual Peace: A Philosophical Essay'. Available from: https://www.gutenberg.org/files/50922/50922-h/50922-h.htm (accessed on 15 August 2020).

Kant, I. (1797) *Metaphysics of Morals*. Available from: https://ld.circuitdebater.org/w/archive_files/%5BImmanuel_Kant%5D_Kant_The_Metaphysics_of_Morals.pdf/507955836/%5BImmanuel_Kant%5D_Kant_The_Metaphysics_of_Morals.pdf (accessed on 2 June 2023).

Kuehn, M. (2009) *Kant: A Biography*, Cambridge: Cambridge University Press.

Langlands and Bell's (1991) *UN Security Council*. Available from: http://www.langlandsandbell.com/portfolio-item/un-security-council-1991/ (accessed on 10 February 2023).

Lijphart, A. (2012) *Patterns of Democracy: Government Forms and Performance in Thirty-Six Countries*, New Haven, CT and London: Yale University Press.

Lyotard, J.-F. (1988) *Le Différend*, translated by G. Van den Abbeele, Minneapolis: University of Minnesota Press.

McGilchrist, I. (2009) *The Master and his Emissary: The Divided Brain and the Making of the Western World*, London: Routledge.

Mouffe, C. (2004) 'Pluralism, Dissensus and Democratic Citizenship', in F. Inglis (ed.) *Education and the Good Society*, Basingstoke, UK: Palgrave Macmillan, pp. 42–54.

Mouffe, C. (2013) *Agonistics: Thinking the World Politically*, New York: Verso.

Mumford, L. (1961) *The City in History: Its Origins, Its Transformations, and Its Prospects*, New York: Harcourt, Brace and Jovanovich.

Palmquist, S.R. (2005) 'Kant's Ideal of the University as a Model for World Peace', in H. Ayatollahy (ed.) *Papers of International Conference on Two Hundred Years after Kant*, Tehran: Allame Tabataba'i University Press. Available from: https://philarchive.org/rec/PALKIO (accessed on 12 September 2020).

Plato (385 BC [2008]) *Republic*, Oxford: Oxford University Press.

Rauscher, F. (2017) 'Kant's Social and Political Philosophy', in E.N. Zalta (ed.) *The Stanford Encyclopaedia of Philosophy (Spring Edition)*. Available from: https://plato.stanford.edu/archives/spr2017/entries/kant-social-political/ (accessed on 20 September 2020).

Roberts, J. (1988) *German Philosophy: An Introduction*, Cambridge: Polity Press.

Schmitt, C. (1928 [2008]) *Constitutional Democracy*, Durham, NC: Duke University Press.

Serlio, S. (1611 [1983]) *The Five Books of Architecture*, New York: Dover Books on Architecture.

St Augustine of Hippo (fifth century AD [2006]) *The City of God*, Documenta Catolica Omnia, EU. Available from: http://www.documentacatholicaomnia.eu/03d/0354-0430,_Augustinus,_De_Civitate_Dei_Contra_Paganos,_EN.pdf (accessed on 13 May 2022).

Strauss, L. and Cropsey, J. (eds) (1987) *History of Political Philosophy*, Chicago: University of Chicago Press.

Sudjic, D. and Jones, H. (1999) *Architecture and Democracy*, London: Laurence King and Glasgow City Council.

Virilio, P. (1997) *Open Sky*, London: Verso.

Vitruvius, M.P. (first century BC [1960]) *Ten Books on Architecture*, New York: Dover Publications.

von Mohl, R. (1833) *German Policy Science According to the Principles of the Constitutional State (Die deutsche Polizeiwissenschaft nach den Grundsätzen des Rechtsstaates)*, Tübingen.

Welcker, K.T. (1813) *Die letzten Gründe von recht, staat und strafe, philosophisch und nach den gesetzen der merkwürdigsten völker rechtshistorisch entwickelt*, Giessen: Heyer. Available from: https://archive.org/details/dieletztengrnde00welcgoog (accessed on 10 February 2023).

24

Degrees of opposition and cooperation

How seating plans and parliament layouts reflect and give rise to political cultures

Kerstin Sailer

Background: layouts as built social and cultural form

Building layouts have a profound impact on the way humans interact and relate to one another. Walls, ceilings, partitions and furniture placed in one way or another create meaning through the manner in which they are assembled, since the resulting configuration affords humans to perceive, move about and use space in specific patterns. For instance, spatial openness creates awareness, visibility and publicity. Occluded space may invite exploration, but also engenders privacy. A concrete example for the relation between spatial form and culture is offered by Robin Evans in his comparison of Renaissance and seventeenth-century floor plans. While the former plans were structured as interconnected rooms, accommodating the societal 'fondness for company, proximity and incident' (Evans 1997, p. 69) typical of the time, the latter plans were characterised by the emergence of the corridor as a 'device for removing traffic from rooms' (Evans 1997, p. 70), reflecting a society aimed at avoiding human contact. In his seminal book *Space Is the Machine*, Hillier argued that 'space is more than a neutral framework for social and cultural forms. It is built into those very forms' (Hillier 1996, p. 29).

Parliaments come in many physical shapes; likewise, political cultures, voting systems, representation and debating practices vary significantly across the globe, rendering parliament buildings a fascinating phenomenon for further research. While previous work has mapped layouts in relation to country characteristics such as population size, government type and democracy index (XML 2016), this chapter investigates the micro interior layout of debating chambers from a configurational perspective, bringing aspects of visibility, proximity and group solidarities to bear in order to describe political cultures in relation to their built form. Culture in this context can be defined as a way of 'how things are done here' (Deal and Kennedy 1982), or more formally as a pattern of basic assumptions valid within a given group as 'the correct way to perceive, think, and feel in relation to ... problem [solving]' (Schein 1990, p. 111).

The main contribution of this chapter lies in the nuanced reading of how parliamentarians sit together in the chamber and how this engenders political cultures, challenging some of the views purported by an abstract, top-down understanding of political ideals, particularly in the case of the European Parliament.

Theoretical framing: interfaces and correspondence

Two specific configurational theories are applied in the context of parliament buildings in this chapter, each applied to a different case: the theory of interfaces and the theory of correspondence and non-correspondence.

Interfaces, Hillier and Hanson (1984) argued, are the relationships between different user groups, mainly visitors (those with temporary usage patterns) and inhabitants (whose social knowledge is inscribed into the building) as orchestrated by built forms. This interpretation of interfaces will be taken up in this chapter by investigating how buildings create interfaces between different political parties via the structuring of chamber spatial layouts alongside seating plans. The plans of the UK Parliament versus the German Bundestag will be used for the analysis. This allows the mapping of two contrasting examples – an opposing bench model as is prevalent in the UK and some of its former colonies, versus the semicircular model of the German parliament, which is typical of many continental European countries.

The second part of the chapter builds on the theory of correspondence and non-correspondence, which was defined by Hillier and Hanson (1984) as the relationship between social and spatial groupings. Systems where spatial closeness and categorical membership (such as kinship, class or ethnicity) did not match, so-called non-correspondent systems were argued to create solidarities thriving on openness, inclusivity and equality. Peponis subsequently called non-correspondence 'a social insurance policy, whereby the strengths deriving from affiliation to social groups are complemented by the strengths derived from affiliation to spatial groups' (Peponis 2001, pp. xxiii–xxiv). Correspondence, in contrast, describes a strong overlap between social and spatial groupings, resulting in more insular solidarities. This concept will be investigated using the seating plan and layout of the European Parliament in Brussels based on proximity as spatial relation and political grouping as well as represented nation as categorical relation.

The conceptualisation of architectural space as a combination of a layout and a seating plan builds on the work of Hillier and Hanson describing physical form as configuration but also the idea of configuration-in-use (Sailer 2010), for example, the strategic utilisation of physical space, which in this case can be seen in the decision of who should sit where.

Data and method

Two different methods and data sets were used for the analysis. First, plans for the German and UK parliaments were redrawn from existing sources (XML 2016). DepthmapX software, a specialised tool to analyse spatial relationships in floor plans, was used to construct partial isovists (Benedikt 1979) from a subsample of parliamentarians – for example, the 120-degree viewshed from their seat – in order to analyse the interfaces between political parties afforded by building configuration. This was evaluated on a visual basis.

Second, data on the European Parliament, including seating plans as well as information about the parliamentarians (political affiliation, country), was obtained from their website (European Parliament 2020) and analysed in QGIS, a standard geographic information software, in order to understand degrees of cooperation through correspondence or non-correspondence. Close spatial proximity between MEPs (members of the European Parliament) was defined as someone sitting within a 3.6-metre radius from the seat of an MEP, which includes four people either side sitting in the same row, as well as some of those in the rows adjacent (see Figure 24.1). The average number of this definition of 'close MEPs' was 16.9 with a standard deviation of 2.7.

The degree of non-correspondence in the seating plan was calculated following the example of workplace seating arrangements provided by Sailer and Thomas (2019). They proposed a single measure called Yule's Q, which is a standard statistical measure based on an odds ratio[1] and is applied here to seating arrangements. It calculates the likelihood of finding similar others (by affiliation or country) close by, given the overall size of groupings. A Yule's Q of +1 denotes complete positive correspondence, where only similar others are in proximity, whereas a Yule's Q of –1 means

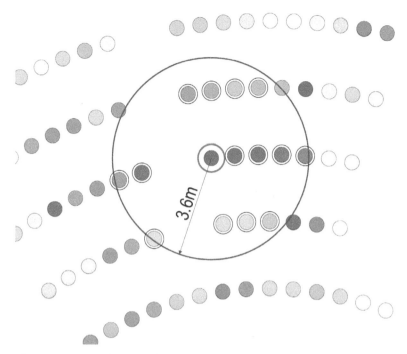

Figure 24.1 Definition of spatial closeness in the European Parliament in Brussels. All proximate MEPs within a 3.6 m radius are counted as close. © Kerstin Sailer

complete negative correspondence, where no one physically close by is similar. A value near zero reflects non-correspondence, a balance of same and different others in one's own proximate bubble, as well as further afield.

Oppositional and cooperative interfaces

The degree to which a building's layout and seating plan afford different interfaces becomes immediately obvious when comparing two parliamentary plans with each other: the plan of the Reichstag, the German parliament building (Figure 24.2), which was designed by Norman Foster in 1999 and is arranged in a semicircle, and the plan of the House of Commons, the UK parliament building (Figure 24.3), which was rebuilt after destruction during the Second World War in 1950, with its opposing benches layout.

The 120-degree isovists in the German Bundestag all face towards the front, where the lectern is placed, but also where the government is seated

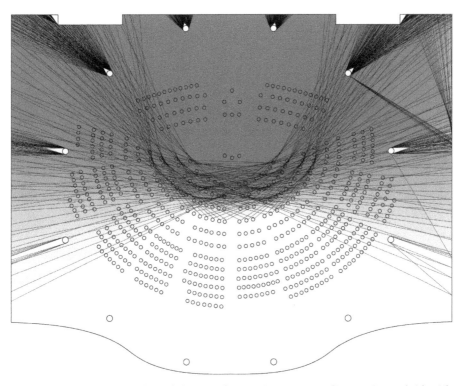

Figure 24.2 Seating plan of the Bundestag (German parliament) overlaid with 120° isovists for the first four rows of parliamentarians. © Kerstin Sailer

(to the left of the plan) and the Bundesrat, representatives of the second legislative chamber (to the right of the plan). The political groupings sit in wedges, with party leaders seated in the front row. Due to the curvature of the semicircle, parliamentarians of each political grouping have members of other groups in their visual field, yet the overall viewing direction, as illustrated in Figure 24.2, is directed towards the country's legislature. This signifies a more cooperative culture.

In contrast, the opposing benches of the House of Commons (see Figure 24.3) mean that the governing party, seated on the left side of the plan, is facing the parties of the opposition, seated on the other side. The front rows are reserved for the executive, led by the prime minister as well as the leader of the opposition and their shadow cabinet. In particular, those so-called front benchers do not see any of their own party members in their visual fields, they only face members of the other side in their day-to-day viewing perspective in Parliament. This hints at a more confrontational political culture.

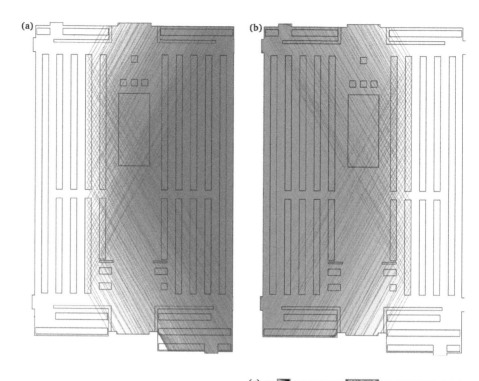

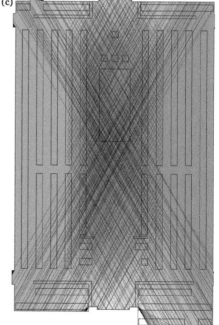

Figure 24.3 Seating plan of the UK House of Commons overlaid with 120° isovists for the first two rows of parliamentarians. Isovists from government benches are coloured in blue and isovists from opposition benches in red: (a) Government viewsheds; (b) opposition viewsheds; (c) all viewsheds overlaid. © Kerstin Sailer

Correspondence and non-correspondence in the European Parliament

The seating plan in the European Parliament is organised by affiliation to one of seven political groups (see Figure 24.4): the European People's Party (EPP), the Progressive Alliance of Socialists and Democrats (S&D), Renew Europe (Renew), the Greens/European Free Alliance (Greens/EFA), Identity and Democracy (ID), European Conservatives and Reformists (ECR), and the Confederal Group of the European United Left/Nordic Green Left (GUE/NGL). Members without group affiliation are called non-attached (currently $n = 29$).

We would therefore expect high levels of correspondence regarding political opinions, so MEPs in close proximity are those with the same political affiliation. This indeed is the case with Yule's $Q_{group} = 0.903$. There is only little variation if this is split by political group with values ranging from 0.868 (EPP, sat centrally) to 0.987 (non-attached, seated at the back with little interface to the other groups).

Within the seating space assigned to each political grouping, the front row seats are reserved for the group leaders, yet the remainder are mainly allocated alphabetically. MEPs from different countries should therefore generally find themselves sitting next to a wide range of representatives from different European nations. Investigating Yule's Q by country confirms this (Yule's $Q_{country} = 0.370$), since the overall value suggests non-correspondence as expected, with a slight tendency towards having others from the same nation within one's close bubble. Partially, this is due to the number of representatives, especially from larger nations.[2] If broken down further by country, the analysis reveals interesting patterns, as shown in Table 24.1.

Some of the smaller countries such as Luxembourg, Latvia or Slovenia show complete negative correspondence ($Q = -1.0$), which means none of their compatriots sit close to them. In contrast, some of the smaller countries, such as Cyprus, tend towards positive correspondence ($Q = 0.762$), as shown in Figure 24.5a below, where two pairs of MEPs sit close to each other within their political groupings.

This leads to another observation on countries leaning more towards one side of the political spectrum than others. Poland and Greece are interesting cases in that regard (see Figures 24.5b and 24.5c), as both show a tendency towards correspondence ($Q = 0.567$ and $Q = 0.591$) due to a clustering of high numbers of Polish MEPs on the right affiliated with the ECR and ID, and high numbers of Greek MEPs affiliated with the left GUE/NGL grouping.

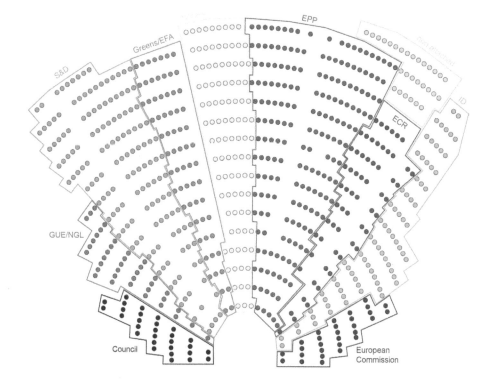

Figure 24.4   Seating plan of the Brussels European Parliament by political grouping. © Kerstin Sailer

Some of this correspondence is explained by language idiosyncrasies, such as a clustering of names beginning with the same letter within a particular country. For example, three MEPs of the GUE/NGL grouping named Kokkalis, Kouloglou and Kountoura sit next to each other. This patterning is not consistently evident, though, and would warrant further research. Finally, countries with a balanced mix of nationals from other countries as well as their own can be found, evident by a Q value close to zero, such as Sweden (Q = −0.231, see Figure 24.5d).

Conclusion

The relationship between building layouts and political cultures can be described by bringing both arguments together, the one on interfaces and the one on correspondence and non-correspondence.

Table 24.1 Numbers of MEPs in total as well as by country, including average group sizes of those close/distant and from same/other countries; and resulting Yule's Q

Country	No. of MEPs	My country close	Other country close	My country distant	Other country distant	Yule's Q
TOTAL	703	2.2	14.1	45.3	640.5	0.370
Austria	19	0.8	14.4	17.2	669.6	0.390
Belgium	21	0.6	15.2	19.4	666.8	0.127
Bulgaria	17	0.7	15.6	15.3	670.4	0.330
Croatia	12	0.5	16.5	10.5	674.5	0.321
Cyprus	6	0.7	14.2	4.3	682.8	0.762
Czech Republic	21	1.5	16.0	18.5	666.0	0.549
Denmark	14	0.6	16.1	12.4	672.9	0.316
Estonia	7	0.3	15.3	5.7	680.7	0.380
Finland	14	0.6	14.5	12.4	674.5	0.363
France	79	3.4	12.7	74.6	611.3	0.375
Germany	96	3.9	12.3	91.1	594.7	0.352
Greece	21	1.5	14.1	18.5	667.9	0.591
Hungary	21	0.9	15.4	19.1	666.6	0.320
Ireland	12	0.2	16.1	10.8	674.9	−0.215
Italy	76	4.3	10.5	70.7	616.5	0.564
Latvia	8	0.0	15.0	7.0	680.0	−1.000
Lithuania	11	0.4	16.9	9.6	675.1	0.202
Luxembourg	6	0.0	17.5	5.0	679.5	−1.000
Malta	6	0.3	14.0	4.7	683.0	0.554
Netherlands	29	0.8	15.1	27.2	658.9	0.140
Poland	52	3.4	12.7	47.6	638.3	0.567
Portugal	21	1.1	14.5	18.9	667.5	0.472
Romania	33	1.2	15.0	30.8	655.0	0.240
Spain	59	1.8	13.6	55.2	631.4	0.211
Slovakia	14	0.3	15.7	12.7	673.3	−0.019
Slovenia	8	0.0	17.4	7.0	677.6	−1.000
Sweden	21	0.3	15.5	19.7	666.5	−0.231

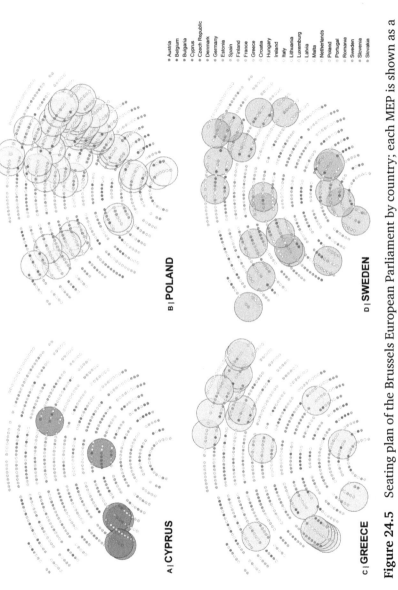

Figure 24.5 Seating plan of the Brussels European Parliament by country; each MEP is shown as a small circle, coloured by country; proximity bubbles of selected countries are shown in larger circles: (a) Cyprus; (b) Poland; (c) Greece and (d) Sweden. © Kerstin Sailer

A | **CYPRUS**

B | **POLAND**

C | **GREECE**

D | **SWEDEN**

- Austria
- Belgium
- Bulgaria
- Cyprus
- Czech Republic
- Denmark
- Germany
- Estonia
- Spain
- Finland
- France
- Greece
- Croatia
- Hungary
- Ireland
- Italy
- Lithuania
- Luxembourg
- Latvia
- Malta
- Netherlands
- Poland
- Portugal
- Romania
- Sweden
- Slovenia
- Slovakia

The configurational comparison of the German and UK parliaments with their two different layout alternatives, superimposed by a strategic seating plan, highlighted the creation of two different types of interfaces following configurational analysis: on the one hand, a German political culture of pragmatic cooperation, which is reflected in a system of proportional representation and a practice of coalition governments; and on the other hand, the UK political culture of fierce opposition, which is characterised by a competitive first-past-the-post representation and narratives surrounding the parliament building, such as that the distance between the two opposing benches is supposedly two sword lengths apart.

The examples also highlight the constraints arising from layouts and seating plans. The UK chamber is built on the idea of a roughly balanced number of MPs on either side. In the 2019 general election, the Conservatives won 365 seats (out of 650), making their side of the layout of the House of Commons much more densely populated than the opposition benches. Another example is the change in seating following the general election in Germany in September 2021 and the formation of a left-liberal coalition government. The three governing parties de-cided to move the liberal FDP from the right wing of the chamber into the centre in order for them to sit together. This caused an outrage in the conservative CDU/CSU as they did not want to sit next to the right-wing AfD and did not want to be perceived to be anything other than centre-leaning. Interestingly, opposition in this layout is expressed by distance rather than opposing benches. Seating plans indeed are highly political, and it matters who sits where, not just symbolically but also as a material representation of culture.

In addition, different cultures of scrutinisation emerge from the spatial layout. Following the argument brought forward by Maclachlan, who argued that 'scrutinisation in the UK parliament works by maximising encounters for confrontation' (Maclachlan 2001, p. 7), it could be argued that scrutinisation happens to the same degree in the German parliament, albeit with a different political culture, one whereby all members of parliament face the legislature together. Further insights into detailed parliamentary configurations through visibility can be gleaned by two other chapters in this volume authored by Psarra and Maldonado Gil and Gibson, Psarra and Maldonado Gil.

Several insights can be drawn from the correspondence analysis presented in the second half of this chapter: first, the seating plan of the European Parliament in Brussels enables an experience of togetherness, whereby parliamentarians from all EU nations work together side by side on European policies. Unity and cohesion lie at the heart of the aspirations of the European project, and as such the layout of the Parliament reflects this vision. However, this could be challenged by everyday practices providing a more nuanced picture, since second, it can be noted that the experience of togetherness is not consistent throughout, as some nations have less exposure to parliamentarians from other countries. Not everyone benefits from the 'social insurance policy' that Peponis assigned to the phenomenon of non-correspondence, despite best intentions to mix parliamentarians up. Obviously, nationalism is a complex phenomenon fed by a variety of socioeconomic factors, yet some of the countries with nationalist and partisan tendencies on the rise (Kelemen 2017) show some of the highest correspondence patterns. Therefore, inward-looking tendencies might become exacerbated by the seating plan and a lack of opportunities for mingling arising from the layout and seating plan. Of course, political decision-making in the European Parliament is not confined to the chamber, and committees play an important role, yet this analysis offers a new viewpoint on the subtle ways in which layouts constitute underlying mechanisms for intermingling.

In his analysis of power and built form, Dovey argued that 'buildings necessarily both constrain and enable certain kinds of life and experience' (Dovey 2008, p. 208). The contribution of this chapter lies in the analysis of layouts and seating plans and how they constrain and enable political cultures with a differential degree of opportunities built into them. It was shown how cultures of nuanced opposition and cooperation are built into each parliamentary chamber with its own physical form and strategic usage. As an expression of shared values and beliefs, or more simply, the way things are done within a given setting, political cultures are both reflective of spatial arrangements and shaped by them.

Notes

1 Yule's Q is calculated as: Yule's $Q = (a \times d - b \times c)/(a \times d + b \times c)$, where a is the number of MEPs that were spatially close and conceptually close to someone; b is how many were spatially distant, but conceptually close; c is how many were spatially close, but conceptually distant; and d how many were spatially and conceptually distant. For more details on the metric, please refer to Sailer and Thomas (2019).

2 Germany, France and Italy have the largest contingents with a total number of 96, 79 and 76 MEPs in the European Parliament, respectively. The numbers of other MEPs from the same nation within their close proximity bubble are 3.9 (DE), 3.4 (FR) and 4.3 (IT), which are the highest overall.

References

Benedikt, M.L. (1979) 'To take hold of space: isovists and isovist fields', *Environment and Planning B: Planning and Design*, 6(1), pp. 47–65. DOI: 10.1068/b060047.

Deal, T.E. and Kennedy, A.A. (1982) *Corporate Cultures: The Rites and Rituals of Corporate Life*, Reading, MA: Addison-Wesley Publishing Group.

Dovey, K. (2008) *Framing Places: Mediating Power in Built Form*, London and New York: Routledge.

European Parliament (2020) Interactive seating plan of the hemicycle of the European Parliament. Available from: https://www.europarl.europa.eu/hemicycle/index.htm?lang=en&loc=bru (accessed on 12 October 2020).

Evans, R. (1997) 'Figures, Doors and Passages', in R. Evans (ed.) *Translations from Drawing to Buildings and Other Essays*, London: Architectural Association, pp. 55–91.

Hillier, B. (1996) *Space Is the Machine: A Configurational Theory of Architecture*, Cambridge: Cambridge University Press. Available from: https://discovery.ucl.ac.uk/id/eprint/3881 /1/SITM.pdf (accessed 1 August 2023).

Hillier, B. and Hanson, J. (1984) *The Social Logic of Space*, Cambridge: Cambridge University Press.

Kelemen, R.D. (2017) 'Europe's other democratic deficit: national authoritarianism in Europe's Democratic Union', *Government and Opposition*, 52(2), pp. 211–238. DOI: 10.1017/gov.2016.41.

Maclachlan, B. (2001) 'Scrutiny and consensus in the Palace of Westminster', in J. Peponis, J. Wineman and S. Bafna (eds) *3rd International Space Syntax Symposium*, Atlanta, GA: A. Alfred Taubman College of Architecture and Urban Planning, University of Michigan, 44.41–44.47.

Peponis, J. (2001) 'Interacting questions and descriptions: how do they look from here?' in J. Peponis, J. Wineman and S. Bafna (eds) *3rd International Space Syntax Symposium*, Atlanta, GA: A. Alfred Taubman College of Architecture and Urban Planning, University of Michigan, xiii–xxvi.

Sailer, K. (2010) 'The space-organisation relationship: on the shape of the relationship between spatial configuration and collective organisational behaviours', PhD thesis, Faculty of Architecture, Technical University of Dresden.

Sailer, K. and Thomas, M. (2019) 'Correspondence and non-correspondence: using office accommodation to calculate and organization's propensity for new ideas', *12th International Space Syntax Symposium*, Beijing, China, 166:161–166:117.

Schein, E.H. (1990) 'Organizational culture', *American Psychologist*, 45(2), pp. 109–119. DOI: 10.1037/0003-066X.45.2.109.

XML (2016) *Parliament*, Amsterdam: XML Architecture.

Part VII

Sovereignty, scale and languages of representation

25

Peripheral parliament

Sovereignty, Indigenous rights and political representation in the architecture of the Sámi Parliament of Finland

Samuel Singler and Sofia Singler

Introduction

This chapter undertakes a politico-architectural analysis of one of two Arctic parliamentary buildings in the European Union, the Sámi Parliament of Finland.[1] It addresses the relative silence within political theory on the political significance of architecture and built spaces (Bell and Zacka 2020). It seeks not so much to understand the political views and debates that shaped the design process as to analyse the architecture of the Sámi Parliament of Finland with reference to the broader political tensions between nation-states and Indigenous peoples.

The nomadic Sámi people have historically inhabited the Sápmi region, which today stretches across the northern territories of Finland, Norway, Russia and Sweden (Sarivaara 2012, p. 27). Since the rise of modern state power, the geographical mobility and economic, political and cultural autonomy of the Sámi people have been threatened by the territorial division of Sápmi, concurrent with state policies designed to assimilate the Sámi people into their respective mainstream national cultures (Sarivaara 2012, p. 35). Examining state–Sámi relations is particularly fruitful for moving beyond state-centric analytical frameworks in international relations and political theory, as the Sámi 'never had anything resembling sovereign authority', nor have they formulated political claims according to dominant statist norms (Oksanen 2021, p. 96). Instead, similarly to other Indigenous peoples, the Sámi have challenged state authority in 'a language exterior to the states-system's ontology of sovereign statehood and rigid mutually exclusive territoriality' (Oksanen 2021, p. 103). Thus, tensions between the Sámi people and the Finnish state are relevant beyond the remit of Indigenous politics; they provide insights into the nature of sovereignty, human rights and the spatial imaginaries that underpin contemporary understandings of the political (Mayall 1999).

Building Indigenous self-determination in Finland

The cultural-administrative centre Sajos, which houses the Sámi Parliament of Finland, was completed in Inari in 2012 to the design of Finnish firm HALO Architects (Louekari 2012) (Figure 25.1). The parliament, established in 1973, had assembled in a mid-century school dormitory in Inari for the first decades of its existence.[2] Having deemed the dormitory substandard for parliamentary operations both practically and symbolically, the parliament resolved to build a 'Sámi cultural centre' in 2000, which would house the parliament alongside various Sámi educational and cultural organisations (Sámediggi Saamelaiskäräjät 2000; Oikeusministeriö 2005).[3] An open international competition was announced in 2008 (Senate Properties 2008).

Figure 25.1 HALO Architects, Sajos, Inari, 2012. Exterior view, south elevation (photograph by Mika Huisman, 2012). © Decopic Oy

The competition followed Norwegian and Swedish precedent. The Norwegian government organised an open competition in 1995 for the Sámi Parliament of Norway (Sametinget) in Karasjok. The winning design, by Stein Halvorsen and Christian Sundby, consciously references Sámi architectural tradition, casting the parliamentary assembly as an exaggerated *goahti* or *lávvu*, vernacular familial dwellings traditionally built of timber, mosses and reindeer hides (Halvorsen and Sundby 2000). The Swedish state property agency organised an equivalent competition a decade later, in 2006, for a site in Kiruna. The crescentic massing of the winning submission Badjáneapmi (Northern Sámi for 'awakening'), designed by Hans Murman and Helena Andersson, tapered in both section and plan, hinting formally at a snowbank formed by Arctic winds (Stannow 2006). The project's realisation has stalled, however, because of the existential threat posed to downtown Kiruna. Due to geological instability caused by the iron ore mine that lies beneath the city, Kiruna is being moved, building by building, some three kilometres east of its current location (Golling and Mínguez Carrasco 2020). The relocation of the city also necessitated the relocation of the Sámi Parliament. A decision was finally reached in 2019 to select a site in Östersund, Jämtland, instead. The Swedish Sámi Parliament's offices are currently located in temporary premises in Kiruna.

The notion of a Sámi public building is inherently paradoxical: traditional Sámi architecture knows neither large scale nor immoveable structures (Lehtola 2008; Huima 2015; Haugdal 2017). The competition programme explicitly acknowledged that although the architectural legitimisation of Sámi self-rule in Finland entailed the acceptance of paradigms foreign to Sámi tradition – most crucially, publicness and permanence – the resultant project would ultimately stand as 'a symbol of Finnish Sámi self-determination as well as their living and developing culture' (Senate Properties 2008, p. 6). The jury, tasked with writing the competition brief and evaluating all submissions, comprised both Sámi and Finnish representatives: five members from Senate Properties, two from the Sámi Parliament, one from the municipality of Inari and two from the Finnish Association of Architects. Additionally, a secretary and four invited experts guided the jury; the latter included Veli-Pekka Lehtola, Professor of Sámi Culture in the Giellagas Institute at the University of Oulu. The jury judged that most submissions failed to 'achieve a connection to Sámi cultural tradition' and instead merely 'mirrored today's Finnish and universal stylistic attributes' (Senate Properties 2009a, p. 7). The first prize was awarded to architects Janne Laukka, Tuomas Niemelä and Milla Parkkali, whose design encompassed 'significantly more themes from which the Sámi might recognise symbolic content related to their culture than any of the other submissions' (Senate Properties 2009a, p. 14; Ilonoja 2009, p. 10).

Territory, citizenship and Sámi expression

The ambition to build an Indigenous parliament within the borders of a nation-state is inherently fraught with contradictions. The competition brief and evaluation process reflect the self-contradictory nature of the project as well as more general tensions between Indigenous understandings of space and the spatial imaginaries of state sovereignty (Barnsley and Bleiker 2008). Key to modern sovereignty is its territorialisation – the need to demarcate, assert control over and homogenise the national territory (Scott 1998; Lefebvre 2009; Elden 2013). Indigenous peoples' nomadism and non-cultivation of land have often been seen as a lack of civilisation, justifying their violent exclusion and forced assimilation into the nation (Anghie 2004; Shaw 2008; Nisancioglu 2020). Although the Finnish state no longer undertakes such measures, the Sámi Parliament of Finland nonetheless continues to be shaped by state-centric conceptions of sovereignty and nation. The Finnish state was integrally involved in the planning, development and construction of the parliamentary building, yet simultaneously, negotiations over a Nordic Sámi convention stalled; such a convention would establish a unified framework for the protection of Sámi rights in Finland, Norway and Sweden (Lankinen 2017). Indeed, ambiguity regarding the need to territorialise Finnish sovereignty while recognising Sámi cultural autonomy permeates the architecture of Sajos.

The virtue of Sajos is that it avoids the pigeonholes into which Sámi architecture is too often polarised: either contrived references to traditional dwellings such as *goahti* and *lávvu*, which awkwardly transpose vernacular structures to foreign scales, materials and programmes, or anonymous 'council style' buildings born of the Nordic governments' assimilationist politics, which draw more from postwar prefabrication methods than Sámi culture (Skålnes 2008). Sajos rejected both extremes in favour of a more abstracted interpretation of Sámi tradition – its spacious plan and the rounded formal language of its massing and interior volumes were cited by the jury as recognisable, yet refined, characteristics of a meaningful contemporary Sámi expression. Ambiguity and tension arise, however, from the fact that the very characteristics of Sajos considered evocative of Sámi tradition can be, and have been, read as distinctive traits of Finnish architecture. The building simultaneously creates 'a profound link ... to the Sámi way of life' and 'represents the mainstream of young Finnish architecture' (Louekari 2012, p. 30).

The seemingly contradictory readings of the building echo general difficulties relating to overlapping conceptions of identity, citizenship and belonging. Sámi individuals' Finnish citizenship is sometimes seen to contradict demanding equal rights as a Sámi national (Siivikko 2019, p. 50). In Finland, the construction of a national identity has historically centred on the promotion of equality alongside the assertion that cultural homogeneity ensures social cohesion (Palmberg 2009; Keskinen, Skaptadóttir and Toivanen 2019). The Sámi people have been represented as uncivilised outsiders, a 'people without a history, a primitive remnant of what had been – something opposite to Finns' (Siivikko 2019, p. 53). The promotion of equality has historically been pursued through policies that inadvertently promoted a homogenised Finnish national identity (Sarivaara 2012, p. 35). Education policy is an illustrative example. The Education Act of 1947 made basic education compulsory for all children living on Finnish territory, eliminating structural disadvantages in equality of opportunity. However, Sámi children were often sent to boarding schools due to living in remote areas. In these schools, speaking Sámi was prohibited, students were taught about Finnish culture and history – from which the Sámi people were excluded – and Sámi children were shamed and bullied for their cultural background. Although public boarding schools did provide Sámi children with free education, they also had a significant assimilationist effect (Ranta and Kanninen 2019, pp. 146–171). Balancing the rights of the Sámi as citizens of Finland and as members of an Indigenous people remains fraught with difficulty and ambiguity.

Architectural ambiguity and contesting Indigenous rights

In the architecture of Sajos, the open plan and curved walls illustrate aspects unassignable to exclusively Sámi or Finnish tradition (Figure 25.2). The light filled, high-ceilinged foyers respond to the competition programme's demand for a 'generous and bright' interior that would simulate the sense of openness experienced 'atop fells, where Sámi thought wanders freely' (Senate Properties 2008, p. 7). Attributes of airiness and lightness, however, cited as evidence of Sajos's rootedness in Sámi conceptions of space, are often evoked as typically Finnish characteristics in projects such as Helsinki's central library Oodi (Oikarinen 2019). So, too, the 'soft, rounded forms' of Sajos ostensibly draw from Sámi tradition, according to both critics and the architects themselves, yet can arguably be associated also with the strong lineage of curvaceous, often timber, spaces in Finnish architecture (Senate Properties 2009a, p. 14; Laukka 2012a, 2012b). The timber panelling of the rounded interior walls recalls contemporaneous projects such as the Kamppi Chapel of Silence (Vartola, Holmila and Riikonen 2012).

The ambiguities in distinguishing between Finnish and Sámi architectural elements in Sajos evoke ambiguities in Sámi political representation in Finland, as the remit of Sámi rights remains hotly contested. The Sámi people's status as an Indigenous people – with a collective right to cultural autonomy and practising their traditional lifestyles – was enshrined into the Finnish constitution in 1995 (Ranta and Kanninen 2019, pp. 20–21). The Finnish state objects to more substantive forms of political and economic self-determination, limiting Sámi constitutional protection to cultural issues. Although the state promoted the establishment of the Sámi Parliament in 1973 and the building of Sajos in the 2000s, Finland has not signed the International

Figure 25.2 HALO Architects, Sajos, Inari, 2012. Foyer (photograph by Mika Huisman, 2012). © Decopic Oy

Labour Organization 169 agreement,[4] and the Sámi people continue to be marginalised and ignored in important decision-making processes (Sarivaara 2012). Although the range of Sámi grievances is broad, by far the most contentious issues are those relating to land ownership and land regulatory rights, as the territorialisation of the Finnish state clashes with Sámi understandings of space, nature and land use.

Such clashes materialise in certain themes in Sajos which seemingly amalgamate Sámi and Finnish traditions, but are, in fact, rooted in discord. The sweeping vistas from Sajos into surrounding woodland purportedly express Sámi peoples' intimate relationship with nature; yet similarly, in Finnish architecture, visual links to the outside are considered indicative of a collective subconscious engaged in 'forest dreaming' (Aalto 1925; Louekari 2008). The ample glazing and concave curvature of Sajos's façades magnify views outside, but inevitably impede any direct contact with the elements, thereby reducing the 'tradition of "outside while inside" thought' in Sápmi to a visual simulacrum rather than producing an immersive corporeal experience (Einejord 2007; see Figure 25.3). The compromise pertains to a critical underlying tension: the very term 'nature' refers to wholly different concepts in Finnish and Sámi cultures (Magga 2007). For the Sámi people, 'humans are a part of their environment, and nature is not seen as a distinct entity' (Ranta and Kanninen 2019, p. 87). For the state, the vast areas of uncultivated land in the Finnish parts of Sápmi are, in Martin Heidegger's (1977, p. 17) terms, a 'standing-reserve': natural resources made legible and ordered, that is, transformed from land into territory (Elden 2013).

Figure 25.3 HALO Architects, Sajos, Inari, 2012. North wall (photograph by Mika Huisman, 2012). © Decopic Oy

The architecture of Sámi culture and sovereign authority

Historically, dissonant conceptions of nature have been a central theme in state–Sámi disputes, and a vector for galvanising Sámi political activism as well as transnationalising these disputes. In Sweden, Sámi political movements became more active in the 1950s in response to the state's expansion of hydroelectric dam construction projects in Swedish Lapland, demonstrating how 'the affected reindeer herding Sámi had ontologically constituted the rivers and tundra that were dammed and flooded as homesteads, spiritual sites, pastures, fishing waters and migration routes … these meanings and economic values were rendered exterior by the Swedish state, which gave them little consideration when the dams were planned' (Oksanen 2021, p. 102). A watershed event for the transnationalisation of state–Sámi disputes was the Alta conflict between the Sámi people and the Norwegian state, again over the state's plans for new hydroelectric dams that endangered Sámi livelihoods (Somby 1999). This conflict culminated in barricades and hunger strikes by both Sámi and non-Sámi activists in Norway, as well as international involvement by the World Council for Indigenous Peoples, thus turning the dispute into an 'international media spectacle' (Oksanen 2021, p. 105).

Territory is a key marker of modern sovereignty; states are intensely concerned with guarding their territorial boundaries and exercising their sovereign power within (Elden 2013; Agnew 2015). The Finnish state asserted its sovereignty in the north by appropriating Sámi land in 1886, categorising it as 'excess land' rather than property of the Sámi people (Ranta and Kanninen 2019, p. 44). Evidence of property records stretching back to the seventeenth century has done little to change the state's stance on Sámi land ownership (Korpijaakko 1989). Even a constitutional committee noted in 2004 that state ownership of Sámi land is legally 'questionable' (Hyvärinen 2010, p. 143). Key ongoing land disputes pertain to issues such as the boundaries of reindeer collectives, as well as plans for an Arctic Railway which would pierce through Sámi lands (Lakkala, Alajärvi and Torikka 2017; Lakkala 2019). In both cases, the Finnish state has marginalised the Sámi in decision-making processes, despite multiple denouncements by the deputy chancellor of justice and various constitutional committees, which have argued that the state has repeatedly failed to fulfil its legal obligation to negotiate with the Sámi people (Ranta and Kanninen 2019, p. 229). Internally, Sámi land rights challenge 'the current distribution of political power' by limiting the authority of the state (Buchanan 1993, p. 99). Externally, exercising sovereignty in the north functions as a performance to an international audience, allowing Finland to retain membership within the society of sovereign states (Salter 2019). To justify ignoring Sámi land ownership claims, the state argues that they are unrelated to the Sámi constitutional right to cultural autonomy (Hyvärinen 2010, p. 141). For this reason, the very definition of Sámi culture has become a key political stake in state–Sámi disputes.

Critiques of Sámi architecture are anchored in the disputes concerning definitions of Sámi culture. As a project that consciously avoided repeating, let alone relying on, stereotypical visuospatial and structural motifs in its evocation of Sámi tradition, Sajos has largely evaded debates on architectural appropriation and exoticisation. Timber, the traditional material of all Sámi building, is used throughout the design, but in an idiom decidedly distinct from vernacular precedent; interior elements such as furnishings derive their tones from the Sámi flag, but refrain from reproducing Sámi patterns or symbols; the formal syntax of spaces such as the parliamentary assembly hall allude geometrically to Sámi handicraft (*Duodji*), but do not resort to objectification (Senate Properties 2009b). To a large degree, such nuances were products of post-competition development of the initial submission. The assembly, for instance, was judged excessively 'cave-like' by the jury in its proposed form, and redesigned entirely (Senate Properties 2009b, p. 13). Given that the realised version of the assembly, clad in birch panels, bears resemblance to mainstream Finnish architecture, it might be cynically viewed as a 'Finnicisation' of an original proposal more closely related to Sámi tradition (Figure 25.4). Based on the competition programme and evaluation minutes, however, it appears more plausible that the jury, composed of both Sámi and Finnish members, consciously guided the project away from elements that veered too close to cliché (Senate Properties 2008, 2009a, 2009b). The end result thus avoided becoming an architecture more closely related to the Lapland travel industry than Sámi culture itself, a phenomenon Sámi architectural scholar Joar Nango calls the 'Giant Lávvu Syndrome' (Nango 2009).

On the one hand, parliamentary architectures of non-sovereign polities might seek to underscore similarity to the architectures of sovereign states, in order to imply or legitimise hopes of eventual coequality; on the other, they might communicate their dissociation from sovereign precedents and counterparts. The parliamentary buildings of Greek tributary states, for instance, simultaneously embody the architectural conventions of their suzerain in plan, and reject them in elevation (see Kotsaki in this volume). The elevations and plans of Sajos subtly but subversively communicate the differences between the Sámi Parliament of Finland

Figure 25.4   HALO Architects, Sajos, Inari, 2012. Parliamentary assembly chamber. The wall relief is *Eatnu, Eadni, Eana* ('Stream, Mother, Ground') by Outi Pieski, 2012 (photograph by Mika Huisman, 2012). © Decopic Oy

and its nation-state counterpart, completed to the design of J.S. Sirén in 1931 in Helsinki. Whereas the main façade of the Finnish Parliament communicates a robust, heroic sense of unending civic solemnity – its claim to ancientness magnified by the Egyptianate references that complement the Corinthian granite colonnade – that of Sajos bows to the timelessness of nature instead (Hakala-Zilliacus 2002). The lively and uneven spruce panelling of the exterior suggests parallelism between the building mass and the tree trunks that surround it. The auditorium and the assembly hall sit on the ground floor of Sajos like nuclei in a cell, their bulbous irregularity a conscious counterpoise to the unyielding symmetry of Sirén's assembly (Figure 25.5). Significantly, members of the Sámi Parliament are seated around a circular negotiation table in the assembly hall, where not even the chair is distinguished spatially, in marked contrast to the literally and metaphorically elevated positions assumed by the speaker and ministers in the Finnish Parliament.

Conclusion

The celebration of Sámi culture in Sajos is a welcome rectification of earlier cultural appropriation and exoticisation of the Sámi as tourist attractions and even zoo exhibits (Siivikko 2019, p. 58; Ranta and Kanninen 2019, pp. 127–129). Cases such as the 2017 Finnish-Norwegian Teno River Fishing agreement, however, framed by Sámi groups as threatening their cultural autonomy, demonstrate that defining Sámi culture remains politically contentious (Ranta and Kanninen 2019, p. 175). Even in cases where Sámi culture and lifestyles are clearly impacted, the Finnish state continues to ignore its 'obligation to negotiate' with the Sámi enshrined in Section 9 of the 1995 Act on the Sámi Parliament, despite repeated legal complaints even by international actors such as the United Nations Office of the High Commissioner for Human Rights (Ranta and Kanninen 2019, p. 180). However, recent developments have given the Sámi limited hope that their right to cultural autonomy might be taken more seriously in the future. In 2017, the Administrative Court of Northern Finland overturned and submitted for reconsideration the state's decision on the boundaries of the Näkkälä reindeer collective, due to shortcomings in the state's background investigation process and the lack of hearings involving affected Sámi individuals (Lakkala 2017).

Among the Sámi themselves, choosing how to respond is a divisive issue. Maintaining a positive relationship is desirable, but agreeing to partially problematic proposals might be interpreted by the state as having

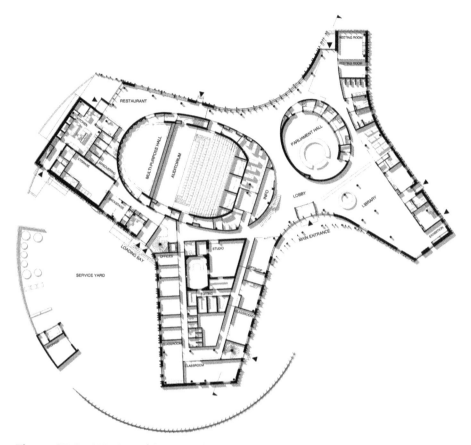

Figure 25.5 HALO Architects, Sajos, Inari, 2012. Ground floor plan, originally at 1:300 (drawing by HALO Architects, 2012). © Janne Laukka, Tuomas Niemelä and Milla Parkkali

done enough. Conversely, refusing to negotiate might result in the Sámi becoming even more marginalised. Sámi MP Jan Saijets recently asked of a contentious Nordic Sámi convention: 'If the convention is rejected, will there ever be a new one on the table?' (Lankinen 2017). These difficulties reverberate directly into architectural reception. Major commissions such as Sajos have been received overwhelmingly favourably in Sámi communities, yet their architectural successes have not correlated with, let alone triggered, analogous political successes.

Discourse on contemporary Sámi architecture has hitherto focused largely on issues of authenticity: 'How Sámi is a building?' An interrogation of Sajos with reference to tensions between Finland and

Sámi rights complements prior discourse by evaluating not merely its authenticity as a Sámi building per se, but as a product and expression of the relationships between Indigenous peoples and nation-states, and their continued contestation over the boundaries between the cultural and the political. The events and practices that have taken place within Sajos since its inauguration in 2012 amplify the ambiguities of the architecture itself; at least equally telling are those events that have not. The assembly hall at Sajos has been the site of protests by Sámi MPs against violations of Sámi self-determination, and the building has hosted several cultural events, ranging from Sámi art workshops to the Indigenous film festival Ijahis Idja.[5] Alongside the cultural centres, research complexes, museums and other public buildings erected in Sápmi since the 1970s, Sajos curates events that directly critique the political relationship between the Sámi and the Nordic nation-states. Countless film screenings, dance shows, debates, art exhibitions and installations constitute a neglected dimension of Sámi public architecture: the ephemeral and extra-architectural activity provoked and hosted by buildings like Sajos serves to underscore the political conflicts faced by the polity which they serve. The importance of considering bodily movement, activity and ritual through an ethnographic lens in the analysis of architectures of power is evident (see Johansen in this volume).

Meanwhile, decisions regarding land rights and other crucial issues – which, according to the state, fall beyond the remit of Sámi cultural autonomy – continue to be made outside the walls of Sajos, often free from Sámi input, despite their significant impact on the future of the Sámi people.[6] The building that was conceived as a symbol of Sámi autonomy, and that is broadly considered an exemplar of meaningful contemporary Sámi architectural expression, threatens to remain a backdrop and symbol of their continued struggles for political recognition.

Notes

1 The other is the Sámi Parliament of Norway in Karasjok.
2 Finland was the first of the three Nordic countries with Sámi populations to establish a Sámi political body in 1973, known as the Sámi Delegation 1973–1995 and the Sámi Parliament from 1996. The Sámi Parliaments of Norway and Sweden were established in 1989 and 1993, respectively.
3 All translations are made by the authors.
4 The International Labour Organization Indigenous and Tribal Peoples Convention (No. 169) contains important provisions for protecting Indigenous peoples' collective rights, including provisions regarding land ownership and regulatory rights (Article 14), natural resource ownership and use (Article 15), taking Indigenous customs into account when applying national laws (Article 8), and an obligation to consult Indigenous peoples with regard to any legislative or administrative measures directly affecting them (Article 6). See Josefsen (2010, pp. 6–7).

5 Although group acceptance is usually seen as a central requirement for membership within an Indigenous people (Sarivaara 2012, p. 54), in 2011 the Supreme Administrative Court of Finland overruled the Sámi Parliament's decision to refuse the electoral register applications of some individuals they did not accept as Sámi. The following year, the UN Committee on the Elimination of Racial Discrimination condemned the decision as contrary to the Sámi right to cultural autonomy. In 2015, the Court again overturned tens of Sámi Parliament refusals of electoral register applications, leading to two formal complaints by Sámi individuals to the UN Human Rights Committee, which determined that the Court had violated the Sámi right to self-determination (OHCHR 2019). A number of newly elected Sámi MPs were individuals deemed non-Sámi by the Sámi people themselves, resulting in protests by two Sámi MPs against the Court's ruling at the first meeting of the new 2016–2020 Sámi Parliament in the assembly hall at Sajos (Aikio, Näkkäläjärvi and Alajärvi 2016). Despite condemnation by the UN Human Rights Committee, the Supreme Administrative Court has upheld their ruling (KHO 2019).

6 State–Sámi relations in Finland are, of course, continually changing due to new legal rulings and political initiatives. Recently, the Lapland District Court at Utsjoki ruled that the 2017 Teno River Fishing agreement violates the Sámi people's constitutional and international rights (Leisti 2019). The case has now been appealed to the Supreme Court of Finland and represents a potential landmark case for Sámi rights (Ranta and Kanninen 2019, p. 182). A crucial development has been the establishment of the Truth and Reconciliation Commission Concerning the Sámi People by the government of Finland (Valtioneuvosto 2021). The Commission will examine how the Sámi people have been and continue to be discriminated against and how their rights have been violated; it is also expected to recommend ways to 'strengthen connections between the Sámi people and the Finnish state' (Vaarama 2021).

References

Aalto, A. (1925) Keskisuomalaisen maiseman rakennustaide, *Sisä-Suomi*, 26 June, pp. 2–3.

Agnew, J. (2015) 'Revisiting the Territorial Trap', *Nordia Geographical Publications*, 44(4), pp. 43–48. Available from: https://nordia.journal.fi/article/view/64824.

Aikio, K., Näkkäläjärvi, P. and Alajärvi, M. (2016) Nuoret radikaalit protestoivat Saamelaiskäräjien järjestäytymiskokouksessa [online], *YLE*. Available from: https://yle.fi/uutiset/3-8695940 (Accessed on 16 October 2020).

Anghie, A. (2004) *Imperialism, Sovereignty and the Making of International Law*, Cambridge: Cambridge University Press.

Barnsley, I. and Bleiker, R. (2008) 'Self-Determination: From Decolonization to Deterritorialization', *Global Change, Peace & Security*, 20(2), pp. 121–136. DOI: 10.1080/147811 50802079797.

Bell, D. and Zacka, B. (2020) *Political Theory and Architecture*, London: Bloomsbury Publishing.

Buchanan, A. (1993) 'The Role of Collective Rights in the Theory of Indigenous Peoples' Rights', *Transnational Law & Contemporary Problems*, 3(1), pp. 89–108. Available from: https:// heinonline.org/HOL/LandingPage?handle=hein.journals/tlcp3&div=12&id=&page=" https://heinonline.org/HOL/LandingPage?handle=hein.journals/tlcp3&div=12&id =&page=.

Einejord, O.H. (2007) 'Saamelaiset tilat – saamelainen nykyarkkitehtuuri ja julkisten rakennusten suunnittelu', in T. Elo and P. Magga (eds) *Eletty, koettu maisema – näkökulmia saamelaiseen kulttuurimaisemaan*, Rovaniemi: Lapin ympäristökeskus, pp. 111–117.

Elden, S. (2013) *The Birth of Territory*, Chicago: The University of Chicago Press.

Golling, D. and Mínguez Carrasco, C. (2020) *Kiruna Forever*, Stockholm: ArkDes & Arkitektur förlag.

Hakala-Zilliacus, L. (2002) *Suomen eduskuntatalo: kokonaistaideteos, itsenäisyysmonumentti ja kansallisen sovinnon representaatio*, Helsinki: Suomalaisen kirjallisuuden seura.

Halvorsen, S. and Sundby, C. (2000) 'Sametinget', *Byggekunst*, 8, pp. 10–21.

Haugdal, E. (2017) 'Strategies of Monumentality in Contemporary Sámi Architecture', in S. Aamold, E. Haugdal and U. Angkjær Jørgensen (eds) *Sami Art and Aesthetics: Contemporary Perspectives*, Aarhus: Aarhus University Press, pp. 211–238.

Heidegger, M. (1977) *The Question Concerning Technology and Other Essays*, New York: Garland Publishing.

Huima, P. (2015) 'Ihmisen jälki – Käsivarren porosaamelaisilta opittuja ajatuksia arkkitehtuurista', Diploma thesis, Aalto University.

Hyvärinen, H. (2010) 'Saamelaisten kulttuurin ja elinkeinojen sääntely', in K. Kokko (ed.) *Kysymyksiä saamelaisten oikeusasemasta*, Rovaniemi: Lapin yliopiston oikeustieteellisiä julkaisuja, pp. 120–148.

Ilonoja, P. (2009) Saamelaisille oma kulttuurikeskus. *Arkkitehtuurikilpailuja*, 5, pp. 3–31.

Josefsen, E. (2010) *The Saami and National Parliaments: Channels for Political Influence*. Geneva: Inter-Parliamentary Union.

Keskinen, S., Skaptadóttir, U.D. and Toivanen, M. (2019) 'Narrations of Homogeneity, Waning Welfare States, and the Politics of Solidarity', in S. Keskinen, U.D. Skaptadóttir and M. Toivanen (eds) *Undoing Homogeneity in the Nordic Region: Migration, Difference, and the Politics of Solidarity*, Abingdon: Routledge, pp. 1–17.

KHO (2019) Korkein hallinto-oikeus, KHO:2019:90. Available from: https://www.kho.fi/fi/index/paatoksia/vuosikirjapaatokset/vuosikirjapaatos/1562217155914.html (Accessed on 16 October 2020).

Korpijaakko, K. (1989) *Saamelaisten oikeusasemasta Ruotsi-Suomessa: Oikeushistoriallinen tutkimus Länsi-Pohjan Lapin maankäyttöoloista ja -oikeuksista ennen 1700-luvun puoliväliä*, Helsinki: Lakimiesliiton Kustannus.

Lakkala, A. (2017) 'Näkkälän paliskunta sittenkin kahtia? – AVI joutuu käsittelemään asian uudelleen' [online], *YLE*. Available from: https://yle.fi/uutiset/3-9728285 (Accessed on 16 October 2020).

Lakkala, A. (2019) 'Saamelaisilta täystyrmäys Vesterbackan Jäämeren rata-suunnitelmille – Saamelaiskäräjät yllätettiin jo toistamiseen' [online], *YLE*. Available from: https://yle.fi/uutiset/3-10775103 (Accessed on 16 October 2020).

Lakkala, A., Alajärvi, M. and Torikka, X. (2017) 'Mistä Näkkälän laidunkiistassa oikein on kyse? Asiasta ollaan montaa mieltä' [online], *YLE*. Available from: https://yle.fi/uutiset/3-9730681 (Accessed on 16 October 2020).

Lankinen, J. (2017) 'Pohjoismainen saamelaissopimus ei vastaa saamelaisten odotuksia' [online], *Turun Sanomat*. Available from: https://www.ts.fi/uutiset/kotimaa/3173632/Pohjoismain en+saamelaissopimus+ei+vastaa+saamelaisten+odotuksia (Accessed on 16 October 2020).

Laukka, J. (2012a) 'Suunnittelijan ääni = Architect interviewed', *Arkkitehti*, 109(5), pp. 38–39.

Laukka, J. (2012b) 'Beaten by the four winds' (trans. Nicholas Mayow), *PUU*, 1, pp. 8–15.

Lefebvre, H. (2009) *State, Space, World* (ed. N. Brenner and S. Elden), Minneapolis, MN: University Press.

Lehtola, V.-P. (2008) 'Saamelaisten visuaaliset maisemat, rakentaminen ja muotokieli. Virikkeitä saamelaisalueen julkiseen rakentamiseen', *Saamelaiskulttuurikeskus. Arkkitehtuurikilpailun ohjelma*, Helsinki: Senate Properties, pp. 26–32.

Leisti, T. (2019) 'Lapin käräjäoikeus on hylännyt kaikki Utsjoen saamelaisten syytteet luvattomasta kalastuksesta Vetsijoella ja Utsjoella' [online], *YLE*. Available from: https://yle.fi/uutiset/3-10675382 (Accessed on 16 October 2020).

Louekari, L. (2008) 'Architecture of the Forest. Observations on the Relationship between Spatial Structures in Architecture and Natural Spaces', *Nordic Journal of Architectural Research*, 20(3), pp. 98–114.

Louekari, L. (2012) 'Saamelaiskulttuurikeskus Sajos', *Arkkitehti*, 109(5), pp. 28–37.

Magga, P. (2007) 'Rakennuksia, kotasijoja, muistoja – saamelaista kulttuuriympäristöä inventoimassa', in T. Elo and P. Mahha (eds) *Eletty, koettu maisema – näkökulmia saamelaiseen kulttuurimaisemaan*, Rovaniemi: Lapin ympäristökeskus, pp. 11–24.

Mayall, J. (1999) 'Sovereignty, Nationalism, and Self-Determination', *Political Studies*, 47(3), pp. 474–502. DOI: 10.1111/1467-9248.00213.

Nango, J. (2009) 'The Saami building tradition: a complex picture', in E. R. Røyseland and Ø. Rø (eds) *Northern Experiments: The Barents Urban Survey 2009*, Oslo: 0047 Press, pp. 188–191.

Nisancioglu, K. (2020) 'Racial Sovereignty', *European Journal of International Relations*, 26(S1), pp. 39–63. DOI: 10.1177/1354066119882991.

OHCHR (2019) 'UN Human Rights Experts Find Finland Violated Sámi Political Rights to Sámi Parliament Representation' [online], *OHCHR*. Available from: https://www.ohchr.org/en/press-releases/2019/02/un-human-rights-experts-find-finland-violated-sami-political-rights-sami?LangID=E&NewsID=24137 (Accessed on 4 August 2023).

Oikarinen, E. (2019) 'Oodi kaikelle: Helsingin keskustakirjasto Oodi', *Arkkitehti*, 116(1), pp. 36–51.

Oikeusministeriö (2005) *Saamelaiskulttuurikeskus. Toimikunnan mietintö*. Helsinki: Oikeusministeriö.

Oksanen, A. (2021) 'The Indigenous Dimension of the Intersocietal: Dussel, Exteriority and the Sámi People', *Millennium: Journal for International Studies*, 50(1), pp. 83–109. DOI: 10.1177/03058298211050671.

Palmberg, M. (2009) 'The Nordic Colonial Mind', in S. Keskinen, S. Tuori, S. Irni and D. Mulinari (eds) *Complying with Colonialism: Gender, Race and Ethnicity in the Nordic Region*, Abingdon: Routledge, pp. 75–104.

Ranta, K. and Kanninen, J. (2019) *Vastatuuleen: Saamen kansan pakkosuomalaistamisesta*. Helsinki: S&S.

Salter, M.B. (2019) 'Arctic Security, Territory, Population: Canadian Sovereignty and the International', *International Political Sociology*, 13(4), pp. 358–374. DOI: 10.1093/ips/olz012.

Sámediggi Saamelaiskäräjät (2000) '8§ Sh 25.5.00', *Minutes of Sámi Parliament Meeting 15 June 2000*, Sámediggi Saamelaiskäräjät, Inari.

Sarivaara, E.K. (2012) *Statuksettomat saamelaiset: Paikantumisia saamelaisuuden rajoilla*, Rovaniemi: University of Lapland.

Scott, J.C. (1998) *Seeing Like a State: How Certain Schemes to Improve the Human Condition Have Failed*, New Haven, CT: Yale University Press.

Senate Properties (2008) *Saamelaiskulttuurikeskus: Arkkitehtuurikilpailun ohjelma*, Helsinki: Senate Properties.

Senate Properties (2009a) *Saamelaiskulttuurikeskus: Arkkitehtuurikilpailun arvostelupöytäkirja*, Helsinki: Senate Properties.

Senate Properties (2009b) *Saamelaiskulttuurikeskus: Arkkitehtuurikilpailun 1. Palkinto*, Nro 37, nimimerkki 'ađa', Helsinki: Senate Properties.

Shaw, K. (2008) *Indigeneity and Political Theory: Sovereignty and the Limits of the Political*, Abingdon: Routledge.

Siivikko, N. (2019) 'Finnish Media Representations of the Sámi in the 1960s and 1970s', in S. Keskinen, U.D. Skaptadóttir and M. Toivanen (eds) *Undoing Homogeneity in the Nordic Region: Migration, Difference, and the Politics of Solidarity*, Abingdon: Routledge, pp. 50–66.

Skålnes, S. (2008) 'Samtidig samisk arkitektur', *Arkitektur N.*, 3, pp. 20–27.

Somby, A. (1999) 'The Alta-case: A Story about How Another Hydroelectric Dam Project Was Forced Through in Norway', *Indigenous Affairs* (3–4).

Stannow, M. (2006) 'Sametinget Kiruna', *Arkitektur*, 5, pp. 46–49.

Vaarama, V. (2021) 'Saamelaisten totuus- ja sovintokomissio sai viimeisen sinetin – Sanna Marin: "Meidän pitää yhdessä käydä läpi vaikeatkin kysymykset"' [online], *YLE*. Available from: https://yle.fi/uutiset/3-12164570 (Accessed on 17 February 2021).

Valtioneuvosto (2021) 'Saamelaisten totuus- ja sovintokomissio aloittaa työnsä Suomessa'. Available from: https://valtioneuvosto.fi/-/10616/saamelaisten-totuus-ja-sovintokomissio -aloittaa-tyonsa-suomessa?languageId=fi_FI (Accessed on 17 February 2021).

Vartola, A., Holmila, P. and Riikonen, V. (2012) 'Kimmo Lintula, Niko Sirola, Mikko Summanen: Kampin Kappeli', *Arkkitehti*, 109(3), pp. 24–33.

26

Forms of parliamentarism in modern Greece and their architectural-spatial reflections

Convergence, debate, imposition

Amalia Kotsaki

Introduction

Democracy is a difficult topic to discuss. Similarly, architecture and space are difficult to put into words. Exploring the possible relations between them is even more complicated. In our attempt to approach the direct connection between architecture and democracy, we study those buildings that are most strongly connected with political developments, namely the 'theatres of democracy', parliament buildings, and more specifically, those situated in Greece.

The architectural typology of parliament buildings has not changed much since the nineteenth century, when most of these buildings were built in Europe. As a result, there is little reference to them in the history of architecture, particularly in general publications on public architecture and neoclassicism, or in individual chapters of books of general interest.

There are no relevant publications on this subject in the Greek literature, and the relation between modern Greek architecture and politics remains unexplored, which does not mean that this subject is not interesting. It is therefore important to consider: to what extent does democracy influence the architectural style of parliamentary buildings? Does architecture have the power to enhance the concept of democracy and boost parliamentarism?

In contemporary Greece (after independence in 1821, the gradual liberation from the Ottoman Empire in the nineteenth and twentieth centuries, and the foundation of the modern state on 3 February 1830) the Greek Parliament has been housed initially in four different buildings:

- the Parliament of Nafplion (1823–1827 and 1829–1836);
- the Parliament of Aegina (1827–1829);
- the first parliament in Athens, being the capital of the Greek state (known as the Old Parliament); and
- the current parliament at Syntagma Square in the centre of Athens, the Old Palace.

Nafplion and Aegina were the first capitals of the new Hellenic State established in 1821 following the war of Greek independence, before Athens was declared the capital of Greece in 1836. In today's Greek territory there are, moreover, the Parliament of the United States of the Ionian Islands and the Parliament of the Principality of Samos.

Only three of those six buildings were designed and built specifically to house a parliament: the Old Parliament in Athens, the Parliament of the United States of the Ionian Islands and the Parliament of the Principality of Samos. The Old Palace in Athens was specifically designed to function as a parliament building in that its interior was significantly transformed for this purpose.

Vouleftiko (parliament) in Nafplion, first capital of the newly established Hellenic State

In Nafplion, the original plan was to use a private house as parliament ('Vouleftiko'), following the usual practice of transforming big private houses into public buildings. The lack of space for an audience led to a change of plans (Amygdalou and Kolovos 2018) and in 1825 it was decided to renovate a mosque (Brouskari 2008) in order to house the Vouleftiko, after extensive changes in its interior.

The new building had two galleries: an upper gallery for the general public and a second, which could be used by audience members with special permission. The members were seated on ground level in a radiating pattern with the chairman sitting in the centre, following the layout of the contemporary European parliaments, and symbolising the transition from the Ottoman world to the world of western democracies. In 1827, a bomb shell hit the building and, as a result, the Vouleftiko was no longer used.

The Parliament of the Hellenic State in the Metropolis church of Aegina

From 1827 to 1828 the parliament of the newly founded state was in operation in the Metropolis church in Aegina, a building which holds an important and symbolic role in political developments in modern Greece.

The 'courtyard of the Metropolis of Holy Mary which at the moment serves as Parliament' (*General Newspaper of Greece* 1828) is where the official welcome 'on behalf of the Nation' of the first governor of Greece, Ioannis Kapodistrias, took place.

There are written testimonies that inform us of the way the meetings were conducted in the interior of the church (General State Archives 1828a, 1828b). Meetings were held by the 50 proxies of the politicians' government, later joined by the corresponding proxies of the military. The women's gallery, a section of the church, operated as a balcony from where the public could observe the meetings – this being one of the reasons, apart from its size, why this building was selected (Giannoulis 1996).

The Old Parliament House in Athens, the first building designed specifically to house the parliament in Greece

After Athens became the capital of Greece in 1833, King Otto, first king of Greece from 1832 to 1862, had selected the house of the Athenian politician Alexandros Kontostavlos as his temporary residence. A large octagonal dance and banquet hall was added to the house in 1835, and after the Revolution of 1843 that forced King Otto to grant a constitution and convene a National Assembly, this Assembly convened in that hall. In October 1854, however, the house burned down in a fire.

Construction of a new building began in August 1858, from plans by French architect François Boulanger (Biris 2017), who was invited by the Greek government to take part in the construction of public projects in Greece. Boulanger was representing the French tradition of architecture. The initial plan of 1858 foresaw two assembly halls, for the parliament and the senate, and façades that were simple and austere, in the style of Athenian classicism. Construction was halted the following year, however, due to lack of funds.

The plans for the façades were then modified by the Greek architect Panagis Kalkos, and construction was completed in 1871. The layout of the assembly hall remained unchanged and followed the standard amphitheatrical arrangement of European parliament buildings of the nineteenth century, inspired by the amphitheatrical Assemblée Nationale in Paris. The amphitheatre plan, however, was also a direct reference to the ancient Greek Vouleftirio. In this way, the assembly hall (Figure 26.1) both unites the prevailing spirit of European neoclassicism and has, as a vision, the revival of the Athenian democracy (Ober 1996; Sakellariou 2000). The Hellenic Parliament was housed in this building from 1875 until its move to its current location in the Old Palace in 1935.

Figure 26.1 Interior of the Old Parliament House in Athens 27 April 2019 (National Historical Museum). © George E. Koronaios, Wikimedia Commons, reproduced on the basis of Public Domain. Available at: https://en.wikipedia.org /wiki/Old_Parliament_House,_Athens#/media/File:Inside_the_Old_Parliament _House_in_Athens_on_27_April_2019.jpg (accessed 25 July 2023)

The Old Palace – the Hellenic Parliament

The same spirit combining ancient Greek and European references prevails in the design for the conversion of the Old Palace, designed in 1836 as a residence for King Otto, first king of Greece (architect Friedrich von Gärtner) into the Hellenic Parliament (Demenegi-Viriraki 2007, pp. 311–387). In 1929, the government of Eleftherios Venizelos decided the relocation of the parliament proper and the senate to the Old Palace building, and announced an architectural competition (Hestia 1929). The conversion of the Old Palace to a parliament and senate building was done by the architect Andreas Kriezis and constitutes the most radical transformation since the building's initial construction. The plans involved major structural changes.

Once again, the assembly halls have an amphitheatrical layout (see Figure 26.2). In addition to situating the Greek parliament at the interface of contemporary European affinities and ancient Greek origins, as discussed, this layout promotes consensual politics in the process of collective decision taking. It expresses a parliamentarism of convergence, aiming at the maturity and the high level of democracy. The first session of the senate in the building took place in 1934 and the first session of parliament in 1935.

The Ionian Parliament, 'Parliament of the United States of the Ionian Islands'

The United States of the Ionian Islands was an atypical, political entity, a Greek state and amical protectorate (Manitakis 2008) of Great Britain from 1817 to 1864, when Great Britain conceded the Ionian Islands to Greece. In 1855 a new parliament building was built in Corfu, designed for this specific use.

This new Ionian Parliament replaced an older building destroyed by fire in 1852, on which we have no information. It is located in the centre of the town of Corfu and was designed by Ioannis Chronis (Agoropoulou-Birbilis 1983), who was the architect of many important buildings on

Figure 26.2   Greek Parliament swearing-in ceremony, 14 October 2009. © ΠΑΣΟΚ, Wikimedia Commons, reproduced on the basis of CC BY-SA 2.0 licence. Available at: https://commons.wikimedia.org/w/index.php?curid=8279513 (accessed 20 July 2023)

the island. The plans are no longer available, but we have accounts by his student Spiros Deviazis (Deviazis 1909). The proposal for the building had won a prize in an architectural competition for the design of this parliament building in 1852.

The building is built in a neo-Renaissance style and makes extensive use of mannerist decorative elements. It expresses its public use and character, without any exterior characteristics referencing British architecture and the British rule. The interior of the assembly hall, by contrast, does not follow the amphitheatrical layout, but rather has a rectangular pattern which is generally thought to be adversarial (see Figure 26.3), effectively presenting a small-scale version of the British House of Commons in Westminster. It is interesting to note that the hall of the Parliament of Malta, which was also a protectorate of Great Britain, has an identical layout. In both the Ionian Parliament and the Parliament of Malta, the layout of the assembly hall is similar to that of the parliament of the suzerain state, Great Britain, which promotes the use of the same form of parliamentarism: a parliamentarism of debate.

The Parliament of the Principality of Samos

Samos, before it was united with Greece in 1912, had been an autonomous tributary state of the Ottoman Empire since 1832. The so-called Samos Hegemony (Laiou 2014) was an atypical political entity, a semi-independent state, similar to those of the Ionian Islands and Crete. The semi-independent character of this state stemmed from the nomination of the prince by the Ottoman authorities and the election of the members of the parliament from the local Greek people.

The Parliament of the Samos Hegemony was in session only for one and a half months a year, and had limited powers. Proposals for administration and laws were brought in by the prince (who was nominated by the Sublime Porte), while the role of the members of parliament was limited to the ratification of the prince's will.

The parliament building (Vouleftirion) of the Samos Hegemony was built in 1898–1901, according to plans by the engineer Michael Efstathiades. In 1902, the new parliament building was established as the seat of the senate, as which it was in use until 1914. Today the building is the Town Hall of Samos.

It is a typical neoclassical building, demonstrating its public use and character, without any exterior characteristics referencing Ottoman architecture or Ottoman dominance. The interior of the assembly hall follows neither the amphitheatrical layout of the Greek Parliament

Figure 26.3 Plan of
the Ionian Parliament.
© Amalia Kotsaki

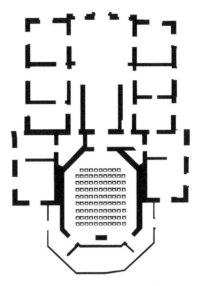

Figure 26.4 Plan of the
Parliament of the Principality
of Samos, Samos Hegemony.
© Amalia Kotsaki

in Athens nor the adversarial pattern of the Ionian Parliament. Rather, the plan shows the layout of a lecture hall, with an inclined seating arrangement in order to ensure unobstructed views of the prince's seat, and a gallery to accommodate an audience (see Figure 26.4).

This layout was identical to that of the parliament in Istanbul, housed in the Dolmabahçe Palace. It is significant that we find the same layout in the parliament of the Hegemony of Eastern Rumelia in Plovdiv. Eastern Rumelia was a semi-independent vassal state of the Ottoman Empire. The Hegemony in both cases follows the layout of the parliament of the suzerain state, and accordingly the form of parliamentarism it promotes: a parliamentarism of imposition, at the limits of democracy.

Conclusion

In conclusion, a few general patterns can be identified from this brief discussion of the architecture of parliament buildings in the Greek territory, which may point the way for further research.

Since the establishment of the Hellenic State, the main factor determining the choice of the building that would house the parliament was its capacity to accommodate a public audience, usually in a gallery. This indicates a desire for the transparency of the parliamentary process. The Hellenic State follows the example of the European architectural standard parliament building as it is expressed in the French Assemblée Nationale. At the same time, following the dominant neoclassical movement and the ideal of the revival of the Athenian democracy, Greece adopts the layout of the amphitheatre, a direct reference to the Vouleftirion in the Agora of ancient Athens.

The parliament buildings of the semi-autonomous tributary states of the Greek territory, by contrast, and more specifically the Parliament of the Cretan State, the Ionian Parliament and the Parliament of the Principality of Samos, did not follow the Hellenic model. Their layout follows the model of the parliament of the suzerain state, along with the parliaments of other semi-autonomous tributary states under the same suzerainty. The parliaments of the Ionian Islands and Malta, for instance, referenced the parliament building in London, whereas Samos, Plovdiv (East Rumelia), referenced the Istanbul parliament. Suzerain states thus have a strong presence, imposing their own form of parliamentarism when it comes to decision-making processes as well as architectural form. The architectural treatment of the façades of the parliament buildings in the Ionian Islands and Samos, on the other hand, adopts the prevailing neoclassical style, avoiding any morphological references to the architecture of the suzerain power, such as British neo-Palladian forms or Ottoman architectural forms (pointed arches, tile decoration, half-domes), the presence of which become less evident in the built environment of the tributary state. This contradiction between the layout of the plan (where the presence of the suzerain state is manifest) and the design of the façade (where it is disguised) is an eloquent architectural expression of a sham autonomy that the tributary states had, and Greek-inspired European influences in the formation of the Greek state.

The three parliament buildings designed and built specifically for this use – the Athenian, Ionian and Samos parliaments – are architectural expressions of three different concepts of parliamentarism: a parliamentarism of consensual politics (σύγκλιση), of debate (αντιπαράθεση) and of imposition (επιβολή). The existence of three spatially different types of parliament buildings in Greece, which express three different forms of parliamentarism, offers the opportunity to explore the role of space in structuring political practices.

To conclude, the parliament buildings in the Greek territories discussed in this chapter cast a light on how politics or parliamentarism and architecture interrelate and shape each other in modern and contemporary Greece. The study of this relationship contributes to the interpretation of the evolution of Greek parliamentarism, using architecture and space as tools, and offering a rare opportunity to enrich our understanding of this crucial issue.

References

Agoropoulou-Birbilis, A. (1983) 'The Work of the Corfiot Architect Ioannis Chronis' [Το έργο του Κερκυραίου αρχιτέκτονα Ιωάννη Χρόνη], Corfiot Chronicles [Κερκυραϊκά Χρονικά], 27, pp. 115–158.

Amygdalou, K. and Kolovos, E. (2018) 'The spatial dimension of the transition from the Ottoman Rule to the Greek State: The transformation of the mosque of Nafplion to the "first Parliament in Greece" (1825)', History Files [Ταΐστορικά], 67, pp. 58–76.

Biris, K. (2017) 'The new Athens, capital of the Greeks', in Alexander Papageorgiou-Venetas (ed.) Historical and Ethnological Society of Greece, National Historical Museum, Αθήνα, pp. 344–345.

Brouskari, E. (2008) The Ottoman Architecture in Greece, Athens: Ministry of Culture, Directorate of Byzantine and Post-Byzantine Antiquities.

Demenegi-Viriraki, K. (2007) The Old Athens Palace: The Building of the Hellenic Parliament, Athens: Hellenic Parliament.

Deviazis, S. (1909) 'Ioannis Chronis' [Ιωάννης Χρόνης], Pinakothiki [Πινακοθήκη], volume 107, Athens, pp. 211–212. https://lekythos.library.ucy.ac.cy/bitstream/handle/10797/25930/pin_issue107.pdf?sequence=10&isAllowed=y

General Newspaper of Greece (1828) Γενική Έφημερίςτῆς Έλλάδος, no. 38, Aegina, 14 January.

General State Archives (1828a) Minor Collections [ΜικροίΚλάδοι], B, Folder 1, 10 December.

General State Archives (1828b) 'To His Excellency the Governor of Greece', General Secretariat, Folder 32/March 17.

Giannoulis, E. (1996) The "Big Church": The Metropolitan Church of the Island of Aegina, Aegina: Giannoulis Editions.

Hestia (1929) (Έστία) newspaper, Μαρτίου, 7 March, p. 5.

Laiou, S. (2014) Constitutional Texts of the Samos Hegemony [Συνταγματικάκείμενα Ηγεμονίας Σάμου], Athens: Hellenic Parliament Foundation for Parliamentarism and Democracy.

Manitakis, A. (2008) 'The diplomacy-dependent transition from the "old Venetian Rule" of administrative autonomy to a national and democratic integration', in A. Nikiforour (ed.) Constitutional Texts of the Ionian Islands [Συνταγματικάκείμενατων Ιονίωννήσων], Athens: Hellenic Parliament Foundation for Parliamentarism and Democracy, pp. 23–27.

Ober, J. (1996) The Athenian Revolution: Essays in Ancient Greek Democracy and Political Theory, Princeton: Princeton University Press.

Sakellariou, M. (2000) The Athenian Democracy [Ηαθηναϊκήδημοκρατία], Heraklion: Cretan University Press.

27

The opening ceremony of the Swedish Riksdag

Tormod Otter Johansen

Introduction

Every year in early autumn the Swedish Riksdag starts its parliamentary session with an opening ceremony that the king attends. Between 1974 and 1975 this ceremony changed dramatically. The opening of the parliamentary year serves, as we will see, as a condensation of the Swedish constitution. In 1974, a new Instrument of Government was enacted which codified the modern constitutional order. The main fundamental law of the Swedish constitution, the Instrument of Government, had persisted since 1809, and although amended it gradually had become more and more out of sync with the actual political system, which included parliamentarism. This major shift in formal constitutional order was not only represented but, I argue, embodied and enacted through the transformation of the opening ceremony. One of several crucial aspects of this transformation was the change of venue for the ceremony from a hall in the king's palace to the parliament building of the Swedish Riksdag.

My theoretical starting point is that ritual and ceremony are important, and that the analysis of such phenomena is valuable to the general discipline of constitutional theory and constitutional law.[1] I concur with Shirin Rai and Rachel Johnson in that 'what has often been seen as the banal backdrop to politics proper, accumulated tradition or necessary rules of procedure should in fact be the starting point for our analyses of modern democratic institutions' (Rai and Johnson 2014, p. 2). Philip Manow has critiqued the idea that 'democracy has no imagery' (Manow 2010, p. 9). Manow is right to insist that modern democracy, as much as all other forms of rule, has its own specific symbolic imagery and symbolism. The methodological approach in this study is, in general terms, an ethnographic analysis from a legal constitutional perspective.[2]

Sweden, tradition and reform

As a nation, the Kingdom of Sweden has a peculiar relation to its own constitutional and symbolic history. The country is one of the remaining constitutional monarchies, with a past stretching back into at least the early Middle Ages, but still sees itself as a distinctly modern and secular nation. As a democracy, with a decent legacy on protecting human rights, and an image of being a rational, humanitarian, industrious and forward-looking nation, Sweden still retains its royal family and hereditary head of state, Carl XVI Gustaf.

Today the main principle of the Swedish constitution is popular sovereignty, expressed in the Instrument of Government: 'All public power in Sweden proceeds from the people' (Chapter 1, section 1). This sovereign power is invested in the 349 parliamentary members of the Riksdag. At the same time, the king is head of state and the Act of Succession, one of the four fundamental laws of Sweden, regulates the order of succession.[3] The relationship between the Riksdag and the king forms the constitutional locus of the Swedish state.

The 1809 Instrument of Government was based on the separation of powers, where the king and the parliament had their own and shared legislative powers.[4] While amended during the nineteenth century, by the early twentieth century it was in large part dead letters. Parliamentarism and universal suffrage were not even represented in the written constitution, even though these were constitutionally entrenched and practised.[5] Fredrik Sterzel thus called the period from 1921 to 1974 the 'constitutionless half-century' (Sterzel 2009, p. 18). In 1974, a new Instrument of Government was adopted in line with political reality and which declared a state ideology of popular sovereignty.[6] The king remained as the head of state, but without retaining any political power (the result of the Torekov compromise, between the social democrats and the right-wing parties) (Stjernquist 1971, p. 377). In addition to the representative functions under international law (such as receiving ambassadors), the head of state has, above all, ceremonial functions.

Two sovereigns

This means that the Swedish constitution, in a sense, contains two sovereigns: the Riksdag and the king. In the case of the king and the royal family, the whole year is filled with ceremonies and public events such as openings, state visits, celebrations of national holidays, royal birthdays, audiences, meetings with patronage organisations, royal orders or excursions at public agencies and businesses. All these can be analysed in terms of their constitutional function, since the king is the head of state. The most significant of such events are those where the head of state interacts with other central state organs. Two such interactions of constitutional importance stand out: the *konselj* (cabinet council) meetings when the king meets the prime minister and cabinet, and the yearly *Riksmötets öppnande*, the opening of the Riksdag session.[7]

Once a year the two sovereigns, the Riksdag and the king, interact directly with each other as constitutional actors. While a full history of the opening of the Riksdag would be interesting, it would be a daunting task, covering a period stretching back to at least the first formalised openings in 1617, and previous medieval ceremonies held as early as 1435 in Arboga. At the same time, a description of the ceremony only as it takes place today[8] would risk being ahistorical. I have chosen a middle path, using two specific historical instances, together representing a paradigm shift in the long history of the ceremony.

A ceremony transformed

To set the stage for comparison and analysis of the new and old opening ceremonies, two condensed descriptions of the ceremonies will follow. The final instance of the old one took place on 11 January 1974. The first instance of the new ceremony took place on 10 January 1975. The second instance was on 15 October 1975, at the time of year (September or October) at which it has since taken place annually.[9]

I will focus on the central symbolic and ritual aspects of the ceremony. My ethnographic approach means that both extravagant aspects as well as seemingly insignificant details can be of relevance (see the approach in Manow 2010). The description here is based on observation of the recorded television broadcasts of the live events.

Riksdagens högtidliga öppnande, 11 January 1974

The broadcast begins with a view of the greater coat of arms, panning over to a view of the empty Silver Throne (a gift to Queen Christina in 1650), draped in an ermine coat. The location is *Rikssalen* (The hall of state) at Stockholm Palace. On each side of the throne two tables are placed that hold royal regalia, a crown and sceptre, guarded by chamberlains in uniform (Figure 27.1).

Spectators stand along the walls, and benches are waiting for members of the Riksdag. The right side of the throne has benches where

Figure 27.1 Silver throne and regalia. All illustrations in this chapter are captured frames from two publicly available video recordings of the openings of the Riksdag session on 11 January 1974 and 15 October 1975, originally broadcast by Sweden's public broadcaster, © Sveriges Television, available at https://youtu.be/8hIjIN3ADwI and https://youtu.be/AO09OLazDYQ (accessed 6 July 2022)

court ladies and spouses of ministers are seated. The left side has benches where ambassadors and their wives are seated (Figure 27.2).[10] Dress code is white tie and full dress uniform.

First to arrive from the mandated church service are members of the Riksdag. Not all 350 are present due to space constraints. They sit on benches, surrounded by heads of public agencies and large corporations. Military officers, officials from the royal court, knights of the highest royal order (*Serafimerorden*) and justices arrive (Figure 27.3). They bow or salute the flag before entering the hall. Orders and other honorary signs are worn.

Military parade music is played. Princess Christina (the king's sister) arrives in an ermine coat. Everybody stands and the princess curtsies to foreign representatives and the members of the Riksdag. A ceremonial guard arrives in solemn march and takes place behind the throne. King

Figure 27.2 Wives of ambassadors. © Sveriges Television

Figure 27.3 Serafim order knights in front of court ladies. © Sveriges Television

Carl XVI Gustaf arrives, preceded by the Marshal of the Realm carrying a staff of office (Figure 27.4). Behind the king are the prime minister and foreign minister, then-heir to the throne Prince Bertil, followed by the other ministers. The king and the prince are dressed in general's uniform with honorary signs.

Soldiers from the royal Life Guards (wearing historical uniform) enter the hall in a loud stomping march that heralds the king's arrival. Silence falls, and the king enters. 'The King's Song' is played and sung. The king and heir bow to the members, the ambassadors and the princess.

The king sits down. He reads a crown speech, written by the government, in which he thanks the Swedish people, the members of the Riksdag, and acknowledges the sorrow of the death of his predecessor and grandfather, Gustav VI Adolf (Figure 27.6). Then a political declaration of the social democratic cabinet follows. Calling for God's blessing of the members, he declares the parliamentary session opened.

The speaker of the Riksdag then gives a speech. It expresses sorrow over the passing of the late king and some political notes relating to foreign policy and other matters. The finance minister hands over the yearly budget proposition and the chancellor a yearly report to the speaker. The

Figure 27.4 Marshal of the Realm, king with prime minister and foreign minister.
© Sveriges Television

Figure 27.5   Charles XI's Trabants in stomping march. © Sveriges Television

Figure 27.6   King reads crown speech. © Sveriges Television

ceremony master gives a sign and the ceremony is over. Everybody leaves in the reverse order to that in which they arrived.

Riksmötets öppnande, 15 October 1975[11]

Svea livgarde troops in parade uniform with bear fur hats stand at attention on Sergel's Square.[12] Military music is played.

In the parliamentary chamber, members of the Riksdag are convened. Dress code is business suit. The hall is covered in blond birch veneer, with several Swedish flags hanging below the spectator benches (Figure 27.8).

Five hundred guests are present, high public officials and diplomatic corps, as well as the commander-in-chief, the archbishop and royal family members. Music composed for a royal wedding in the eighteenth century is played by a civilian orchestra in the chamber.

Police cars escort the king and the heir Prince Bertil, who arrive in a black automobile together with the speaker of the Riksdag and the Marshal of the Realm. They chat informally while riding up. They are followed by military officers in service dress uniform. At the top of the escalator they meet Prime Minister Olof Palme and the vice speakers and they shake hands.

Figure 27.7   Music corps. © Sveriges Television

Figure 27.8 View from behind the speaker's podium. © Sveriges Television

Figure 27.9 King, speaker, prince and prime minister chat on an escalator. © Sveriges Television

Figure 27.10 'The King's Song' is played and sung. © Sveriges Television

Figure 27.11 King declares Riksdag session opened. © Sveriges Television

Figure 27.12 Prime minister gives policy statement. © Sveriges Television

The king enters to the sound of fanfares and drums. When the king and company arrive at the central podium, 'The King's Song' is played and sung (Figure 27.10). All stand. The speaker of the Riksdag requests that the king opens the 1975–76 parliamentary session. With a short speech, beginning 'Mr Speaker, honoured members!' the king declares the session opened (Figure 27.11). Fanfares sound. Everybody sits and chamber music is played.

The prime minister gives a government policy statement, addressing first the king and the heir to the throne, then the speaker and members (Figure 27.12). More music and fanfares are played. The king rises, everybody rises, and the king leaves together with the prime minister.

Interpretation of change from old to new ceremony

The opening of the Swedish Riksdag is a ceremony with certain ritual components.[13] These rituals also contain symbolism, both in physical artefacts and ritual actions. Hobsbawm and Ranger focus on the 'invention of tradition' as a constructive act where ritual and ceremony are used for specific purposes (Hobsbawm and Ranger 1983, p. 6). Important among these is the 'historical innovation [of] the "nation"' (Hobsbawm and Ranger 1983, p. 13). On a more general anthropological level, David Kertzer has argued that rite and symbolism are essential to creating political reality in every type of society. All types of organisations, not least nations and states, 'can only be represented symbolically' (Kertzer 1988, p. 16). The opening of the Swedish Riksdag is one of those instances where a ceremony contains ritual elements that symbolically represent the Swedish state, nation and its democracy (Yanow 1993, pp. 51f.).

Several distinct differences between the two ceremonies can immediately be identified: the change of location and the fact that the king becomes the guest of the Riksdag (instead of vice versa); the decrease in formality; the change from military to civilian character of the ritual and symbols present. This is also apparent in the architectural shift from the classical feudal hall to the modern, birch-clad venue – a recurring theme in Scandinavian architecture (see Singler and Singler in this volume).

Sovereignty: feudalism to democracy

The ceremony correlates in many ways to the change in the formal written constitution. In the old ceremony, the king was the centre of sovereignty, and he invited the people (historically as the four estates) to his palace.[14] In the new ceremony, the centre of sovereignty is the Riksdag, where the king is a guest. The king does not unilaterally open the Riksdag; he does so at the request of the speaker. This embodies the notion that popular sovereignty is the basic principle of the new constitution.

A non-obvious detail is that under the new rules the session has already begun before the opening ceremony is held.[15] This further strengthens the shift away from the declaration of the king being the constitutionally significant act, replacing it instead with the election and its confirmed result.[16]

The speech and declaration by the king in the old ceremony addressed 'Swedish men and women, elected representatives of the Swedish people'. But in the new ceremony, the king begins his declaration addressing the speaker of the Riksdag, as is customary for all who speak in the chamber: 'Mr Speaker, honoured members!' The king no longer speaks directly to his people; he addresses the sovereign body of the Riksdag.

The new from the old

The crucial innovation of the new opening ceremony is that the main ritual component is retained while the change of setting fundamentally alters the symbolic nature of the ceremony. It is not just a change of venue, but an inversion of the old feudal, military and royal ceremony into a democratic, civil and popular ceremony. As Kertzer has pointed out: 'New political systems borrow legitimacy from the old by nurturing the old ritual forms, redirected to new purposes' (Kertzer 1988, p. 42). Just as the Swedish constitution is an amalgam of monarchical tradition and modern democracy, its central ceremony contains conflicting symbols.[17] The ceremony, then, can both contain conflicting symbols as well as functioning as an embodiment of the Swedish state and its constitution. It does not require consistency or unambiguity, rather it functions because symbols can have a 'rich diversity of meanings', understood by people in different ways and thus staying ambiguous (Kertzer 1988, p. 11).

In the old ceremony, following a feudal logic, the king was the obvious sovereign – however restricted by the rights of his people, represented by the estates gathered in the Riksdag. In the new ceremony, this question is left unresolved, and perhaps this is what makes the ceremony function and the ritual components effective.[18] The ceremony does not just represent the constitution; it embodies it and performatively creates the Swedish state in a constitutional sense through this embodiment. While it is easy to think that the Riksdag and the king simply existed before and autonomously from the opening ceremony, in an important sense they can only continue to exist through such rituals.

Sacred body

If we look at those present at the ceremony, it is clear that there are two bodies which are most central. The other parties present are primarily an audience and while they legitimate the ritual as such, they do not take part in it actively. The two bodies, present in the flesh, are the king's body and the collective body of the gathered members of the Riksdag. It is significant that the current king did not crown himself (as did previous Swedish monarchs) and no longer carries the royal regalia: crown, sceptre, sword, orb and key.[19] This gradual separation of the body of the king and sovereignty had already begun to take place under the old constitution and ceremony (see Benveniste on sceptre, crown and sovereignty, book 4, p. 325).

The king's body is at the centre of the ceremony. In the old version he was surrounded by his adjutants and guards, court members and foreign diplomats. In the new ceremony, those placed closest to him are the members of the Riksdag, just as he is closest to them, rather than his court and entourage. In the contemporary iterations, since the return to the permanent parliamentary building in 1983, the king is seated even lower on the ground than in the 1975 version, no longer on a platform, but facing the speaker's podium, from which he, like everyone else, addresses the chamber. We must remember that the king still has immunity from prosecution; in this sense his body is clearly marked as sacred (Chapter 5, section 8 of the Instrument of Government). The use of him as the ritual master still clings to his sacred sovereign status.

It has even been recently suggested that the constitutional shift taking place in 1974 did not amount to a change in the constitutional status of the king as such, but rather the unilateral sanctioning of the new constitutional order and political system by the king (see Sunnqvist 2021, pp. 405–407). This would mean that many of his old privileges (over land, other possessions, certain decision-making concerning royal estates and the royal court, and so on) are not granted to him under the present constitution, but rather retained by him and his house. The popular sovereignty only reaches so far, and leaves intact, this argument goes, the longstanding constitutional status of the monarch. I must note that I find this argument constitutionally unconvincing, considering the supreme and sovereign status of the Riksdag according to the 1974 reform. The notion that the king still retains constitutional and sovereign power is, of course, one possible interpretation of his important symbolic function in the new ritual. That this would simply override the parliamentary sovereignty seems difficult to square with the 1974 Instrument of Government. One must in any case admit that the constitutional situation is not easily interpreted just one way or the other.

To return to the ceremony, we can see that it is now no longer a ritual with a legal and constitutional effect, but rather a pure symbol. But it still embodies in a ceremonial form the constitution of the nation and country. The presence of the body of the king contributes to the constitution of the body of the Riksdag, as the members are gathered. Vice versa the Riksdag, through the ceremony, legitimises the constitutional role of the king's body. The opening ceremony is not merely a cordial visit or a favour granted by the old sovereign towards the new. It is also a yearly reconstitution of the constitutional status of both the Riksdag and the king. The ambiguity of the 1974 reform – so clear on the main issues of the political order, but so deferring and unclear on the constitutional status of the king – is perhaps in the end best represented in this very ritual.

Notes

1 Legal scholars and other disciplines for a long time have identified the courtroom as a symbolically charged milieu, a place where symbols and rituals matter. However, rituals connected to political activity and ceremony have not to the same extent interested scholars of constitutions (Manow 2010, p. 2). See also Kertzer on the peripheral position of ritual in mainstream western ideology (Kertzer 1988, p. 12).

2 Scheppele (2004, p. 395) defines such an approach like this: 'Constitutional ethnography is the study of the central legal elements of polities using methods that are capable of recovering the lived detail of the politico-legal landscape.' Scheppele also discusses the range of ethnographic approaches available outside of traditional field studies (Scheppele 2004, p. 396). This is similar to Manow (2010) but could also be described as a sort of praxiography, (see Bueger 2014, p. 287). It is connected to political theology (Kahn 2011, p. 26).

3 The four constitutional laws are called fundamental laws: the Instrument of Government, the Act of Succession, the Freedom of the Press Act, and the Fundamental Law on Freedom of Expression.

4 Shared legislative power over fundamental, civil and criminal law. The king had exclusive power over economic and administrative legislation and the Riksdag had the main say on budget and taxation (Sveriges Riksdag 2016, p. 13).

5 The 1809 Instrument was amended several times, but the most radical changes happened during the first decades of the twentieth century. After reforms in 1866 the four estates were replaced by a bicameral system, the increased parliamentarism and successively expanded franchise (universal male suffrage 1909, female suffrage 1921) led to the old 1809 Instrument of Government no longer describing or prescribing how the actual constitutional system worked.

6 Many other points can be made about the Swedish constitution, historically and today, for example concerning the centrality of freedom of the press and expression, which is seen both in the second sentence in the Instrument of Government ('Swedish democracy is founded on the free formation of opinion …') and in that two of the fundamental laws concern freedom of the press and expression.

7 These are primarily regulated in Chapter 6 section 6 of the Instrument of Government, and Chapter 3 section 6 of the Riksdag Act.

8 At the time of writing, the last one was held on 14 September 2021.

9 The old ceremony took place at the beginning of the calendar year. This tradition stemmed from the time when parliaments were not constantly convened or in session. The new ceremony was moved to the beginning of the yearly parliamentary session to follow the modern schedule, when there is always a session, being named after the two years during which it takes place (the first being the *1975–76 års riksmöte* (the 1975–76 parliamentary session). During the first half of 1975 there was a shorter session, lasting until the 1975–76 session started.

10 Gustav III, who arranged several aspects of the ceremony during the latter part of the eighteenth century, decided that the wives of ambassadors should sit in front of their husbands since they were prettier to look at.

11 In what follows I will describe the second instance of the new ceremony held in 1975. The reason for this is that the first instance of the new ceremony was unavailable to me during the research process. I have, however, had the chance to see it shortly before submitting this text, and it does not in any significant way change my analysis of the two ceremonies, even though it strengthens the argument I take from Hobsbawm and Ranger, that political ceremonies and rituals are, often continually, invented. Small details (like whether the speaker and prime minister arrive together with the king or before him) are

different between the two instances of the new ceremony in 1975, and they can of course also be analysed in terms of their symbolic meaning. Choices have been made to alter the ceremony.

12 The Riksdag was housed in a temporary location in the newly built *Kulturhuset* while the main building was renovated.

13 This study does not rest on any specific definitions of the concepts of ritual and ceremony. Relevant are the definition of ritual as a 'rule governed activity of a symbolic character which draws the attention of its participants to objects of thought and feeling which they hold to be of special significance' (Lukes 1975, p. 291).

14 This is the same structure as when the prime minister and his cabinet (who historically were the council and advisers to the king) constitute themselves at a council (meeting) with the king.

15 Compare article 34, of the 1866 Riksdag Act with Chapter 3, section 6 of the current Riksdag Act. The members of the Riksdag meet before the opening ceremony, listen to a speech by the speaker, followed by a roll call of the members. The Riksdag is already constituted in practical terms and has started their working year when the king arrives for the formal opening ceremony. Therefore, the ceremony no longer fulfils a necessary legal-constitutional function. Also, if the king cannot attend (or one might presume, refuses) to fulfil the request from the speaker, the speaker will declare the session opened.

16 Kertzer points out that the election is perhaps 'the most important ritual of legitimation found in modern nations' (1988, p. 49). Consider here also the notion of play kings, becoming real kings, and again play kings in Graeber and Wengrow (2021, p. 117).

17 'One of the most striking features of ritual, in fact, is its ability to accommodate conflicting symbols while reducing the perception of incongruity. Thus in many societies, symbols of egalitarianism are combined with symbols of power and authority through rites involving elected officials. The grammatical rules of ritual symbolism are of a different sort than those of natural language, still less do they follow the rules of logic' (Kertzer 1988, p. 51).

18 'The strength of political organizations comes less from any homogeneity of their members' beliefs than from the continuing expressions of allegiance through ritual' (Kertzer 1988, p. 69).

19 They are still present, although not worn or carried, in royal ceremonies such as baptisms, weddings and funerals.

References

Benveniste, É. (2016) *Dictionary of Indo-European Concepts and Society*, Chicago: HAU.

Bueger, C. (2014) 'Pathways to practice: praxiography and international politics', *European Political Science Review*, 6(3), pp. 383–406. DOI: 10.1017/S1755773913000167.

Graeber, D. and Wengrow, D. (2021) *The Dawn of Everything: A New History of Humanity*, London: Penguin.

Hobsbawm, E. and Ranger, T. (1983) *The Invention of Tradition*, Cambridge: Cambridge University Press.

Kahn, P.W. (2011) *Political Theology: Four New Chapters on the Concept of Sovereignty*, New York: Columbia University Press.

Kertzer, D. (1988) *Ritual, Politics, and Power*, New Haven: Yale University Press.

Lukes, S. (1975) 'Political ritual and social integration', *Sociology*, 9(2), pp. 289–308. Available from: https://www.jstor.org/stable/42851629.

Manow, P. (2010) *In the King's Shadow: The Political Anatomy of Democratic Representation*, Cambridge: Polity.

Rai, S.M. and Johnson, R.E. (2014) *Democracy in Practice: Ceremony and Ritual in Parliament*, Hampshire: Palgrave Macmillan.

Scheppele, K.L. (2004) 'Constitutional ethnography: an introduction', *Law & Society Review*, 38(3), pp. 389–406.

Sterzel, F. (2009) *Författning i utveckling: tjugo studier kring Sveriges författning*, Uppsala: Iustus.

Stjernquist, N. (1971) 'Grundlagberedningskompromiss i statschefsfrågan', *Statsvetenskaplig tidskrift*, 74, pp. 377–379.

Sunnqvist, M. (2021) '"Under konungens enskilda styrelse": Statschefen, kungahuset, hovet och ordensväsendet i konstitutionellt och rättshistoriskt perspektiv', *Statens Offentliga Utredningar*, 74. Available from: https://lup.lub.lu.se/record/cfe63e9c-f5ed-4e94-b311 -b0adfd79f31d.

Sveriges Riksdag (2016) *The Constitution of Sweden. The Fundamental Laws and the Riksdag Act.* Available from: https://www.riksdagen.se/globalassets/05.-sa-fungerar-riksdagen/demo krati/the-instrument-of-government.pdf

Yanow, D. (1993) 'The communication of policy meanings: implementation as interpretation and text', *Policy Sciences*, 26(1), pp. 41–61. DOI: 10.1007/BF01006496.

Part VIII
Building parliaments for the future
Guest editor: Jeremy Melvin

28

Introduction to Part VIII

Jeremy Melvin

Since the start of this millennium, there has been a significant amount of activity in the architecture of parliament buildings in the UK. These include a major refurbishment of the Palace of Westminster, the symbolically charged home of the national parliament, two new parliaments resulting from devolution in Scotland and Wales (the latter being upgraded from an assembly to a parliament in 2018), and the re-establishment of the Northern Irish parliament at Stormont as part of the Good Friday Agreement reached in 1998. Just in advance of these projects, the British architectural firm Foster and Partners won the competition to recreate the Reichstag in Berlin as the home for the parliament of the newly reunited Germany, which opened in 1999.

Alongside this, the initially selected winner to design, the Iraqi parliament, Assemblage, and the firm to which the commission was ultimately awarded, Zaha Hadid Architects, are both based in the UK (Wainwright 2013; Bar Hillel 2013). In 1994, there was the opening of the headquarters for the regional government of the Department of the Bouches du Rhone in southern France, designed by Will Alsop. Alsop's firm had narrowly won the competition against Foster and Partners in 1990. Additionally, Foster and Partners have designed city halls for two major metropolises, London and Buenos Aires, as well as a capital precinct including a parliament for the proposed new capital of the Indian state of Andhra Pradesh, Amaravati. Even though the Scottish parliament building was designed by an architect from Catalonia, the institution was conceived in the UK.

In addition to these projects and activities, the UK Parliament is currently considering strategic options for the refurbishment of the Palace of Westminster (Restoration and Renewal Programme).[1] All this suggests that for the last quarter of a century or so, the UK has seen some of the most intensive work on architecture for parliaments and other democratic institutions.

The purpose of Part VIII of this volume is to explore several of those projects specifically related to parliaments – the proposal for a temporary chamber for the House of Commons to use while the Palace of Westminster undergoes refurbishment by AHMM, the Reichstag by Foster and Partners, the Scottish Parliament by EMBT and the Welsh Assembly by RSHP. It should be noted that, as of September 2022, the temporary chamber is in abeyance despite being at an advanced design stage. Parliament and various bodies it has created have expended considerable effort in trying to address the implications of this refurbishment, which will be extremely complex and expensive. It is almost certain to cost billions and be Europe's largest refurbishment project. Amid all the uncertainty for strategy and expense, it is clear that decanting the whole building rather than keeping it in phased occupation will save time and money. This is the main spur for the temporary chamber. Despite all this effort, it seems the potential for significant changes in constitutional or parliamentary procedure have attracted little attention, and various unofficial polemical proposals have gained little support.

Each of the architects for the temporary chamber, the Reichstag and the Scottish Parliament and the Welsh Assembly has contributed a chapter to this part, describing the projects from the designers' points of view. Also included is a brief account of the evolution of the precinct and Palace of Westminster with a particular focus on the House of Commons, which sets the context for the temporary chamber.

The House of Commons evolved slowly within the wider process of the evolution of government within first England and later the United Kingdom. First summoned to parliament in 1264, the Commons only acquired a purpose-designed chamber with the construction of the nineteenth-century palace to designs by Charles Barry and Augustus W.N. Pugin after a fire destroyed most of the existing palace – much of it medieval – in 1834. Previously it had sat in adapted buildings, since the mid-sixteenth century in the former St Stephen's Chapel in the Palace of Westminster.

The long process of irregular incremental change characterises the history of the British Parliament. This is especially important in light of the comment by the temporary chamber's architect, Paul Monaghan, that his team was asked in essence to recreate the form and character of the existing chamber, just as Winston Churchill argued for it to be reconstructed after it was destroyed by enemy action in 1941 (Churchill

1943). Changing its shape, Monaghan comments, would require an Act of Parliament. While it may have taken more than 500 years for the house to be given its own purpose-designed chamber, once it did, that chamber acquired an enormous authority and symbolic value, which as Churchill claimed, had a strong bearing on the nature of British democracy and governance. How it acquired that status is explained in part by the evolution of the precinct and Palace of Westminster in relation to the evolution of governance, as discussed in the following chapter.

Together, these four projects exemplify several points on the spectrum of contemporary parliamentary architecture. Two, the Reichstag and the House of Commons, involve refurbishment in part because of the symbolic power and authority that appears to derive from the existing buildings.

In the case of the House of Commons, it is the necessary refurbishment of the Palace of Westminster that in turn requires a temporary chamber, specifically designed to replicate the atmosphere and layout, if not the exact detail of it, to which the house will, in theory, return. The new chamber is within the reconstruction of an essentially 1980s office building called Richmond House, with little symbolic value at least for its interiors, though it has retained an early-nineteenth-century façade with an entrance from Whitehall, designed by William Whitfield to recall the gateway to the Tudor Whitehall Palace, designed by Hans Holbein, which is known from paintings. Being one of the few structures within the security perimeter of the parliamentary estate that is not listed (apart from the façade), this building offered the possibility of complete reconstruction.

Apart from being a refurbishment and reconstruction, the Reichstag shares little with the House of Commons. Built for the parliament of the newly created German Empire, the original building opened in 1894. Although the history of parliaments within Germany is as similarly long and convoluted as their counterparts in the UK (and much more geographically diverse), no single building or urban precinct is as intimately and incrementally connected with parliamentary history as Westminster. The history of the Reichstag on the other hand, since the architectural competition for this building in 1894, has mirrored the history of German politics with a series of dramatic ruptures, rather than a process of incremental evolution. As an imperial parliament, it lasted less than a quarter of a century, as the German Empire was abolished with the end of the First World War in 1918. Its use as the parliament for the Weimar Republic ended with the fire of 1933, which was shortly followed by the collapse of the republic as the Nazis solidified their grip on power. This turbulent history was encapsulated in *Wrapped Reichstag*, a project by the artists Christo and Jeanne Claude in 1995.

Having been used for a variety of purposes under the Nazis, the symbolic value of the Reichstag made it an important target for the Red Army when it captured Berlin in 1945, and the battle for it made it unusable. German reunification in 1990 and the decision to make Berlin the capital the following year led to a new focus on the building. David Nelson from Foster and Partners explains the subsequent reconstruction in this volume.

The Scottish Parliament and the Welsh Assembly were both new buildings and new institutions. Neither country had any extant memory of independence from which to derive authority or symbolic value. Scotland had not had its own parliament since the Act of Union with England in 1707, while Wales fell under the political control of England in the thirteenth century, a point where the governance of England began to assume some of its present characteristics.

What led to their creation was the overwhelming victory of the Labour Party in the UK's general election of 1997. Its manifesto promised a significant overhaul of the country's governance, including reform of the Westminster Parliament, the creation of a supreme court to replace the Judicial Committee of the House of Lords as the country's highest legal authority, and to offer referenda on devolution in each of Scotland and Wales 'not later than the autumn of 1997' (Labour Party 1997). Moreover, the manifesto promised to continue the peace process in Northern Ireland to which the outgoing Conservative government under John Major had devoted considerable attention, in conjunction with Northern Irish politicians, the Irish government and the US senator, George Mitchell, who chaired the round table talks.[2]

None of these commitments explicitly promised new buildings. But once devolution was approved in the two referenda (by a large margin in Scotland and a smaller one in Wales), the momentum for new buildings became unstoppable. Neither capital city, Edinburgh or Cardiff, had an obvious building for the new parliaments, and there was debate in both about the choice of site. These are explained by the two architects, Benedetta Tagliabue and Ivan Harbour in this volume. What is significant is that both sites had very significant historical and cultural symbolism, which informed the design of the two buildings as they sought to encapsulate the possibilities of the future for their countries.

The Westminster Parliament enabled the creation of both. As many of their early members had also been MPs at Westminster, there was a significant influence from the older institution on the younger ones, though this could be measured as much by a reaction against rather than an adaption of existing parliamentary traditions. Both, for example, adopted circular geometries for their chambers, though there were practical considerations behind this decision as well as symbolic ones.

Each of these institutions depicts a different version of continuity and change as the drivers of parliamentary architecture. And while architecture alone cannot guarantee democracy or good governance, the range of architectural approaches, each interacting with the historical fabric or the locations, suggests that architecture can and does play a significant role in the way parliaments are conceived, how they evolve and how they act as communicators between their members and their electorates.

Notes

1 This has become necessary as the condition of the nineteenth-century Palace has deteriorated, which, understandably, the nineteenth-century design did not anticipate and so does not comply with twenty-first-century requirements for fire, health and safety, and security. Over the years substantial amounts of asbestos were inserted into it, posing significant health risks, while fire marshals have to monitor it 24 hours a day for fire safety, at considerable cost, quite apart from the inherent danger of fire.

2 The peace process reached its apogee with the Good Friday Agreement of 1998, so the shape of the settlement was still unclear in 1997. It included reviving and reforming the Stormont assembly, originally founded as the seat of government for Northern Ireland, the six counties of the island of Ireland that remained part of the UK when the other 26 formed the Republic of Ireland in 1921.

References

Bar Hillel, M. (2013) 'An architectural puzzle: why is Zaha Hadid building the Iraqi Parliament in Baghdad', *The Independent*, 15 November. Available from: https://www.independent.co .uk/voices/comment/an-architectural-puzzle-why-is-zaha-hadid-building-the-iraqi -parliament-in-baghdad-8942580.html (accessed on 13 September 2022).

Christo and Jeanne-Claude (1995) *Wrapped Reichstag*. See: https://christojeanneclaude.net /artworks/wrapped-reichstag/ (accessed on 10 February 2023).

Churchill, W. (1943) Speech on the House of Commons Rebuilding, 28 October. Available from: https://api.parliament.uk/historic-hansard/commons/1943/oct/28/house-of-commons -rebuilding (accessed on 14 September 2022).

Labour Party (1997) 'New Labour because Britain deserves better,' manifesto, *Archive of Labour Party Manifestos*. Available from: http://www.labour-party.org.uk/manifestos/1997/1997 -labour-manifesto.shtml (accessed on 13 September 2022).

Wainwright, O. (2013) 'An Assembly by Assemblage? Iraq plans $1bn parliament building', *The Guardian*, 14 January. Available from: https://www.theguardian.com/artanddesign /architecture-design-blog/2013/jan/14/iraqi-parliament-design-assemblage-zaha-hadid (accessed on 30 May 2023).

29

Westminster, its Palace and the House of Commons

An outline of the House of Commons chamber and its context

Jeremy Melvin

Introduction

So commonly is 'Westminster' used in many forms of political journalism and common speech that it has become almost synonymous with 'Parliament', at least in a British context. The evolution of English governance is bound up with the evolution of this district, and especially its architectural development. The UK Parliament's home is indeed the Palace of Westminster, whose silhouette since its rebuilding in the nineteenth century with its pointed and four square towers at either end of a long, low block has become an easily recognisable symbol of London. Its clock chimes make an equally familiar audio analogue.

This extraordinarily powerful association in popular consciousness between architecture and parliament may seem to depend on the present Palace, its design and operation. Unlike the piecemeal buildings it replaced after a fire of 1834, the architects for the new Palace, Charles Barry and Augustus W.N. Pugin, created a work of architecture that was specifically a home for and a symbol of parliament, embedded both in its overall planning and in various levels of decoration.

The Palace's complicated and heterogeneous history combines the development of English (and later British) governance. The grandeur of the medieval Palace, most of whose builders were anonymous, and the involvement from the seventeenth century of a roll call of notable British architects including Christopher Wren, James Wyatt, John Soane, Charles Barry, A.W.N. Pugin and Giles Gilbert Scott, suggests at least a tenuous link between the governance of Britain and British architecture. That alone makes it worthy of serious investigation, but it also tends to obscure individual episodes of happenstance, opportunism and deliberate policy that have led to the building and its precinct becoming what it is today, both as a physical condition and its embedding in popular perception.

Yet from that history has evolved a building of such resonance that the basic layout of the House of Commons chamber designed by Barry and Pugin was considered sacrosanct. In turn, that led to it being rebuilt to almost exactly the same pattern after it suffered bomb damage in 1941. Its authority persists, as the proposed temporary chamber to accommodate the House of Commons during the impending refurbishment is also intended to replicate the layout of the nineteenth-century model (Churchill 1943; Monaghan in this volume).

By focusing on a limited number of episodes and sites in the House of Commons' history, this chapter attempts to show how this spatial template emerged, and why it acquired and still has such authority. Its scope is far more limited than a history of the house itself. From the point where the House of Commons acquired the former St Stephen's Chapel as its permanent home in 1547, the chapel's rectilinear form exerted a strong influence over parliamentary procedure and practice. It underwent numerous alterations and various unfulfilled proposals to rebuild it, few of which challenged the basic configuration and several of which reinforced it.

By the time of the rebuilding after the fire which destroyed the old Palace in 1834, the Commons' spatial configuration had acquired such authority – despite, or perhaps because, it emerged more from an accretion of accident, opportunism and reaction to practical necessity than conscious political theory – that it was more or less repeated in the new Palace. Charles Barry's 'improvements' to that spatial template were largely to make it and the procedures that flowed from it work more effectively, with better accommodation for members, visitors and the press as well as for voting.

Just over a century later, when the House of Commons was destroyed by a German bomb in 1941, the authority of this spatial template was, if anything, even greater. Winston Churchill, in his speech on the rebuilding of the house in 1941, made a strong case for its virtues which led to replicating it closely.

For the purposes of this chapter, we will look briefly at the historical evolution of three particular loci – the precinct of Westminster, the Palace and the chamber of the House of Commons – to suggest how this has come about. It is important to note that some form of parliament was long established before the 'commons' – burgesses of towns and knights of the shires – were first summoned to Parliament in December 1264.

J.R. Maddicott, a recent historian of Parliament, dates the origins of the institution to 924 (Maddicott 2010).[1] It was only over a long period that both Parliament and the buildings started to assume their present form. In this process, the House of Commons, both as an institution and a building, emerged fairly late.

Precinct and Palace

Edward the Confessor (reign 1042–1066) initiated the transformation of Westminster into a centre of divine, royal and ultimately parliamentary power with his rebuilding of Westminster Abbey in the innovative Romanesque style, building (or rebuilding) a palace alongside it. His death, childless at the beginning of 1066, accelerated this process. None of the claimants to succeed him had an overwhelming claim to the throne. Being designated as successor by a dying king was an important part of a claim to Saxon kingship (Brooke 1967, pp. 21–49) and two of the leading claimants, Harold Godwinson and William of Normandy, believed Edward had designated them. In any case Harold was able to act quickly and chose Westminster Abbey for his coronation on the same day that Edward was buried, a clear attempt to establish the legitimacy of his claim in part through the aura of the new Abbey. When William (the Conqueror) defeated Harold later the same year, he also chose to be crowned in Westminster Abbey, cementing its status as the site of royal coronations.[2] By these two coronations in quick succession, the Abbey became recognised as the locus for the flow of divine power into the secular authority of the king. The Palace quickly became a symbol and extension of royal authority over the realm. By 1100 it had acquired some of its most important and sumptuous spaces, notably Westminster Hall (built under William Rufus, reign 1087–1100) and the king's bedchamber (reputedly where Edward the Confessor died, and rebuilt as the painted chamber in the thirteenth century). Both would become significant as settings for parliamentary meetings and other administrative functions.

So, some of the constituent parts in the partnership between building and governance that characterises Westminster were in place in the early Middle Ages. Some embryonic form of parliament existed, and the use of buildings to symbolise, serve and extend royal power was established.

Henry III (reign 1216–1272) rebuilt the Abbey and made significant alterations to the Palace. This period saw extraordinary developments both in the practice of governance and the evolution of architecture to serve it. This is when the term 'parliament' first enters the records, though in the historian David Carpenter's words, it was already 'a new name for an old institution' (Carpenter 2020, pp. 193–194). This period also saw the first summons of the Commons to Parliament at the end of 1264. The various disputes and debates about the nature of power that characterised Henry's reign led to England becoming irrevocably a 'parliamentary state', as Carpenter claims, under Henry's son and successor Edward I (reign 1272–1307) (Carpenter 2004, pp. 466–494).

Henry transformed the Palace, Abbey and precinct of Westminster into 'a dynastic shrine, cult centre, palatial residence and seat of government' (Maddicott 2010, p. 163). The first two were embodied in the rebuilding of Westminster Abbey, the second two in the extended Palace, but it is how they worked in conjunction with each other that is significant. His building works, serendipitously and accidently, started to provide architectural form to the nascent House of Commons, which also originated as one of the innovations in governance during his long and fractious reign.

Carpenter fleshes out Maddicott's comment about Henry's transformation of Westminster, with detail about the rebuilding of the Abbey and alterations of the Palace. He gives an account of how the Palace was used (Carpenter 2020, pp. 365–371). The hall remained its centrepiece, but the king's, or painted chamber, and the queen's chamber, both subsequently used for parliamentary meetings, were also built during this period.

The chambers

As indicated above, the House of Commons emerged sometime after the institution of parliament was established. Although when first summoned to Parliament, the commons and the great magnates sat together, by the early fourteenth century the two groups began to meet separately, thus beginning the division of Parliament into the two houses of Lords and Commons. At this point the chapter house of Westminster Abbey was the most frequent location for the commons, though they also met in the Abbey's refectory.

Carpenter's account of the chapter house is suggestive (Carpenter 2020). It was both 'the place where the monks met daily' and 'where Henry intended to address the realm (a country ruled by a king or queen). Everything about the chapter house was designed to impress' (Carpenter 2020, p. 347). In using the chapter house for this purpose, Henry was perhaps performing a symbolic act of channelling divine power into secular authority, reinforced by its magnificence.

Figure 29.1 Westminster Hall in the Palace of Westminster, London. © Thomas Rowlandson and Augustus Pugin, 'Westminster Hall in the Palace of Westminster, London', December 1809, from *The Microcosm of London: or, London in Miniature*, London: Rudolph Ackermann. Great Britain. Coloured aquatint. Source: Houghton Library, Harvard via Wikimedia Commons, reproduced on the basis of Public Domain. Available at: https://commons.wikimedia.org/wiki/File:Houghton_Library_MS_Hyde_76_(1.1.2.2)_-_Westminster_Hall.jpg (accessed 29 November 2022)

The significance of the chamber as a venue for the House of Commons is twofold. In the early fourteenth century, as the Abbey's centre of governance, it was the only space in the area which was deliberately designed to debate and consider decisions, and even to allow for some sort of democratic resolution (between the monks). Second, being octagonal in plan, it is a closer approximation to a circular layout than any subsequent chamber (except, perhaps, for configurations when Parliament met in other venues for which there are no, or at best, scanty records of the layout). If the first point about debate would become the essence of the House of Commons, the second, its form and layout, would fall by the wayside, though probably more by accident than through deliberate decisions.

To appreciate this, we have to move forward several centuries to the next episode in the architectural evolution of the House of Commons. The middle of the sixteenth century was another period of major changes in governance. Much of that originated with the Reformation, and the break between England and the Roman Catholic Church which was cemented by the Act of Supremacy in 1534.[3] By that Act, the Pope lost all legal authority in England, and the supreme sovereign body of the country was defined as the King-in-Parliament (effectively a trinity of the Houses of Lords and Commons and the monarch).

That in itself had enormous architectural ramifications as it led directly to the dissolution of the monasteries (including Westminster Abbey) and, with the Abolition of the Chantries Act in 1547, of St Stephen's Chapel. This was the king's private chapel while the Palace was a royal residence. What became the chamber for the House of Commons originated as a chapel begun in 1292 by Edward I.[4] It was specifically intended to rival Sainte-Chapelle in Paris in magnificence with sumptuous materials and fine decoration, including paintings. It was also very tall. In 1348, Edward I's grandson, Edward III, refounded it as a 'college' to offer prayers for the dead, with up to 48 staff. It was this institution that was dissolved to allow the House of Commons to take possession in 1548.

There is little record of what alterations were made at that time. The rectilinear shape of the chapel suggests that members sat on opposite sides of the speaker's chair, and that considerable alteration would have been needed to adapt it to accommodate 341 MPs rather than the 48 priests who made up the college. The choir stalls were replaced by tiered seating, and the roof lowered to improve acoustics. Eventually a gallery was added to give space for more MPs.

It is certainly notable, and possibly ironic, that while the House of Commons sat in St Stephen's Chapel from 1548 until 1834, the building became ever more inadequate as the Commons became ever more important and assertive. The principal problem was size: it was simply not large enough, even if rather fewer than the full complement of MPs attended. This problem became worse with the Acts of Union with Scotland (1707) and Ireland (1801) which abolished those countries' parliaments and brought MPs from them into the Westminster House of Commons. In 1834 there were 658 MPs, almost double the number in 1548.

During these three centuries, the House of Commons' status changed enormously. In the seventeenth century it directed the winning side in the civil war between Charles I and Parliament, while the constitutional settlement following the 'Glorious Revolution' of 1688 confirmed the supremacy of Parliament in the sovereign concept of the King-in-Parliament. Thereafter, monarchs reigned with approval from Parliament and became increasingly detached from the heart of political power. During the eighteenth century, Great Britain (as the country had become with the Act of Union between England and Scotland) became a global power, though the independence of the 13 American colonies in the 1780s challenged this status. That, together with the social pressure of economic growth and the changing intellectual ideas of the Enlightenment, intensified the challenges of governance. Pressure for parliamentary reform came to a head around the Great Reform Act, which was finally passed in 1832 and began a century-long process which fundamentally altered the electorate and composition of the House of Commons.

The architecture of the chamber itself was remarkably static during this period of extraordinary upheaval. Christopher Wren, as surveyor of the king's works, undertook modifications to the chapel in the 1690s. This involved lowering the height of the building, as he thought the stonework unsafe, and giving the interior timber panelling to create a classical feel. In 1707, to provide space for another 40 MPs, he widened the galleries. From the surviving records,[5] its architecture hardly captured the enhanced role of the House of Commons. If Henry III had sought to use architecture to convey the flow of power from God through him to the country, Wren's remodelling made little attempt to express the new supremacy of Parliament over the monarch.

Rebuilding the chamber

The state of the House of Commons building was frequently criticised during the eighteenth century. There were occasional proposals for radical rebuilding of the entire Houses of Parliament.[6] By 1800 the problems with the chamber, such as size and ventilation, could no longer be ignored. The following year, James Wyatt, chief architect to the Office of Works, did adapt the chamber to try to suit the influx of members following the Act of Union with Ireland.[7] That was, in effect, the chamber that passed the Reform Act in 1832 and burnt down two years later.

Behind the scenes, however, there had been numerous proposals for rebuilding the house over the previous 40 years. John Soane, appointed as clerk of works to the Palace of Westminster in 1791, was asked in 1794 to propose the location and design of a new chamber. He obviously felt proud enough to refer to it both in evidence he gave to committee decades later, and to include it in a pamphlet he wrote almost at the end of his life (Soane 1835).

A great flurry of proposals came on either side of the date of the Reform Act, starting with the Commons establishing a select committee, which met on 17 August 1831 to:

> consider the possibility of making the House of Commons more commodious and less unwholesome; and who were empowered to report their observations and opinion, together with minutes of evidence taken before them, to the House, and who were instructed to inquire in what manner adequate accommodation can be best afforded for its members (Parliament 1831).

Despite taking evidence through August and September of that year from distinguished architects including Sir Jeffry Wyatville, Benjamin Wyatt and Robert Smirke, the committee came to the following resolutions: that the present House of Commons does not afford adequate accommodation for its members; no such alterations or improvements could be made in the present House of Commons as would afford adequate accommodation for the members, due regard being had to their health, to general convenience and so the dispatch of public business; and finally, that the committee could not contemplate any other alternative than to recommend the construction of a new House of Commons, but that they were unwilling to pursue the consideration of a subject of such magnitude, and involving so much expense, without recurring to the opinion of the house.

At another committee, convened in 1833, Sir John Soane was the first witness, giving evidence from 14 March until 1 May.[8] Aged almost 80, he had worked at the Palace of Westminster for more than half his life, including his masterful addition of the law courts around Westminster Hall (Sawyer 1999).[9] On 14 March 1833, he pointed out that he was first asked to design a new chamber for the House of Commons in 1794. Then, as he recalled, he proposed solving the long-running problems of the existing chamber with a new one, on the space (156 feet, he measured) between the closest point of the existing chamber and the riverbank (House of Commons 1833). Nearly 40 years later, the case for this solution was even more compelling, as his own design for the House of Lords library further constricted the existing site, leading to the conclusion that even if the existing chamber was demolished, 'I consider it [the existing site] to be a very bad situation for a new house of commons' (House of Commons 1833). Soane's revised design of 1833 rested on his having:

> considered [how to resolve the problems of the chamber by adapting it] from time to time, from the year 1794, for at least 30 years; and the result of the best consideration I could give the subject was that it was totally impossible, by any means whatever, to enlarge the House of Commons sufficiently to make it commodious and for the accommodation of the members (House of Commons 1833).

His drawing for the new design was appended to the select committee report. It projected from and was entered through the existing chamber, which became a large lobby. The new site, he explained, would allow for an antechamber, a voting lobby and a chamber of 'adequate' 75 by 85 by 45 feet dimensions with a corridor around it. Allowing 2 feet width per member, with 3 feet 4 inches depth for seats, this size would hold 600 members. He considered suitable acoustics and sight lines to be achievable, with a strangers' gallery, its front row reserved for the press, over the speaker's chair. It would, in short, address most of the perceived shortcomings.

Over the next two months the committee took evidence from a roll call of distinguished architects, including Robert Smirke, Edward Blore, Decimus Burton, Thomas Hopper and George Basevi, as well as two MPs, John Crocker and Rigby Wason.[10] Many of their plans were appended to the select committee minutes, and show a wide variety of architectural styles and layouts, although all follow Soane's lead over the site. Some are essentially Gothic, others classical, while a few use modern materials such as iron to span the roof. Several follow Blore in proposing an octagonal plan (close to circular); one is elliptical, with a classical portico.

Without the space to analyse them in any detail, it is clear that the poor and inadequate condition of the chamber was well recognised before the fire (perhaps intensified by the business of parliamentary reform);

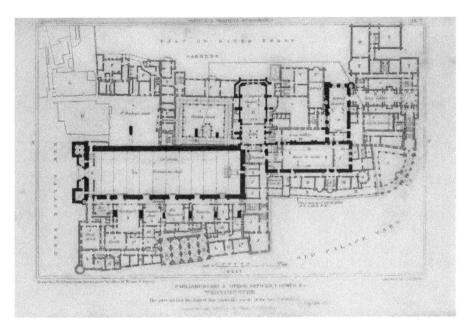

Figure 29.2 Floor plan of the Palace of Westminster prior to the 1834 fire. Author: Edward Wedlake Brayley, John Britton, 'Parliamentary & Other Offices, Courts &c. Westminster. The part within the dotted line shows the extent of the fire Oct. 16, 1834', 1836, from *The History of the Ancient Palace and Late Houses of Parliament at Westminster: Embracing Accounts and Illustrations of St Stephen's Chapel, and Its Cloisters, - Westminster Hall, - The Court of Requests, - The Painted Chamber, &c.* London: John Weale, Architectural Library. Great Britain. Engraving. Source: Wikimedia Commons, reproduced on the basis of Public Domain. Available at: https://commons.wikimedia.org/wiki/File:Brayley_Plate_II.jpg (accessed 29 November 2022)

that a new chamber would be required; and that apart from choice of site, a wide variety of configurations was possible. Much of what became the specification for Barry's chamber was already prefigured by Soane and his contemporaries. All this was rendered redundant by the fire which destroyed most of the Palace on 16 October 1834.

The story of rebuilding has been recounted frequently (Shenton 2016). A competition to find a design for a new Palace was held and won by Charles Barry with contributions from Augustus W.N. Pugin. The competition was a long and complicated saga, the actual rebuilding longer and even more complicated.

How it came about is beyond the scope of this chapter, bar two salient points. The first is that while a temporary chamber in which the Commons could meet was rigged up, the practice of 'divisions' for taking votes changed (Rix 2021). Although Soane hinted at this, his design did not fully develop the idea of two lobbies, one for those voting 'aye' (yes, or in favour of the motion) the other for 'nay' (no, against), which became crucial for Barry and remains integral to the design of the temporary chamber. As Kathryn Rix explains (2021), it was tied up with a new sense of accountability, as the list of members walking through each lobby (voting) was published, instead of the previous practice of publishing just the tellers (those who count the votes). Electors could see how their MP voted.

The second point in the journey from adapting the existing Palace to the necessary rebuild after the fire comes, almost inevitably, from yet another select committee, established in 1835 'to consider and report on such plan as may be most fitting and convenient for the permanent accommodation of the Houses of Parliament' (Parliament 1835). Its resolutions included: to hold a competition for the design of the new Palace; to rectify the shape of the existing chamber; to provide space for 420–460 members, plus galleries for the remainder of MPs, an outer lobby and gallery for 'strangers' (non-members); and adequate ventilation. After taking evidence about functional and operational requirements, the select committee handed over the judging of the competition to a commission, with some members familiar from the 1833 committee, notably Charles Hanbury-Tracy (1778–1858), who chaired the commission.

In recommending the selection of Barry's design (subject to reassurances on cost), and providing assurances that the convenience of internal accommodation was not sacrificed to the 'beautiful elevations', Hanbury-Tracy commented that 'considering the magnitude of the building it is impossible to conceive a[nother] design equally magnificent', and that Barry's internal arrangements and beauty were 'unquestionably far superior overall'. The select committee, to whom the commission reported, agreed to the commission's recommendation (House of Commons 1835, quoted in Shenton 2016, p. 52).

Barry's 'superior arrangements' included, for the first time, placing the House of Lords and House of Commons at either end of an axis, centred on the public lobby, as well as apparently meeting all the specifications set out in the House of Commons. While the design would evolve considerably from the competition, that feature remained, and indeed became the building's central spine.

All this notwithstanding, there was nothing inevitable or predestined in the design of the House of Commons chamber. Barry's overall layout for the Palace cleverly resolved practical problems and requirements (for example, the new idea of separate voting lobbies) and imbued the building with symbolic significance for the institution. So why did this chamber achieve such a value that it was rebuilt to the same pattern after the bombing of 1941, and for the temporary chamber to take the same form?

Churchill's influence and the chamber

One explanation for this comes from a speech Winston Churchill made in October 1943, introducing a motion to create a select committee to consider the issue of rebuilding after bomb damage (Churchill 1943). It is probably the single most cogent argument for a rectilinear debating chamber with not enough space to accommodate all members simultaneously.[11]

To précis a long and complex argument: Churchill starts by citing his 40 years of experience as an MP and his personal preference for the existing layout, from which he had 'derived great pleasure and advantage' (Churchill 1943, p. 403). He acknowledged that preference for this size and shape 'sound odd to foreign ears', but supported that preference with a combination of theoretical and historical points. The theoretical points start with a distinction between the party and group systems, the former served by a rectangle and the latter by a semicircular layout. The group system and its layout 'enables every individual … to move around the centre, adopting various shades of pink according as the weather changes', and accordingly the group system had destroyed 'many earnest and ardent parliaments' (Churchill 1943, p. 404). He contrasted that fluidity with his own experience of 'crossing the floor' of the house (changing his party allegiance), a 'difficult process [which] requires serious consideration'.[12] The rectangular shape and party system imply greater conviction on the part of individual politicians.

On size, he pointed out that if there is space for all members, 'nine-tenths of its Debates will be conducted in the depressing atmosphere of an almost empty chamber', an impediment to 'the essence of good House of Commons speaking … the conversational style, [with] the facility for quick informal interruptions and interchanges'. In turn that raises a sense of responsibility because 'on great occasions [there is] a sense of crowd and urgency' as 'great matters are being decided, there and then, by the House' (Churchill 1943, p. 404). So a 'small chamber and a sense of intimacy' are essential for parliament to be 'a strong, easy flexible instrument of free debate'. Indeed, he goes on to imply that the nature of this type of parliamentary debate had played a part in the conduct of the Second World War, which in the year before his speech had shifted irrevocably in favour of the allies, as 'a rock upon which an Administration … has been able to confront the most terrible emergencies' (Churchill 1943, p. 405).

The history of the House of Commons also lent it authority. 'The vitality and the authority of the House of Commons and its hold upon an electorate, based upon universal suffrage, depends … on its great moments, even upon its scenes and rows' (Churchill 1943, p. 405). Although 'not free from shortcomings … our House has proved itself capable of adapting itself to every change which the swift pace of modern life has brought upon us'. All this, he suggested, had enabled the survival of parliamentary democracy, which would continue to play a vital role in postwar reconstruction. 'Politics may be very fierce and violent in the after-war days. … We shall certainly have an immense press of business and, very likely, of stormy controversy. We must have a good, well-tried and convenient place in which to do our work' (Churchill 1943, p. 408).[13] Churchill's views were obviously persuasive. There was little dissent from

Figure 29.3 Aerial view of the Palace of Westminster. © André Zehetbauer, 'Aerial photographs of Westminster Palace from the London Eye', 29 September 2006. Source: Wikimedia Commons, reproduced on the basis of a CC BY-SA 2.0. licence. Available at: https://commons.wikimedia.org/wiki/File:Westminster_Palace_-_2.jpg (accessed 29 November 2022)

other members and the house was reconstructed to almost the same form (with 'improvements' for ventilation as well as press and public access) and simplified detail by Giles Gilbert Scott.[14]

It might be tempting to dismiss this praise to the design of a parliamentary chamber whose salient features even its author admitted would 'sound odd to foreign ears' as the views of a single individual. But this is Churchill the parliamentarian speaking, which is not quite the same as Churchill the politician, still less Churchill the Conservative leader. Given though that his arguments also set the pattern for the reconstruction of the chamber in the late 1940s, and for the design of the proposed temporary chamber, it is reasonable to assume that it inaugurated or represented a view that the chamber's design is the terminal point of a long, fraught and fluid evolution. It embeds or reflects a great deal of constitutional theory and practice, itself flowing from the history of the site and relationship between different buildings and institutions.

Notes

1 Maddicott places Parliament's origins in the late Saxon era, from the accession in 924 of Aethelstan, the first monarch to be described as Rex Anglorum (King of the English). Defining the origins of the English Parliament as 'a leader, usually a king, taking council with his great men' (Maddicott 2010, p. 1), Maddicott notes that Aethelstan's reign 'saw the first appearance of truly national assemblies' (p. vii).

2 The coronation ceremony was devised by the Archbishop of Canterbury St Dunstan when he crowned King Edgar in Bath Abbey in 971. Adapted from Byzantine and Frankish rituals, it is still the basis for modern coronations.

3 A slow evolution in statecraft had begun earlier, under Henry VII (r. 1485–1509), as the Middle Ages gave way to the early modern world, and in line with what the cultural historian Jacob Burckhardt described as 'The State as a Work of Art' (Burckhardt 1954, pp. 2–99).

4 For more detail, see https://www.parliament.uk/about/living-heritage/building/palace /estatehistory/the-middle-ages/early-chapel-st-stephen.

5 See https://www.parliament.uk/about/living-heritage/building/palace/ststephenschapel /ststephensthehouseofcomonns/adapting-the-chapel/christopher-wren-and-james -wright. See also this image from 1710: https://www.wikiwand.com/en/St_Stephen%27s _Chapel#Media/File:Commons_In_Session.jpg (accessed on 14 September 2022).

6 Among these were more or less complete design proposals by William Kent and James Adam (probably modified by his brother Robert). Frank Salmon (2013) has studied Kent's proposals (Cambridge University 2013). Drawings for the Adam design are at Sir John Soane's Museum. Soane also produced a design in 1779 'without regards to expense, or limits to space, in the gay morning of youthful fancy', as he described it much later (Soane 1835).

7 Wyatt expanded the chamber by pushing outwards sections of the wall between the structural supports, though this did not solve the entire problem.

8 In the interim, in 1832, the Great Reform Act had been passed, significantly changing the franchise of the House of Commons. This committee had several members who would have an important influence on the rebuilding of the Palace after the 1834 fire, such as Sir Robert Peel (future prime minister), Charles Hanbury-Tracy (who chaired the commission to judge entries to the competition for rebuilding after the 1834 fire), Benjamin Hall (commissioner for works who oversaw the later stages of the reconstruction).

9 Soane had been appointed clerk of works to the Palace of Westminster in 1791. He would go on to produce some of his finest work for the Palace, including the law courts and adaptations to the House of Lords, but his initial impact was limited.

10 Crocker, MP for South Devon, seems to have been an amateur architect, remodelling his own residence, Flete House, in Devon.

11 The speech also includes what is probably Churchill's most famous comment on architecture: 'We shape our buildings and afterwards our buildings shape us' (Churchill 1943, p. 403).

12 Churchill 'crossed the floor' not once but twice, from the Conservatives to the Liberals in 1904, and back when he re-entered Parliament after a period without a seat in 1924.

13 Benedetta Tagliabue echoes this point in her statement that the Scottish Parliament set out to 'turn power into conversation' (see Tagliabue in this volume).

14 The most notable dissent in the debate which succeeded Churchill's speech came from the 'Red Clydesider' James Maxton. He argued that most of Parliament's qualities had emerged before Barry's and Pugin's rebuilding, though his most serious point was to expand the remit of the proposed select committee, so it could consider 'premises built on a fine site, in good English parkland ... some 20 miles' from London served by a train station and aerodrome, and in 'the finest building that British architecture can devise' (Churchill 1943, pp. 411–412).

References

Brooke, C. (1967) *The Saxon and Norman Kings*, London: Fontana.

Burckhardt, J. (1954) *The Civilisation of the Renaissance in Italy*, New York: Random House.

Cambridge University (2013) *Putting Our House in Order: William Kent's Designs for the Houses of Parliament* [online video]. Available from: https://www.youtube.com/watch?v=87fIgM33qAU (accessed on 14 September 2022).

Carpenter, D. (2004) *The Struggle for Mastery: The Penguin History of Britain, 1066–1284*, London: Penguin Books.

Carpenter, D. (2020) *Henry III*, New Haven, CT and London: Yale University Press.

Churchill, W. (1943) Speech to the House of Commons, HC Deb 28 October, vol. 393 cc403–73. Available from: https://api.parliament.uk/historic-hansard/commons/1943/oct/28/house-of-commons-rebuilding (accessed on 12 September 2022).

House of Commons (1833) Collection of Official Documents issued between 1833 and 1843, London 1843.

Maddicott, J.R. (2010) *The Origins of the English Parliament 924–1327*, Oxford: Oxford University Press.

Monaghan, P. (2021) 'Touchstones for a twenty-first century parliamentary building: a temporary chamber for the House of Commons, UK', *Parliament Buildings Conference*, UCL, 18–19 February. The Bartlett School of Architecture and UCL European Institute.

Parliament (1831) Select Committee Report. Ordered, by the House of Commons, to be printed, London, 6 October.

Parliament (1833) Report from the Select Committee on the House of Commons' Buildings, London.

Parliament (1835) Report from the Select Committee on rebuilding Houses of Parliament. Ordered, by the House of Commons, to be printed, 3 June.

Rix, K. (2021) 'Adapting Westminster's architecture: the division lobbies in the nineteenth century Houses of Commons', *Parliament Buildings Conference*, UCL, 18–19 February. The Bartlett School of Architecture and UCL European Institute. Available from: https://www.parliamentbuildings.org.uk/abstracts/adapting-westminsters-architecture-the-division-lobbies-in-the-nineteenth-century-house-of-commons/ (accessed on 25 August 2022).

Salmon, F. (2013) 'Public Commissions', in S. Weber (ed.) *William Kent: Designing Georgian Britain*, New Haven and London: Yale University Press, ch. 13.

Sawyer, S. (1999) 'The Law Courts', in M. Richardson and M. Stevens (eds) *John Soane, Architect: Master of Space and Light*, London: Royal Academy of Arts, pp. 268–275.

Shenton, C. (2016) *Mr Barry's War*, Oxford: Oxford University Press.

Soane, J. (1835) *Three Designs for the Two Houses of Parliament 1779, 1794 and 1796*, London: library@soane.org.uk.

30

Touchstones for a twenty-first-century parliamentary building

A temporary chamber for the House of Commons, UK

Paul Monaghan – Allford Hall
Monaghan Morris (AHMM)

In 2017 Allford Hall Monaghan Morris was commissioned to design a temporary chamber for the House of Commons to use while the Palace of Westminster undergoes refurbishment. The circumstances behind the commission and the challenges it poses are complicated and do not necessarily follow the conventions of linear logic. They include the reasons for refurbishing the Palace, the implications for parliamentary operations while it happens, questions of heritage and tradition – both architectural and political – and various other considerations.

The main purpose of this chapter is to describe our proposals for the chamber. In order to do that it is first necessary to sketch the most salient points of this context. The immediate area around the Palace, which includes Westminster Abbey, Parliament Square, together with sections of the River Thames' north bank and Whitehall, has enormous historical significance. Here the institution of Parliament emerged and developed, in part because of the association between royal and divine authority which the abbey and medieval palace, whose only significant surviving relic is Westminster Hall, represented. The word 'Westminster', though, is now more or less synonymous with 'Parliament', indicating how the source of authority has shifted from Church to monarch to a representative body, though the association between them remains constitutionally and symbolically important.

In its current form, the Palace is largely a building of the nineteenth century, the work of Charles Barry and Augustus W.N. Pugin, incorporating some earlier fabric such as the hall, and with a near total

Figure 30.1 Illustrative aerial view of Parliament's Northern Estate, including Richmond House. © Secchi Smith

rebuild of the House of Commons chamber after bomb damage during the Second World War, by Giles Gilbert Scott. Over the last 70 years, much of the building has had little maintenance to the point where it is now unsafe. Riddled with asbestos and with fire safety risks that require 24-hour marshals to be in place, adding millions of pounds every month to running costs, it is close to being uninhabitable. The decision to resolve this situation dates back to 2008, though it took another decade to ascertain how this would be achieved.

Just as the rebuilding of the House of Commons after the war provoked debate about the sort of space that might replace the Victorian chamber, so the Palace's current condition has provoked consideration of how and whether it should be refurbished, and if so, how might the Commons continue to operate during what would inevitably be a lengthy – between eight and ten years – and expensive process. The numerous twists and turns of that debate are beyond the scope of this chapter and mainly predate our involvement, but a summary of the salient points is as follows:

- The Palace should undergo a comprehensive refurbishment.
- In the interest of cost and time, the Palace should be completely decanted while this work proceeds.
- Accordingly, temporary accommodation would have to be procured for both the House of Commons and the House of Lords.

- The House of Lords would move to the Queen Elizabeth Conference Centre opposite Westminster Abbey.
- After much discussion and appraisal of various options, it was decided that a new chamber on the site of Richmond House on the northern edge of the parliamentary estate would be built as temporary accommodation for the House of Commons with possible future uses to be determined.
- The temporary chamber should, as closely as possible, replicate the shape and spatial configuration of the existing chamber, including the division lobbies and other ancillary accommodation, with improvements to accessibility for members and the public (including more accommodation for the latter).

That was distilled into a brief to provide a new chamber and division lobbies; to echo at least some aspects of the ceremonial route between the Lords and Commons chambers; to update and upgrade the possibilities for public engagement; to provide committee rooms as well as improving technical functions in line with the goal for sustainability.

Providing sufficient space for the chamber and associated spaces such as lobbies and office accommodation for the prime minister, the speaker and their staffs, as well as security, were vital factors in selecting the site. Security put an enormous premium on remaining within the existing parliamentary estate. Providing a secure perimeter on a different site would add hugely to the cost – even for nearby locations, such as Horseguards' Parade just along Whitehall. For the same reason, several more or less speculative proposals by different architects on different sites would not have been feasible either. Parliamentarians, too, wanted to be able to move from their offices to the house without crossing public roads.

But with the estate already densely built up and many of the buildings listed, there were few options, the only practical one being the site of Richmond House, a 1980s ministerial building designed by William Whitfield, incorporating the façade of the early nineteenth-century Richmond Terrace (Figure 30.3). Although listed Grade II*, the listing applied primarily to the historic façade and the entrance onto Whitehall, designed by Whitfield as an homage to the gateway to the Tudor Whitehall Palace which stood close by and is known from a Holbein painting. The rest of the building is fairly standard office space. It dates from just before the IT revolution, and before concerns about wellbeing and sustainability transformed expectations. So it was verging on obsolescence.

Figure 30.2 Illustrative view looking from the Cenotaph towards the retained Whitehall façade. © Allford Hall Monaghan Morris Limited

Nonetheless, we spent the better part of a year trying to refurbish it. We found the floor to ceiling heights were far lower than contemporary standards, and the staircases far too narrow for the number of people who would use them. It was also hard to create the necessary spaces and relationships between them. Rebuilding it was the only viable option.

Rebuilding made it possible to ensure the preferred configuration of spaces for the chamber and the lobbies, the best possible options for improving public accessibility to Parliament, including providing MPs offices, the cafes and tea rooms where a great deal of informal business takes place. It also allowed a two-and-a-half storey basement to be created for an energy centre serving other buildings on the estate, such as the two Norman Shaw buildings. Shaw originally designed these buildings as the headquarters for the Metropolitan Police (known as Scotland Yard). Being listed Grade I, it would have been more or less impossible to add the modern plant needed to bring them up to contemporary environmental performance standards.

Barry and Pugin's Palace was designed for ceremony as well as day-to-day operations. Reproducing the spirit of those rituals and their interaction with 'normal' business is an important part of our brief. Barry devised a long axis with the throne in the House of Lords and the speaker's chair in the House of Commons facing each other, which is cut at the central lobby with a direct route from the entrance. Here, members of the public can, in theory at least, 'lobby' their members

Figure 30.3 Illustrative view of Richmond House next to the existing Norman Shaw North building. © Secchi Smith

of Parliament. The axis has a vital ceremonial role at the annual State Opening of Parliament, when the Commons are 'summoned' to hear the monarch's speech (which sets out the government's proposed legislative programme) delivered from the throne in the Lords, and process along the access to the entrance of the 'upper chamber'.

We have tried to understand the site and its history, which has led us to adopt a flexible strategy. This is based on using what is there in the most appropriate way, but making intelligent and sensitive responses to the existing fabric where replication simply does not work. Our purpose was to use these adjustments to inculcate the necessary improvements to aspects such as accessibility and environmental performance.

Our design cue comes from understanding the buildings that are there, such as Richmond House, the Norman Shaw buildings, Whitfield's façade to Parliament Street and two rather fine buildings on that street.

Barry had to fit his new forms into the pattern of the old structures. Similarly, we insert the chamber and its associated spaces into the existing pattern of the Northern Estate. As the whole area is steeped in history and heritage, possibilities for building on it are defined by planning regulations and other legislation. Our brief, for instance, is to replicate as far as possible the form of the existing chamber, as to change it would in any case require an Act of Parliament.

The resulting dialogue with history can be seen in many aspects of the design. It is apparent, for instance, in how we have tried to convey the ceremonial aspects of the building. Already on the site is a narrow alleyway, Canon Row, which runs from Westminster Bridge to Richmond Terrace (Figure 30.4). We propose to upgrade this as the main entrance for MPs coming to the new chamber from their offices in Portcullis House, which also spurs an upgrade of the landscaping of other narrow streets across the site which are mainly used for bicycle couriers.

Figure 30.4 Illustrative view of the proposed members' entrance to Richmond House from Canon Row. © Secchi Smith

Similar in proportion to St Stephen's Hall, which leads from the main entrance to the central lobby in the existing Palace, this upgraded route will also echo some of the detail of the historic buildings, such as the diagonal grid of Whitfield's design. We turn that pattern into a structural system which also loosely recalls the neo-Gothic vaulting of the Victorian architecture. References to Barry and Pugin's Palace are even more explicit in our new central lobby (Figure 30.5), whose structure is quite visible and echoes Pugin's belief that 'there should be no features about a building which are not necessary for convenience, construction or propriety' (Pugin 1973 [1841], p. 1).[1]

This space serves an analogous purpose to its predecessor, providing somewhere for all visitors and users of the building to mingle. Members of the public from VIPs to pupils on school trips will enter via one of the buildings on Parliament Street, merging with the route along Canon Row

Figure 30.5   Illustrative view of the proposed central lobby at Richmond House. © Secchi Smith

which MPs will use most of the time. Our design for it is another synthesis of existing, adjoining fabric, together with adopted and adapted features from the Palace itself to simulate the ceremonial character of the original. Resolving the varied levels of the existing buildings results in three new levels: the ground where everyone enters, passes through and can meet, with education and public galleries above. Whitfield's façade onto Parliament Street with its distinctive oriel windows sets the pattern for the space behind, establishing its three-storey height, and its shape, which picks up on the diagonals of the oriels.

History shapes the building of the future in two senses: the first is the existing fabric discussed above, while the second is parliamentary tradition. Parliamentary tradition is ever present in the chamber itself (Figure 30.6). We were instructed to recreate the form of the existing House of Commons, while improving accessibility. That included

Figure 30.6 Illustrative view of the proposed temporary House of Commons chamber. © Secchi Smith

retaining the division lobbies on either side (one of those voting 'aye' or yes for the motion, the other for those voting 'nay' or no) of the chamber. Our design will be instantly familiar to anyone who knows the existing House of Commons. It will not imply constitutional change by stealth. The new chamber is, however, slightly wider than its model and far easier for wheelchair access.

Working with theatre design specialists Charcoal Blue, we have expanded and greatly improved the views of the floor of the house from the visitors' and press galleries, to establish better connections with the public, and spread understanding of how Parliament works and what it does. This area too has greatly improved accessibility.

Above the chamber are two floors of committee rooms, where a great deal of parliamentary work is done to improve legislation as it passes through Parliament, and to extract testimony of various matters from knowledgeable witnesses. The grandest of these committee rooms spills onto a terrace with views onto Parliament Street and that great symbol of national unity in grief, the Cenotaph. This terrace reflects another aspect

Figure 30.7 Illustrative view of the proposed rooftop pavilion at Richmond House. © Secchi Smith

of the brief, to provide as much outdoor space and accommodation for planting to encourage inner city biodiversity. That reaches its apogee at roof level, which is largely given over to garden space with a special, multipurpose function room at its centre (Figure 30.7).

Another driving force behind the design is the need to adopt modern methods of construction. Improving the standards and working practices of the construction industry has long been a goal of British governments of all parties, so working with Lend Lease, we are developing components which can be manufactured offsite and brought to it by barges using the River Thames. The intention is to drive up quality and efficiency of construction.

But, as explained above, the overwhelming consideration is to work with historic structures and parliamentary traditions, interpreted and expressed in a way that is meaningful to the contemporary society which Parliament serves. So we have picked up on the context – Whitfield's oriel windows and geometry, Norman Shaw's string courses, the classical division of almost all buildings on or around the site into a base, middle and top, to create a new and more accessible setting for a near facsimile of the existing House of Commons. Our design is, then, in a long tradition of both the British Parliament and its buildings, of incremental evolution rather than episodic, radical changes.

Addition, March 2022

Since this paper was delivered at the Parliament Buildings conference at The Bartlett School of Architecture, UCL, in February 2021, the future of the entire renewal of the Palace of Westminster – which created the need for a temporary chamber – has been thrown into doubt. The commissions of both houses overseeing the project announced in February 2022 that the Restoration and Renewal sponsor body, established in 2020 to deliver the process, would be replaced. This was apparently after a significant increase in the estimate for the total cost and timescale, up to £14 billion and 20 years. At the time of writing, it is unclear how this will proceed.

Note

1 A.W.N. Pugin (1973 [1841]) *True Principles of Pointed or Christian Architecture*, London: Academy Editions.

31

Integrating the building into the land

The Scottish Parliament

Benedetta Tagliabue – Miralles Tagliabue EMBT

The Scottish Parliament was designed more than 20 years ago, but I still think it is the most important project we have built. After it stirred controversy at the beginning, its qualities gradually gained appreciation, and now it is one of Scotland's most popular visitor attractions.

We knew designing a parliament would be very difficult, but we wanted to create a building that seemed natural and right for its purpose. One way of illustrating what we set out to achieve is the painting of the Reverend Robert Walker skating, by Henry Raeburn in the National Gallery of Scotland. In our building we wanted to capture the same sense of doing something very difficult, like skating on a frozen loch, and making it appear to be easy and effortless. One of the difficulties in designing parliaments is that their histories are very complex, with much blood and war. Struggles for power are inevitable, but our goal was to turn struggle into *conversation*, a wonderful idea but not easy to achieve.

Our most important idea at the outset was to create not just a building, but a landscape across an area larger than the site itself. That meant absorbing a piece of land adjacent to and within the same ownership as Holyroodhouse, at the time the Queen's official residence in Scotland. Ultimately, and generously, the late Queen authorised the donation of this land to the Parliament, allowing our vision to become reality.

The thinking behind this vision was to imply that the parliament belongs physically and metaphorically to the land, which we thought more profound and appropriate than the common association between democracy and transparency. The spectacular geology of the Salisbury Crags, including the extinct volcano of Arthur's Seat, shapes the site; this form assumes something of the character of a great natural amphitheatre.

Figure 31.1 The Scottish Parliament and Edinburgh, facing the Palace of Holyroodhouse (right). © ZACandZAC

Figure 31.2 The Parliament and the Salisbury Crags. © ZACandZAC

To us that seemed a suitable backdrop for a parliament, a place where we proposed to put a very important object.

Within this natural landscape we formed a true amphitheatre as the setting for the parliament itself. The building has a very complex geometry. We developed the geometry through drawings, and then represented that evolution with models which we keep in our studio. They were an important tool as they allowed politicians, who are not experts in architecture, to understand the design. With the drawings and models, we could convey every idea, and involve politicians in the conversations about design.

The relationship between the parliament and the architecture, history and culture of the city of Edinburgh is also very important to the design. My partner and codesigner, Enric Miralles, studied English there as a teenager and loved the city. A year before we won the competition, he took me to it. We stayed in the station hotel, the Balmoral, which is set at a very important point in the city's urban fabric, at the junction between the old city and the Georgian new town. From this position we could observe the city and begin to develop an understanding of how it works. We realised that the Royal Mile, running between the old castle and Holyroodhouse, plays a vital part in determining its character.

Figure 31.3 Stairs descending to the garden lobby and meeting place. © ZACandZAC

When we came to design the parliament, we tried to draw on the natural landscape and the urban fabric and to make our building belong to both of them. Our complex geometry also relates to the natural and the human made. Natural objects like leaves inspired us to make it very light and delicate, giving the building a sense of being a natural form which would occupy the historic setting in front of Holyroodhouse. More inspiration came from what we saw during a tour of Scotland, and in particular boats upturned to make them habitable on the seashore. Delicate and precise in their construction, they suggested how we might create volumes for the building using wood. As well as echoing how artificial objects can be placed in the Scottish landscape, they could also recall the sea and how Scottish people travelled across the world.

Integrating the building into the land – landscape, people and culture – was a vital element in creating an identity for the parliament (Figure 31.4). That led us to bring inspiration from nature as well as human-made objects. This also helped to define a relationship with the historic Queensbury House on the site. Rather than remove it altogether (as other competitors did) we incorporated it into a collage of old and new built fabric.

The entry to the parliament is opposite Holyroodhouse, as mentioned above, official seat of the monarch in Scotland. The big pergola underlines that this parliament is not a fortress, a bunker or an isolated castle. Instead, it is dedicated to the people; it is open to the people and invites them in. It took a great effort to conceal the security, but this design approach shows that this is a democratic building.

This strategy continued into the design of the members of Scottish Parliaments' (MSPs) private offices. From the inside we wanted the offices to be as comfortable and cosy as workspaces, but from the outside we wanted to express that although the members are servants of the people, they are also individuals. We achieved this with the bay windows, which make comfortable seats within and give views out towards the garden, while on the exterior each bay is expressed separately, revealing that behind it is a distinct individual.

Our first ideas for the chamber were very different from what was eventually built. When we started the design, the Parliament as an institution did not exist. It was founded in 1999, and gradually, as it developed its own traditions and procedures, members began to acquire a better understanding of what they needed from the new building. During this process, we were asked to give it a semicircular form. The idea was to express, in an understandable way, that the Scottish Parliament would not be a replica of the confrontational layout at Westminster. The

Figure 31.4 Integrating the parliament building into the landscape. © ZACandZAC

intention also was not to slavishly follow the semicircle, which is common on the European continent, but to place Scotland somewhere between the UK and European parliaments.

Using wood implied a connection to the boat forms described above, but the semicircle also supported our intention that the public should be able to get very close to the members, adding to the feeling

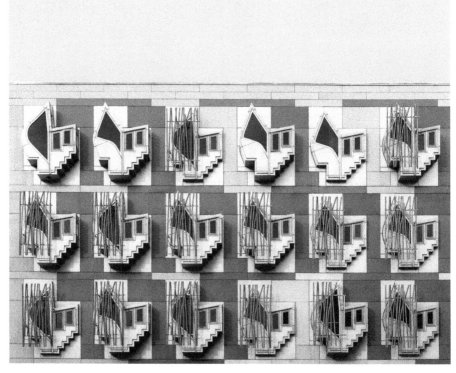

Figure 31.5 The bay windows to the MSPs' private offices, each with a distinctly individual expression. © ZACandZAC

that the public actually takes part in debates. We were also aware the building is a set for broadcasting, which is a very important part of the debating chamber's function, so we had to accept artificial light despite the beautiful natural light and views.

Another change that came from the experience of the first members was the foyer between the garden and the existing fabric. This became the entry point for MSPs and the press, and a place where people can meet. Despite a lack of space, we believed that it makes a necessary link between the old and new structures, and that we could make it very beautiful.

One of the building's most important features is the wall onto Canongate (Figure 31.7). We always knew this would be a crucial element in the design as it would be the point to introduce the new building to Edinburgh's historic fabric, and to prepare people for their encounter with it. Enric Miralles had many ideas for it, which he noted in his sketchbooks, but nothing was finalised.

Figure 31.6 Inside the chamber, the timber ghosts of upturned boats sheltering the MSPs' seats below. © ZACandZAC

Figure 31.7 Canongate and the concrete mural by artist Soraya Smithson. © ZACandZAC

After Enric died, the artist Soraya Smithson was commissioned to develop the concept for the wall. As the daughter of Peter and Alison Smithson, she knew how architects think and how they might achieve their visions. So together we went through Enric's sketchbooks to try to understand his thinking as a base for developing the concept. Her idea was for a collage of Scottish stones, and texts drawn from Scottish literature cast in concrete panels. Thus the building is symbolically a Scottish landscape, a palimpsest of Scottish urban fabric and an anthology of Scottish literature. It can be read on many different levels by anyone who approaches the Scottish Parliament, and prepares them for engaging with the building and the institution, which it introduces to the city, the country and its people.

On 9 October 2004 the Queen opened the building with the president of the parliament, Sir David Steel. Among other notable Scots present was the great actor Sean Connery.

32

A continuation with history and a significant new experience

The Reichstag in Berlin

David Nelson – Foster and Partners

Reconstructing the Reichstag in Berlin to house the Bundestag (the parliament of the Federal Republic of Germany which absorbed the former East Germany on unification) was the result of a two-stage competition. The first stage came about with unification in 1990. Unification was popular in all parts of the country; everybody felt bringing together 80 million people in one nation was an unimagined opportunity.

At this stage the brief for the project was suitably ambitious, requiring effectively twice the floor area of the nineteenth-century Reichstag building. The government encouraged us to modify the surviving fabric and also build outside of the existing envelope, making the task bigger than a project that would be confined by four walls.

The choice of architect was meant to be unanimous, but the judges for the first stage could not reach such a decision. Three entrants were asked to continue to another stage. Two significant shifts occurred between the two stages. First was a change of mood in Germany after the euphoria wore off, as the full economic implications of stitching the country together became clearer. This resulted in a more modest strategy and reduced accommodation to about half the area of the existing building. Second was a public consultation, much of which took place within the 1960s configuration of the Reichstag building. An open forum was created and, over several days, many issues were raised. One was the idea of keeping more of the historic fabric (and the memories it evoked) and interior spaces, even though no one knew how much still existed and in what condition, as it had all been covered up by the 1960s refit. By this time, we knew so much about the working parliament, we were able to suggest additional uses for the rest of the building.

Figure 32.1   The Reichstag building today. © Reinhard Görner

We knew something of the history of the building and of the institution. The building was completed in 1894 as the home for the German parliament, which had a longer history. The country had unified in 1871, but the process of getting a parliament built was frustrated for 20 years. During this period, it had been moving from temporary accommodation to temporary accommodation.

Completing the building was a remarkable milestone. From 1815, all German states had constitutions and parliaments. In 1815 the German Confederation ('Deutscher Bund') was founded as successor of the Holy Roman Empire. Article 13 of the *Bundesakte* (the constitution of the German Confederation) forced the German states to pass constitutions and implement parliaments called *Landstände* or *Landtage*. The Frankfurt parliament (or Paulskirche) of 1848 was the first freely elected parliament for all of Germany (before it was unified as a nation state in 1871), but on the whole there was no single concept of a parliament that covered the entire territory of the new Germany. Even after unification, the emperor – Kaiser – (formerly King of Prussia) could issue edicts to determine policy. So, unlike the UK for example, the German parliament was not sovereign.

This condition informed how the building was designed. Interestingly, a seating configuration with origins in classical Greece was chosen,

Figure 32.2 The Reichstag building at the turn of the twentieth century. 'Berlin, memorial to Otto von Bismark in the original position in front of the Reichstag around 1900', before 1904, *Album von Berlin*. Berlin: Globus Verlag, Germany. Source: Wikimedia Commons, reproduced on the basis of Public Domain. Available at: https://commons.wikimedia.org/wiki/File:Berlin_Reichstag_mit_Bismarck_Den kmal_um_1900.jpg (accessed on 29 November 2022)

reflecting the identification of the educated bourgeoisie with that civilisation. This was hierarchical, with the most important people sitting towards the front, less prominent people towards the rear and all those of equal importance sitting on the same row. There seating was also divided into two sides, which embodied the split between the executive and the government. Two viewing galleries for the general public were included to give democratic accountability.

This parliament continued until the end of the First World War in 1918. The influence of the Prussian members was substantial. They would delay votes by filibustering. As many of the Prussians lived in or near Berlin, the delay meant that members from other parts of Germany would have to return home as they were not paid for extra time, leaving the Prussians to vote.

Der große Sitzungssaal im Reichstagsgebäude.

1. Tisch des Hauses. 2. Sitz des Reichskanzlers. 3. Sitz der Mitglieder des Bundesrates. 4. Sitz des Präsidenten. 5. Plätze der Schriftführer. 6. Rednertribüne. 7. Tisch der amtlichen Stenographen. 8. Journalisten-Tribüne. 9. „Kein-Thüre".

Figure 32.3 Reichstag plenary hall, 1903. Augsburger Postzeitung, 'Großer Sitzungssaal des Deutschen Reichstages Berlin', 1903, Unterhaltungsblatt zur Augsburger Postzeitung, Nr. 38, 16(5). Source: Wikimedia Commons, reproduced on the basis of Public Domain. Available at: https://commons.wikimedia.org/wiki /File:Reichstag_Sitzungssaal_1903a.jpg (accessed on 29 November 2022)

The decision to finance the conflict that became the First World War was taken in the Reichstag. After the war and during the Weimar Republic, various coalitions presided over Germany as it experienced a succession of traumas from the impact of the Armistice, hyperinflation and the 1929 Wall Street crash.

On 30 January 1933, Adolf Hitler was appointed chancellor, and four weeks later the Reichstag was burnt in mysterious circumstances, severely damaging the plenary chamber and forcing a relocation. The Kroll opera house nearby was designated as the new home for the parliament. All the political action occurred on the stage, where the people with power sat and everyone else was merely part of an audience. Speakers would address parliament from a rostrum in the middle and debate was not part of the agenda. It was not in any way a democratic arrangement.

Interestingly, Hitler was very concerned to keep the name 'the Reichstag' as it encapsulated the union of people and parliament. That lasted from 1933 until 1942, during which period all instructions and directives were issued under the banner of 'Reichstag'.

This is the reason why the Russians focused on attacking the Reichstag, the name transferred from the institution of parliament to the building itself, as a symbol of their goal to end the war. In this spirit, individual soldiers then made their own marks within the building to record the end of the war. When we stripped away some of the 1960s lining, we discovered not just the original fabric but also some of this graffiti. That provoked a political debate. The Russian ambassador helped us to identify some of the unsavoury remarks, but many were kept and incorporated into the rebuilt fabric as part of the Reichstag's, and the country's, history.

Meanwhile, in 1949, a parliament had been established in Bonn, which became the capital of West Germany. The Bundestag was housed in a repurposed pedagogic academy. The plenary chamber in the buildings now housing this democratic institution also used the half circle layout, but had a larger diameter, primarily due to the increased number of politicians. This had the effect of pushing the front benches closer to the podium and the speaker. The significance of that emerged later during our research and design work. To reinforce the democratic nature of this new parliament, there was ever greater access for the public to scrutinise its activities.

In 1989, however, the West German parliament was in temporary accommodation in the former Water Works in Bonn. They had decided some time before the Berlin Wall fell that they needed a new chamber to better represent them, and this was under construction in 1989. It was in the Water Works that two votes were taken, first to move the whole of the government and parliament to Berlin, and second that the Reichstag would be the home for the new parliament. On Monday, 19 April 1999, the Bundestag took up its new seat in the Reichstag building.

First though, in 1992, the Bundestag moved into the new chamber in Bonn designed by Günter Behnisch, which now had a limited lifespan. In consultation with parliamentarians, Behnisch's design put all the members in a complete circle, the ultimate democratic diagram. The speaker stood close to the centre, with the government to the left and the Bundestag to the right. The chancellor was in the chair closest to the rostrum.

The Behnisch building in Bonn became a full size working prototype for the parliament and us to study while progressing our design. The

Figure 32.4 The new weaves through the historic fabric of the interior spaces.
© Nigel Young / Foster + Partners

Figure 32.5 Graffiti from the end of the Second World War preserved within the Reichstag. © Nigel Young / Foster + Partners

Figure 32.6 Protesters and wallpickers at the Berlin Wall by the Reichstag (left). © Alexander Mayer, 'Berlin Wall behind Reichstag Building (left), protestors and "wallpickers"', 28 December 1989, Germany. Source: Wikimedia Commons, reproduced on the basis of a GNU Free Documentation License. Available at: https://commons.wikimedia.org/wiki/File:Mauer_hinter_Reichstag.jpg (accessed on 29 November 2022)

politicians quickly identified some shortfalls. The completeness of the circle put all the leading politicians in the front row; however the diameter of the inner circle was too wide, and it was difficult to see the facial expressions of the speaker and anyone else, even from the front row. They missed being able to see into the eyes and read the body language of those addressing parliament, which they had built into the embodied original 1949 Bonn layout. What persuaded them of the desirability of shorter distances was a visit to the House of Commons in London. Although they did not like its confrontational layout, preferring the more consensual form of a circle, they did like the proximity of being able to see people while making statements.

The design of the chamber in the Reichstag started by inserting the Bonn chamber into the plan, which proved to be a tight fit. We then began to evolve it with the overall development of the debating chamber. Everything we proposed found its way to the press (through leaks) in order to gauge public opinion. We did many studies and geometrical work, ending with the arc of the circle interacting with a different circular geometry, for the government and Bundestag benches.

Our main client contact was with the parliament's building committee. We made full size mock-ups for them and assembled them in a temporary building in front of the Reichstag in Berlin. Towards the end of the design process but still during construction, when the seating had already been chosen, Chancellor Helmut Kohl came to see it with the president of the parliament, Rita Süssmuth, and the rest of the committee. He made it clear he did not want to sit in the traditional chancellor's seat on the front row near the rostrum, but in the seat behind. However, by the time the building was constructed, there was a new chancellor, who found the traditional position to be acceptable.

The new chamber is flooded with daylight and far larger than the original one in the 1894 building. Even more emphasis is now placed on

Figure 32.7 Floor plan for the Reichstag with the plenary hall at the heart of the building. © Foster + Partners

the 'tribunes', where the members of the public who come to see their parliament in action sit. The newest influence on design was the need to televise all sessions of the Bundestag with an elevated platform provided for this, and for the inclusion of a very sophisticated acoustic system. Ultimately, despite the long and sometimes tumultuous history of the nation's parliament, the effects of that history are made manifest within the new plenary chamber. It achieves a remarkable consistency and an appropriate continuation with what has gone before, at the same time as being a significant new expression and experience.

33

A natural gathering place

The National Assembly for Wales – the Senedd, 1998–2004

Ivan Harbour – RSHP

As with Scotland's Parliament at Holyrood, devolution was the catalyst for the National Assembly for Wales, which became a parliament in 2020 and is now known as Senedd Cymru, or the Senedd.

Wales was last independent in the thirteenth century, which perhaps reflected the lukewarm response of the Welsh people to devolution. At the 1997 referendum, turnout was only 50 per cent, with a very narrow majority of 50.3 per cent in favour. By contrast, in Scotland there had been overwhelming support.

Prior to designing the new Assembly there had been much debate about its location. Unlike the Scottish Parliament, the Welsh Assembly did not have a 'spiritual home' (like Holyrood) to which it could return. Wales' capital city, Cardiff, in the south, is by some margin its most populated city. Although most support for devolution came from the less populated north, the selection process for the site eventually narrowed down to two locations in Cardiff: Cardiff City Hall in Cathays Park, described by Nikolaus Pevsner as the finest civic centre in the British Isles; and, the ultimately successful location, a new docklands development site on Cardiff Bay.

For 150 years, Cardiff Bay had accommodated the largest coal exporting port in the world, the source of South Wales' great wealth. The new docklands development was marketed as a place for the future. Being remote from the city centre, it was considered a neutral, nationally significant ground. Coal had no need for warehouses and once closed, the docks were a relatively clean slate. At the prime spot on the bay, however, is the Pierhead Building, a Grade I listed terracotta jewel that housed the docks' accountants and is a reminder of the great wealth that coal brought to the city.

Figure 33.1 Competition drawing. © RSHP

In 1998, when the design competition was launched, the news focus was very much on Holyrood. I was consequently acutely aware of the political and general interest such a public project would have, but also of the different circumstances in Wales, which played my design thinking.

The site did not have the same built historic context as Holyrood and had essentially been master planned as a business park on sea. The empty plot taken by the Assembly was separated from the water's edge by an access road with the Pierhead Building as its immediate neighbour. Crickhowell House, now known as Tŷ Hywel, to the back of the site had been earmarked for the Assembly's offices, so the design was to be for 'front of house' to the Welsh government: the public and symbolic part only. The site of Zaha Hadid's groundbreaking but ultimately ill-fated opera house was next door. Its journey had ended controversially a few years before the competition. For all these reasons we were not optimistic when we set out to conceive a home for the new Assembly.

Former British prime minister and chair of the jury James Callaghan – a longstanding Cardiff MP – wrote an inspiring foreword to what was a short brief. He said that it offered the architectural profession the opportunity to express a democratic Assembly that would listen to and lead a small democratic nation into the next millennium. It would 'not be overly adversarial in shape or argument' and this ambition resonated with my own feelings. In parallel, the brief referred to the Home Office requirements for the design of public buildings, which broadly state that they must be bomb-proof, presupposing concrete or masonry walls with punched windows and blast curtains.

When working on a competition, our 'house rule' is not to ask questions as the answer is inevitably 'no', so we put the Home Office guide to one side and went with our hearts in conceiving the design. The last line of the foreword, 'In due course, we would dare to hope that it will become a visible symbol, recognised and respected throughout the world, whenever the name of Wales is used', however, induced an unbelievable pressure even before we started.

Callaghan's hopes for the scheme suggested that we might look back to consider first principles about our essential human nature to progress the design. This approach, rather than any symbolism or reference, informed our concept. There was, after all, no precedent or memory of a previous assembly in Wales, and as the building would have to last at least 100 years, following the whims of fashion would not be appropriate. To be relevant it would have to look forward to appeal to young people – the politicians of the future. All this led us to start with a design that would engage passersby and welcome them with open arms. We wanted the building to present a future of the possible to that sceptical electorate. We envisaged a natural gathering place like an old tree, its canopy extended,

Figure 33.2 People gather on the steps of the Senedd. © Edmund Sumner

where people have convened since time immemorial for shelter and debate.

The second important influence was the location. As seen from the site, the sky stretches across the bay. Looking across it to the headland of Penarth, behind which the sun sets, the light seemed to lead beyond, to the rest of Wales and the world. This was a place that could make connections.

At the time we began to design the Welsh Assembly, I had recently completed the Bordeaux Law Courts. We had conceived that building as open and legible to those who had to visit it. Our aim was to demystify the law court and give hope to, and underline its accountability to, the people. We felt that, at the Senedd, the relationship between the electorate and the elected body should be similarly open and transparent. So, for example, visitors should be free to engage on a number of levels, rather than be herded through a 'visitor experience'. The relationship should not depend on a doorway that can be shut in your face at any time,

Figure 33.3 The debating chamber public viewing gallery. © Katsuhisa Kida/ FOTOTECA

but should be across a space or between floors where visual connections are always maintained. We developed the relationship by placing the space for the electorate above the elected body. The public, thereby, have commanding glimpses over the Assembly areas below.

The concept was summarised as a public living room with openings in its floor surface, extending from the sea, up and over the Assembly functions. It follows a simple diagram derived from the view towards Penarth, where the sea, the sky and the world beyond define the place. Drawing down the roof brings daylight in and the two surfaces coming together form the principal spaces, where the electorate meets the elected. Taking inspiration from the water's edge led us to reach back to the water beyond the edge of the site to encourage passersby to look outwards from the building to connect to the rest of the country. As the required floorspace was rather small in comparison to its neighbours', making the building reach out like this would make it feel much larger from the human perspective.

Figure 33.4 Interior view of the public space around the debating chamber funnel.
© Katsuhisa Kida/FOTOTECA

We wanted to provide shelter beyond the building's interior, to encourage people to gather and make their presence known at the seat of government. By putting the façade in shadow, the large oversailing roof would enhance the building's transparency, which was imperative in inviting people to look towards light rather than darkness, to encourage people to approach.

The submission deliverables were a lesson in the necessary minimum to understand a proposal, particularly compared with today's overmanaged, information-heavy demands. These expectations for the submission allowed us to focus on presenting the idea, with images, a small model and a short report to explain the concept. As a process it depended on architects advising the lay jury to help them discern whether the idea had merit and whether it was buildable. The public, though, benefited from an artist's impression, which the late, great visualiser Alan Davidson produced for us for the press announcement.

A milestone moment in design development came when the first Assembly was elected. The new first minister and other members were excited to be involved in creating their new home. They were horrified when not all their constituents agreed that the home was fit for them.

Wales has a significantly larger than average proportion of disabled people.[1] What we had seen as being inviting, many of them saw as barriers. Our response followed my belief that the best buildings come from the interaction between criticism and a strong concept. They must engage the client – here, broadly, the people of Wales – who has to be willing to believe in the concept and, in effect, become part of the team to realise it.

The mix between architecture and politics is complicated. Architecture is far too slow for many politicians and political systems. It requires clear and consistent decision-making, occasional leaps of faith and not a little risk-taking.

Without our critics, though, the Senedd would not have evolved into being a place of exemplary accessibility. The section of the building, which describes its spatial sequences most eloquently, became clearer and simpler as a result, but retains the spirit of the public realm rising from the sea.

When, in the process of detail design, Rhodri Morgan, who had taken over the position of first minister from Alun Michael, suggested that the Senedd might be overshadowed by the new Millennium Centre (the replacement for Zaha Hadid's beautiful opera house), we made another sketch to demonstrate how the smallest building can appear to be the largest when experienced from a human perspective. Morgan thought something more banal, like an Assembly chamber in a car park, might have been preferable to our proposal on the waterfront. We demonstrated how difficult Morgan's suggestion would be but, fortunately, public opinion was warming to the idea of a new parliament building, and so these side studies went no further.

Alas, our troubles were not over yet. The saga of the building's final realisation mirrored the angst around creating the Palace of Westminster in the nineteenth century. We persisted, were sacked, then vindicated as we were re-employed. Finally, we delivered the building a few years late. The Senedd learned the hard way, but once the team coalesced with the client who made decisions, it was a unique experience.

Today the Senedd does appear more prominent than the Millennium Centre at the water's edge. It is open and steps down to the bay. The roads have gone, so it no longer feels like a business park but a place that encourages participation.

Halfway through the design, the impact of 9/11 required major changes to incorporate heightened security. Fortunately, this happened just in time for us to make those changes without unduly compromising the building's transparency. As it is, all visitors (apart from ceremonial guests) approach via a route which keeps the paraphernalia of security control outside the principal public room.

It has become a living room for Wales, a great democratic meeting place with overlapping activities and events, but also a place where you can come and do nothing. Encouraged by the form of the daylight funnel, there is a natural draw to the chamber, and the degree of engagement with the democratic process is a personal choice.

The chamber itself is intimate as there are only 60 members, though it can expand to include 30 additional members. It would fit comfortably into the House of Commons chamber. It started off on our initial drawings as a pink circle, which was a placeholder for later discussion, that became the defining form. In a sense, the circle is the ultimate democratic form as it is neither presentational nor confrontational. As it developed, the dividing line between government and opposition remained completely flexible, answering Jim Callaghan's dictum that it should not be overly adversarial.

A key moment in the debating chamber's realisation came wher the client agreed to commission a full-scale mock-up in plywood to agr its arrangement. We advised them they could not afford to get it w' and that this process would enable all of the members to have the The model was invaluable in reaching agreement about the stepr spacing between the aisles to gauge intimacy, and most impo'

Figure 33.5 Watching the Assembly from a public viewing gallery. © Edmund Sumner

get all the Senedd members to buy into it before finalising the design for construction.

Despite being conceived more than 20 years ago, the Senedd remains one of our most environmentally sustainable buildings. When I visited for its tenth anniversary, I learned that the backup mechanical plant for ventilation had never been needed. Instead, the natural ventilation system had successfully operated, driven by buoyancy and wind, drawn through a labyrinth of ducts within the thermal mass of the slab below the building to temper incoming air.

The façade of the living room is single glazed. It is a 'coats on' space, with temperature appropriate to functions. Daylight is maximised throughout, and top light is used in offices and committee rooms. Low grade heating comes from ground earth heat exchangers and heat pumps. Top-up heating uses biomass. There are opening windows, and bands of vents to allow night purging of the thermal mass. Materials were selected to minimise embodied energy, including transportation, with temporary site works adopting the same approach.

Intelligent sensors embedded in the building fabric help the building to learn, allowing the data to be followed up for many years after occupation. It easily met the BREEAM 'excellent' criteria and would have made 'outstanding' had that been in place at the time. All this was integral to the design from the start. The lead environmental engineer, Klaus Bode, was present as I drew the first sketch that summarised our collective thoughts.

The building is also built to last. The design life of 100 years was behind decisions such as the choice of single glazing. The slate will last for longer. I believe the most successful aspect of the Senedd is its scale. It has an intimacy which few civic buildings have matched. It feels very human, inviting and intriguing. I could never hope to compare it to the Parthenon as an architectural achievement, but perhaps not surprisingly, it is the same size.

One thing that has not changed in the 2,500 years since democracy originated in ancient Athens is our innate sense of being and how we feel in our environment. The Senedd handles this very well.

Note

1 'In England, 18.7% of females and 16.5% of males were disabled in 2021, while in Wales 22.3% of females and 19.8% of males were disabled'. Disability by age, sex and deprivation, England and Wales: Census 2021. https://www.ons.gov.uk /peoplepopulationandcommunity/healthandsocialcare/disability/articles/disabilitybyag esexanddeprivationenglandandwales/census2021 (accessed on 10 February 2023).

Index

Locators in *italics* refer to illustrations, t after locator refers to tables

power 13–19, 284
assemblies 337–9, 342
buildings for the future 437, 465
contemporary parliament in historic
building 93, 99, 114–15, 161
culture of 208
divine 442
exercise of 339–41
material structure of parliaments 172, 176,
185, 209, 215–16
royal 194, 442
separation of 417
transitions and legitimacy 224, 266
vertical 246
and visibility 336–7
practices, political 19–21
President Vladimir Putin making a speech,
March 2020 242
press 179, 261, 315, 463, 488
prestige 212
Prime minister gives policy statement 426
Prisoner, The 301, 302, 309
privatisation 227
privileges 429
Production Sites and Production Sights of New
Broadcasting House, The 308
propaganda 251, 271
Proportional representation of spaces 187
protagonists 86–7
Protesters, Berlin Wall 480
protests (protesters) 307
Romania 232–3
see also Bulgaria; riots
proximity 480
Psarra, Sophia 385
public access 453
publications 211, 240
public consultation 473
public debates 279, 284, 287
publicity 317
public opinion 271, 284, 318, 371, 480, 489
public parks see Abington Street Gardens
public participation 290
public resistance, Malta 263
public space, interior view 487
public spaces 209, 246, 266, 271
see also Abington Street Gardens
public viewing gallery of debating chamber 486
Public Whip 313
Pugin, Augustus Welby N. 299–300, 335
buildings for the future 441, 449, 455, 461
contemporary parliament in historic
building 104, 112, 136, 150
Putin, Vladimir 242, 246
Puwar, Nirmal 54, 314

Rai, Shirin 107, 210, 416
rallies 250–1, 253
see also protests (protesters)
Ranger, T. 426–7
Rathbone, Eleanor 42–3
rationality 365

Rauscher, F. 364
Reagan, Ronald 283
speech, protests 284
reappropriation 333
rebellion 233–4
Rechtsstaat 365
recognition, political 403
reconstruction 192
records, historic 64
redesign 105
referendum, UK 286
reflexivity 238, 245
Reform Act 1832 447
Reformation 445
refurbishment 104, 456
Reichstag building 169, 170, 184, 257, 473–82
see also Palace of Westminster and
Reichstag building
Reid, David Boswel 64
reindeer collectives 398, 401
relationships 61, 98, 240, 308
across Europe 333
assemblies 330–2, 335, 344
buildings for the future 468, 486–7
mediated parliamentary and digital
interactions 307
sovereignty, scale and representation 401,
403, 415
spatial typologies 331
relations, permeable 176–9
religion 230, 300, 365–6
relocation 393, 410, 476
Bulgarian 250
see also Bulgaria
renewal see imagination, architectural
renovations 242, 244, 245
representation 203, 350
representation, political
cultural and spatial turns in political history
208–9
exterior and interior 211–15
interdisciplinary and comparative approach
215–16
interpreting architecture of parliaments
209–11
representation, sovereignty, scale and
language 27
representation, symbolic 130–1
corporate identity 125–6
corporate (non)identity 129–30
engagement and identity 122–5
parliaments 126–9
representation versus participation 290–3
representative claim 126
repression 247
responsibility 451
restoration see imagination, architectural
restoration and renewal (R&R) programme
44–6, 171, 192, 464
historical contexts 104–8, 116, 119, 126–7
reunification 196
revolutions 227

Milton Keynes UK
Ingram Content Group UK Ltd.
UKHW020203220624
444453UK00002B/17